First Person Plural

First Person Plural

Multiple Personality and the Philosophy of Mind

Revised Edition

STEPHEN E. BRAUDE

ROWMAN & LITTLEFIELD PUBLISHERS, INC.

ROWMAN & LITTLEFIELD PUBLISHERS, INC.

Published in the United States of America
by Rowman & Littlefield Publishers, Inc.
4720 Boston Way, Lanham, Maryland 20706

3 Henrietta Street
London WC2E 8LU, England

British Cataloging in Publication Information Available

Library of Congress Cataloging-in-Publication Data

Braude Stephen E.
First person plural : multiple personality and the philosophy of
mind / Stephen E. Braude.
p. cm.
previously pub.: New York : Routledge, 1991.
Includes bibliographical reverences and index.
1. Philosophy of mind. 2. Multiple personality. I. Title.
BD418.3.B73 1994 616.85'236'001—dc20 94–40570 CIP

ISBN 0–8476–7996–9 (pbk. : alk. paper)

Printed in the United States of America

♾™ The paper used in this publication meets the minimum requirements of
American National Standard for Information Sciences—Permanence of
Paper for Printed Library Materials, ANSI Z39.48–1964.

For Jule Eisenbud

CONTENTS

CONTENTS

CONTENTS

ACKNOWLEDGMENTS

The preparation of this book has been a long-term project. It involved gaining more than a passing familiarity with the literature on hypnosis, the history of psychiatry generally, and of course the extensive clinical and theoretical literature on MPD. Along the way, specialists in these areas have graciously helped me to achieve what I hope is at least a respectable command of the relevant issues. I am particularly indebted to Jule Eisenbud, Alan Gauld, Frank Putnam, and Onno van der Hart for their patience and generosity and for their good-natured tolerance of my frequently naive questions. Rachel Downing, Michael Gainer, and Walter Young also shared their time and ideas with me at important stages of my research, and I thank them as well. Thanks also to Carlos Alvarado and Rhea A. White for their historical and bibliographic expertise and resources, and to Karen A. Olio for helpful criticism and for keeping me up-to-the-minute concerning the controversy over false memories. And of course, I am deeply grateful to the multiples who have shared their lives, pain, and perspectives with me and who have given me a kind of understanding of MPD I could not possibly have derived solely from the literature.

My philosophical colleagues have also frequently come to my rescue and have helped me at least to reduce the number of embarrassing errors in this book. My thanks, especially, to Robert Almeder, Bruce Aune and John Heil, and to my Maryland colleagues Michael Slote, Ray Martin, Bruce Goldberg, Annette Barnes, Alan Tormey, and Doug MacLean.

A very early version of Chapter 9 was presented in London as the 19th F.W.H. Myers Memorial Lecture at the Society for Psychical Research, and was subsequently published as 'Mediumship and Multiple Personality', *Journal of the Society for Psychical Research* 55 (1988). I would like to thank the Society and the editor of the *Journal* for their permission to use substantial portions of that material.

And a very special thanks to my wife, Audrey, for numerous valuable insights and for her love, understanding, and patience with my distractions during the writing of the book.

INTRODUCTION

Back in the good old days of philosophy — say, around 400 B.C., philosophers played a rather prominent role in the community at large. One reason is that the various sciences were not yet the largely self-contained disciplines they are today. Nowadays, one can study and become proficient in a science without examining the highly abstract philosophical assumptions on which it rests. In ancient Greece, however (as students of Aristotle are well aware), those abstract assumptions were generally kept quite close to the surface. In fact, back in the good old days of philosophy and for quite a while thereafter, the boundaries between philosophy and science were far from clear. All (or at least some) of the now relatively autonomous main areas of science were simply parts of what was called *natural philosophy*. So for a long time it was not uncommon for philosophers to play an active role in various fields of empirical investigation.

For that matter, philosophers frequently discussed issues of concern to the community as a whole, and sometimes their views had a real impact within that community. Of course, the good old days of philosopy were not *that* good. Socrates's efforts to influence the thinking of his fellow Athenians earned him the ridicule of Aristophanes and eventually cost him his life. But at least people were paying attention. They also paid attention to Socrates's less-abrasive student, Plato, who likewise sought to address a general audience. Although Plato's dialogues were philosophically substantive, they usually dealt with matters of considerable public interest.

In the twentieth century, however, philosophy became as specialized as the sciences from which it had become detached. For more than 2,000 years, philosophers had concentrated increasingly

1

on difficulties confronting their predecessors and on the *methods* they used to solve basic philosophical problems. And as a result, the field became increasingly insular. One could forge a career in philosophy devoted entirely to issues of concern to no one but a handful of other philosophers. In fact, one could earn a Ph.D. in philosophy without seriously studying topics of general philosophical import; in many cases it was enough to demonstrate a reasonable command of the specialized interests of one's mentors. It is not surprising, then, that many in the field considered it a *virtue* to deal exclusively with problems couched in a meta-meta-meta-language mastered by a few philosophical initiates. That was supposed to be a sign of philosophical sophistication (although it was clearly not a reliable mark of profundity). Hence, philosophers distrusted and derided their colleagues' attempts to address the wider academic and non-academic community — even the community of scientists, as if those efforts were reprehensible examples of pandering to people incapable of doing 'real' philosophy.

Although I recognize the value — indeed, the indispensability — of highly technical and specialized issues which only a philosopher could love, it seems to me that for a while at any rate, philosophy as a whole lost its focus and purpose. Granted, some in the field continued to address issues of broad concern. But many suffered from a kind of professional myopia. And as a result, philosophers generally served no significant role in the wider academic community, and they played an even smaller role in the lives of laypersons. Happily, in recent years this has begun to reverse itself; philosophy is apparently rediscovering its links both to other disciplines and to people outside the halls of academe. For example, philosophers are once again dealing with basic ethical issues, as opposed to arcane problems in deontic logic or the analysis of normative discourse. Moreover, we have recently witnessed the birth of various fields of practical or applied philosophy, such as bio-medical and business ethics. The assumption underlying this turn of events is similar to one that apparently motivated philosophers back in the good old days of philosophy: Ideally at least, laypersons and scientists can benefit from philosophers' training in critical thinking, as well as their deep acquaintance with abstract issues and assumptions taken somewhat for granted in the sciences and in everyday life. Of course, in real life matters are seldom this pretty; in fact, philosophers are often as

2

incompetent and confused as non-philosophers. Nevertheless, one can only welcome the restoration of philosophy to a more active role in the intellectual community generally. Every field has its share of fools and incompetents, but it is still good to have a specialist when you need one.

I mention all this as a prelude to explaining my view of the present work. I believe that the topic of multiple personality has much to offer a broad range of traditional — and even specialized — philosophical concerns. I also believe that philosophy has much to offer non-philosophers trying to come to grips in their distinctive ways with the phenomena of 'multiplicity' (e.g., psychologists, clinicians, cognitive scientists, and even laypersons who might simply be friends with or relatives of a multiple). I hope, therefore, that this book has something to offer both philosophers and a wide range of non-philosophers, and that it will contribute to progress in the philosophy of mind while at the same time advancing the course of more thoroughly empirical approaches to the topic of multiple personality (and perhaps some relatively practical concerns as well).

I am aware, however, that serving these distinct sets of interests is no easy matter, and that sooner or later one must resort to types of analysis or description beyond either the competence or interest of members of one's intended audience. For example, I cannot expect clinicians either to follow or even care much about many of the issues addressed in Chapter 6 or some of the terminological intricacies of Chapters 3 and 4. Similarly, philosophers may have little interest in some of the issues raised in Chapters 2 and 9, or little patience with the slightly oversimplified accounts of some philosophical issues which I considered important enough to render accessible to non-philosophers. I had to face the same sort of strategic dilemma in my previous two books, and I'm sorry to say I still have found no way to avoid it. So as before, I hope that readers will be tolerant of portions of the text tailored to those with somewhat different interests or areas of competence.

Before sketching the stucture of the book, let me clarify the respect in which I think a philosophical study of multiple personality has value outside the field of philosophy. Contrary to what many scientists and clinicians probably think, no study of multiple personality can be entirely empirical. Like all empirical scientific investigations, that inquiry is philosophical as well. Indeed, like other scientific investigations, it is *fundamentally* philosophical.

Every branch of science rests on numerous, often unrecognized, abstract presuppositions, both metaphysical and methodological — for example, concerning the nature of observation, the nature of properties, or the appropriate investigative procedures for a given domain. Hence, the integrity of the discipline as a whole hinges on the acceptability of its root philosophical assumptions. If those assumptions are indefensible or incoherent, that particular scientific enterprise has nothing to stand on, no matter how attractive or promising it might be initially, or on the surface. In fact, this seems to be the case in certain rather prominent areas of science — for example, in memory trace theory and (for that matter) in many areas of so-called cognitive science. Theorizing in those fields is often no more than bad philosophy dressed up in the imposing technical language of the electrical engineer (Braude, 1979, 1986a; Bursen, 1978; Goldberg, 1982; Heil, 1978, 1981).

Compared to many areas of scientific research, the study of dissociation is relatively recent and that of multiple personality even more so. These branches of science have not yet hardened into relatively procrustean systems of thought. They are not yet so thoroughly developed or firmly entrenched in the academic community as to be greatly threatened by the prospect of fundamental conceptual housecleaning. Indeed, they are still at the stage where such an enterprise can dramatically and positively affect the course of their development.

My aim in this book is to examine issues central to our thinking about multiple personality. I want to discuss some concepts that have not been given the attention they deserve, clarify frequently-used and important terms (e.g., 'dissociation') that have not been used with sufficient care, and dispel some confusions that have plagued theorizing about multiplicity for many years — probably, since the end of the eighteenth century.

To set the stage for all that, I begin the book with a brief history of hypnosis, in which we discover the conceptual developments which paved the way for the recognition (and perhaps for the very existence) of multiple personality. As I explain in later chapters, there are good reasons for regarding multiple personality as the product of a kind of self-hypnosis. If so, it would apparently belong to the broad class of phenomena classified as *dissociative*. Therefore, to understand multiple personality, it should help to have some understanding of hypnosis and dissociation generally, not only to appreciate the variety and apparent ubiquity of this

4

broad class of often peculiar psychological states, but also to see how the phenomena of multiplicity connect with a wide assortment of sometimes quite puzzling human capacities, dissociative and non-dissociative. Furthermore, the history of hypnosis has played a pivotal role in the development of theories of the unconscious or subconscious, aspects of which multiple personality quite naturally forces us to confront.

Chapter 2 surveys the often striking phenomena of multiple personality disorder (MPD) and examines critically the currently accepted profile of multiplicity within the clinical community. Rather than describe one or more cases of MPD in detail, I have chosen to summarize the evidence gathered from numerous cases. The drawback to that procedure, I am afraid, is that the reader does not get much of a 'feel' for the phenomena. But since detailed case reports are readily available and since the most detailed and dramatic cases, taken by themselves, can provide a distorted picture of multiplicity, I have thought it best to provide a more well-rounded sketch of MPD by surveying the totality of cases.

With Chapter 3, matters become more abstract. The central goal of this book is to clarify the nature of the mental discontinuities or divisions produced in MPD and in other forms of dissociation, and to determine how best to describe them. But to do that, it is necessary to decide whether (or to what extent) dissociative phenomena require explanation in terms of functionally distinct agents, and whether (or to what extent) the explanatory strategies appropriate to MPD are appropriate to normal, non-dissociative psychological phenomena. Chapter 3 takes a necessary first step in that direction, by considering in what way the psychic divisions produced through 'splitting' in MPD are deeper than those produced (say) in ordinary hypnosis, psychogenic fugue, and certain kinds of role playing. In the process, I offer a novel view of what accounts for the distinct sense of self that each alternate personality seems to enjoy.

Whereas Chapter 3 considers differences between multiplicity and other dissociative phenomena, Chapter 4 considers similarities. In that chapter, I examine and attempt to clarify the concept of dissociation. I identify what seem to be the concept's central features and presuppositions, expose the flaws in definitions found in the literature, and compare the concept of dissociation to others often connected or confused with it (e.g., repression and suppression). Finally, I offer a new definition of 'dissociation', which avoids the pitfalls of the unsatisfactory definitions already examined, provides a way of distinguishing dissociation from repression, etc., and which at the very least should provide a useful foundation for further discussion.

Chapter 5 examines a seductive but confused principle that has been widely accepted, at least tacitly, for well over a hundred years, and which has led to a seriously distorted picture of the importance of dissociation (and especially MPD) for our understanding of the mind. This principle, which I call the principle of *compositional reversibility*, is a hidden (and mistaken) premise in numerous arguments inferring the structure of the pre-dissociative self from the nature of post-dissociative divisions. I also show how a variant of this 'Humpty Dumpty Fallacy' plays an important role in the literature on brain bisection.

But not all arguments for divisions of the self (or the disunity of consciousness) concern the peculiarities of dissociation. Some apply only to quite normal sorts of mental phenomena. In Chapter 6, I examine the most prominent of such arguments (fashioned, usually, after Plato's argument for a tripartite soul). I attempt to show that these arguments are either deeply flawed or that they simply show too little (at most, the mere utility of speaking figuratively of 'parts' of the self or psyche). I also consider a rather different (Freudian) argument for multiple consciousnesses, which commits a different set of errors.

Chapter 7 is a kind of climax to the book. Chapter 3 defends a certain kind of profound distinctness between alternate personalities. But in Chapter 7, I consider whether there is nevertheless some unity behind that diversity, some even more profound respect in which a multiple's alternate personalities are merely functionally distinct parts of a more primitive whole. I argue that we need to posit an underlying unity to explain certain central features of multiplicity, including the adaptational nature of alter formation and the conspicuous overlapping of many memories and abilities. In the process, I examine closely the nature of abilities generally and expose the flaws in applying certain mechanistic concepts of cognitive science to the phenomena of MPD.

Chapter 8 considers whether (or to what extent) the phenomena of MPD force us to think differently about persons. I argue that there are numerous, quite different, concepts of a person, no one of which is privileged or preferred independently of a context of inquiry, and that MPD at best challenges only some of these.

6

Moreover, I discuss how MPD might expand the range of situations in which we can appropriately consider persons to be mere agents or subjects, even if that undermines our familiar presumption of a one:one correspondence between persons and bodies. I also explore the relationship between personhood and the concept of a personality and examine some confusions in the clinical literature concerning that relationship.

Chapter 9 examines the similarities and differences between multiple personality and the phenomena of mediumship or 'channeling'. I consider whether a comparison of the two sets of phenomena helps us decide if mediumship is simply a dissociative phenomenon or if it is at least sometimes quite different from dissociation (and to that extent indicative of survival of bodily death). I also consider the more unusual hypothesis that some alternate personalities are really discarnate communicators.

Finally, Chapter 10 (new to this edition) considers recent conceptual developments and controversies concerning MPD — in particular, the elimination of the category of multiple personality in the DSM-IV, and the raging debate over the iatrogenic creation of so-called 'false memories'. The first topic concerns a pragmatic justification for treating multiples as if they are unitary. The second raises interesting questions about the accuracy and durability of memory and the assumptions underlying attempts to recover hidden memories of abuse.

1

A BRIEF HISTORY OF HYPNOSIS

1.1 INTRODUCTION

The condition now called multiple personality was first identified as such only relatively recently — apparently toward the end of the eighteenth century. In fact, it may well be that before that time there *was* no multiple personality, at least in the form familiar to most laypersons and even to most clinicians. Some claim that multiple personality is a distinctive 'idiom of distress' (Kenny, 1986) or *symptom-language* (Crabtree, 1985b) for psychological disturbances that manifested differently in other cultures and at other times.[1] But whether or not one agrees with that position, it is clear that the modern phenomena of multiple personality have various historical antecedents and that their similarities may be more than superficial.

Precursors of the phenomena of multiple personality can be found in the rich traditions of early medicine and shamanism, as well as in numerous forms of apparent spirit possession. And of course, one finds additional reports of kindred phenomena throughout the history of mesmerism and in the more systematic investigations of modern hypnosis. In fact, the discovery and study of hypnosis may have helped to set the stage both socially and conceptually for multiple personality as we know it today. It seems appropriate, therefore, to begin this study of multiple personality with an examination of that period in medical and intellectual history.

Not surprisingly, there are various ways to conduct such a survey. For example, one could highlight the role of hypnosis — or *suggestion* generally — in healing, and consider its place in the lengthy chronicle of possibly allied techniques, from the earliest

8

practice of the laying on of hands and the allegedly supernatural rituals of medicine men to recent studies of placebos and biofeedback control. Another approach would be to emphasize the role of hypnosis in the history of psychology, particularly in connection with the development of theories of the unconscious or subconscious. One could also examine the social and legal aspects of hypnosis, with an eye on the ways hypnosis has shaped our conception of persons, agency, and moral responsibility. Finally, one could focus on the *para*psychological aspects of hypnosis and consider its apparent role in ostensible cases of ESP and psychokinesis.

Each of these approaches has something to offer the present study of multiple personality and its philosophical significance. My emphasis, however, will be on the second approach: the examination of hypnosis in relation to depth psychology. The pioneers of hypnosis appeared to discover hidden strata and resources of the mind, which operated somewhat surreptitiously during periods of normal consciousness, but revealed themselves rather dramatically in various forms of psychopathology.

1.2 ANIMAL MAGNETISM[2]

Although he did not actually discover the healing powers of hypnotic procedures, it was Franz Anton Mesmer (1734-1815) who first brought hypnosis (which he called *animal magnetism*) to the attention of the European public. But perhaps more importantly, he stimulated the systematic investigation of hypnosis within the intellectual community.

Mesmer's theory of animal magnetism was based initially on an already robust practice of using magnets to heal disease. But Mesmer eventually arrived at the belief that magnets were not the healing agents. Instead, he proposed that the physician has powers analogous to those of a magnet. Just as a mineral magnet channels certain invisible universal forces to produce familiar effects of various kinds, a medical magnetizer channels a universal 'magnetic fluid' into the body of a patient to heal disease.

Mesmer proposed that the universe is filled with a subtle physical fluid, connecting objects of all kinds and permeating the human body. Specific ailments, he suggested, resulted from specific types of imbalance or uneven distribution of this fluid within the body, and recovery accordingly demands the restoration of fluidic balance or equilibrium. Mesmer also proposed that the magnetizer has the *power* to cure, and that certain techniques allow the fluid to be channeled, stored, and transferred to others. First, the magnetizer must establish *rapport* (a kind of physical 'tuning in') with the patient. Then, he can exercise his healing power by making 'magnetic passes' (i.e., sweeping hand movements) over the body. These passes redirect the magnetic fluid within the body, and eventually provoke the 'crises' that Mesmer considered necessary for healing. Crises were artificially-induced and ostensibly cathartic instances of the disease to be cured, and were thus specific to the disease. For example, when healing an asthmatic or an epileptic, the magnetizer would attempt to induce (respectively) an attack of asthma or epilepsy.

Mesmer also believed that collective healing could be achieved through the use of a *bacquet*, a large tub that was supposed to contain and concentrate the fluid, and around which groups of people could sit. The bacquet had special bottles arranged on the bottom, and was then filled with water, iron filings, and bits of glass. Iron rods protruded out from the bacquet at various heights, corresponding to different parts of the body where ailments might occur, and to which the rods could then be applied. Mesmer believed, further, that if the patients held hands, they could strengthen the magnetic current by forming a circuit.

Mesmer enjoyed a period of enormous popularity, fueled by his flamboyant personality and (of course) by numerous reports of astounding cures. He established two clinics in Paris, one for the rich and one for the poor, and they both reported many successes. But the medical community in Paris was generally unsympathetic to Mesmer's theory and techniques. In 1784, the King of France appointed two commissions to investigate animal magnetism. The first, chaired by Benjamin Franklin (the American Ambassador to France), was composed of prominent members of the Royal Academy of Sciences (including Lavoisier) and the Faculty of Medicine. The second commission consisted of physicians from the Royal Society of Medicine. Both commissions filed reports highly critical of mesmeric theory and practice. Interestingly, however, they never directly challenged the contention that Mesmer's patients often recovered or that the patients attained psychological states conducive to healing. (In fact, they attributed cures to a combination of imagination and imitation.) Rather, they focused on the adequacy of Mesmer's *theory* (and also the morality of his pro-

10

cedures) and concluded that there was no evidence for the existence of a magnetic fluid.

Mesmer and his followers wrote vigorous objections to the reports (some of them quite sensible). But, unlike those reports, they had little impact on public opinion, and Mesmer's reputation suffered a sharp decline. Indeed, after a few additional public-relations setbacks, Mesmer's image was a shambles. Although he retained some loyal disciples, he left Paris and disappeared from public view.

Mesmer's reputation apparently was damaged beyond repair. Even today, most regard him as more of a quack than a visionary. But animal magnetism (also called 'mesmerism') did not join Mesmer's descent into obscurity. One major factor in its survival was the work of the Marquis de Puységur (1751-1825), a French nobleman and student of Mesmer, whose prestige and conspicuous successes kept the movement alive. In fact, for the purposes of this study, Puységur is a more central figure than his mentor.

Puységur, like Mesmer, believed in the existence of a magnetic fluid pervading and animating all of nature, and he likewise contended that both disease and healing were functions of the distribution of the fluid within the human body. But Puységur's approach differed in some important ways from those of Mesmer. Mesmer stressed the formal similarity between animal and mineral magnetism, asserting that one needed to understand the nature of the magnetic fluid in order to understand the magnetic healing process. Moreover, Mesmer considered the rapport between magnetizer and patient to be a kind of physical, or quasi-electrical linkage, allowing for the 'transmission' of the magnetic fluid. Indeed, rapport could be established with objects other than the magnetizer, including inanimate objects. For example, Mesmer believed that patients could be in rapport with each other, or with the bacquet, provided that the appropriate 'connections' were made. Puységur demurred. Although he agreed that the fluid is partially responsible for disease and physical well-being, he denied that knowledge of it was necessary to understand the healing process. And although he initially accepted Mesmer's view on the nature of rapport (and throughout his career made extensive use of inanimate transmitters of magnetic fluid, such as a magnetized tree and a version of Mesmer's bacquet), he later came to interpret rapport in terms of psychological intimacy rather than fluidic connectivity.

In fact, as Puységur's thinking evolved, he recognized that his theory of animal magnetism had taken a distinctly anti-materialist turn. To begin with, he considered the real healing agent to be the power of an immaterial *will*, which he called the 'principal driving power' of animal magnetism. Ordinarily, the will directs the motion of the animal electricity within our own bodies. But according to Puységur, a magnetizer can alter the motion of that fluid in *another* person through the process of rapport, in which the magnetizer and patient become as one person, almost as if the patient is an extention of the magnetizer's body. The rapport is so intimate that the magnetizer's will directly affects the magnetic fluid in the patient, just as it affects the fluid in his own body.

There are also less exotic (or theoretically contentious) respects in which Puységur's theory of animal magnetism has a psychological focus missing from Mesmer's original version. He not only considered an immaterial will to be the primary causal agent in healing, but also believed *good* will to be essential to healing. Furthermore, Puységur pointed to other apparently central psychodynamic features of the healing process — for example, the importance of and methods for establishing a sufficiently intimate degree of rapport with the patient, and also the psychotherapeutic utility of accessing relevant information, feelings, or thoughts hidden from the subject in the waking state.

Curiously, however, Puységur never realized — or at least he never emphasized — the importance of putting the subject into a psychological state conducive to healing. From the point of view of Puységur's theory, that is hardly surprising. Since he considered the magnetizer and patient to be intimately linked during the state of rapport, he believed that the magnetizer affects the patient's body directly and that the patient's will is literally *bypassed* in the process. Nevertheless, at certain points in his writings, Puységur seems to acknowledge the importance of the subject being in a healing-conducive state. For example, he had noticed often that previously treated patients would fall into a trance before arriving at his house. But on one occasion, that happened to a patient he'd never magnetized before. Puységur explained this by saying that once the man *decided* to be on his way to get magnetized, he was already entering into an appropriate preliminary state for becoming entranced.

Puységur's greatest contribution to the history of hypnosis was his identification of the sleeplike trance state that he called 'magnetic sleep'. He may not have been the first to notice the condition, but he was apparently the first to consider it an important feature of hypnosis and to study its properties in detail. Puységur found that some of his patients fell into this trance state after being magnetized. Although they appeared superficially to be asleep, they could nevertheless respond to questions and move about intentionally. But when they emerged from the trance, they claimed to remember nothing of what had transpired during that period. Since there were conspicuous similarities between magnetic sleep and the spontaneous condition called 'somnambulism' (i.e., sleepwalking), Puységur called the former 'magnetic somnambulism', or 'artificial somnambulism'.[3] Later, James Braid would call it 'hypnosis'.

Naturally, Puységur was intrigued by this condition, which turned out to have a number of unusual features. On many occasions, his entranced subjects exhibited a kind of 'lucidity', in which they seemed able to diagnose and predict the development of their own illnesses as well as those of others, and also to prescribe successful treatment. Puységur called this a state of 'perfect crisis',[4] and he frequently induced it in several persons simultaneously to carry out collective treatment on large groups of people. Those in crisis (now called 'physicians') would execute the command of the magnetizer to diagnose disease and prescribe remedies for those awaiting treatment. Furthermore, some entranced patients would demonstrate various forms of ostensible telepathy and clairvoyance. Mesmer had already mentioned a 'sixth sense' manifested through the application of the fluid. Puységur claimed that this sixth sense allowed persons to describe distant events and predict the future.

Puységur also observed what seemed to be a kind of state-specific memory in his magnetized subjects. While in trance, they could recall what occurred during previous states of magnetic sleep, although in the waking state they seemed to remember nothing of those periods. Magnetized subjects also were able to remember what transpired during the waking state. Furthermore, magnetized subjects tended to speak of themselves in the waking state with a kind of detachment, as if the waking self were another person. Indeed, magnetized subjects tended to exhibit a number of traits or attitudes not characteristic of the waking state. They were frequently more objective about — and even indifferent to — their problems and in general tended to adopt a different perspective on life than the one manifested while awake. Puységur took all this to show that a person's mental life was — or at least could be — deeply divided. He believed that by magnetizing a subject, he was gaining access to a kind of second self, with its own memories and characteristics. Puységur called the magnetized and waking states 'two different existences', and his follower Deleuze likewise referred to a person in these two states as 'two different beings' (Crabtree, 1985b, pp. 136-7). In fact, Deleuze noticed how some of his somnambulistic patients would speak in the third person, as if the magnetized and non-magnetized patients were distinct individuals. He concluded eventually that humans had a dual nature, composed of an external man (engaged in everyday affairs) and an internal man (a spiritual being accessed through magnetism).

Of course, the concept of a divided self did not originate with Puységur. For example, Plato argued in *The Republic* (IV. 435-441 C) that one must posit parts of the soul, with their own distinct drives and traits, to explain even ordinary conflicts of desire. (This argument is examined in Chapter 6.) But Plato's view never caught on, and it seems as if Puységur helped to resurrect and (for the first time) popularize a position very much like it. As Crabtree (1985b, 1993) has noted, Puységur helped to establish a profoundly new *tradition* of understanding the nature of psychological disturbances. The received view, prior to Puységur, was that such disturbances resulted either from purely organic malfunctions (even Mesmer adopted this position) or from the intrusion of a spirit (living or dead). But it seemed to many as if Puységur had discovered a second self or second consciousness, which could co-exist along with our ordinary waking consciousness. Apparently, this second self could have drives, thoughts, and feelings quite different from those of the waking self, some of which might impinge on our waking states and cause us to act, think, or feel in ways that appear quite foreign.

The psychological orientation of Puységur's theory divided the community of magnetists into two opposing (if not always clearly distinct) camps: *fluidists* and *animists*. Although these were not terms widely used (or used at all) at the time, one can see in retrospect that the mesmerists tended to side with one faction or the other. At any rate, the fluidists (following Mesmer) adhered to a physical explanation of animal-magnetic phenomena, arguing that changes in the patient resulted primarily from changes in the bodily distribution of a magnetic fluid. By contrast, the animists (following Puységur) attempted to explain magnetic phenomena largely in psychological terms. But members of the latter group were not strict disciples of Puységur. Puységur took the intermediate position that an immaterial will directed the movements of a magnetic fluid. By contrast, the animists placed a greater emphasis on the psychological components of the healing process, and they had their own ideas about which of those components mattered most.

1.3 THE NANCY SCHOOL

The most significant next step in the formulation of a psychological theory of animal magnetism was taken by the Portuguese priest, Abbé Faria (1755-1819), and his view was then developed further by Alexandre Bertrand (1795-1831). Faria believed, contrary to both Mesmer *and* Puységur, that there was no magnetic fluid, and that explanations of animal-magnetic phenomena should be given exclusively in psychological terms. Hence, Faria advocated, not simply a psychological, but also an anti-fluidic, theory of animal magnetism. Moreover, Faria noticed that some patients would enter a trance even before he had attempted to magnetize them — for example, as they crossed the threshold of his salon. He therefore challenged Puységur's claim that healing depends on the directing or coercive power of the healer's will. Faria proposed, instead, that the magnetizer utilizes only the more modest power of *suggestion*, which is particularly useful (but not necessary) for inducing a state of 'lucid sleep' in the subject. According to Faria, lucid sleep is the principal cause of magnetic healing, and he believed that the healing powers unleashed during that trance state are present in, though not accessible to, everyone. He considered lucid sleep to result from a type of extreme concentration, the ability or capacity for which varied from one person to another. In this state, the subject is unusually susceptible to suggestions from the healer, and that, in turn, allows the suggestions to take hold and have very powerful effects.

It was Faria who introduced the technique of having a subject fixate on an object in order to induce magnetic sleep. He called the process 'fascination', and combined it with the verbal command to sleep.

Bertrand, trained in both medicine and engineering, originally subscribed to a fluidic theory of animal magnetism. In fact, in the first of his two books he takes seriously as evidence a phenomenon reported initially by Tardy de Montravel — namely, subjects' visions of the magnetic fluid emanating from the magnetizer's fingers. Three years later (in 1826), however, he had concluded that the fluid did not exist, and that those visions could be explained in terms of the preconceptions of both magnetizer and subject, and the way they affect their expectations and imagination. Hence, Bertrand (like Faria) acknowledged the role of suggestion in producing the phenomena associated with animal magnetism. Also (like Faria), he adopted the technique of fascination for inducing magnetic sleep. Moreover, Bertrand stressed the existence of what were later called subconscious or unconscious mental processes, and he experimented extensively with the phenomenon of post-hypnotic suggestion. In fact, Janet had the greatest respect for Bertrand, and praised him for having been the first to investigate hypnosis objectively and systematically.

An even more prominent figure is James Braid (1795-1860), who spread magnetism to England in the 1840s, using Faria's and Bertrand's technique of fascination. In 1842, he coined the terms 'hypnotism' and 'nervous sleep' as substitutes for 'animal magnetism', in an attempt to sever the links with fluidic theory. And in fact, Braid's innovations in nomenclature succeeded in making the study of hypnosis more acceptable in certain medical and scientific circles. Instead of crediting mesmeric phenomena to the action and properties of an invisible fluid, Braid at first explained them in terms of a rapid weakening of the sensory and nervous systems. Later, however, he placed greater emphasis on the role of suggestion, not only in producing the hypnotic state, but also in activating the healing process. Ultimately, he described hypnotism as a psycho-physiological state to which people had varying degrees of susceptibility, and which can be either self-induced or induced by an external agent.

Although Braid adopted Faria's technique of fascination, he realized that fixing the subject's gaze was not essential, since he could hypnotize blind subjects. What mattered instead, he claimed, was to get the subject to concentrate on *something*, whether it be an object or even an idea in the mind. The importance of focused attention was later echoed by John Bramwell (1852-?), who recognized that since the *deaf* could be also hypnotized, verbal messages were likewise not essential to the hypnotic process.

About twenty years later, Braid's work made an impact in France. And before long, discussions of that work by Broca, Azam, and others came to the attention of the provincial physician, Ambroise Liébeault (1823-1901). Liébeault was curious to see if hypnotism could assist him in his medical practice, and so he offered his patients a choice. They could receive standard medical treatment for his usual fee, or else be given free hypnotic treatment. Not surprisingly, many chose the latter alternative, and Liébeault quickly attracted a large patient pool on which to experiment.

Liébeault, too, believed that suggestion was the key to hypnotic healing. He claimed that hypnotic sleep was identical to natural sleep, except that in the former, a rapport existed between patient and hypnotist. Because of that rapport, the hypnotized patient was acutely susceptible to healing suggestions from the physician. Incidentally, Liébeault was apparently something of a virtuoso when it came to inducing hypnotic sleep, owing perhaps to his innovative induction technique. Unlike Faria and his followers, who tended to combine fascination with the *command*, 'Sleep!', Liébeault hypnotized his patients by having them look into his eyes as he gently suggested that they were becoming increasingly sleepy.

Although Liébeault was a great success within his own community, his reputation spread no further, and his book *Du sommeil*, remained virtually unknown. But in 1882, he attracted the attention of Hippolyte Bernheim (1840-1919), professor of medicine at Nancy, by curing a patient whose six-year affliction of sciatica Bernheim had been unable to treat successfully. Bernheim was so impressed by Liébeault and his methods that he brought the physician to Nancy and began hypnotizing patients at the medical hospital there. Since Bernheim already had earned a considerable reputation for his research on typhoid fever as well as heart and lung disease, his endorsement of and successes with Liébeault's techniques brought belated fame to Liébeault. Together, the two men attracted a small group of hypnotic practitioners, including Henri Beaunis (1830-1921) and Jules Liégeois (1833-1908), all of whom were convinced that suggestion was the principal cause of hypnotic effects. This group founded what became known as the Nancy School of hypnotism, and its influence spread rapidly and widely throughout Europe. (Ironically, toward the end of his life, Liébeault abandoned the teachings of the school he helped to establish, and endorsed the existence of a magnetic fluid.)

After about two years' worth of collaboration with Liébeault, Bernheim published his very successful book, *De la suggestion*, which outlines his theory of hypnosis (and compares it to the slightly different theory of Liébeault). Bernheim had been using hypnosis successfully to treat a variety of ailments, including gastrointestinal diseases, diseases of the nervous system, rheumatism, and menstrual disorders. Hence he argued, contrary to Charcot (see section 1.4), that hypnosis is not a pathological condition akin to hysteria but is rather the result of suggestion, which he defined as 'the aptitude to transform an idea into an act'. Following the tradition begun with Faria, Bernheim maintained that *all* persons are suggestible, although not to the same degree. He regarded hypnosis as a condition of heightened suggestibility, induced by suggestion, and he claimed that hypnosis is easiest to induce in persons accustomed to obedience and passivity — for example, soldiers and factory workers. As time went on, Bernheim relied less and less on formal hypnotic induction, and practiced healing by suggestion in the waking state (which he and his colleagues called 'psychotherapeutics'). The influence of Bernheim and the Nancy School spread throughout Europe and to the United States. Among its foremost adherents were Schrenck-Notzing and Albert Moll in Germany, Vladimir Bechterev in Russia, Milne Bramwell in England, and Boris Sidis and Morton Prince in the U.S.

1.4 CHARCOT AND THE SALPÊTRIÈRE SCHOOL

Jean Martin Charcot (1825-1893) was one of the nineteenth century's most distinguished neurologists. In 1862, he became chief physician at the Hospice de la Salpêtrière in Paris and transformed the huge but antiquated facility into a thriving state-of-the-art hospital. He was a colorful and influential teacher, and his dynamic personality earned him many disciples and more than a few enemies. In 1878, he began experimenting with hypnosis, using as subjects some of the hysterical women he was treating at his hospital. Apparently, Charcot never used hypnosis therapeutically. Moreover, most, if not all, of his subjects were prepared (some say *coached*) by his loyal assistants, who, in effect, trained them to exhibit the hypnotic behaviors Charcot expected and later elicited in his demonstrations. This is probably the main reason why some critics charge that Charcot never hypnotized anyone. At any rate, fortified by what seems to have been a rather limited range of experience with hypnosis, Charcot asserted that one could hypnotically reproduce the hysterical symptoms (e.g., paralysis, anesthesia) plaguing his patients. He concluded, therefore, that hypnosis was merely an artificial neurosis similar to hysteria and that hypnotic phenomena were rooted entirely in physiological processes. According to Charcot, hypnosis has three physiologically distinct stages: lethargy, catalepsy, and somnambulism, which he claimed are always present in hypnosis and which always occur in the same order. Moreover, Charcot maintained that these stages do not result from suggestion. Hypnosis, he argued, was nothing more than a pathological organic disturbance.

In retrospect, it seems that Charcot's grasp of hypnosis was almost comically shallow. Although some were quick to point out that his three stages of hypnosis were by no means essential to the phenomenon, many adopted his view that hypnosis is merely an organic condition related to hysteria. That became the basis for a different 'school' of hypnosis, the so-called Salpêtrière School. The rivalry between that school and the Nancy School revived, to some extent, the older dispute between animists and fluidists.

But whatever the defects of his theory may be, Charcot deserves credit for making the study of hypnosis respectable within the scientific community. In 1882, he presented his alleged findings on the three stages of hypnosis to the Academy of Sciences, and his paper was a tremendous success. As Janet noted, it was a major achievement to have hypnotism accepted by the very same Academy that had already condemned it three times under the name of 'animal magnetism'.

1.5 HYPNOTIC ANESTHESIA

Although Charcot had observed various types of apparent hypnotic anesthesia similar to the conditions he found in hysterical patients, he neither used the phenomenon constructively nor significantly advanced our understanding of it. For example, he apparently never even absorbed, much less clarified or added to, the extensive body of data accumulated during the 1840s, when hypnotic anesthesia had been the subject of considerable controversy. Forty years before Charcot made hypnosis a legitimate area of scientific investigation, debate raged over the possibility of using hypnosis to relieve the pain of surgery. Although the writings of Faria suggest that he knew of major surgery performed under hypnosis (see Laurence and Perry, 1988, p. 140), the first well-documented surgical use of hypnosis took place in Paris, in 1829. The mesmerist Pierre Jean Chapelain and the famous surgeon Jules Cloquet hypnotized a 64-year-old woman in order to remove a cancerous breast. And in 1836 in the United States, a mesmerist named Bugard used hypnotic anesthesia to extract a tooth. But it was two British physicians who first used and recommended hypnotic anesthesia as a standard procedure for surgery.

Working independently of each other (at least initially), and certainly outside the mainstream of practitioners on the Continent, John Elliotson (1791-1868) and James Esdaile (1808-1859) made rather different sorts of contributions to this phase of the history of hypnosis. Even before his involvement in mesmerism, Elliotson had earned the reputation of a medical maverick for having been the first in England to use the stethoscope. Moreover, since he combined his advocacy of hypnosis with an interest in phrenology, many in the medical community regarded him with suspicion and hostility. Elliotson was familiar with the view that hypnosis resulted largely from suggestion, but he was a hard-core materialist who believed, instead, that hypnosis could be explained in terms of a physical influence. Furthermore, although he used hypnosis in his medical practice, Elliotson's role seems primarily to have been that of an advocate. He deplored the brutality of surgery without anesthesia, as well as other prevailing medical treatments such as bloodletting, and he sharply attacked the widespread skepticism among physicians to the use of hypnosis for relieving pain and curing disease.

In his monograph, *Numerous Cases of Surgical Operations without Pain in the Mesmeric State...* (1843/1982), Elliotson describes how the surgeon W. Squire Ward and the magnetizer William Topham operated on a man named James Wombell, amputating his leg above the knee. During the procedure, Wombell lay motionless, except for emitting a low moan as if he were having a troubled dream. In fact, there was no observed change in the patient even when the surgeon touched the severed end of the sciatic nerve. The medical community was (to put it mildly) unsympathetic to reports of the operation, and Elliotson was equally unimpressed by their skepticism. (For a recent and very clear-headed challenge to skepticism about hypnotic analgesia, see Gauld, 1988.) Several critics charged that the patient was faking, and one physician even argued that nature knows best and that patients *ought* to suffer pain during surgery. In 1843, Elliotson established and for thirteen years edited *The Zoist*, a journal devoted to the study of mesmerism.

While Elliotson was waging his campaign for hypnotic anesthesia, in India the Scottish surgeon Esdaile was using it successfully in scores of major operations. He found hypnosis to be useful not only as an anesthetic, but also as a means for reducing surgical shock. Esdaile's interest in the professional applications of hypnosis had been aroused by reading Cloquet's account of the mastectomy mentioned above. Eventually Esdaile produced two books (1846, 1852), which outline his theoretical position, record the details of many of his surgical procedures, and report numerous fascinating observations and experiments made along the way. And as we will see, Esdaile's experiments with hypnotic anesthesia anticipated studies conducted around the turn of the century.

At the beginning of his first book, *Mesmerism in India*, Esdaile lists seventy-three operations performed under hypnotic anesthesia during the previous eight months. These included amputations of an arm, a breast, and a penis; several cataract operations; the removal of great toe nails by the roots; and the removal of seventeen scrotal tumors weighing from 8 to 80 pounds. Esdaile notes that no deaths resulted from these procedures. During Esdaile's six years in India, he used hypnosis for more than 261 major operations and many more minor procedures. Two hundred of the major operations were for the removal of scrotal tumors, resulting from the relatively common affliction of elephantiasis. At least twenty of the tumors weighed from 50 to 103 pounds, and many of the patients were more than 50 years old. Furthermore, only 8 percent of those 200 patients died immediately after surgery, compared to the prevailing mortality rate of between 40 and 50 percent for the same procedure using conventional non-hypnotic techniques. When Esdaile's patients died, it was usually days or weeks later, and resulted from cholera, lockjaw, or dysentary, probably attributable to the impoverished and filthy conditions in which they lived.

21

Like Elliotson, Esdaile subscribed to a fluidic theory of mesmerism. He considered it to be 'a physical power exerted by one animal over another' (1852, p. 222), and he claimed that he would just as soon 'adopt the *diabolical* theory' (p. 222) as accept an explanation of hypnotic phenomena in terms of the action of the imagination. He claimed that all his patients were mesmerized with their eyes closed, in a dark room, and that he preferred to leave the patients ignorant (when possible) of his intention to mesmerize them. According to Esdaile, the physical mesmeric power can affect people when asleep or in a coma, or without their knowledge, and he claimed it can affect brutes as well. Moreover, he believed that only a physical theory could adequately explain his ability to mesmerize patients by having them drink water that they did not know he had already magnetized.

Probably one reason why Esdaile's methods attracted few converts is that an effective chemical anesthesia was discovered the same year he published *Mesmerism in India*. But quite apart from that obstacle to success, Esdaile (like Elliotson) was the target of frequent attacks from members of the medical establishment, to which he reacted sharply with charges of stupidity and dishonesty. In response to the familiar allegation that his patients merely pretended to feel no pain in order to please the doctor, Esdaile often claimed that this would not explain the change in subjects' *involuntary* responses during certain tests he conducted. These tests are forerunners of important experiments conducted fifty years later, and they merit a brief examination.

Consider, for example, the following reports.

September 13th, 1847. — Hurronundo Saha, the former owner of the *monster* tumour (weight 103 lbs.), occasionally comes to the hospital to make his *salaam*, and did so to-day. He is as plump as a quail, and in excellent health. I had only occasionally tried if he still retained his mesmeric susceptibility, and found that he could still be readily entranced or thrown into somnambulism.

He was blindfolded to-day, and, his nose being mesmerised for a few minutes, he was given snuff, and desired to draw it up his nostrils: this he did with force, saying that he felt nothing. A bottle of carbonate of ammonia was placed under his nose, and he breathed it as tranquilly as common air: but, the moment he was demesmerised, he showed the most violent signs of irritation in his nostrils and eyes. He was again blindfolded, and, without mesmerising him, the bottle was made to touch his nose *with the cork in it*, with the usual non-effect; but, the moment it was opened, he drew back in disgust. The nose was again mesmerised, and he now breathed the irritating fumes without a symptom of annoyance.

(Esdaile, 1852, pp. 134-5)

December 4th, 1847. — Luckynarain Dey, preparing for operation, was found deeply entranced to-day: he was pricked and pinched with no effect, and could not be roused by the loudest noises. His mouth was opened, and sulphate of magnesia was placed upon his tongue, which remained quite passive, and *there was no increase of saliva.*

His nose was also put into a bottle of carbonate of ammonia, and he inhaled the fumes like common air. He could only be awakened by syringing his eyes with cold water, and the moment he came to his senses he retched violently, and said that his mouth was disgustingly bitter — why he could not tell.

(Esdaile, 1852, pp. 135-6)

Esdaile also observed, among other things, the high selectivity of hypnotic analgesia. For instance, sensitivity to pain apparently differed from sensitivity to temperature. Esdaile noticed that mesmerized patients sometimes complained of or otherwise showed sensitivity to cold drafts from open windows or air from a cold operating room, although they were apparently anesthetic to the major surgical procedures being performed on them (1852, pp. 172ff). On the basis of related observations, Binet (1896, p. 292) later distinguished *total* from *complete* anesthesia. Anesthesia is total when a given region is insensible to *all* forms of stimulation; it's complete when there is no conscious experience of the stimulation, no matter how great its intensity. Hence, anesthesia can be rated for totality with respect to just one region of the body, and it can be rated for completeness with respect to just one sense modality.

Although Binet's distinction seems worthwhile (at least in principle), it may be of little practical utility. For one thing, it is not clear that anesthesia is ever total. For example, Binet reported that anesthetized subjects might still be sensitive to electrical stimulation, no matter how effective hypnotic anesthesia is in other respects. Binet also claimed that some patients seem totally insensible, except with regard to certain *objects* (1896, p. 295). Moreover, it is unclear what to say about Esdaile's anesthetized patients, who nevertheless displayed apparent sensitivity to temperature. For example, it's unclear whether the patient's *whole* body was insensitive to pain. Hence, it's unclear whether those patients were sensitive to temperature in exactly the same regions in which they were anesthetized.

(Incidentally, various researchers were quick to recognize that areas of hypnotic anesthesia do not correspond to natural physiological regions of sensitivity − for example, as would be affected by neurological damage. Hence, a subject might become anesthetic in an area he merely *believes* to be a natural region of sensitivity, or in an area of symbolic or other form of personal significance − for example, a band around the arm.)

1.6 HYPNOSIS AND SECONDARY CONSCIOUSNESS

Although mental health professionals and many lay readers have at least a superficial understanding of the work of Freud, relatively few know anything at all about Pierre Janet (1859-1947). Yet some consider Janet − rather than Freud − to be the real pioneer of depth psychology. Beginning in the late 1880s, Janet attempted to describe and explain the behavior of persons suffering from hysterical symptoms as well as those exhibiting a 'doubling of the personality'. He seems also to have been the first to use the term 'subconscious', at least in anything close to its present-day sense. At any rate, Janet's use of that term and his accounts of subconscious processes laid the groundwork for modern dynamic psychiatry, including (of course) Freudian theories of the unconscious.

Janet began his career as a philosopher, and through his interest in hallucinations and the philosophy of perception he learned (in 1885) of a subject named Léonie, who allegedly could be hypnotized at a distance. Janet's interest in psychopathology was so stimulated by his subsequent investigation of Léonie and several other subjects that in 1889 he decided to pursue a degree in medicine, a career move that he had already been contemplating for several years.

Janet published the results of his early investigations in a series of three articles in the *Revue Philosophique* (1886, 1887, 1888), and these formed the basis for his doctoral thesis in philosophy at the Sorbonne (also, his first book) *L'Automatisme Psychologique* (1889). Although this research was based on the study of fourteen hysterical women, five hysterical men, and eight psychotics and epileptics, Janet's work concentrated on four women: Rose, Marie, Lucie, and Léonie. Overall, Janet was deeply impressed by the way in which hypnosis seemed to uncover information that could explain a variety of symptoms. For example, he linked Marie's depression and hysterical shivers, spasms, and pains to an apparently forgotten episode uncovered during hypnosis. Marie had been so acutely ashamed by her first menstrual period that she plunged herself into a bucket of cold water to stop the bleeding. Evidently, each month Marie was reliving the violent shivers and delirium she had experienced at the time. Janet also used hypnosis to trace a blindness in Marie's left eye to a traumatic experience that occurred when she was six years old.

Similarly, Lucie suffered fits of terror for no apparent reason. But through the automatic writing she produced under hypnosis, Janet uncovered what seemed to be the cause of those fits. At the age of seven, Lucie had been frightened by two men hiding behind a curtain. Janet also found that a second personality, Adrienne, was reliving this experience during Lucie's fits of terror. Léonie, too, turned out to have several personalities, whose characteristics and relationships to one another Janet described in detail.

Perhaps the most novel and important thesis in Janet's early work is the claim that certain ideas, thoughts, feelings, memories, etc., may be isolated from the rest of one's mental activity, although they can be uncovered through hypnosis. They are, in other words, *dissociated* or split-off from the individual's consciousness. (See Chapter 4 for a detailed discussion of the concept of dissociation.) Nevertheless, dissociated ideas will remain within the field of another consciousness, where they develop or are simply sustained more or less autonomously. These *subconscious* fixed ideas, which are often caused by a traumatic event, may then manifest in automatic writing, hallucinations, compulsions, and other hysterical symptoms. Moreover, there may be more than one subconscious field or 'mind', and when a cluster of subconscious fixed ideas becomes sufficiently systematic, these may manifest in behavior as alternate personalities.

Janet believed that the development of subconscious fixed ideas resulted from a narrowing of the field of consciousness, and he believed, further, that this contraction of consciousness resulted from a weakness in our ablity to maintain conscious unity. Hence, he described hysteria as a

> malady of the *personal synthesis...*, *a form of mental depression characterized by the retraction of the field of personal consciousness and a tendency to the dissociation and emancipation of the systems of ideas and functions that constitute personality.*
>
> (Janet, 1907/1920, p. 332)

To uncover the fixed ideas plaguing his patients, and also to communicate with the subconscious mind or second self, Janet sometimes employed a technique called *distraction*. From his theoretical viewpoint, this technique took advantage of the hysteric's severely narrowed field of attention. First, Janet would get the subject engrossed in an activity, such as reading aloud or talking. Then he would position himself behind the subject and utter various commands or questions in a low whisper. Apparently, Janet's patients were not consciously aware of these utterances. Nevertheless, they would respond, evidently without realizing it and without interfering with the task at hand. For example, Janet found that he could elicit responses through gestures and automatic writing, and even cause his subjects to perform a series of complex and awkward bodily movements.

Janet's famous case of Achilles illustrates his use of this technique, as well as his diagnostic application of hypnosis. Achilles was a thirty-three-year-old man, apparently suffering from demonic possession. When Janet met him in 1890, he was in an extremely agitated state. He would strike himself repeatedly, utter blasphemies, and at times speak with the voice of the devil. This condition had begun about six months before, after the patient had gone on a short business trip. When he returned, his wife noticed that he was preoccupied, depressed, and uncommunicative. Doctors examined him, but found nothing wrong. Suddenly, Achilles burst into a two-hour fit of laughter and claimed that he saw hell, Satan, and demons. Then he tied his legs together and threw himself into a pond. When he was retrieved, he explained that this had been a test to see whether he was indeed possessed. By the time Janet met him, Achilles had been exhibiting the classic signs of possession for several months. But Achilles would not speak to Janet, and he resisted the latter's attempts at hypnosis.

So Janet decided to take advantage of Achilles' absorption in his demonic manifestations. He placed a pencil in the patient's hand and whispered questions to him from behind. When the hand responded, Janet asked, 'Who are you?', and the hand wrote 'the Devil'. Janet then requested proof of the Devil's identity. First, he asked the Devil to force Achilles to raise his arm against his will. The Devil complied. Then he asked the Devil to put Achilles into an hypnotic state, also against the latter's will. Evidently, the Devil again complied, and because Achilles was hypnotized, he began to answer Janet's questions directly and tell his own story. During the business trip six months earlier, Achilles had been unfaithful to his wife. When he tried to forget about the episode, he discovered that he was unable to speak. He also began to dream often about the Devil, and shortly thereafter he found himself to be possessed.

It is easy to see why the use of distraction and automatic writing led many to claim that at least two distinct selves, minds or consciousnesses were at work. For example, it seemed as if one consciousness was engrossed in conversation, while another was engaged in automatic writing. The former would apparently be unaffected by the writing of the latter and would continue conversation as if nothing out of the ordinary were occurring. Similarly, the intelligence guiding the writing seemed either unaware of or unconcerned with the activities or interests of the primary consciousness.

Along the same lines, hysterical and hypnotic anesthesias seemed to provide evidence for the existence of a secondary consciousness. The hypnotized subject could report painful sensations of which the waking subject was apparently unaware. In fact, through automatic writing, subjects could report the phenomena even while they were occurring, and while the remainder of the subjects' behavior showed no sign of feeling the experimentally-induced pain. To many, this suggested that 'during the times of anaesthesia, and coexisting with it, *sensibility to the anaesthetic parts is also there, in the form of a secondary consciousness* entirely cut off from the primary or normal one, but susceptible of being *tapped* and made to testify to its existence in various odd ways' (James, 1890/1891, p. 201).[5] (See also James, 1889/1986.) Studies of hypnotic anesthesia have continued to the present day, most notably in Hilgard's experimental efforts to elicit reports of a 'hidden observer' (Hilgard, 1986).[6]

Even more impressive, perhaps, were phenomena occurring in connection with post-hypnotic suggestion. Researchers had known for some time that if an entranced subject is told to hallucinate or perform an act at a certain time after waking, the subject will obey. But they were understandably puzzled by the subject's ability not only to register the command but also to carry it out at the proper time. For one thing, it appeared as if the waking person remembered nothing of the instructions given during hypnosis. In fact, waking subjects would often appear puzzled by the actions or sensations resulting from prior suggestion, and they would invent contrived and unconvincing stories to account for their mysterious impulses and experiences. And for another, it was unclear how the subject marked the passage of time while he was apparently engrossed in a different activity.

The first major breakthrough in this puzzle was provided by Edmund Gurney (1847-1888), one of the most clever and original nineteenth-century investigators of hypnosis (see Gurney, 1887a). In an intriguing series of experiments, subjects gave accounts of the ways in which they subconsciously calculated the right moment to execute a post-hypnotic command. Hence, these experiments seemed to show that a secondary consciousness persisted and carried out its own agenda of activities even when the subject was performing different tasks in the waking state.

For example, on March 25, 1887, the hypnotized subject was told to put his hat on and take it off 20 minutes after his arrival for their next session. He was also instructed to write automatically (when given an instrument for doing so) how many minutes had passed and how many remained. The next day the subject arrived at 7:13, and participated in a few experiments. At 7:31, in the waking state, he wrote (by means of a planchette) '18 minutes gone 1½ more'. (Gurney's usual procedure was to hold a large screen in front of the subject's eyes in order to block his view of his writing hand, and at the same time to engage the subject in conversation or to have him read aloud.) At 7:35, the subject walked over to his hat and carried out the suggestion to put it on and then remove it. When he was then re-hypnotized and reminded that 18 and 1½ do not equal 20, the subject replied that he had allowed half a minute for the writing. Although Gurney had not timed the automatic writing, he noted that it did, in fact, seem to take less than a minute.

Another subject, while hypnotized, was told that 7 minutes after awakening he was to look out the window, and that during that 7-minute period he was to write how the time was going. He was brought out of trance at 7:34:20 and given a planchette. Writing began at 7:36:30, with Gurney holding the screen in front of the subject's eyes as usual. Although Gurney did not watch him write, he was close enough to the subject's arm to realize that the writing was being produced at distinct intervals, and he commented aloud that it seemed 'to be going by fits and starts' (1887a, p. 313). At 7:40 the subject stopped writing, stood up, drew aside the blind, and looked out the window. When Gurney examined the paper, he found that the subject had written

$$25 \quad 34 \quad 43 \quad 52 \quad 61 \quad 7$$

Evidently, he had been recording, at each minute from the time he began to write (2 minutes after being brought out of trance), the number of minutes that had passed and the number that remained.

1.7 FURTHER EXPERIMENTS IN HYPNOSIS

Gurney's experiments were part of a late nineteenth-century flurry of experimentation on hypnotized subjects, intended to probe both the workings of hypnosis and the nature of secondary consciousness. One reason these experiments are important is that they seemed to uncover processes in normal healthy subjects that paralleled those investigated in hysterical patients. Hence, they suggested that the peculiar phenomena of secondary consciousness were not necessarily pathological and that they could be generalized to the population as a whole. Among the major figures in this period were William James, Boris Sidis, and Morton Prince in the U.S., Gurney in England, and Janet and Alfred Binet in France.

Possibly the most fascinating experiments involved the induction of what Binet called *systematized anesthesias* and what others (following Bernheim in 1884) called *negative hallucinations*. Binet's term was selected because subjects were made to suppress 'a system of sensations and ideas pertaining to particular objects'

(1896, p. 296). Bernheim's term was intended to emphasize that subjects could be made unaware of objects they would ordinarily be perceiving, contrary to the more familiar form of (positive) hallucination in which they would apparently perceive non-existent objects. One reason these experiments are so interesting is that they seem to demonstrate, apparently paradoxically, that subjects must in some sense recognize objects in order not to perceive them. And of course that is why many considered them to provide additional evidence for the existence of a secondary consciousness. Hence, Binet wrote,

> the perception forbidden by suggestion undergoes the same fate as the sensations arising [spontaneously in hysterics] from anaesthetic regions. It is relegated to a second consciousness, where it determines ideas, judgments, and actions, which are all equally unconscious to the principal personality.
>
> (Binet, 1896, p. 297)

Later, in Chapters 3, 5, and 7, we will consider whether or to what extent dissociative phenomena indicate that more than one consciousness (mind, or self) exists in an individual. It should be clear, in any case, why such a view is appealing, and it should help to examine briefly the kind of evidence that many have found compelling. Consider, for example, James's comments on a class of experiments apparently demonstrating that

> a subject *must distinguish the object from others like it in order to be blind to it*. Make him blind to one person in the room, set all the persons in a row, and tell him to count them. He will count all but that one. But how can he tell *which* one not to count without recognizing who he is? In like manner, make a stroke on paper or blackboard, and tell him it is not there, and he will see nothing but the clean paper or board. Next (he not looking) surround the original stroke with other strokes exactly like it, and ask him what he sees. He will point out one by one all the new strokes, and omit the original one every time, no matter how numerous the new strokes may be, or in what order they are arranged. Similarly, if the original single stroke to which he is blind be *doubled* by a prism of some sixteen degrees placed before one of his eyes (both being kept open), he

will say that he now sees *one* stroke, and point in the direction in which the image seen through the prism lies, ignoring still the original stroke.

(James, 1890/1891, pp. 208-209) (see also, p. 1207)

According to Binet,

in facts of this kind...[t]here is always an unconscious judgment that precedes, prepares, and guides the phenomenon of anaesthesia. The perception of the forbidden object continues to operate, but it becomes unconscious.

(Binet, 1896, p. 302)

Certain experiments merit a fairly detailed examination. For one thing, they provide fascinating illustrations of the phenomenon of systematized anesthesia. And for another, they demonstrate standards of experimentation on human subjects that many today would find ethically suspect. Consider an experiment conducted by Bernheim on an eighteen-year-old servant girl, Elise B___. (Bernheim's account is quoted verbatim in Binet, 1896.)

I easily developed negative hallucinations in her. During her sleep I said to her, 'When you wake you will no longer see me, I shall have gone'. When she awoke she looked about for me and did not seem to see me. I talked to her in vain, shouted in her ear, stuck a pin in her skin, her nostrils, under the nails, and thrust the point of the pin in the mucous membrane of the eye. She did not move a muscle. As far as she was concerned, I had ceased to exist, and all the acoustic, visual, tactile, and other impressions emanating from myself made not the slightest impression upon her; she ignored them all. As soon, however, as another person touched her with the pin unknown to her, she perceived it quickly, and drew back the member that had been pricked.

(Binet, 1896, p. 305)

It was useless to tell her that I was there and that I was talking to her. She was convinced that they were simply making fun at her expense. I gazed at her obstinately and said: 'You see me well enough, but you act as if you did not see me. You are a humbug, you are playing a part!' She did not stir and continued to talk to other people. I added, with a confident manner: 'However, I know all about it.

31

You can not deceive me. It is only two years since you had a child and you made away with it! Is that true? I have been told so'. She did not move, her face remained peaceful. Wishing to see, on account of its medico-legal bearing, whether a serious offence might be committed under cover of a negative hallucination, I roughly raised her dress and skirt. Although naturally very modest, she allowed this without a blush. I pinched the calf of her leg and her thigh. She made absolutely no sign whatever. I am convinced that she might have been assaulted in this state without opposing the slightest resistance.

That established, I asked the head of the clinic to put her to sleep again and suggest to her that I should again be there when she awoke. This she realized. She saw me again and remembered nothing that had happened in the interval. I said to her: 'You have just seen me. I talked with you'. She was astonished, and said: 'Why, no, you were not there'. 'I was there and did talk with you. Ask these gentlemen if I didn't'. 'I saw those gentlemen very well. M. P.___ tried to persuade me that you were there. But that was only a joke. You were not there'. 'Very well', I said, 'but you remember everything that happened while I was not there — all that I said and did to you!' 'But how could you say and do anything to me when you were not here?' I insisted; speaking seriously and looking her in the face, I laid stress on every word: 'It is true I was not there, but you remember just the same'. I put my hand on her forehead and declared: 'You remember everything, absolutely everything. There, speak out! What did I say to you?' After a moment's concentrated thought, she blushed and said: 'Oh no, it is not possible, you were not there. I must have dreamed it'. 'Very well; what did I say to you in this dream?' She was ashamed and did not want to say. I insisted. At last she said, 'You said that I had had a child'. 'And what did I do to you?' 'You pricked me with a pin'. 'And then?' After a few minutes she said: 'Oh no, I would not have allowed you to do it; it is a dream'. 'What did you dream?' 'That you exposed me', etc.

(Binet, 1896, pp. 306-308)

Similar experiments were conducted by Jules Liégeois

(1833-1908), a lawyer at Nancy who worked closely with Lié-beault and Bernheim. He was particularly interested in forensic aspects of hypnosis, and is perhaps best known for having induced hypnotized subjects to commit (and then have amnesia for) what they believed were strongly objectionable criminal acts. In the present context, however, we must focus on some novel results he obtained with suggestions for systematized anesthesia. The most curious, perhaps, is a method he discovered for communicating with subjects acting on the suggestion that he was not there. Liégeois, like his colleagues, had noted that these subjects seemed totally unaware of his presence, no matter how it was manifested. For example, he, too, found that he could thrust pins in the subjects and get no response, whereas they reacted immediately to the same stimulation from others. But Liégeois found that if he spoke to the subjects impersonally, speaking only in the third person, and (he says) as if the subject's own internal voice was speaking, he could get the subject to carry out various of his suggestions.

Consider, for example, some remarks he made about the subject Camille, 18 years old (also quoted in Binet, 1896).

I assured myself of the state of her sensibility....[T]his existed for all the assistants, but did not exist for anything emanating from me. If anyone else pricked her she quickly drew her arm back. If I pricked her she did not feel it. I stuck pins in her that remained hanging from her arms and cheek. She complained of no sensation....

In the same way, if I held a bottle of ammonia under her nose she did not push it away. but she turned away from it when it was presented to her by a strange hand.

...if I speak directly to Camille...if I ask her, for example, how she is, how long it has been since she stopped growing, etc., her countenance remains impassive. She neither sees nor hears me — at least she is not conscious of so doing.

I then proceed...impersonally, talking not in my own name, but as if an internal voice of her own was speaking, and expressing such ideas as the subject would be likely to get from his own private thought. Then somnambulistic auto-matism shows itself in this new and unexpected guise, as complete as any of the other forms already known.

(Quoted in Binet, 1896, p. 312)

I said aloud: 'Camille is thirsty; she is going to the kitchen for a glass of water that she will bring back and set on this table'. She did not seem to have heard me, and yet in a few minutes she acted as I had said, and carried out the suggestion with that brisk and impetuous manner...frequently noticed in somnambulists. She was asked why she brought the glass that she put on the table. She did not know what was meant. She had not moved. There was no glass there.

(Binet, 1896, p. 313)

Another interesting set of experiments concerns hypnotically induced hallucinations and color reversal. For example, James (1890/1981) notes how suggested hallucinations may be followed by a negative after-image. He reports that when the subject is made to hallucinate a colored cross on a sheet of white paper, he will see a cross of the complementary color if he shifts his gaze to a different sheet (p. 204). Similarly, Johnson (1900) induced his subject to experience hallucinations of various different pictures on sheets of white paper. After about 30 minutes, he asked her to look again at the sheets and describe what she saw. The subject reported the same images but with the colors reversed. For example, she described a blue cross on a yellow ground, whereas previously she had reported (and apparently experienced) a yellow cross on a blue ground.

James noted similar results in connection with negative hallucinations, and (like other such hallucinations) they seemed in particular to indicate the presence of a secondary consciousness.

if you make a red cross (say) on a sheet of white paper invisible to an hypnotic subject, and yet cause him to look fixedly at a dot on the paper on or near the cross, he will, on transferring his eye to a blank sheet, see a bluish-green after-image of the cross. This proves that it has impressed his sensibility. He has *felt* it, but not *perceived* it. He has actively ignored it, refused to recognize it, as it were.

(James, 1890/1891, p. 1206)

1.8 REMARKS ON AUTOMATIC WRITING

Just as formal hypnotic induction can produce subjective and behavioral phenomena similar to those reported arising spontaneously in cases of hysteria, the automatic writing elicited in connection with experimental or therapeutic hypnosis has its counterpart in spontaneous automatisms. Of course, spontaneous automatic writing might still result from hypnosis — in this case, self-hypnosis. However, spontaneous automatisms are an unusually rich source of information concerning both the apparent nature of secondary consciousness and the experience of that consciousness.

The literature on ostensible demonic possession is filled with reports of spontaneous automatisms of various sorts. But even when humdrum automatic writing occurs in contexts or epochs where possession is not considered a viable explanatory option, it still has the appearance of possession of some kind or other — if not, demonic, then by another part of oneself. Since many people actually and quite voluntarily began to *practice* automatic writing toward the end of the last century, they have been able to report on those episodes in ways unlikely to have been elicited in experimental or clinical settings. And in fact, the data reveals certain regularities.

For one thing, as James observed, the automatist often falls into a sleepy or trance-like condition while writing, and seems to be 'abstracted from the outer world' (James, 1889/1986, p.43). Before writing begins, the subject might experience peculiar sensations or spasms in the writing arm or hand. But perhaps most important,

> the writing and speech announce themselves as from a personality other than the natural one of the writer, and often convince *him*, at any rate, that his organs are played upon by someone not himself.
>
> (James 1889/1986, p. 45)

Consider, for example, the oft-quoted remarks by Sidney Dean, 'member of Congress from Connecticut from 1855 to 1859, who has been all his life a robust and active journalist, author, and man of affairs' (James 1889/1986, p. 45). Dean, who produced automatic scripts for many years, says,

> when the work is in progress I am in the normal condition, and seemingly two minds, intelligences, persons, are practically engaged. The writing is in my own hand, but the dictation not of my own mind and will, but that of another...; and I, myself, consciously criticise the thought,

35

fact, mode of expressing it, etc....Sentences are commenced without knowledge of mine as to their subject or ending.

(James, 1889/1986, p. 46)

It is an intelligent *ego* who writes, or else the influence assumes individuality, which practically makes of the influence a personality. It is *not* myself; of that I am conscious at every step of the process.

(James, 1889/1986, p. 47)

Another man, John N. Arnold, writes about his automatic personality (named 'Automat') as if he was dealing with a distinct person.

the Automat and I got disgusted with one another years ago. We had a falling out, and haven't been on good terms since. The Auto got tired with my lack of patience, and I got tired with the Auto's lack of truthfulness.

(James, 1889/1986, p. 48)

Since automatisms occurred spontaneously in people apparently not suffering from some form of psychopathology, it seemed to many as if secondary consciousness might be a pervasive feature of human consciousness generally. Also (as we have seen), some frequent automatists seemed to have a secondary consciousness that manifested regularly and that appeared quite personality-like. Hence, this body of data provides a handy transition to the even more dramatic phenomena of multiple personality.

2

MULTIPLE PERSONALITY DISORDER: A SURVEY OF THE EVIDENCE

2.1 INTRODUCTION

At the outset, we should note that the currently accepted profile (especially the etiological profile) of a multiple may be based on a biased sample of cases — namely, those subjects finding their way to mental health professionals. In later chapters, we will consider the possibility that some types of multiple personality are not forms of psychopathology — hence, that they should not be classified as types of multiple personality *disorder*. For example, this would be the case if (as some claim) we are all multiples — that is, a colony or synthesis of lower-order functionally distinct selves. But for now, we need only remember that the following is a sketch of multiple personality disorder. And I doubt that this tactic should be cause for concern. Certainly, MPD patients are the most thoroughly investigated class of ostensible multiples. Hence, it seems reasonable to focus on them initially and to proceed as if their manifestations — although admittedly dramatic - are largely paradigmatic of multiplicity generally.

Until recently, multiple personality was generally considered to be quite rare. Now, however, a rapidly growing body of scientists and clinicians consider it to be relatively common — or at least prevalent enough to justify the formation in 1984 of the International Society for the Study of Multiple Personality and Dissociation (ISSMP&D, shortened in 1994 to ISSD), whose membership approached 2,000 at the end of the decade.

To some extent, no doubt, the current frequency of MPD diagnoses reflects recent clinical insights into MPD's more subtle manifestations. But it is also partly a function of larger cultural and social influences. In an earlier epoch, cases now diagnosed as MPD probably would have been classified as cases of demonic or spirit possession (Crabtree, 1985b; Ellenberger, 1970; Laurence and Perry, 1988; Ross, 1989). But beginning in the eighteenth century, the conceptual climate changed gradually and profoundly. Puységur's accounts of magnetic sleep and an apparent doubling of consciousness, the general rise of interest in hypnosis (particularly in the nineteenth century), and Janet's introduction of the concept of dissociation, all contributed to fostering the view that personality or behavioral disorders — and, to a degree, psychological processes generally — could best be explained in terms of deep divisions of consciousness. Hence, diagnoses of multiple personality became fairly common, while reports of possession declined sharply. (In addition to the works already cited, historical essays by E.T. Carlson also merit examination — in particular, 1981, 1984, 1986, and 1989.)

But then the intellectual climate changed again. Between 1910 and 1970, diagnoses of MPD dwindled dramatically. Freudian dynamics (and the concept of repression) displaced dissociation theory, and many came to regard dissociation as nothing more than a form of repression (see Chapter 4 for an account of the difference between these two concepts; and see Ross, 1989, for criticism of Freud's influence on the diagnosis and treatment of dissociative disorders; also, Marx, 1970). Moreover, around 1910, Bleuler introduced the term 'schizophrenia', which seemed to range over many of the phenomena of MPD and which clinicians were quick to embrace. Accordingly, some argue that enthusiasm over the concept of schizophrenia led to the misdiagnosis of many multiples as schizophrenic (see, e.g., Rosenbaum, 1980). At any rate, it is clear that since 1970, many patients diagnosed as schizophrenic were re-diagnosed as multiples. Furthermore, due in part to the prevailing enthusiasm for Freudian dynamics, some believed that MPD, like hysteria, was an artifact resulting from the demand characteristics of the therapeutic setting (especially in cases where hypnosis was used). In other words, they regarded MPD as *iatrogenic*, unwittingly created by the physician or therapist, and aided by the subject's heightened suggestibility and desire to please (see section 2.6).

It is not altogether clear why diagnoses of MPD increased again, beginning around 1970. It may be connected to a gradual dissatisfaction with certain aspects of the Freudian conceptual framework, and perhaps also to a growing disenchantment with behaviorism in psychology (and its myopic focus on outer behavior to the exclusion of inner experience). It may also have to do with the interest generated by the popular cases of Eve (Thigpen and Cleckley, 1957; Sizemore and Pittillo, 1977) and Sybil (Schreiber, 1974). Moreover, if it is true (as many clinicians claim) that multiples tend to be misdiagnosed and that many cases *had* been misdiagnosed prior to 1970, the present MPD explosion may reflect a backlog of hitherto misdiagnosed cases rather than a sudden glut of MPD appearing *de novo*. But whatever the reason, the number of diagnoses of MPD has risen significantly in recent years, and although some remain skeptical about the genuineness of multiple personality, the clinical community on the whole (particularly in the U.S.A.) seems to have re-evaluated MPD conceptually. For example, before the appearance of the DSM-III (Diagnostic and Statistical Manual of Mental Disorders, Third Edition) in 1980, the American Psychiatric Association did not officially recognize MPD as a distinct diagnostic category. The DSM-II had listed MPD merely as a *symptom* under 'hysterical neurosis, dissociative type'. In the DSM-III, however, it appeared as a separate category under the more general heading of 'dissociative disorders'. (See Chapter 10 for a discussion of subsequent developments.)

2.2 A GENERAL SKETCH OF MPD

According to the received view of MPD, which has evolved steadily during the past twenty years, multiple personality has two main causal determinants. The first is a capacity for profound dissociation; in fact, MPD patients tend to be highly hypnotizable. The second is a history of (usually severe and chronic) childhood trauma — typically, a combination of emotional, physical, and sexual abuse.

The significance of high hypnotizability (in this case, really, *self*-hypnotizability) is that MPD patients have a coping mechanism at their disposal not available to victims of abuse or trauma who do not become multiples. To put it picturesquely, through dissociation, the subject is able to avoid experiencing or dealing with an intolerable episode by turning it over to an alternate personality (or *alter*) who undergoes those experiences in his place. Those lacking such a dissociative coping mechanism may resort instead to denial or repression, and as a result they may develop different sorts of disorders (e.g., various forms of sexual dysfunction).

A large majority of MPD patients report a history of sexual

abuse, and a majority of those report instances of incest. Witnessing a violent death (usually of a parent or sibling) is another frequently reported trauma. Sometimes, the abuse appears to have been ritualistic and quite grisly, especially (but not exclusively) certain ceremonial acts reportedly performed in connection with religious or satanic cults. For example, the mother of a male MPD patient performed the following ritual: She would use a thermometer to push pearls into her son's penile urethra. She would then retrieve the pearl by pulling on a thread to which the pearl had been attached (Braun and Sachs, 1985). In another case, a five-year-old girl was made to watch her father throw a live cat into a furnace. He then promised to retrieve it on the condition that they have sexual intercourse (Bliss, 1986).

Clinicians realize that adult reports of childhood abuse may be distorted by time and memory, and that many of the reports are, in fact, unverified (see, e.g., Ganaway, 1989). Nevertheless, some adult multiples do have a verified history of childhood abuse. Moreover, in the past few years, a project at the National Institute of Mental Health has focused exclusively on children with MPD having a documented history of trauma or abuse.

At least three-quarters of known cases report or exhibit personalities claiming to be under the age of twelve. About half of the cases exhibit personalities of the opposite sex. And of course, a multiple's alternate personalities tend to display distinctive sets of mannerisms, values, lifestyles, and abilities. Although alternate personalities may be classified in many different ways, certain obvious types appear frequently, and their general functions tend to be quite clear (Putnam, 1985c). For example, child personalities often retain or protect the subject from pain or trauma. Persecutor personalities torment one or more of the other alters in various ways (e.g., by inflicting pain, playing mischief, or by attempting mutilation or murder of another alter). On the other hand, helper personalities provide guidance or advice, and assist with tasks other alters find difficult. There are also recorder or memory personalities, who maintain continuous awareness of the individual's activities (and sometimes mental states), even when other alters experience periods of amnesia. When one identifies personality types according to their attitudes, general dispositions, or orientation, one frequently finds that pairs of personality types are present, exhibiting a particular dichotomy — for example, male/female, hostile/friendly, aggressive/passive, liberal/conser-

MULTIPLE PERSONALITY DISORDER

vative, rebellious/obedient, extroverted/introverted, sexually pro-
miscuous/inhibited.

The earliest reported cases of MPD tended to be dual personalities, with the occasional exception of a patient having three or four
alters. But according to several recent surveys (Bliss, 1980; Coons,
Bowman, and Milstein, 1988; Kluft, 1884a, 1988b; Putnam, *et al.*,
1986; Schultz, Braun, and Kluft, 1989), the average number of
personalities in cases of MPD ranges (roughly) from six to sixteen.
Some cases reportedly exhibit well over one hundred alters. Kluft
(1988b) so far holds the record for the highest number of reported
alters: more than 4,500. (One can only wonder about the accuracy
of such an estimate; see section 2.4.) Many of these are perhaps
better described as personality *fragments*, since their functions
tend to be highly circumscribed and because they do not exhibit
the more extensive range of traits and dispositions found in
more personality-like alters. Ross (1989) prudently notes that in
these cases of 'polyfragmented' MPD 'the [splitting] process may
not be the same as the formation of alters' (p. 81). He suggests,
somewhat more contentiously, that the creation of mere fragments
may not even be a dissociative phenomenon. Instead, he proposes that the person may merely label different memories with
distinct names. However, considering the functional specificity
of alter-fragments, Ross should perhaps have said that different
functions belonging to the same alter may simply be given different
names.

But quite apart from the status of highly specialized personality
fragments, it remains true that clinicians now report greater
numbers of relatively robust alternate personalities than they did
previously. And not surprisingly, it is unclear how to interpret
these recent findings. On the surface, it appears as if multiples
now have more alternate personalities than they did around the
turn of the century. But it is unclear whether this is really a change
in the nature of multiple personality itself, or whether it is best
explained in terms of therapists' increasing readiness or ability to
discover alters who do not manifest overtly. (The skeptical appeal
to iatrogenesis, however, is transparently inadequate. See section
2.6.) As Putnam suggests (1989, p. 40), the answer may become
clearer as we continue to monitor this trend.

Switching between personalities ranges from one or two seconds
to several minutes, and it can be voluntary or involuntary. Apparently, many (if not most) multiples fail to exhibit the rapid or

'clean' switching characteristic of some classic cases, and as portrayed in movies. Indeed, the popular movie, *The Three Faces of Eve*, may have helped to foster a distorted picture of MPD's clinical features. Putnam summarizes the general features of switching as follows.

> In most, but not all, instances where I have been able to videotape and study a switch, the initiation of the switch is signaled by a blink or upward roll of the eyes. There may be a rapid fluttering of the eyelids. Transient facial twitching or grimacing often accompanies a switch. In addition, there may be bodily twitches, shudders, or abrupt changes in posture. If the switch takes several minutes to complete, the individual may go into an unresponsive, trance-like state with blank, unseeing eyes. A few multiples have convulsion-like switches that have, on occasion, been mistaken for epileptic seizures.

(Putnam, 1989, pp. 120-21)

Although a patient might have a single alter in executive control of the body for extended periods, a large majority of therapists report frequent spontaneous switching in their patients. At its most extreme, switching occurs so frequently and so rapidly that no personality has control over the patient's behavior. Generally speaking, this condition occurs when a new crisis initiates a struggle for executive control, or a general relinquishing of control by all the central personalities. During these periods, the patient may shift chaotically between brief bursts of different emotions and produce incoherent strings of words or syllables rather than sentences. If the rapid switching is between only a few personalities, one might be able to detect abrupt interruptions of one sentence, followed by portions of another sentence, and then a continuing portion of the previous sentence-fragment, and so on.

Switching generally leads to various physical and psychological changes in the multiple, and these may be very dramatic or quite subtle. Not surprisingly, one often sees differences in facial expressions, voice quality, speech patterns, posture, and bodily movements, as well as sudden shifts in affect. The most dramatic changes tend to occur between alters of different sexes and significantly different ages, or between alters of significantly different psychological styles or abilities. Moreover, as one becomes better acquainted with the distinct characteristics of different alters, even

42

subtle differences may become obvious after a while (e.g., gesturing with different sides of the body, or distinctive sorts of inflections at the end of sentences or phrases).

The first thing many alters do after assuming executive control of the body is to adjust to their surroundings. Therapists call this process 'grounding', and it is most dramatic in the case of alters emerging from a period of lost time. At these times, patients may look rapidly around the room or display other signs of restlessness, and they often touch their body or nearby objects, as if they were adapting to the novelty of being in executive control.

One of the most commonly reported phenomena in cases of MPD is *asymmetrical awareness*,[1] in which personality A is aware of B's thoughts or actions, but B is not aware of A's existence. In the majority of cases examined, at least one personality denied that other personalities existed, even though another personality claimed to be aware of all the other alters, or claimed to have complete memory of the (total) individual's life history. In fact, in most cases the personality submitting itself for treatment was unaware that other personalities existed. That personality was merely aware that something was amiss (as the result, say, of lost time, and finding strange clothes or other possessions around the home).

Researchers report some form of amnesia (e.g., fugue episodes, or inter-personality amnesia) in virtually all cases, and alters often develop subtle and refined ways of camouflaging the fact that they have lost time. For example, when the periods of amnesia are brief, an alter might say 'I'm sorry, my mind wandered. Will you repeat that?' Larger gaps can be handled in a similar way — for example, 'Forgive me, I was so preoccupied yesterday, I forgot what you said. I promise to pay better attention this time'. And of course, failures to keep appointments can be explained by claiming illness, car trouble, falling asleep from exhaustion, etc. Persons who are good at such ploys can escape detection as multiples for a long time.

Similarly, since multiples generally want to conceal their condition, they tend also to devise various ways of covering up the switching of personalities, not only in the presence of friends and acquaintances, but also during sessions with mental-health professionals. For example, alters who are aware of the mannerisms of other alters might try to emulate those mannerisms as much as possible. Moreover, multiples can mask their inability to communicate successfully during switching (or any period when alters vie for executive control of the body) — for example, by clearing their throat, turning away, or covering their faces. And it may be some time before one realizes that the multiple is not simply displaying a curious mannerism. Hence, therapists on the lookout only for dramatic manifestations of MPD may be unaware that personality changes have occurred. Some argue that many misdiagnoses of multiples have resulted from the mistaken supposition that the manifestations of different alters will be as dramatic as that observed in certain classic cases (see, e.g., Kluft, 1985c). And, of course, the multiple's close friends might not even realize what is going on. To them, their friend might seem merely rather changeable, moody, distracted, forgetful, or unusually eccentric.[2]

Many alternate personalities claim to have a continuing existence when not in executive control of the body. In fact, they often claim to interact during those periods with other alters who are also covert. For example, the interactions could take the form of 'council meetings' to supervise the emergence of the various personalities (e.g., to ensure that the children have an opportunity to play with their toys and that the artist alter has a chance to paint, or to conspire to keep the sociopathic alters under wraps). Some personalities claim to live subconsciously (often for long periods) before first taking control of the body. Others appear to come into existence without any previous subterranean life. An alter may appear only once, as if for a single task or mission, and then remain dormant or perhaps continue to exert unconscious influence (e.g., by interfering with the experiences of the personality in executive control).

In fact, it is important to note that an alter can apparently influence the multiple's behavior and subjective experiences even when it is not in executive control of the body. For example, the submerged alter might induce hallucinations (positive and negative) in the alter assuming control of the body or prevent that alter from acting or speaking. (Some good examples of this are described in M. Prince, 1905/1978.) Moreover, interference with the emerged alter's behavior often looks quite different from (say) ordinary examples of indecisiveness or hesitancy. Actually, it *can* be as dramatic as Dr. Strangelove fending off his own hand. More frequently, however, the subject displays peculiar sorts of reticence and hesitations, distinctively different from more conventional behavioral waverings and inhibitions. Indeed, one sometimes glimpses mannerisms of the otherwise hidden alter, as if (for a moment) the alter in control had been subdued by the struggle.

Switching personalities enables a multiple to cope with exhaustion, pain, or other impairments to normal or optimal functioning. For example, if *A* is tired or drugged, *B* can emerge fresh or clear-headed. When in pain, *A* can switch to an anesthetic personality. Or, personalities can keep passing the pain to each other in turn, switching when the persistent pain becomes intolerable.

Similarly, cooperation between personalities, when it occurs (which apparently is not all that often), allows a multiple to cope with various life demands. For example, helper personalities might emerge to buy groceries, drive a car, balance a checkbook, eat, or go to work in the morning, all of which the presently dominant personality might be unable to do (say, if that personality's principal function is to experience grief or pain, or if it is generally helpless for some other reason). The more functional multiples often distribute activities between alters in creative ways, or at least in ways that do not command attention. For example, a college student might divide course work among personalities with the appropriate abilities (e.g., the alter good at math will take the statistics course). Kluft (1986c) describes a highly functional multiple, a prominent research scientist, only one of whose personalities did the research. The function of the presenting personality was to handle interpersonal relationships. As with many functional multiples, certain of her alters emerged only in private. For example, one alter practiced (in solitude) a sport the patient had enjoyed in her youth. Similarly, the child alters of adult multiples might emerge only in situations where their behavior would not be noticed or out of place. The children might emerge only in the privacy and solitude of the multiple's home, or (say) in the context of buying toys in a store, where childlike behavior in an adult might appear simply to be a somewhat eccentric form of exhuberance.

Some of the more militant functional multiples maintain (quite vigorously) that it is better to be a multiple than a 'single', and they might disdainfully refer to non-multiples as people suffering from 'single personality disorder'. This stance is understandable for several reasons. First (as I have noted), multiples do indeed have ways of handling pain and exhaustion available (apparently) only to such virtuoso dissociators. Second, multiples often feel that they have many valued and intimate friends among their alters, whom they would hate to lose in the process of integration. And third, multiples who (as adults) have had no experience living as a single would quite naturally prefer the familiar to the unknown. Hence, as in a bad marriage, multiples will sometimes prefer to maintain a life with individuals (i.e., alters) whose ways they understand, even if that life is a nightmare.

However, in all the cases I know of where a multiple has been integrated extensively enough to feel what it is like to be a person with different and often conflicting desires, preferences, and interests, the integrated state has been preferred. Granted, the internal group of friends may have disappeared, but the integrated mutiple recognizes that their distinctive qualities tend to remain. In fact, the integrated multiple will tend to experience those qualities in a somewhat enhanced and enriched way, as they blend for the first time with and become augmented by other attributes previously limited to specific alters. Moreover, the experience of integration is liberating, in the sense that the multiple no longer needs to fear periods of lost time or the situations that used to trigger switching of personalities. Hence, the loss of an intimate inner network of friends and acquaintances seems more than compensated for by a profound gain in the subjective richness of life.

Moreover, the need for an anesthetic personality may dimish considerably, especially since the multiple's somatic pain frequently disappears during therapy (and later, integration), after early traumatic experiences have been confronted successfully. Besides, only the most highly functional multiples can control switching to such a handy alter whenever it would be desirable. Quite often, a multiple's life is dominated by alters coping with demands or issues that take precedence over the need for physical comfort. Hence, even though fully integrated multiples can no longer cope with pain or exhaustion by switching to an anesthetic or energetic alter, generally speaking that loss seems compensated for by an overall gain in tranquility and control. To my knowledge, multiples generally retain a positive assessment of integration even when disintegration recurs, so long as dominant alters remember what integration was like. (For those lacking a population of multiples to interview directly with regard to these and other matters, I recommend two newsletters, written by, for, and about people with MPD. One is the now-defunct *Speaking for Our Selves*, and the other is its successor, *Many Voices*.)[3]

Furthermore, despite the protestations of those who argue for the superiority of life as a multiple, it is quite clear that such a life has numerous obvious disadvantages and pitfalls, even in the case of highly functional multiples. As I have already suggested, the ability to navigate smoothly through the day's activities will always depend on the proper alter being in control of the body at the appropriate time. But such juggling of alters can be precarious even in the best of cases, so long as the multiple is still vulnerable to the many unpredictable and uncontrollable situations that can induce spontaneous switching. Indeed, when the multiple has little or no control over switching, an alter might find him/herself in awkward, dangerous, or repulsive situations. Moreover, the frequency of those occurrences can be multiplied when alters carry out vendettas on each other (e.g., by hiding or destroying another's valuables, school work, or letters, or by intentionally placing another alter in a situation the latter can't stand). But even when such competition is not intentional, the multiple might find it extremely difficult to get through the most mundane sorts of activities. For example, if alters switch frequently and spontaneously, the multiple might take several baths, or change clothes and hair styles several times, simply as a preliminary to leaving home for the day. Moreover, since some personalities do not perform vital bodily functions (such as eating or eliminating), uncontrolled switching can imperil the subject or at least cause the subject considerable discomfort.

The reader might have wondered why a multiple would develop very large inventories of alters (say, from 85 to 200). Must we assume, implausibly, that there were in the patient's life that number of distinct kinds of major traumas? The standard answer to this question is that dissociation might initially have been used as a defense against what the patient found to be intolerable trauma or abuse. But if it is used repeatedly in response to continuing trauma or chronic abuse, then it might become the patient's habitual way of handling all sorts of uncomfortable situations that otherwise might not have been severe enough to trigger dissociation. That is why large inventories of alters contain many highly specialized members (or fragments), apparently formed to deal only with quite limited (and often seemingly trivial) activities or situations.

But why should patients who dissociate defensively become multiples, rather than developing fugue states or some other less drastic dissociative response? The received view on this issue is

47

that there seems to be a link between types of dissociative responses and the developmental stage at which trauma occurs. In general, the earlier the trauma, the more likely one is to fragment profoundly into a multiple. Hence, someone who experiences severe trauma after passing through major developmental stages is more likely to experience a less drastic form of dissociation (e.g., fugue, hysterical amnesia, anesthesia, or paralysis). The reason, presumably, is that early in life our sense of self is somewhat primitive and our personalities are still relatively malleable. However, the sense of self becomes more robust and rigid with time, as our memories and attachments accumulate. Indeed, various surveys suggest that the initial split occurs in childhood, between the ages of four and six. Some personalities, in fact, seem to have developed gradually from imaginary playmates (see Kluft,1984b, 1985a, 1986e; Putnam, Guroff, *et al.*, 1986; Riley and Mead, 1988).

2.3 COGNITIVE, SENSORY, AND PHYSIOLOGICAL DIFFERENCES BETWEEN ALTERS

I have already noted that some alters have abilities or sensory capacities not found in other alters. For example, one alter might be good at mathematics, or have knowledge of shorthand or foreign languages, while other alters do not. Differences in cognitive abilities also can be more general. Some alters might simply be unable to reason abstractly or comprehend language. In fact, a multiple might have one alter who is a brilliant student and another who is autistic. Sensory differences can also be either general or specific. Some alters might be anesthetic, totally or partially, and partial anesthesias may be distributed in accordance with traumas connected to the corresponding sense modality. For example, a blind personality might be formed to deal with childhood experiences of being locked in dark places. Deafness or muteness might be found in alters whose traumas or abuse concerned the covering of the subject's ears or mouth. Other alters might lack only tactile sensations or the ability to taste. And, of course, memories might be trauma-specific as well. For that reason, an alter can sometimes be called forth by means of verbal or behavioral cues that have a special significance only for that alter.

Sometimes, differences in cognitive or sensory modalities are not so sharp and seem to be more a matter of degree. For example, alter *A* might have difficulty writing directions dictated to him, while *B* might have an easy time writing and reading, but experience difficulty comprehending spoken words. An alter might be unable to eat, drink, or taste only specific foods and liquids, or be insensitive to the touch only of certain persons or objects.

Of course, phenomena of this sort are not unprecendented. The pioneers of hypnosis discovered or reproduced most of them. Similarly, the history of hypnosis contains numerous parallels to the reports of striking physiological differences between alters. And those differences can be quite dramatic. Alters may vary with regard to voice quality, handedness, color blindness, the need for eyeglass prescriptions, tolerance to drugs or medication, and allergic responses (e.g., to cats or cigarette smoke).

For example, Braun (1983b) described a male multiple who was allergic to citrus juice in all personalities except one. If that personality ate an orange, and was able to digest and metabolize it before another personality took over, the subject's body showed no allergic symptoms. But if switching occurred too soon, the body tended to develop a rash that itched and blistered. If the non-allergic personality then resumed control, the itching would cease gradually, as if the subject had taken an antihistamine. If the non-allergic personality retained executive control for a while, the blisters would disappear more quickly than if one of the other personalities had been in control. They would not disappear miraculously or instantaneously; the bodily damage that had already occurred simply healed more rapidly. Another multiple had been tortured by her mother and brother. One of the tortures was the extinguishing of cigarettes on her skin. When the personality who experienced the burns controlled the body, spots about the size of cigarette burns appeared on her skin. And in the classic case of Miss Beauchamp (M. Prince, 1905/1978), personalities B1 and B4 could be rendered unconscious with chloroform, while at the same time, Sally would remain unaffected. (For additional discussions of physiological differences between alters, see Coons, 1988; Miller, 1989; and Putnam, 1984a. For reports on the hypnotic production and treatment of analogous physiological symptoms, see, e.g., Kroger, 1979; Mason, 1952, 1955; and Bowers, 1979. And see Selye, 1956, for a discussion of the relation between stress and vulnerability to infection and allergies.)

With regard to possible neurophysiological differences between alters, the data is currently too preliminary and inconclusive to provide a satisfactory profile of a multiple (see Coons, 1988, for a recent review of the literature). Nevertheless, some of the data looks intriguing (although it is too complex to merit a discussion here). Readers interested in pursuing the matter are directed in particular to Brende, 1984; Larmore, *et al.*, 1977; Loewenstein and Putnam, 1988; Ludwig, *et al.*, 1972; Mathew, *et al.*, 1985; and Putnam, 1984a and 1989. Some very interesting neurophysiological studies of conditions other than MPD (e.g., trance states) are also relevant to the topic, especially, Dawson, 1980; Ervin, *et al.*, 1988; Simons, *et al.*, 1988; Sidtis, 1986; Thomson, Forbes, and Bolles, 1937.

2.4 FURTHER ASPECTS OF MULTIPLICITY

Unless one knows (or is) a multiple, undoubtedly the best way to get a feel for the distinctive complexities of a multiple's existence is to read the more thoroughly documented cases (as well as the newsletters mentioned above). Some popular accounts succeed rather well in conveying a sense of the novelties and difficulties of life as a multiple (especially, Bliss and Bliss, 1985; Schreiber, 1974; and Sizemore and Pittillo, 1977). But the best sources remain two turn-of-the-century cases, the studies of Miss Beauchamp (M. Prince 1905/1978) and Doris Fischer (W.F. Prince, 1915/16). The former, despite its wealth of detail, is nevertheless incomplete and misleading in crucial respects, especially with regard to the psychogenesis of Miss Beauchamp's disorder.[4] Some of the puzzle's missing pieces may be found in Rosenzweig's fascinating exercises in 'psychoarcheology' (1987, 1988). The case of Doris Fischer is probably the most thoroughly and painstakingly documented case of all time. The subject lived in the home of her investigator/therapist, W.F. Prince; the full account of the case consumes 1400 printed pages; and the material for the published report was 'drawn from nineteen hundred pages of manuscript record of a study continued without the intermission of a day for more than three years' (W.F. Prince, 1916, p. 73). Prince also published a considerably abridged, but still illuminating (and probably also more accessible) version of the case (W.F. Prince, 1916). Contemporary descriptions of multiples in the professional literature are extremely cursory and will be of little help to those seeking a more robust sense of MPD.

Although it would certainly be interesting to examine one of the major cases in detail, for present purposes I suspect it would be best to maintain the level of generality of the preceding sections and offer some additional observations about MPD. Some of these will be of particular value later, when we look closely at the distinctness of alter personalities and consider the bearing of MPD on the concept of a person.

The reader might have wondered how multiples deal with having personalities of the opposite sex. Clearly, the best general strategy is to adopt an outwardly unisex style of hair and dress, thereby sparing the male/female personalities the awkwardness of appearing too feminine/masculine. Hence, such multiples often keep their hair short and prefer trousers to dresses or skirts. Of course, that strategy may not satisfy alters whose functions center around certain styles of masculinity or femininity, and it may be necessary to set aside time for those alters to dress according to their self-image. Moreover, as I mentioned earlier, when management of the personality system is not under control, the multiple may make numerous inopportune and time-consuming changes of dress within the course of a day, even among personalities of the same sex.

It is important to note that although the differences between alternate personalities can be dramatic, the divisions are not always very sharp or complete. According to Putnam (1989, p. 115), 'the more emotionally charged or traumatically linked an idea or affect is, the more it will tend to be isolated within an alter and segregated from the larger domain of consciousness'. In other respects, however, alters might differ only slightly. Hence, not only might alters interfere with one another; sometimes they seem to *overlap* as well — say, by sharing memories, body language, and verbal habits. Of course, such personalities might still differ overtly, but those differences will simply be manifested in other ways — for example, physically with respect to voice quality and facial expressions, and psychologically with respect to attitudes, beliefs, interests, and other dispositions. The overlapping of alters is particularly dramatic when child personalities exhibit numerous adult traits. For example, a young alter might share the vocabulary of older alters, but simply speak in a childlike way (see Orne, 1951, and O'Connell, Shor, and Orne, 1970, for similar observations in connection with hypnotic age regression). At other times, however, the childlike behavior will be accompanied by an apparent and appropriate reduction in vocabulary.[5]

Alternate personalities may also be limited with respect to the sorts of awareness they have of one another. For example, A might be aware of B's thoughts but not B's actions, or B's actions but not B's thoughts (see Chapter 3 for a discussion of these and more subtle varieties of inter-alter awareness). And, of course, in cases of conflict, an alter can take advantage of another's limitations in awareness. For example, in the Miss Beauchamp case Sally knew what B4's actions were, but she did not have access to B4's thoughts. Hence, Sally had to infer B4's thoughts from knowledge of her actions, just as most people come to know the thoughts of others. When B4 realized this, she knew she had a weapon she could use in the struggle between the two personalities for control. She could deceive Sally by acting as if she were having thoughts other than those she was actually having. In some respects, this ploy was successful. Interestingly, however, Sally was clever enough to figure out from B4's behavior that the latter knew nothing of Miss Beauchamp's life for the previous few years, even though B4 pretended otherwise. Sally grasped that B4 was always 'fishing' for information, and in fact she seemed to be astonished that B4 should know so little.

In some cases, whether an alter is aware of other alters depends on which personality is in executive control of the body. A very clear example of this comes from the Doris Fischer case (it is also easy to explain, because Doris had only a small number of alternate personalities). The arrow in the diagrams below (adapted from W.F. Prince, 1915/16, pp. 840-41) indicates the 'direction' of awareness. Hence, an arrow running from A to B symbolizes that A is aware of B (we needn't worry here about what sort of awareness this is; see Chapter 3, and also W.F. Prince, 1915/16, pp. 838ff, 1916, pp. 109ff).

Recently, Kluft (1988b) has argued that the terms 'splitting' and 'division' make it needlessly difficult to understand how alters can overlap and have many properties in common. He proposes, instead, that alter-creation be understood as a process of *reduplication* or *reconfiguration* of personality ingredients. I suspect, however, that Kluft's concern is unwarranted. The concept of division (or splitting) can be understood in various ways. Some sorts of division, such as the reorganizing of a cutlery set into subsets of knives, forks, and spoons or the splitting of a light beam with a prism, separate a whole into parts with conspicuously distinct sets of properties. Others, such as dividing a cutlery set

52

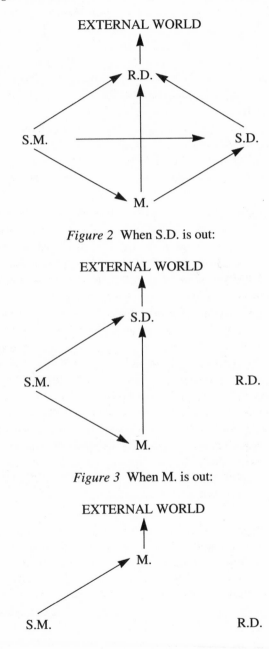

Figure 1 When R.D. is 'out' (i.e., in executive control):

EXTERNAL WORLD

R.D.

S.M.   S.D.

M.

Figure 2 When S.D. is out:

EXTERNAL WORLD

S.D.

S.M.   R.D.

M.

Figure 3 When M. is out:

EXTERNAL WORLD

M.

S.M.   R.D.

S.D.

into identical place-settings and the slicing of a pie into pieces, split a whole into discrete parts that may be quite similar to one another. And still others, such as cell division, split a whole into parts that may be very similar to the original whole. Hence, the overlapping of alters does not seem to conflict with the concept of division. That concept accomodates numerous types of splitting processes. Moreover, the evidence for attribute-distribution and attribute-depletion (section 2.5) suggests that the terms 'splitting' and 'division' are particularly apt. Accordingly, I think we may use those terms without fear of confusion, so long as we remember that the division of the self that seems to occur in multiple personality is not of a kind that must result in markedly distinct parts.

Probably one of the least understood aspects of multiplicity is the process of integration. Although a full discussion of the topic exceeds the modest scope of this brief survey, a few comments are in order. To begin with, integrations may only be (and frequently seem to be) partial, and the incompleteness of integration may be of two sorts. First, the *degree* of integration between two personalities may not be total, and this may lead to a curious state of affairs called *co-presence* (see Chapter 3). Second, integration may involve only some of the personalities within the total system of alters. Partial integrations, however, are often a first step toward total integration, and when either sort of integration occurs, characteristics seem to blend and reorganize rather than disappear. For example, if the voice of A had a brittle, hard quality and that of B was very soft, the voice of the new AB might have a quality somewhere between those poles. Or, if A gestured largely with the right side of the body and B largely with the left, AB might balance gestures evenly between the two sides. Furthermore (and perhaps more relevantly), the experiences and psychological characteristics of AB can apparently be a composite of the distinctive inner lives of A and B — a kind of cognitive cocktail. For example, AB might combine A's formerly exclusive feelings of heightened sexuality and self-confidence with B's formerly exclusive sexual inhibitions and uniquely self-deprecating sense of humor, or A's formerly exclusive ability to experience tactile sensations with B's formerly exclusive ability to experience tastes. Similarly, if A was childlike and B was an adult, AB might be a mixture of the two (e.g., an adult who now has the capacity to be childlike — hopefully, when appropriate).

Unfortunately, integrations are quite fragile and may be only temporary, especially if familiar sorts of triggering situations recur. Moreover, if the multiple splits again, the divisions between alters may occur along different functional lines, reflecting either novel sorts of stresses in the multiple's life or perhaps only novel dissociative strategies for handling old stresses. Hence, although a multiple's inventory of alters can evolve, this process is not analogous to that in which athletic teams or orchestras change personnel. For example, the orchestra analogy (favored by Beahrs, 1982) has some utility, but generally speaking, an orchestra's functional divisions remain pretty much the same through personnel changes (e.g., conductor, strings, winds, brass, percussion, and finer divisions within each group). By contrast, changes in alters are more akin to the way a philosophy department (say) might reorganize around a different set of areas of specialization.

Furthermore, it is very difficult to determine when integrations are total. Actually, taking a census of alternate personalities is never straightforward, even prior to attempts at integration, simply as a matter of principle. For one thing, since alters are capable of dishonesty, deception, and confusion, there is no surefire way to identify two distinct alters as opposed to one alter calling itself by two names. Moreover, during pseudo-integrations, one alter might pretend to be another or otherwise conceal its existence. For example, when an alter is deeply committed to retaining its individuality (as is often the case), it might simply go undercover for awhile, or emerge only in very non-conspicuous ways, and thereby contribute to the appearance of successful integration. In the meantime, the multiple might be considerably more integrated than before and appear to have no unintegrated alters remaining. Indeed, there might be one relatively well-integrated personality that experiences itself as a quite complex whole, with many of the conflicting desires and impulses of a typical non-multiple. And that personality might not even realize that one or more alters has yet to be integrated. It is possible, also, that this integrated personality is committed to retaining a distinct non-integrated alter as a companion (or guardian, or helper). And both might conspire to feign total integration.

Furthermore, clinicians can (at best) claim to have integrated only the personalities they know about, and sometimes there are alters that have never emerged in their presence, and about whom the various presenting personalities are also ignorant. These might

55

be deeply submerged alters formed in connection with profound and possibly very early traumas that have yet to be uncovered in therapy. They might also be relatively recent alters who are simply motivated to remain hidden. Moreover, clinicians are often inexperienced at treating multiples, and others (to put it bluntly) are simply inept. Hence, they might unwittingly discourage crucial alters from revealing themselves, or at least not probe deeply or thoroughly enough to elicit a multiple's full set of alters. Generally speaking, then, one should be very wary of clinicians' assertions that they have integrated their patients, especially when they claim to have orchestrated many successful integrations. Not only might such claims (particularly the inflated ones) be naive; they might also reflect the clinician's own investment in being both competent and successful.

2.5 PERSONALITIES AND 'PRIMARY' PERSONALITIES

One striking feature of the the recent literature on MPD is that one sees almost no references to *primary* personalities. By contrast, around the turn of the century it was commonplace to refer to alters as either primary or secondary. There seem to be two main reasons for the current reluctance to designate an alter as primary. First, within the personality system discovered by the clinician, there may be no personality whose *role* within that system is primary in any deep way, although it may of course be quite important. One might think that the *presenting* personality should be considered primary. But that alter often turns out to be relatively recent and fairly peripheral in the multiple's total system of alters. Similarly, there might be an alter who acts as *host* for the others, or who initially shows his or her face to the world before yielding to alters awaiting their appropriate times to emerge. And there might be alters who − for a time, at least − dominate the multiple's life. But host personalities might serve no vital function other than serving as 'master of ceremonies' (so to speak), and both they and dominant personalities generally may be replaced by others who dominate for a while or act as host. Therefore, if an alternate personality deserves to be considered *functionally* primary, it is very unlikely to be in virtue of its permanent role within the total system of alters. At best, it would

56

be primary only for certain (possibly very brief) periods in the multiple's life.

Generally speaking, however, the point of calling an alter 'primary' has not been simply to indicate its function within the total system of alternate personalities. Rather, the term 'primary personality' has been used traditionally to refer to the alter presumed to be *historically* primary. I do not know of any attempts to question this presupposition explicitly. But it seems as if the clinical community has come to recognize gradually that there is little or no justification for regarding any alter as primary in that sense either. An historically primary personality, presumably, existed prior to the individual's becoming a multiple. Hence, it most likely would have been the personality of a non-dissociated child or adolescent, possessing its full complement of abilities and dispositions. But rarely (if ever) does an alter seem to be *that* personality, or any clear evolution or descendant of that personality.

The principal reason for this concerns the quite obvious functional specificity of alternate personalities and a pair of related phenomena we might call *attribute-distribution* and *attribute-depletion*. In general, clinicians believe that as alters are created to deal with quite specific sorts of traumas, the traits and abilities manifested by or latent in the pre-dissociative personality begin to get distributed throughout the members of the personality system. Moreover, as alters proliferate, they apparently become increasingly specialized, and one is less likely to find any personality having the complexity or range of functions presumably possessed by the subject prior to the onset of splitting. Hence, Coons suggests that when a multiple begins the process of dissociation,

> the original personality is depleted of affects and impulses. Each secondary personality fulfills a precise function such as to express anger or depression, discharge sexual or aggressive impulses, act as a repository of memories, or serve as a protector or rescuer.
>
> (Coons, 1984, p. 53)

Similarly, in the Doris case, W.F. Prince claimed,

> each of the secondary personalities made certain subtractions

57

from the keenness of the senses of the various types of physical sensation of the primary member.

(W.F. Prince, 1916, p. 93)

Of course, clinicians seldom (if ever) have direct knowledge of their patients' pre-dissociative personalities. Hence, although they may eventually get a fairly clear picture of the reasons for splitting and of the corresponding functional appropriateness of the various alters, their assumptions about the nature and complexity of the pre-dissociative personality remain speculative. Still, these assumptions may be quite reasonable, considering what we know generally about childhood development.

In any case, the passage from Coons is oddly anachronistic, since he refers to personalities as *secondary* and *original*. It is also somewhat confusing, since it is not clear whether Coons uses the term 'original personality' to refer to an alter or to the patient prior to becoming a multiple. In the passage just quoted, one would think he means the latter. However, in his next paragraph Coons says, 'the original personality is usually quiet, shy, and reserved', and here he seems to be referring to an alter (possibly the one who originally came for treatment), not the historically original pre-dissociative personality. By contrast, Prince quite clearly uses the term 'primary member' to refer to an alternate personality (albeit one having uniquely intimate links with the pre-dissociative personality). He even called that alter 'Real Doris'. Of course, it is not surprising that Prince would designate an alter as primary; that was simply the familiar terminological convention of his day. But quite apart from Prince's readiness to assume that one alter was identical to (or a uniquely direct descendant of) the historically original personality, his observations about attribute-distribution and attribute-depletion are similar to those made today. Moreover, Prince even noted an apparent reversal of those processes. He observed that when one alter *lost* a certain kind of sensation during the process of integration, Real Doris would often seem to acquire it at approximately the same time.

Perhaps Prince, too, would have abandoned the concept of a primary personality if Doris had displayed the large number of alters found in many recent cases, or at least if Prince had known about the prevalence of such cases. One would think (and, indeed, it appears) that the combined effect of attribute-distribution and attribute-depletion becomes more noticeable as a multiple's inven-

58

tory of alters increases, and (accordingly) as the causal links between the alters and the pre-dissociative personality become progressively obscure. Hence (for reasons I shall explain more fully below), as alters proliferate it becomes increasingly unlikely that any one of them can be identified with or directly (or uniquely) linked to the pre-dissociative personality.

At any rate, many today find it unjustifiable or simply futile to identify one alter as historically primary (see, e.g., Putnam's remarks on the 'original' personality in 1989, p. 114). Moreover, that attitude extends even to alters claiming to be children, including those who claim to have continuous memories of the life of the subject. And once again, the principal reason is the combination of attribute-distribution and attribute-depletion. Almost invariably, those child alters are noticeably limited in function, behavior, and sensation. In fact, as Putnam has noted recently, child alters (unlike normal children) tend to be 'frozen in time; they are locked into a given age until late in the course of therapy when, relieved of their psychological burden, they may "grow up" prior to integration' (Putnam, 1989, pp. 107-8). Hence, it seems unreasonable to suppose either that the pre-dissociative child had those limitations or that one of those alters is a uniquely direct causal descendant of the pre-dissociative personality.

Of course, alters often develop and mature, especially as they have more time in executive control of the body. (The behavioral repertoire of others, however, remains relatively fixed.) When some alters first appear, their roles tend to be well-defined and quite simple. But as they spend more time in the world interacting with others, developing interests, and forming attachments, they accumulate many new experiences and become more well-rounded and complex. For example, Bliss (1984a) notes how one of his patient's personalities was created to be bitter toward men. Eventually, however, she acquired additional roles and characteristics; she became the leader of a women's liberation group, an auto mechanic, and a lesbian. And although Bliss doesn't mention it, during this period of growth she presumably developed idiosyncratic tastes, behaviors, and opinions. Hence, like a young person growing up, an alter may evolve and develop a distinctive and increasingly varied set of behaviors and characteristics.

Nevertheless, clinicians treating MPD tend to agree that even well-developed alters are two-dimensional compared to normal persons, even a very young child. Of course, adult alters will have many traits not found in children, and they may have established a complex set of roles for themselves in the world. But continued interaction with the alters tends to reveal profound sorts of character (and often sensory or other physiological) limitations which most children do not have. This is hardly surprising, considering that complex alters are still merely elaborations of alternate personalities created (as in the case of Bliss' patient) to serve a quite specific and limited set of functions. That is why Ludwig says that the concept of a personality is 'exemplified almost in caricature in the manifestations of multiple personality' (1984, p. 161), and why Greaves calls alters 'woefully incomplete as personality systems' (1980, p. 591). (I think it would be hasty to conclude, however, that alters are *unlike* persons, or that they are *conspicuously* flat as personalities. See Chapter 8 for further remarks on these issues.)

Hence, even though alters may mature and increase in complexity, there seems to be no reason (or need) to identify any of a multiple's more developed personalities with an historically primary, pre-dissociative personality. Nor is there a reason to regard one of them in particular as a uniquely direct causal descendant of the original personality. For one thing, the pre-dissociative personality clearly lacked many of the characteristics of the subsequently developed alters (e.g., adult traits, skills, and attachments). Hence, if an alter is identical to the historically original pre-dissociative personality, they would be identical only in the relatively loose sense in which an ordinary infant is the same as the adult he becomes (or in which an acorn is the same as the oak it becomes). But considering the functional specificity and attribute-depletion of most adult alters (even well-developed ones), there is no reason to single out one alter in particular as that kind of sole direct descendant of the pre-dissociative personality. In fact, as more and more alters take over roles or functions that the pre-dissociative personality would have assumed in the natural course of maturation, the choice of any one alter in particular as historically primary seems increasingly arbitrary. And to make matters worse, during the course of a multiple's life, mini-integrations may occur between specific alters or groups of alters. But if these split again, and if the splits result in *novel* functional divisions, the causal line going back to the original pre-dissociative personality becomes even more obscure.

Incidentally, there is reason to believe that an alter's maturation or development might occur even when that alter is seldom or

60

never in control of the body. Of course, if the alter *never* assumes control prior to its maturation, we can only take that alter's word after the fact that it has evolved (or the word of other alters that a subliminal personality is evolving). At any rate, it is not difficult to imagine how a totally subliminal personality might still undergo various kinds of change or development, especially if that personality maintains awareness of other alters' thoughts and interactions in the world. In that case, the subliminal personality could gather many new experiences, which in principle could help to form increasingly well-rounded and idiosyncratic sets of dispositions. M. Prince believed that such a process occurred in the case of Sally (see M. Prince, 1939, p. 205).

2.6 IS MULTIPLE PERSONALITY ARTIFACTUAL?

As I mentioned in 2.1, some skeptics argue that MPD is an iatrogenic artifact of the therapeutic setting (especially in cases where hypnosis is used) and that the clinician (presumably unwittingly) capitalizes on the subject's heightened suggestibility and desire to please. For example, Harriman (1942a, 1942b, 1943), Janet (1907/1920), Kampman (1976), and Leavitt (1947) have all maintained that hypnosis can *create* multiple personality. Janet also had noted how hypnosis can sharpen and solidify an alternate personality. Even the mere act of naming it, he claimed, helps to define the personality more clearly. Along similar lines, Orne (1979) has argued that it is difficult in general to distinguish what is observed from what is created under hypnosis.

Several social psychologists have taken a slightly different approach. They charge that patients in therapy may simply be encouraged to act *as if* they had multiple personalities (see, e.g., Aldridge-Morris, 1989; Kenny, 1986; Spanos, 1986; Spanos, Weekes, and Bertrand, 1985; Spanos, Weekes, Menary, and Bertrand, 1986).[6] Generally speaking, the proponents of these alternative accounts hope to show that MPD is not characterized by radically distinctive inner states, and that it is continuous with and not profoundly different from other forms of highly self-absorbed role enactments or compliant behavior. Moreover, they often attempt to buttress their view with a rejection of the claim that *hypnosis* is likewise not a distinctive inner (or altered) state, and that it, too, can be explained thoroughly behaviorally as a form of social compliance.

Space does not permit a comprehensive examination of all these skeptical positions. (The reader will find references throughout this book to the more thoughtful and plausible critical responses to them.) In fact, for the purpose of this book, it would be enough to consider the philosophical import of MPD *should it turn out to be a genuinely deep form of psychological disunity*. Still, it seems to me that the skeptical analyses of MPD range from merely implausible to quite preposterous and that the charge of iatrogenesis is relatively toothless on the whole. Hence, a few remarks on the topic are in order.

To begin with, multiple personality has been found in many patients who have never been hypnotized or in therapy, including children with a documented history of trauma or abuse. The childhood cases also suggest strongly that MPD is not simply a form of role-playing or social compliance, much less conscious malingering or play-acting. In fact, the hypothesis of iatrogenesis is difficult to square with the evidence for severe trauma or abuse and its apparent role in the psychogenesis of MPD. Moreover, the alleged personalities created hypnotically (in attempts to simulate the symptoms of MPD) differ in important respects from those apparently arising spontaneously. Not only are the former substantially lacking in depth and breadth as personalities when compared to many alters, they also have no life histories and serve no particular function in the emotional life of the patient (i.e., they are dynamically fortuitous). In any case, even if full-blown alternate personalities could be created hypnotically, it would not follow that all arise from some form of suggestion. Analogously, although warts and rashes may be produced hypnotically, they nevertheless have multiple causes. (For additional and more extended discussions, I recommend a recent special issue of the journal *Dissociation*, vol. 2, no. 2 (1989), devoted almost entirely to a critical examination of the charge of iatrogenesis. See, also, Kluft, 1982, 1987c; Braun, 1984a, 1984b; Greaves, 1980; Putnam, 1989, pp. 131-32, 218-19; and Putnam, Guroff, *et al.*, 1986; Ross, 1989, pp. 58-63.)

Similarly, even if some cases of ostensible MPD turn out to be elaborate instances of role-playing, it does not follow that all are. And needless to say, to defend the thesis that MPD is nothing but a form of social compliance or role-playing (even if quite instinctive or unconscious), one must do more than focus principally on cases — such as the Bianchi ('Hillside Strangler') case —

where the probability of role-playing (or malingering) is rather high (see, e.g., Aldridge-Morris, 1989; Spanos, 1986; Spanos, *et al.*, 1985). After all, the hypothesis that MPD is a genuine (and presumably abnormal) psychological phenomenon is *compatible* with the claim that some cases of ostensible MPD may be explained wholly in terms of social compliance or role-playing (see Chapter 7.5 for further remarks on this topic). It would be ludicrous to maintain that a profound psychological disorder *cannot* be feigned or mimicked to some extent — hence, that every case of ostensible or diagnosed MPD would have to be a case of genuine MPD. In fact, treating the Hillside Strangler as a paradigm case of MPD is a clear example of the familiar and disreputable gambit of generalizing from the weakest cases. Unlike the claim that some (and probably many) cases of MPD are instances of a genuine psychological disorder (which is all that partisans of MPD are claiming), the social psychologists' skeptical denial of this position is the *universal* claim that *every* case of ostensible MPD is a case of social compliance or role-playing. Hence, to properly defend that skeptical hypothesis, one must demonstrate its plausibility in those cases where it seems *prima facie* to be least applicable — precisely those cases which most clearly suggest a genuine psychological disorder.[7]

Moreover, quite apart from the difficulties of explaining early childhood cases and the trauma-specificity of alters exclusively along social psychological lines, the better cases are rich in subtle nuances that are very difficult to interpret plausibly as aspects of mere social compliance or role-playing. We already have considered some of these details — for example, the attempts by multiples to conceal or mask the switching process, grounding behavior following a switch, and the consternation and surprise multiples exhibit when an alter apparently finds him/herself in an unexpected situation. It is not that these behaviors cannot be feigned or unconsciously mimicked, especially by those who already know that clinicians have reported them. But there is usually no reason whatever to believe that this is the case. For one thing, clinicians observed the more subtle signs of multiplicity before first describing them in the literature. And there is no reason to suppose that they initially expected to find those (or any) particular indications of switching. Moreover (unlike the Bianchi case), there is usually no reason to suppose that multiples are familiar with the clinical literature in which the fine-grained features of multiplicity are described (although in the past few years, as clinical reports become widely disseminated and as detailed popular accounts of MPD proliferate, one can no longer be so confident of the multiple's prior ignorance). Hence, many — and certainly, the initial — reports of subtle manifestations of multiplicity cannot plausibly be explained in terms of the patients' desire to satisfy clinical expectations, or their unconscious simulation of behavior described in the clinical literature.

Furthermore, although it may be fairly easy to duplicate some of the more obvious features of multiplicity for short periods of time, it is considerably more difficult to display the full and subtle range of behaviors characteristic of MPD, and to do so consistently over an extended period. But those (like Spanos, *et al.*, 1985) who argue that 'enacting the multiple personality role is a relatively easy task' (p. 372) support their claim (at best) only with regard to enactments of the most obvious and superficial sorts. Significantly, but apparently unwittingly, Aldridge-Morris seems to recognize the weakness of Spanos' position. He remarks that 'it is demonstrably more easy to play sharply contrasting roles than it is to offer one's audience subtle nuances of change in personal identity' (1989, p. 91). But that is precisely what one finds in a typical case of MPD (unlike the Bianchi case). It is true that multiples 'typically portray sharply contrasting alter-egos' (p. 91). But many alters differ *only* in very subtle ways, (e.g., fine-grained changes in vocal inflections and body language), and even those that differ sharply still differ *consistently* over a long period in a great number of very subtle respects.

Actually, so long as multiplicity is not simply a form of social enactment or role playing, the issue of iatrogenesis seems largely irrelevant to a philosophical inquiry into multiple personality, although it is clearly of clinical importance. (See Chapter 3, for a discussion of the difference between multiplicity and highly developed role playing.) After all, what matters conceptually is the significance of the characteristic internal states of multiple personality, whether those states arise spontaneously or artifactually. Either way, it would seem, multiplicity raises various issues about the concept of the person and the nature of mental functioning generally. Besides, in a sense *all* alternate personalities are demand personalities, whether they are trauma- or physician-initiated.[8]

If the topic of iatrogenesis is of any concern for present purposes, it would have to do primarily with the question of how personality-like an alter can be — that is, the extent to which an alternate personality displays the depth and breadth of character typically found in non-multiples. If alters were simply created artifactually and served no deep dynamic role in the patient's life, or (more seriously) if they were all as truncated as those created experimentally, then presumably MPD would not pose as great a challenge to the concept of a person. For example, it would not seem particularly important to consider whether different alters deserve to be treated as distinct moral or prudential agents. It seems, however, that many alters are robust enough to be considered distinct individuals in many contexts; indeed, many alters exist in the world without anyone suspecting that they are merely alternate personalities. In the next chapter, we will examine in considerable detail what the distinctness of alters amounts to, and in Chapter 8 we will look more closely at the significance of personality-robustness.

3

THE NATURE OF MULTIPLICITY

3.1 INTRODUCTION

In the last chapter, we examined the received view of MPD and considered what makes it clinically interesting (as well as fascinating to most laypersons). Now I would like to consider some reasons for taking MPD to be of particular *philosophical* interest.

One obvious reason, of course, is that multiple personality appears to challenge various familiar assumptions about the nature of personhood. Most notably (and quite roughly speaking), we tend to assume that a person has no more than one mind, or that there is a one:one correlation between persons and bodies. In Chapter 8, we will examine in detail the concept of a person, and consider whether (or to what extent) it needs to be revised in light of the facts of multiplicity. This chapter, however, will deal with some crucial prelimiary issues. Before we can determine whether the concept of a person (such as it is) needs overhauling, we must try to characterize clearly the features of multiple personality that seem to threaten it. In particular, we must consider why multiple personality apparently differs from other dissociative conditions and why the mental divisions produced in multiple personality seem to be particularly deep. In short, we must consider how to describe those features of multiple personality that tempt us to view a multiple as several persons. Hence, I shall consider in what sense alternate personalities count as different selves or subjects, and in what respects different alters have distinct senses of self. Later (in Chapter 7) we will consider whether these selves — despite their distinctness — are nevertheless deeply unified, and after that (in Chapter 8) we will consider how differences between alters matter to the concept of a person.

3.2 THE DISTINCTNESS OF ALTERNATE
PERSONALITIES

Let us begin by reviewing some intriguing, and surprisingly under-appreciated, characteristics of multiple personality. Even the casual reader on multiplicity knows that alternate personalities seem to have distinct senses of themselves, or centers of self-consciousness. Most people know that a multiple's various personalities have distinct sets of memories, psychological traits, and abilities. Not only do they claim to be distinct persons (and not merely personalities); they will disavow the interests and activities of other alters and pursue goals of their own, sometimes even holding different jobs. Moreover, different alters seem to be of different ages and sexes and appear to have distinct overall body-images. For example, one alter might feel he or she is the wrong sex, or too young, short, or fat, to wear the clothes of another alter. Hence, not only would certain clothes seem inappropriate to some alters but not to others, but an alter might insist (sometimes adamantly) that another alter's clothes are simply the wrong size.

In fact, alters sometimes report experiencing other alters in different locations. For example, during therapy sessions in which various alters communicate with each other and with the therapist, one alter might experience another as seated in a different chair. This is not surprising, in light of the high hypnotizability of most multiples, and the correlated ability to experience both positive and negative hallucinations. Nevertheless, hallucinations of this sort, like those producing different body-images, strongly suggest that alternate personalities are more than merely distinct sets of traits, beliefs, memories, etc. To speak very loosely for the moment, those distinct sets appear to be organized around (or to belong to) discrete centers of self-awareness (i.e., different *selves*).

Another phenomenon suggesting the distinctness of a multiple's centers of self-awareness is the visible struggle between alters for executive control of the body. Granted, certain of these struggles are not as sharply etched as others. For example, an alter might struggle uncharacteristically to complete sentences or actions, and one might properly *infer* from this that another alter is interfering with those tasks. But at other times, one can actually observe and clearly identify the participants in the struggle. For example, as two alters vie for executive control, the multiple's face might shift rapidly between the distinctive features of each. Even more importantly, the clear personality shifts on the subject's face often reflects the alters' idiosyncratic contributions to the conflict. For example, one personality might show anger, tension, or confusion, and the other might display amusement and contempt. And those dispositions can be exhibited in a manner characteristic of the respective personalities. Furthermore, each of the competing personalities might show that it *wants* to be in control. The struggle is not simply as if a single person were alternately trying on different 'masks', or as if an actor were alternating between different 'roles'. Presumably, the dynamic in those cases would be rather different, not only less rich or complex or lacking the quite tangible urgency of the struggle for control, but also lacking the appropriate and long-term connections to the past. For one thing, an alter's behavior connects to traumas and other events in the past, as well as to more recent triggering events, in terms of all of which the details and nuances of the alter's present behavior make sense. Moreover (and perhaps more important), the different behaviors of competing alters tend to be consistent with earlier behaviors. Unlike an actor playing different roles, different alters reflect distinctive behavioral histories and developmental continuity, and they exhibit frequently complex systems of needs and interests.

But there are indications of even deeper respects in which different alters are distinct centers of self-awareness. One of these is the phenomenon of *internal homicide*. It is fairly well-known that alters might intervene in the lives of others, intentionally interfering with their interests and activities, or at least playing mischief on them. For example, in Morton Prince's classic Miss Beauchamp case (M. Prince, 1905/1978), Sally would destroy the school work of Miss B., spend her money, or hide her valuables. She would also take pleasure in putting Miss B. in situations Miss B. found repugnant. In many cases, however, alters pursue a more radical course and actually try to kill other alters. Although therapists point out that such an action would succeed in destroying a common body, the aggressive alter will deny it and claim to be an autonomous individual, mentally and physically.

Of course, one cannot 'get inside the head' of an alternate personality and know its experiences as if they were one's own. But what is striking in the behavior of those homicidal alters is that they often seem to have a strong drive to live. For example, they might see another alter as interfering with or imperiling their own life, and accordingly they may wish to get rid of it. Hence, one cannot simply dismiss the behavior of the homicidal alter as suicidal. While it might be correct to describe the patient *as a whole* as suicidal in such cases (though even that is questionable), it seems false to claim that the homicidal personality is suicidal. *That* personality wants to live and is willing to do what seems necessary to ensure or promote its survival. Moreover, its distinct sense of self is apparently rather sturdy and well-developed, enough so to see no problem in destroying the life of another alter.

But perhaps the strongest indication of the profound distinctness of alternate personalities is the way they frequently describe knowing each other's mental states. Although the terms in which they couch their descriptions raise numerous philosophical questions, two crucial facts nevertheless emerge quite clearly. First, there appear to be different ways in which one alter can come to know the mental states of others. And second, the various methods of acquiring this knowledge seem quite different from the process of coming to know one's own mental states. The Doris Fischer case (W.F. Prince, 1915/16, 1916) contains what is probably the most detailed testimony on this issue. Consider, for example, how 'Sleeping Margaret' describes what happens during periods when 'Real Doris' (R.D.) is in executive control of the body. (The other initials, 'M' and 'S.D', stand for 'Margaret' and 'Sick Doris'.)

S.D. watched when R.D. was out. There would be three of us watching her, each with thoughts of her own. S.D. watched R.D.'s mind, M. watched S.D.'s thoughts of R.D., and I watched all three. Sometimes we had a disagreement. Sometimes a jealous thought would flit through S.D.'s mind — she would think for a moment that if R.D. would not come out any more M. might like her (S.D.) as well as R.D. She never tried to hinder R.D.'s coming, though, but always to help, and only a slight thought of the kind would flit through her mind. But M. would see it and get cross with S.D., and so the disturbance inside would make R.D. go in. Often then the anxiety of the bunch to have R.D. stay out longer would prevent it.

(W.F. Prince, 1915/16, pp. 838-39; 1916, p. 109)

When R.D. was out...S.D. saw her thoughts directly. M. saw them through S.D. By through I mean as reflected from S.D.

There was scarcely any difference in the time of S.D.'s and M.'s getting them. And besides, M. saw S.D.'s own thoughts directly. This was generally the case with M., but there were times when S.D. was so far in that M. got R.D.'s thoughts directly. This was seldom. I don't know why it was. As for me, I saw R.D.'s thoughts as they were reflected by M., and besides I saw M.'s own thoughts directly. This was the case before S.D. went [i.e., disappeared], but after she went I saw, as I do now, R.D.'s thoughts directly. S.D. was a barrier that prevented me from seeing them that way so long as she lasted, but now the barrier is removed.

$$\text{(1915/16, p. 839; 1916, pp. 109-10)}$$

It appears, then, that alternate personalities differ not only with respect to the different sets of behavioral regularities in virtue of which we consider them different *personalities*. They also seem to have quite distinct centers, not just of consciousness, but of self-awareness. In what sense, however, are alters self-aware? And to what extent does that type of awareness distinguish multiple personality from other forms of dissociation? These are the issues to which we must now turn.

3.3 THE SENSE OF SELF

To begin with, we should notice an outstanding difference between multiples and non-multiples, and also between multiplicity and other forms of dissociation. Although non-multiples may dissociate in any number of ways, and even experience amnesia, they tend nevertheless to retain only one center of self-consciousness. No matter how differently a non-multiple might act, think, or feel about himself on separate occasions, those changes generally 'refer' or apply to the same center of self-awareness, even from that person's subjective point of view. That is, not only would an outsider say that the changes were changes *in* the same individual, but that person generally experiences the changes in that way and would refer to successive states as 'mine'. Hence, when we recall a dream or the emotions and behavior experienced during a hypnotic trance, or when our feelings and actions during a period of great stress are quite uncharacteristic, we usually assume ownership (as it were) for those states, no matter how odd or unlike the majority of our states they might be. In the case of MPD, however, successive emotional or cognitive states seem to be assigned and experienced quite differently. For example, alters who claim (and appear) to be aware of another alter's mental states or actions, typically refer to them as 'his' or 'hers', not as 'mine'. Apparently, the inner life of the multiple differs significantly from that of the non-multiple, or even from that of an ordinary hypnotized subject.

This point can be refined somewhat further, with an admiring nod to the taxonomic flourishes of C.D. Broad. It is clear, first of all, that mental states vary in their level of complexity and richness, and some, no doubt, exceed the level of mental functioning of which certain organisms are capable. Presumably giraffes do not experience feelings of irony or whimsy, and quite probably clams and termites do not experience much of what even giraffes do. Some might wish to argue that any organism that perceives has mental states, even if those states are quite rudimentary. But whether or not the simplest organisms have a mental life, it is nevertheless clear that mental states vary considerably in their degree of richness and complexity, both within a given organism and across species. For the most part, those of the lowest organisms could be said to belong at what Broad (1962, p. 391) called the *biotic* level of experience; those of non-human mammals could be said to belong at the *animal* level; and those of humans will occupy a higher, *personal* level. Now it is difficult to say at what level in this heirarchy we should place the capacity for self-awareness, or at what level of organic complexity we would expect to find the sorts of *distinct* centers of self-awareness characteristic of MPD. The two might even be different. For example, perhaps certain higher non-human organisms (such as dogs, pigs, and dolphins) are capable of some degree of self-awareness, but perhaps only human beings are able to have more than one center of self-awareness at a time.

Fortunately, for present purposes it should not be necessary to decide where the possibility of one or more centers of self-awareness breaks off on the ontological scale. Our immediate concern is to determine in which respect(s) and to what extent multiple personality differs from both non-dissociative conditions and also other forms of dissociation. Consider, then, some additional terminology. Let us say that two or more sensory, mental, or behavioral states are *co-referential* when they may properly be assigned to, or when they happen to, the same individual. And let us say that a state is *indexical* when an individual believes it to be his own (i.e., to be assignable to himself). Indexicality, obviously, is not a built-in feature or inherent property of a state. Rather, it is an *epistemological* and hence, a relational property; a state is indexical *for* an individual just in case that individual has a certain belief about it — namely, the reflexive belief that it is his own. One would think, then, that a certain amount of epistemological or cognitive development is required for a state to be indexical, since indexicality exists only in the presence of certain reflexive beliefs — namely, beliefs about the referents of one's states. It is unclear, however, just how much intellectual sophistication or development is required to have beliefs of that kind. For example, it is unclear whether infants are sufficiently developed, or at what point they begin to have primitive versions of those beliefs.

Although we cannot afford to pursue these important developmental issues in any detail, we should keep them in mind, at least temporarily, in connection with a possibly valuable distinction. In addition to being indexical, sensory, mental, and behavioral states can have yet another kind of relational property — in this case, *phenomenological*, rather than epistemological. When an individual *experiences* a state as his own, let us describe that state as *autobiographical*. The difference between believing a state to be one's own and experiencing it as one's own is quite subtle and requires a few words of explanation. First, in using the term 'belief', I do not have in mind only occurrent beliefs, much less episodes of actively avowing or consciously experiencing a belief. Having a belief may also (or only) be a dispositional cognitive state. Second, I do not mean to suggest that the difference between a state's being autobiographical and its being indexical can be neatly and crisply drawn. I want to claim only that there is a somewhat rough but useful distinction here between two different senses of oneself. Similarly, in distinguishing a phenomenological from an epistemological sense of self, there is no reason to suppose that the more general phenomenological/epistemological distinction is sharp. Nor does any of this imply that there can be a purely phenomenological (or epistemological) state or sense of oneself. In fact, it is clear that many qualitative features of experience presuppose a belief-system (or world view) that predisposes us to experience certain types of things rather than others. For example, in virtue of our scientific beliefs, we may have a visual experience of an airplane rather than a great silver god. Similarly, our religious beliefs may incline us to experience certain events as awe-inspiring rather than merely curious.

At any rate, probably the best way to understand the distinction is to examine cases where only one of the two properties seems to obtain. Consider, first, some experiments conducted on a pair of Siamese twins, 'connected on the ventral surface between the umbilicus and the bottom of the sternum, so that they always faced one another' (Stern, 1985, p. 78). The two girls, Alice and Betty, frequently sucked contentedly on each other's fingers. Stern writes,

> About one week before they were to be surgically separated at four months (corrected for prematurity)...I had an opportunity to do a number of experiments....When... Alice...was sucking on her *own* fingers, one of us placed one hand on her head and the other hand on the arm that she was sucking. We gently pulled the sucking arm away from her mouth and registered (in our own hands) whether the arm put up resistance to being moved from her mouth and/or whether her head strained forward to go after the retreating hand. In this situation, Alice's arm resisted the interruption of sucking, but she did not give evidence of straining forward with her head. The same procedure was followed when Alice was sucking on her sister Betty's fingers rather than her own. When Betty's hand was gently pulled from Alice's mouth, Alice's arms showed no resistance or movement, and Betty's arm showed no resistance, but Alice's head did strain forward.

> (Stern, 1985, pp. 78-9)

Moreover, when Alice and Betty were sucking on each others' fingers, Stern and his colleagues ran the same tests simultaneously on the two sisters, with similar results. Now if we consider just Alice for the moment, perhaps it is fair to say that her ability to react appropriately to the different sets of circumstances requires some rudimentary phenomenological sense of self, or ability to experience certain of her sensory (and perhaps volitional) states as her own. At the same time, however, we might be reluctant to attribute to Alice the *belief* (or at least any interestingly robust belief) that those states are her own.

We might also want to make a similar claim with regard to

certain lower organisms. Their ability to experience states as their own may be all the sense of self that is required to carry out various activities, such as eating, avoiding bumping into objects, or seeking shelter from rain or cold. As in the case of Alice, these activities may be accompanied by no beliefs (or nothing more than the most rudimentary sorts of beliefs) about the activities or the agent performing them.

More interesting, however, and possibly more relevant, are cases where a state seems to be solely autobiographical for a normally functional adult. Probably all of us have had moments of relative epistemological poverty, during which we may be properly described as having no beliefs about the referents of our autobiographical states. Those moments tend to occur during periods when our experiences are confined primarily to the animal or biotic level — for example, during a drunken stupor, sexual orgasm, panic, or while fighting for one's life. Granted, at these times we may believe any number of things *dispositionally*, just as a person may be said to have various beliefs while sleeping. Nevertheless, during these periods it is not clear that we believe, even dispositionally, that our *ongoing* mental or bodily states are our own. Those particular autobiographical states are not indexical. Of course, we might remember those states later and believe *retrospectively* that the earlier states *had been* our own. But during the period of deep stupefaction, terror, ecstacy, etc., it would seem that we are not even disposed to have the occurrent belief that our ongoing states are our own. If we do have such a disposition, it would seem to be a far cry from the respect in which (say) a person concentrating fully on purchasing allergy medication believes dispositionally that his itchy eyes and runny nose are his own bodily states. For one thing, a preoccupied person can generally shift or relax attention and report (or at least recognize) that he is suffering from allergy symptoms. By contrast, during periods of deep stupefaction, etc., one might be quite incapable of any such shift of attention, much less the actual formulation of beliefs.

At any rate, what matters here is the difference between these two cases, not whether persons are literally devoid of all beliefs during moments of epistemological poverty. For our present purposes, the crucial point is that during certain brief periods in a normal adult's life, one's phenomenological sense of self can be quite vigorous and acute, even though the ordinarily well-developed epistemological sense of self is either non-existent or radically attenuated. At these times, I submit, there is little to be gained from describing the subject as believing that his ongoing states are his own. And we should remember that these periods *are* quite brief. After a short time, our experiences return naturally to the personal level, and we readily and instinctively adopt our former epistemic attitudes toward them.

But no matter how we decide to describe our sense of self during periods of stupefaction, etc., there are different and more impressive sorts of cases in which an adult's state is apparently autobiographical yet non-indexical. These cases demonstrate that one can both experience a state as one's own and also quite consciously and actively believe that the state is *not* one's own. Hence, they demonstrate clearly that a state's indexicality is not a necessary condition for its being autobiographical, contrary to what some might have thought.

My colleague Raymond Martin has told me about a Zen nun he knew who claimed to believe she had no self, and who sedulously avoided any use of the personal pronoun in order to help counter the *illusion* that she had a self. Hence, she would say 'There's hunger here', rather than 'I'm hungry'. And if you asked her whether the hunger was her own, she would answer in the negative. Now it may be that the nun's deeply-held belief that the hunger is not her own ultimately affects her experience of hunger, so that she eventually experiences it impersonally (whatever, exactly, that would amount to).[1] Nevertheless, it is reasonable to assume that at some point in this process the nun still experiences the state of hunger as her own, even though she does not believe it to be her own. Indeed, it is *that* autobiographical experience of hunger that the nun regards as illusory and that she actively tries to undermine.

We can multiply examples of this sort, provided we are willing to entertain a range of fairly exotic beliefs and experiences. For example, consider the hallucination (or ostensibly psychic experience) that I am possessing (or co-occupying, or telepathically in rapport with) another individual's body. In such cases I might experience various bodily sensations as my own, while simultaneously believing that they are not my experiences. Since *ex hypothesi* I believe myself to possess (co-occupy, or be in rapport with) another person's body, I might simply believe that my acquaintance with those states is *as if* they were mine.

It appears, then, that one important difference between a state's being autobiographical and its being indexical is that the latter is theory- or world-view-dependent in a way, or to a degree, that the former is not. By contrast, although our autobiographical states may eventually be altered by our beliefs, our ability to experience a state as our own seems to be relatively theory-independent.

Some might think that automatic writers (or ostensibly possessed persons generally) furnish additional examples of an individual's states being both autobiographical and non-indexical. On the surface, it appears as if the subject in these cases experiences certain states as his own, but believes them to be states of another conscious entity. But I think that might be the wrong way to characterize such cases. Indeed, we must be very careful in describing an apparent victim of possession or a person engaged in automatic writing.

Suppose, for instance, that during automatic writing it seems as if my hand is expressing the thoughts of a discarnate entity. Is it really correct to say that the *very same state* is both autobiographical and non-indexical? Granted, my hand movements will be autobiographical, because I continue to experience the hand as my own. But that is why I also *believe* the movements to be *my* hand movements, even if I believe them to be guided by another mind. Hence, it would be false to say that those bodily states are autobiographical but non-indexical. On the other hand, I would tend to believe that the thoughts expressed in writing, as well as the volition to write, are not my own states. Hence, those mental states would be non-indexical for me. But in that case I might not *experience* those mental states as my own either. Actually, in cases of automatic writing, failing to believe that the mental states are my own may affect the manner in which I experience them. But even if an automatist's beliefs lack that sort of causal influence, it is still very likely that the thoughts expressed automatically would seem quite foreign to my usual way of thinking. Hence, it is possible that I would experience those alien mental states more or less impersonally as well. Moreover, the volition to write would probably be something of which I am consciously unaware. (Indeed, as we saw in Chapter 1.8, automatic writers tend to describe their experiences in both these ways.) But if I do not consciously experience the volition at all, then clearly I do not experience it as mine. Hence, in cases of ostensible possession, it may be that neither mental nor bodily states are both autobiographical and non-indexical.

Finally, we should consider cases in which a person does not experience a state as his own (i.e., it is non-autobiographical), but nevertheless acknowledges it as his (i.e., it is indexical). For example, in some cases of hallucination, out-of-body experiences, or in the psychopathological condition known as depersonalization, subjects might experience their bodily or mental states as if they were detached or as if they were acquainted with them from the perspective of an outside observer. Nevertheless, the subject might still believe that the experience is phenomenologically delusory and that those states really are his own.

Certain phenomena of post-hypnotic suggestion seem also to be both indexical and non-autobiographical. Suppose, for example, that in response to earlier suggestion, I begin tap dancing when I hear the word 'cowlick'. The behavior might come as a complete surprise to me. Not only would I be unaware of any volition or desire to tap dance; it may, in fact, be quite unlike me to do such a thing. Hence (as before), since I do not experience the volition at all, I obviously do not experience it as mine. Nevertheless, if I'm unaware of having been hypnotized, I might believe that the will to dance was my own (however puzzling it may be). For example, I might believe that I was simply not paying sufficient attention to my deepest behavioral impulses.

It appears, then, that one's states may sometimes be indexical but not autobiographical, while at other times they may be autobiographical but not indexical. This should not be too surprising, because no matter what the phenomenological/epistemological distinction finally amounts to, the two properties are clearly different. The property of being autobiographical is primarily qualitative and phenomenological, requiring perhaps only a minimum of cognitive development or sophistication. A state's indexicality, on the other hand, is more thoroughly epistemological, requiring perhaps a somewhat higher level of cognitive development and sophistication, at least enough to have reflexive beliefs about the referents of one's states.

3.4 APPERCEPTIVE CENTERS

Consider, now, how these observations bear on the analysis of multiple personality. Quite probably, the majority of an alternate personality's mental and behavioral states are autobiographical. But even more impressively, they seem to be indexical as well. Although some alters seem quite rudimentary (e.g., carrying out nothing more than basic bodily functions, such as eating or eliminating), generally speaking there is more to an alter than a phenomenologically distinctive stream of experiences. In most cases, the alter also stands in a distinctive set of relatively well-developed epistemological relations to those experiences. Distinct alters, we might say, tend to be distinct *apperceptive centers*, where 'apperceptive center' is defined as follows.

> '*S* is an apperceptive center' =df (a) *S* is a subject of autobiographical states, both occurrent and dispositional (e.g., sensations, emotions, beliefs, desires, ostensible rememberings, hopes, plans, etc.), and (b) most of those states are indexical for *S* (i.e., *S* believes that those states are its own).

In short, an apperceptive center is an individual most of whose autobiographical states are indexical. And we can say that *X* and *Y* are *distinct* apperceptive centers just in case the autobiographical and indexical states of each are (respectively) largely non-autobiographical and non-indexical for the other. I say 'largely' here for two reasons. First, alters often seem to overlap — for example, by having common memories, and it is unclear whether their memories or experiences are numerically identical, qualitatively identical, or merely qualitatively similar. For example, it is difficult to determine if memories, sensations, etc., are somehow shared while nevertheless belonging to distinctive streams of experiences (e.g., in the way two different persons can observe or recollect the same thing). Second, one occasionally reads (admittedly, rather enigmatic) reports of an alter's mental states 'leaking' into or merging with those of another, as if they were part of the latter's stream of experiences.

I doubt that any sharp or rigid division can be drawn between multiplicity and other forms of dissociation. Nevertheless, multiple personality seems to have some distinctive features, which set it off (in different ways) from most other forms of dissociation. And I suspect that the concept of an apperceptive center, rough as it is, will help us to capture fairly tidily what makes multiple personality a subject of particular philosophical interest.

Probably the most outstanding distinguishing feature of multiplicity is this. Whereas multiples seem to have more than one distinct apperceptive center at a time, this does not seem to be the case for other strong forms of dissociation. For example, a hypnotically-induced 'hidden observer' is not an apperceptive center distinct from the original hypnotized individual, even though hidden observers are similar to alters in some important respects. Hidden observers report experiences of which the hypnotized subject is apparently unaware. The hidden observer's experiences are, therefore, not autobiographical for the subject. But they *are* indexical, at least eventually. Once the subject learns of the hidden observer's experiences, he accepts those states as his own, despite their having been outside conscious awareness. More important, however, most (if not all) of the hypnotic subject's indexical states seem to be indexical for the hidden observer (Hilgard, 1986, pp. 187ff, 209ff). Hence, we could say that the disparities of indexicality found in hidden observer studies are largely *asymmetrical*, whereas in cases (such as MPD) satisfying the conditions for distinct apperceptive centers, they are mostly symmetrical.

It is important to remember, however, that this difference between multiplicity and other forms of dissociation is not always clear-cut and that it often seems merely to be a difference in degree. But that is hardly surprising. After all, the distinctness of apperceptive centers is itself a matter of degree, depending on the *extent* to which the autobiographical and indexical states of one alter are (respectively) non-autobiographical and non-indexical for another. That is why in some cases — especially during a multiple's gradual process of integration — it is unclear whether (or how many) distinct apperceptive centers exist. In fact, the blending of personalities can apparently occur at varying levels of completeness.

Probably the most perplexing times are when two alters merge fairly extensively, but not thoroughly. At these stages of partial integration, a state of affairs sometimes exists that we may call 'co-presence'. This is not to be confused with Morton Prince's 'co-consciousness', which denotes the simultaneous existence in a body of two quite distinct apperceptive centers, only one of which may be in executive control of the body. By contrast, 'co-presence' refers to a state in which two formerly distinct personalities, *A* and *B*, *share* executive control of the body. But because the personalities sometimes appear to integrate partially in the process, it is pretty much of a toss-up whether we should consider *A* and B to be a team of distinct apperceptive centers, or whether A and B blend into a new personality. On the one hand, it may appear as if enough of each remains for the two still to be considered distinct. Although during periods of co-presence it seems as if many of the states autobiographical and indexical for A are likewise autobiographical and indexical for B (and vice versa), there might still seem to be a few remaining disparities of indexicality. On the other hand, the multiple might behave as if a new personality exists, albeit one whose constitution fluctuates (perhaps continually) between different *proportions* of A and B. For example, the multiple might say (somewhat inscrutably), 'I'm mostly A right now'.

Cases of mediumship and apparent possession are also difficult to assess. In these cases, it is unclear whether the communicating or possessing agencies should be considered relatively ephemeral (but nevertheless distinct) apperceptive centers, or whether a single apperceptive center has simply shifted into a dramatically different state of consciousness (as in hypnosis). Of course, if ostensibly possessing entities or mediumistic communicators are what they purport to be, or if they are merely special forms of short-term or intermittent alternate personalities, then presumably they are distinct apperceptive centers. If the former is the case (i.e., if possession really occurs), then multiple personality is clearly not unique in exhibiting the simultaneous presence in a body of distinct apperceptive centers. However, when paranormal explanations seem gratuitous (as they often do), it is very difficult to determine whether subjects display a form of multiplicity or simply a dramatic but less deep — or perhaps simply non-pathological — dissociated state (see Chapter 9 for a discussion of mediumship and multiple personality).

At this point, we should pause to consider whether my account of apperceptive centers is open to a charge of circularity. I can think of two types in particular about which the reader might have wondered. First, it might seem as if the term 'apperceptive center' is suspiciously close in meaning to the term 'subject' or 'subject of autobiographical states' in its definiens. But we must recall that an apperceptive center is only a certain *kind* of subject, one whose autobiographical states tend to be indexical. In fact, we have many ways of individuating or naming subjects, which needn't presuppose that the subjects differ more profoundly than in name, or with respect to a limited set of predicates used to describe them. For example, we can distinguish, as subjects, the Chairman of the Board, Jones's father, and that man expressing his distaste for anchovies, even though those descriptions pick out the same person. That is why we can meaningfully ask or investigate whether those subjects are identical. Similarly, we can ask meaningfully whether (say) a particular hidden observer is a distinct apperceptive center from the hypnotized subject, or whether alters calling themselves by different names (hence, different subjects) are really distinct apperceptive centers.

Second, some might object that it is very difficult (if not impossible) to determine whose indexical states are whose without first drawing boundaries between apperceptive centers. Now I readily concede that this is difficult, but it is not a problem for the *concept* of an apperceptive center. It is merely one way to characterize the practical (not theoretical) problem of distinguishing apperceptive centers. For example, this is the challenge faced by the clinician who tries to decide if ostensibly different alters are genuinely different alters. But that clinical problem seems independent of the more abstract issues under discussion. Our concern here is to describe what is distinctive about multiple personality and (in particular) what distinct apperceptive centers are, no matter how difficult it might be in practice to take an accurate 'head count' of apperceptive centers.[2]

Let us return, then, to our examination of the concept of an apperceptive center, and try to refine it somewhat, in order to specify more precisely how multiplicity differs from non-multiplicity, including other forms of dissociation. We must observe, first, that an ordinary person's mental or bodily states seem sometimes to be *neither* autobiographical nor indexical. The reason is simply that one may be *unaware* of one's own states. For example, just as an athlete or soldier absorbed in his activities may not realize he has sustained an injury or wound, persons generally may be unaware that they are in a certain state, as the result (say) of inattention, absent-mindedness, intense concentration on something else, or hypnotic suggestion. Similarly, ignorance (e.g., a lack of self-understanding) may blind us to the occurrence of our own mental states. For example, I may be unaware of my fear of intimacy and consciously experience only its superficial manifestations (such as my displeasure with a lover).

By contrast, a multiple's states may fail to be autobiographical and indexical in a somewhat distinctive way. Of course alters (like anyone else) may be unaware of their states as the result of inattention, etc. Moreover, they sometimes have amnesia for periods during which another alter assumes executive control of the body. But unlike the case of a non-multiple who is merely unaware of certain states, an alternate personality's states may be non-autobiographical or non-indexical even when the alter is aware of them. Alters often experience mental and bodily changes from an *outsider's* perspective, as if they happened to another person. As the excerpt above (see pp. 69-70) from the Doris Fischer case illustrates, alters sometimes claim to experience another alter's mental states in a way that sounds telepathic, as if they were able to peek into a private room of experiences, or access or 'read' a stream of experiences distinct from their own. And in other cases, alters seem to experience their co-embodied alters in the way non-multiples experience each other. For example, as I've already noted, they will sometimes experience certain sensory or physiological states as belonging to a body different from their own. In fact, as I've also noted, an alter will sometimes experience another as occupying a different spatial location. In these cases, mental states may be inferred from the behavior of an ostensibly distinct body, rather than being experienced (as it were) from the inside.

Hence, there seem to be two main ways in which an individual's states may fail to be indexical. When the individual has no beliefs about whose state the state is — for example, when he is simply unaware of it, or when he is epistemically too undeveloped to have any beliefs about whose state it is — let us describe the state as ostensibly *non-referential*. And when the individual assigns the state to a conscious individual other than himself, as is generally and somewhat distinctively the case in MPD and apparent possession, let us describe the state as ostensibly *extra-referential*. Of course, if the individual is correct in making such assignments (as seems to be the case in MPD, and as would be the case in actual possession), we would say the state is *genuinely* extra-referential.

We can now appreciate one reason why multiple personality seems to challenge certain widespread assumptions concerning personhood. It concerns an alter's tendency to regard as extra-referential many of the non-indexical mental and physical states associated with his body. In our everyday ascriptions of mental and bodily states, we generally and tacitly suppose that a human being's successive states are autobiographically and indexically *continuous*. Apart from ordinary gaps in conscious awareness, such as those occurring during sleep or periods of unconsciousness, we suppose that successive states are autobiographical and indexical for the same individual. The behavior of a multiple, however, tends to undermine that assumption. We are often prepared to accept that a multiple's successive states are autobiographically and indexically discontinuous. It seems to us as if more than one individual inhabits the same body.

Of course, we may (in some contexts) prefer to identify a person entirely (or primarily) with his body, and say that the mental and bodily states of different alters are still states of the same *person* (see Chapter 8 for a discussion of different senses of 'person'). In that sense, I suppose, the states of different alters will still be considered co-referential, and I see nothing inherently wrong with that way of speaking (especially in view of some of the considerations advanced in Chapter 7). Nevertheless, this manner of assigning states to the same individual has limited utility. For certain descriptive purposes, it seems quite inadequate, and that is one reason why multiple personality challenges at least one ordinary concept of a person. When the different states appear to be states of distinct alternate *personalities* — so much so that we are willing to treat the alters as discrete moral or prudential agents — our inclination (obviously) is to treat those states as *non*-co-referential.

3.5 SOME POTENTIAL DIFFICULTIES

Of course, the foregoing suggestions about what makes multiple personality distinctive are no more than rough guidelines. Dissociative phenomena and mental disunities come in many varieties, and in numerous degrees within each variety. In fact, like psychological phenomena generally, they tend to resist neat classification. One can always find or imagine borderline cases that straddle different categories, no matter how useful those categories may be in systematizing the domain in question. For example, we have already seen how the concept of an apperceptive center fails to draw clear boundaries between MPD and cases of ostensible possession. But that is hardly a flaw in the account I have proposed. There may well be deep similarities between those two sorts of phenomena, especially if the latter are not cases of genuine possession.

There are, however, two cases that appear to challenge (in

different ways) the utility of the account I have provided. Although it seems to me that neither uncovers any fatal short-comings, they nevertheless force some important issues to the surface.

What should one say, first of all, about a form of multiplicity in which the different alters are too epistemically primitive to have *any* indexical states? Is it possible that lower organisms, or perhaps severely retarded human beings, manifest a kind of multiplicity? Wouldn't it still be a form of multiplicity if the alters were so primitive or brutish that they operated at only the biotic and perhaps also the animal level? If so, then disparities of indexicality do not seem to be what is important and distinctive about multiple personality. A multiple with only these rudimentary sorts of alters would, at best, display nothing more than disparities between autobiographical states.

I should add that this issue is not entirely theoretical, since some alters apparently exist quite close to a merely biotic or animal level of existence. They seem more or less to perform, rather automatically and blindly, nothing more than a limited range of specific bodily functions. (In fact, some alters seem to be animal personalities, but they needn't be as rudimentary as an alter whose sole function was, say, to urinate.) Naturally, individuation of alters becomes very tricky at this point. Even if one could confidently conclude that one of a multiple's alters was genuinely brutish (and not simply a more highly evolved alter behaving brutishly), it is not clear how one would distinguish two different brutish alters. Probably, that task would be impossible in the absence of testimony *from a more epistemically developed personality* that distinct brutish alters had been in executive control of the body. Hence, if there were multiples *all* of whose alters were brutish, we might never be able to identify them as multiples.

Fortunately, that practical problem is not the issue here. Our present concern is to determine if my analysis of multiplicity would be undermined by forms of multiplicity involving subjects epistemically simpler than apperceptive centers. In such cases, presumably, the autobiographical states of one subject would be largely non-autobiographical for the other(s). Nevertheless, those subjects would have few (if any) beliefs, and hence would not display disparities of indexicality.

A sensible response to this challenge, I submit, has several parts. First, we might concede that there could be a form of multiplicity that is not an instance of multiple *personality*. After all, the alters in these cases would not be personality-like. In fact, even if they remain clinically interesting (which is questionable), they would seem to be clinically intractable. If the alters are all so epistemically primitive that they have no beliefs (at least of any interestingly robust sort), then it would not be possible to communicate with them and learn anything about the case, or even distinguish the different alters. Apparently, the treatment of such a multiple is neither required nor possible. Nevertheless, such a case might still be of theoretical interest, even if it could not be identified in practice, and even if it does not challenge the concept of a person in the way a multiple with more highly developed alters does.

One might think that some forms of dissociation display only this rudimentary kind of multiplicity, but I suspect that most (if not all) do not. Consider, for example, cases of hypnotic anesthesia or amnesia in which a hidden observer reports states of which the hypnotized subject is unaware. As we noted earlier, such cases seem to exhibit merely asymmetrical disparities of indexicality, and, therefore, do not justify positing the presence of distinct apperceptive centers. But it seems as if disparities between auto-biographical states are likewise only asymmetrical in those cases. Although the hidden observer's pains (say) are not autobiographical for the hypnotized subject, the hidden observer's reports suggest that the hypnotic subject's autobiographical experiences *are* also autobiographical for the hidden observer (see Hilgard, 1986). Hence, even a completely brutish multiple would seem to be more deeply dissociated than an ordinary hypnotized subject. It also may be the case that thoroughgoing disparities between autobiographical states would distinguish rudimentary hypothetical forms of multiplicity from cases where *occasional* disparities of that sort seem to occur — for example, some periods in the life of a commissurotomy patient.

But even if a largely or thoroughly phenomenological form of multiplicity is more deeply disunified than other dissociative phenomena, the main reason multiple *personality* is philosophically (and clinically) interesting is that higher-level epistemic disparities of indexicality occur extensively. Hence, even if a lower-level phenomenological form of multiplicity exists in nature, it does not pose as profound a challenge as MPD does to the concept of a person — for example, by tempting us to treat different alters as distinct moral or prudential agents. And since it seems to raise no issues about the explanation of behavior or the structure of the mind not also raised by full-fledged multiple personality, I will simply acknowledge brutish multiplicity as a theoretically possible but practically undetectable form of multiplicity, and continue to focus on the even more vexing type of multiplicity that we can distinguish both in theory and in practice.

The second challenge to my account concerns the difference between role-playing and multiple personality. Now of course, it is easy to distinguish multiple personality from the ordinary sort of role-playing we engage in quite routinely as we assume different roles in different situations. Although our various everyday roles correspond to distinctive sets of mental and behavioral states, those roles nevertheless may all be attributed to a single apperceptive center. States autobiographical and indexical for the subject of one role are generally autobiographical and indexical for the subject of another. That is why, for example, I can speak of the different ways *I* feel or behave in my roles as teacher, professional musician, adoring mate, garrulous dinner guest, insecure eldest child who still can't please his parents, etc. By contrast, the feelings, thoughts, and actions of one alter tend to be ostensibly extra-referential for others.

But what should we say about a person who regularly cultivates awareness of role-playing while it is occurring? Such a person might come to experience what could be called a 'real (or private) self' and distinguish it from one or more 'public selves' that he presents to others. Moreover, the so-called real (or private) self might view or comment on the public selves as if they were distinct and semi-autonomous personalities with their own characteristic traits, interests, and agendas. Should this sort of highly-cultivated role-consciousness count as a form of multiplicity?

We should note, first of all, that role-playing apparently can *evolve* into multiple personality, especially when (as in certain cases of ritual abuse begun in early childhood) it is carefully regimented and coercively enforced. But for ordinary — even highly-developed — role-playing, I suspect that the indexical states of the private and public 'selves' are all indexical for the same apperceptive center. Hence, although one's different roles or 'selves' may be considered different subjects, and although we may attribute different beliefs, feelings, etc. to each, it would seem that to speak here of different selves is to do nothing more than employ an occasionally useful figure of speech.

An example should make this clearer.[3] Sometimes, when I give piano performances, I experience a wave of anxiety before starting to play. Yet I may simultaneously feel some emotional distance from the anxiety and even be amused by it. If I had cultivated my awareness of my role-playing, I might find it natural to describe the situation as follows. 'I see that Steve is experiencing his customary nervousness about performing. He's afraid he hasn't practiced enough, and that he'll forget the music. I'm not worried for him, however, although I understand why he's nervous. In fact, if he'll allow it, I could remind him how groundless such fears have been in the past and thereby help to ease his anxiety'.

Now I do not wish to challenge the utility of this way of speaking. But I suspect that the above soliloquy could easily be re-expressed entirely in the first-person, in which form it would have a different, but equally legitimate, sort of utility. For example, I could have said, 'I see that I'm experiencing my usual anxiety about playing, and I'm worried I haven't practiced enough and that I'll have a memory lapse. But I also know that when I've had this reaction in the past it has rarely (if ever) been justified, and when I reflect on that it helps to relieve my anxiety. If I paid attention to what I know, and didn't simply yield to my fears, I wouldn't be so worried now.' Clearly, this first-person alternative to my soliloquy does not detract from the utility (in some contexts) of conceptualizing one's roles, internal conflicts, or aspects of one's character as if they involved different 'selves'. But it shows that those selves do not display the disparities of indexicality characteristic of multiplicity. The multiple cannot re-express in the first person the analogous differences between alters.

3.6 CONCLUSION

At this point it should help to review, and in some cases to define more precisely, the important terms introduced in this chapter, as well as others with which they are connected.

  (1) 'states x and y are *co-referential*' =df 'x and y happen
        (or are properly assigned) to the same individual'
  (2) 'state x is *indexical* for S' =df 'S believes x to be its own
        state'
  (3) 'state x is *autobiographical* for S' =df 'S experiences x
        as its own'

(4) 'S is an *apperceptive center*' =df '(a) S is a subject of autobiographical states, both occurrent and dispositional, and (b) most of those states are indexical for S (i.e., S believes that those states are its own)'

(5) 'X and Y are distinct apperceptive centers' =df 'the autobiographical and indexical states of each are (respectively) largely non-autobiographical and non-indexical for the other'

(6) 'state x is ostensibly *non-referential* for S' =df 'S has no beliefs about whose state x is'

(7) 'state x is ostensibly *extra-referential* for S' =df 'S assigns x to a conscious subject other than itself'

We also considered the difference between 'co-consciousness' and 'co-presence'. But in fact there are several different sorts of interesting relations which can obtain between alternate personalities, and we now need a more fine-grained taxonomy to capture the most important of them. Let 'A' and 'B' stand for alternate personalities. Then first of all,

(8) 'A is *co-active* with B' =df 'states autobiographical and indexical only for A exist simultaneously with states autobiographical and indexical only for B'

Hence, to say that A and B are co-active is to assert that two autobiographically and indexically distinctive streams of experience occur simultaneously in one person. The life histories of A and B need not be co-terminous; A and B will simply be co-active during the period when their histories overlap. Co-activity is clearly a symmetrical relation, and it is also precondition for the following relations between alters.

(9) 'A is *co-sensory* with B' =df 'both A and B are aware of external events, including the multiple's bodily movements (for example, during periods when B is in executive control of the body)'

(10) 'A is *intra-conscious* with B' =df 'A is aware of B's mental states'

(11) 'A is *co-conscious* with B' =df 'A is either co-sensory or intra-conscious with B'[4]

(12) 'A is *intra-active* with B' =df 'A can influence B's experience or behavior'

(13) 'A is *co-present* with B' =df 'A and B share executive

> control of the body, during which time they may
> undergo partial integration'

It should be clear that although the co-activity of alters is a necessary condition for their being co-sensory, etc., co-activity may occur in the absence of these other relations. In other words, *A* and *B* may be co-active but isolated from each other.

To sum up, then, multiplicity seems to differ from non-multiplicity in the following ways. For one thing, only multiples seem to satisfy the conditions for the existence of two or more distinct co-active apperceptive centers associated with one body. By contrast, psychogenic fugue (say) would seem to demonstrate the *successive*, non-overlapping existence of distinct apperceptive centers associated with one body. Moreover, a non-multiple's mental states, including lower-level dissociative states, are usually autobiographical and indexical (although sometimes just one of these). And on those relatively infrequent occasions when they are non-indexical, those states tend to be ostensibly non-referential. The mental states of alternate personalities, however, are often non-indexical, and in those cases they tend to be ostensibly extra-referential.

Of course (as I've mentioned), cases of *genuine* mediumship and possession would also differ from non-multiplicity in these ways. But we may ignore that possibility for present purposes. Our goal is to gain a deeper grasp of the distinctive features of multiple personality, even if survival and possession are never viable explanatory options. Moreover, some cases of automatic writing and merely apparent possession seem to have some of the distinctive features of MPD. I question, however, whether in these latter cases (and especially in ordinary automatic writing) we have any grounds for asserting that the dissociated subject's autobiographical and indexical states are (respectively) non-autobiographical and non-indexical for the apparent possessor or the subject controlling the hand and expressing thoughts in writing. But if so, we should regard those cases as transient and presumably non-pathological (or at least less pathological) forms of multiple personality — i.e., as types of multiple personality, but not necessarily types of multiple personality *disorder*.

If this account of the distinctive features of multiplicity is on the right track, we can see why Kathleen Wilkes's recent attempt (1988) to address the same issue does not go quite far enough.

Wilkes argues (correctly) that the disunities of hypnosis and commissurotomy do not justify positing the existence of distinct *minds* in one person.[5] The reason, she claims, is that those disunities are due largely to the artificial situations created in experimental contexts and that the apparently disunified behavior occurs against 'a background of 99 per cent unity' (p. 156). Similarly, the apparent mental disunity of akrasia and self-deception stand out against 'a massive background of consistency, coherence, [and] integration' (p. 151), and, therefore, do not indicate the deep pervasive disunity necessary for attributing multiple minds to one person. By contrast, however, the disunities of MPD are pervasive enough to threaten our assumption that a human being has only one mind.

No doubt Wilkes is justified in claiming that multiple personality *disorder* is an enduring and not merely a transient phenomenon. But Wilkes makes it seem as if multiple personality threatens the concept of a person only on statistical grounds — namely, that multiples act or feel disunified a significant portion of the time, whereas hypnotized, brain-bisected, weak-willed and self-deceived persons act and feel unified almost all the time.

I have been suggesting, however, that multiples display a different kind of disunity than the others, and not merely a substantially greater amount of it. For example, when we consider a person whose attention is divided (say, between reading a book and listening to music, or between driving a car and conversing with a passenger), those activities seem to be autobiographical and indexical for the same subject. There is no need to posit distinct apperceptive centers to explain this type of disunity. More generally, what distinguishes multiple personality from other forms of mental disunity is that only multiples exhibit, say, the apparent disparities of indexicality discussed above. In the case of multiples we *have* reason to posit two or more distinct co-active apperceptive centers. And of course, only multiples seem regularly to have non-indexical states that are ostensibly extra-referential.

Contrary to what Wilkes suggests, then, what is of particular theoretical interest about MPD may occur for relatively brief periods (e.g., in cases of mediumship and apparent possesion) — hence, even in conditions that clinicians would not consider instances of multiple personality *disorder*. And when genuine possession is not a viable explanatory option, I see no barrier to considering these cases as short-term and non- (or at least less) maladaptive forms of multiple personality.

Incidentally (and quite apart from issues raised in Chapter 7), we can now see that Wilkes also errs in claiming that 'there is no integration *of any kind*' (p. 147, italics added) between reading a book and listening to music, or between driving a car and arguing with a passenger. Indeed, the integration that does exist in these cases is precisely of the sort that is notably absent in the deeper disunities of multiple personality. To see this, contrast the person whose attention is divided between two tasks with a person engaged in only one of them. For example, I can drive a car and argue at the same time. But having to do both simultaneously prevents me from doing either to the degree possible if I were engaged in it alone. In fact, the interference between simultaneous tasks has been demonstrated even in apparently more thorough forms of dissociation (Hilgard, 1986; Messerschmidt, 1927-8).

Hence, one respect in which we integrate (say) driving a car and arguing with a passenger concerns the way we minimize the interference between the two tasks. We avoid the total involvement in one that would distract too much from the other. Granted, this is not the same sort of integration as in Wilkes's examples of seeing or hearing the same person or describing one's ongoing activities. Those are cases where different sensory or volitional processes correspond to the same external phenomena. But in the case of divided attention, the two tasks are integrated in the sense that they are (as it were) juggled successfully so as to avoid the breakdown in one of the tasks. And that juggling activity makes sense relative to an even deeper sort of integration. The two tasks are autobiographical and indexical for the same apperceptive center. It is a single apperceptive center that juggles the tasks and keeps the total situation under control. (We apparently also need to posit a similar, but even deeper, sort of integration or unity to explain numerous features of MPD. See Chapter 7 for a discussion of this issue.)

It should now be clear how the foregoing analysis of multiplicity in terms of apperceptive centers differs from the definitions of 'multiple personality disorder' in the DSM-III and DSM-III-R. Quite apart from the fact that the DSM definitions attempt to pick out a psychological *disorder*, those definitions are intended only to help the clinician make appropriate diagnoses. For example, the DSM-III-R defined 'MPD' in terms of 'the existence of two or more distinct personalities or personality states (each with its own relatively enduring pattern of perceiving, relating to, and thinking about the environment and self)' (see Kluft, Steinberg, and Spitzer, 1988, for a discussion and comparison of the DSM-III definitions). But (perhaps appropriately) it made no attempt to analyze further the notion of a personality or a personality state. The present account, therefore, has simply taken matters somewhat deeper. I have tried to explain what is distinctive and philosophically interesting about alternate personalities, as compared (say) to other dissociative phenomena (such as hidden observers or well-developed role playing) where there likewise seem to be distinctive *patterns* of perceiving, etc. In the former case there seem to be no symmetrical disparities of indexicality between subjects, and in the latter case there seem to be no disparities of indexicality at all. Hence, I have tried to flesh out a concept apparently presupposed in the DSM criteria for MPD, but which clinicians often seem to take surprisingly for granted — namely, one's *sense of self*. To some extent, that issue has been addressed — although not altogether successfully — in the DSM-IV (see Chapter 10).

One final point, on developmental issues, before moving on to other matters. It may be that the central mystery of MPD is how new apperceptive centers are created. Now to some extent, it seems as if this mystery is not unique to the study of MPD. We are far from understanding how a *single* apperceptive center develops in a non-multiple. Nevertheless, in certain respects the development of apperceptive centers in a multiple seems to be a different process from the development of an apperceptive center in a non-multiple. For a non-multiple, one would think that the appropriate epistemological relations evolve, perhaps in degrees, over a period of time. But it seems that a multiple's new apperceptive centers may develop almost immediately — for example, in response to trauma. Perhaps that can happen only *after* the subject has developed into a single, pre-dissociative apperceptive center. In that case, new apperceptive centers may be able to form rapidly by drawing on an already existing repertoire of cognitive functions. (The discussion in Chapter 7 lends support to that conclusion.)

4

THE CONCEPT OF
DISSOCIATION

4.1 INTRODUCTION

Historians of psychology usually credit Pierre Janet with having originated the concept of dissociation, in connection with his studies of multiple personality and hysteria in the late 1880s (Janet, 1886, 1887, 1888, 1889). But according to van der Hart and Friedman (1989), Janet traced the concept to Moreau de Tours's 1845 treatise on hasish and mental illness. At any rate, it seems clear that the concept of dissociation originated in the nineteenth century. Its foundations, however, reach back into the eighteenth century, to the associationist theories of the British empiricists. Janet and his successors accepted the widely-held view that ideas (i.e., mental states) have associative links to one another, and that when these links are broken (e.g., in amnesia), certain ideas may be said to be split-off or dissociated from the rest.

The concept of dissociation enjoyed a rather brief spasm of popularity around the turn of the century. But with the rise of interest in Freudian dynamics, it was quickly eclipsed by the concept of repression. In fact, many *subsumed* the concept of dissociation under that of repression. But dissociation has recently mounted a comeback, along with the resurgence of interest in multiple personality, and once again many regard it as a concept independent of (although possibly compatible with) the categories of Freudian dynamics. It is not surprising that these changes coincide with a renewed interest in the work of Janet, attributable in part to the publication of Ellenberger's monumental *The Discovery of the Unconscious* in 1970 and E.R. Hilgard's *Divided Consciousness* (1986) in 1977. (For more recent manifestations of this trend, see, e.g., Crabtree, 1986; Decker, 1986; Haule, 1986;

Perry, 1984; Perry and Laurence, 1984.) These days, articles in the leading journals on hypnosis make frequent — indeed, almost casual — references to dissociation. In fact, the *American Journal of Clinical Hypnosis* recently devoted an entire issue to the topic of dissociation (vol. 29, no. 2, 1986). Even more noteworthy is the young but thriving International Society for the Study of Dissociation (formerly, the more cumbersome ISS*MP*&D), whose official journal is *Dissociation*.

One certainly gets the impression, then, that the concept of dissociation is playing a central role in the thinking of many clinicians and theoreticians — perhaps, even a greater role than during its initial heyday. Nevertheless, there is very little agreement or clarity about what that concept is; nor is there a generally accepted inventory of dissociative phenomena to which we may appeal in evaluating proposed definitions or theories of dissociation. Hence, this would seem to be a good time to try to remedy the situation. To do this, we needn't assume that dissociation is a neat enough concept to be captured by a single, crisp, and comprehensive philosophical or scientific analysis. It is hardly unprecedented for widely used (and useful) terms to resist such treatment. Indeed, it would not be surprising if the concept of dissociation is more elastic and fuzzy than many equally important scientific constructs, even if it is not quite as loose a notion as some others with which it is frequently linked — for example, 'consciousness'. Nevertheless, the concept can undoubtedly be made clearer than it is at present, and there is much to be learned, I suspect, from the process of tidying it up. Therefore, I propose that we examine what may loosely be called the *logic* of dissociation. We need first to identify what seem to be the concept's central features and presuppositions, and consider an array of apparently crucial distinctions. We must also compare the concept of dissociation to others often connected or confused with it, as well as examine the conspicuous shortcomings of rival characterizations of dissociation. Finally, with all that out of the way, we will be in a position to consider a tentative definition of 'dissociation'.

4.2 BASIC ASSUMPTIONS

Let us begin by considering some assumptions that seem to be quite reasonable, and essential to any adequate account of dissociation. To begin with, we must observe that dissociation is not only an occurrent psychological condition or state (i.e., the state of being dissociated), but also (among other things) something for which we have a *capacity*. It would be a serious mistake to consider dissociation only insofar as it is the termination of a causal process, the final, occurrent state of dissociation. That would be analogous to considering compassion, sarcasm, indignation, or jocularity to be nothing more than occurrent states. Obviously, no one can attain these terminal states without having the corresponding capacity to do so (e.g., the capacity to be compassionate, etc.). Moreover, it is obvious that these capacities vary from one person to the next; some people are more compassionate, sarcastic, and so on, than others. Similarly, dissociation is one of many things which people are *able* to do, and that capacity likewise varies from person to person.

In fact, there is no reason to think that a person's capacity to dissociate differs in its broad outlines from the vast majority of other physiological or psychological human capacities. On the contrary, it seems reasonable to suppose that the capacity for dissociation will be continuous in various ways with other things we are able to do. If that were *not* the case, we would know it only after empirical investigation. But no evidence uncovered so far suggests that the phenomena considered dissociative are totally unprecedented among organic (or just cognitive) capacities, even if they are distinctive in certain respects. Hence, it is reasonable to begin by assuming that features found generally in human (or other organic) capacities are likely to be found also in the case of dissociation. Let us call this the *non-uniqueness assumption*.

Now as I mentioned above, capacities or abilities are the sorts of things that vary from one person to another. They are also the sorts of things that get expressed in different ways and to varying degrees. Consider, for example, the great range of manifestations of our psychological capacities, such as the capacity for irony, silliness, or malice, or the ability to remember, empathize, reason abstractly, think metaphorically, control one's anger, recover from disappointments, act unselfishly, hold a grudge, produce witty remarks, feel sensual, or make commitments in relationships. It should be clear that most (if not all) such capacities take forms ranging from moderate to extreme, and (in many cases) from adaptive to maladaptive. Moreover, they often take forms highly idiosyncratic to the subject (e.g., a unique sense of humor or intellectual style, or a unique constellation of circumstances in which one can act unselfishly or feel sensual). Similarly, many additional sorts of capacities also exhibit a wide and often idiosyncratic range of manifestations — for example, musical and athletic abilities (or our capacity generally for muscular coordination), or the ability to host TV talk shows, govern a city, or teach a university seminar. Hence, one would expect that dissociation likewise assumes a variety of forms, some of them highly idiosyncratic. In particular, one would expect dissociation to affect a broad range of states (both occurrent and dispositional) and to spread out along several continua (e.g., of pervasiveness, frequency, severity, completeness, retrievability, etc.). We may call this the *diversification assumption*.

The next fundamental assumption underlying the concept of dissociation allows us to distinguish dissociation from what we could call cognitive or sensory *filtering*. In ordinary discourse the term 'filtering' may have various meanings. In fact, it may sometimes function as a synonym for 'dissociation'. More important for present purposes, however, are instances where 'filtering' denotes a process quite different from dissociation. Filtering (in this rather technical sense of the term) is a total shunting aside of information or data that the subject (i.e., human being) does not experience or register, as in cases of blindfolding, audio band-pass filtering, or ordinary (i.e., chemical) local anesthesia. But those situations are quite different from, say, hypnotic anesthesia or negative hallucinations, where the subject merely fails to experience consciously what in some sense are his own states. The hypnotically anesthetized subject can, under hypnosis, report what he had previously not felt. And (as we observed in Chapter 1) there is good reason to think that the person experiencing hypnotically induced negative hallucinations must be aware (in some sense) of the things he fails to experience consciously (e.g., the only card presented to him with an 'x' drawn on it). Very roughly, then, the difference between filtering and dissociation is that in the case of filtering, information or data never reach the subject (consciously or otherwise), whereas dissociation merely blocks the subject's awareness that he has already registered certain information. Hence, we may assume that the things dissociated from a human being are always the individual's own states. Let us call this the *ownership assumption*.

Granted, it is common to speak as if things other than the subject's states are dissociated. For example, in cases of amnesia or automatic writing, we might say that information, data, or material is dissociated. But strictly speaking, what is dissociated are the subject's volitions, knowledge, memories, dispositions, and sometimes even behavior (i.e., of producing automatic scripts). Material produced through automatic writing may be produced *dissociatively* — that is, it may be dissocia*tive*. But that means only that certain of the subject's states that produced the material (e.g., cognitive, volitional, or behavioral states) are dissociated from the subject. Similarly, in cases of hysterical or hypnotic blindness or deafness, visual or auditory information may be experienced dissociatively. And there is probably no harm in saying that this information is dissociated, so long as we remember that, strictly speaking, what is dissociated is the subject's awareness or experience of that information (which can later be recovered hypnotically).

Although some might think that the ownership assumption is too obvious even to mention, some accounts of dissociation appear to overlook it. For example, in what is probably only a verbal infelicity rather than a deep confusion, Young (1988, p. 35) defines 'dissociation' as 'an active inhibitory process that normally screens internal and external stimuli from the field of consciousness'. One might think that Young is claiming only that dissociated items (items screened from consciousness) are *sub*conscious. But due to Young's problematic use of the term 'stimuli', that is far from clear. Strictly speaking, it is not stimuli that are dissociated. The surgeon's scalpel, or its cutting action, may be regarded as external stimuli, but they are not what the hypnotically anesthetized subject dissociates. Rather, the subject dissociates the *experience* of pain those stimuli induce. In fact, the hypnotically anesthetized subject may be aware of the surgeon's actions. Moreover, even when we consider the subject's own internal states, it is misleading to say that stimuli are dissociated. In the case of surgery, for example, we might regard excited nerve fibers or biochemical processes as internal stimuli. But once again, it is the experience produced by those processes, rather than the processes themselves, that the subject dissociates. Indeed, there is no reason to think that the subject was *ever* aware of the relevant neural or biochemical processes.

Young's definition has yet another unfortunate feature, which seems to be somewhat deeper, and which one finds (in different forms) in definitions proposed by several clinicians. Specifically,

Young's approach seems to place unwarranted limits on the range of dissociative phenomena; hence, it may violate the diversification assumption. The term 'stimuli' suggests that only occurrent states are dissociated. But there is reason to think that traits, skills, and dispositional states generally are also capable of being dissociated. Indeed, the dissociation of traits and skills seems to be one of the more striking features of MPD. But perhaps we are now getting ahead of ourselves. Later (in section 4.5), we will critically examine various proposed definitions of 'dissociation'.

A fourth assumption underlying the concept of dissociation seems to be related to the ownership assumption. Although the use of computer analogies in the philosophy of mind tends to be dangerously misleading, in this case one will be helpful. Indeed, even its limitations will be instructive. Suppose some information from computer file A is taken from A and transferred to file B. We could then say that the information had been moved or separated from A. But if that information had been erased, and not located elsewhere, it would be odd (if not simply false) to say it had been moved. After all, that information no longer exists anywhere. Now the concept of dissociation seems roughly analogous to the concept of being moved (or separated) in this respect. When something is dissociated, it is not totally obliterated or irretrievable in principle. Although it may be subjectively hidden or psychologically isolated (at least for a time), it is potentially knowable, recoverable or capable of re-association. Let us call this the *accessibility assumption*.

As the reader may already have surmised, the foregoing computer analogy seems too closely allied with old associationist theories. It suggests that dissociation always separates something from another thing to which it had formerly been associated. But numerous paradigm cases of dissociation suggest otherwise. For example, automatic writing is a phenomenon widely regarded as dissociative. But sometimes automatic writing just begins spontaneously, and in the process the subject may have mental states he has never had before. Apparently, then, some dissociated thoughts expressed in automatic writing were never formerly associated with the observing self. Sometimes, those mental states just seem (like dreams) to bubble up *de novo*.

The moral, of course, is that automatisms — like dreams — have internal causes (we may temporarily ignore cases of ostensible possession) and presumably play a role in the person's overall mental economy. The spontaneous creations of automatic writing will tend to be parts or products of an ongoing process or set of dispositions, which may *already* have been dissociated (separated). Hence, even if the mental states expressed in automatic scripts are being generated for the first time, they could be the outcome of a disposition or process that was dissociated (separated) some time before. The computer analogy, therefore, turns out to be misleading in several ways. First, it suggests that the things that are dissociated are bits of information or content. But as we noted earlier, strictly speaking a subject's *states* are what get dissociated. Second, the analogy suggests that only *occurrent* states get dissociated. But as we have also noted, dispositions (e.g., desires, needs) and even *systems* of dispositions (as in traits or skills) may be dissociated. Third, the analogy suggests that dissociated states are always produced directly through the severing of associative bonds. But as cases of automatic writing help illustrate, they may also be novel by-products of formerly dissociated processes or dispositions — hence, indirect or causally remote effects of associational failures.

This last point merits a slight digression. We have just seen that for a state to be dissociated, it needn't have been previously separated from the thing relative to which it is dissociated. That helps us to see that even when we regard dissociation as an occurrent state of a person rather than a capacity, there may be two distinct — but apparently perfectly acceptable — senses of the term 'dissociation'. The first is a purely relational (or topological) sense, which can be thought of as a kind of *non*-association. In this sense of the term, to say that x is dissociated from y is to say only that a certain kind of barrier exists between them. (Presumably, this barrier would be characterized more thoroughly in a theory of dissociation.) The second sense of 'dissociation' may be viewed as a form of the active verb 'to dissociate', and therefore has a temporal component not found in the first sense of the term. In the active sense of 'dissociation', if x is dissociated from y, then the two were formerly associated but are not now.

Nevertheless, in both senses of the term, 'x is dissociated from y' seems to be a *non*symmetrical relation, like 'x loves y'. (Even though x loves y, the latter may or may not love the former.) The nonsymmetry of dissociation is particularly clear in the relational sense of the term. For example, as certain cases of one-way amnesia in MPD remind us, even if x is dissociated from y, the latter may or may not be dissociated from the former. Similarly, although states of a hidden observer may be dissociated from those of the hypnotized subject, the subject's states may not be dissociated from those of the hidden observer. Some might think that in the active sense of 'dissociation', 'x is dissociated from y' is an *a*symmetrical relation, such as 'x is north of (or older than) y'. (If x is north of (older than) y, y is not north of (older than) x.) As the computer analogy above made clear, saying that x is actively dissociated from y is like saying that the former is *taken* from the latter. And in that case one might think that y is not dissociated (taken) from x. On the other hand, one would think that x and y could be taken *from each other*, just as siblings might be separated in a child custody battle. Hence, even in the active sense of the term, 'x is dissociated from y' seems to be non-symmetrical.

Clearly, automatic writing illustrates both the active and relational senses of 'dissociation'. In cases where the automatism produces material that had at one time been known consciously to the subject, we can say that certain cognitive states of the subject had been actively dissociated (and of course dissociated in the relational sense as well). But automatic writing may exhibit only a relational type of dissociation. For example, we have just observed that the subject's cognitive or behavioral states might be parts or products of a previously (and actively) dissociated system of thought. Hence, their first occurrence might be outside conscious awareness.

The active sense of 'dissociation' would seem to be most important in clinical contexts, where etiological considerations are often paramount. But for our purposes, the relational sense of the term appears to be the more fundamental. Granted, the relational type of dissociation seems to be *historically* parasitic on the active type. Many would argue that if a state is relationally dissociated, then either it was actively dissociated at some earlier time, or else it is a part or product of a state or system of states that was once actively dissociated. Nevertheless, the relational sense of 'dissociation' is *presupposed* by the active sense. Moreover, as far as the philosophy of mind is concerned, what matters is the presence and nature of the dissociative barrier and its implications for our understanding of mental functioning generally. Hence, although I shall occasionally continue to use 'dissociation' in its active sense, we shall concern ourselves primarily with the relational sense of the term, and the nature of the barrier that seems to be created actively. Even when we consider dissociation to be a *process*, we will ignore matters of temporal priority and consider it merely to be a process that erects a dissociative barrier.

Another reason for downplaying the active sense of 'dissociation' is that some clinicians are now seriously questioning its historical primacy. Notice, first of all, that the term 'dissociation', unlike (say) 'non-association', seems to denote a process whereby something is undone. Hence, some feel that 'dissociation' presupposes that the self (or consciousness) tends to be unitary, and that dissociative processes result in a fragmentation or breakdown of that unity. Perhaps the leading member of the opposing view is Putnam (1988, 1989). Following Wolff (1987), he argues that this general picture is mistaken, that the self was fragmentary to begin with, and hence that it never existed in a form that could be split apart by dissociative processes. However, Putnam's view is unconvincing. Quite apart from some possible confusions over the concept of a state and the relationship of states to alternate personalities (some of which are noted in Chapter 8.5, and the remainder of which will be addressed on another occasion), we will see in Chapter 7 that various central features of MPD actually *presuppose* an underlying functional unity of the self, both pre- and post-dissociatively.

Consider, now, some issues related to the diversification assumption. In particular, let us consider what might count as a reasonable partial inventory of dissociative phenomena. Although most investigators believe that dissociative phenomena fall along a continuum, they disagree over — or at least seem unclear about — how broad that continuum is. For example, Bernstein and Putnam (1986) claim that the dissociative continuum runs 'from the minor dissociations of everyday life to major forms of psychopathology such as MPD' (p. 728). But although they maintain that dissociation is both a 'normal process' (p. 727) and a major contributor to various mental disorders, they define 'dissociation' as 'a lack of the normal integration of thoughts, feelings, and experiences into the stream of consciousness and memory' (p. 727). But that seems, rather, to be a definition of the clinical term 'dissociative *disorder*'. Indeed, it adheres closely to part of the DSM-III-R definition, which takes a dissociative disorder to be 'a disturbance or alteration in the normally integrative functions of identity, memory, or consciousness'.

But most would say that dissociation is not necessarily a disorder and that it may be present in many normal experiences. For example, Young says that 'In the service of normal functioning, most of our mental life is dissociated at any given time' (1988, p. 36). Similarly, Braun claims that 'some dissociative phenomena are quite normal' (1988, p. 6), and Ross writes, 'dissociation is an ongoing dynamic process in the normal psyche', 'a pervasive aspect of normal mental function' (1989, p. 87)(see also Beahrs, 1982, and Ludwig, 1984, p. 161). Since this does seem to be the prevailing view, let us also assume that in addition to hypnosis, hysterical amnesia, or anesthesia, and the more dramatic separation of traits and skills in MPD, dissociative phenomena include an array of normal phenomena.

But what are these normal dissociative phenomena? Many would include forms of automatic or overlearned behaviors — that is, behaviors we can perform without apparently thinking or paying attention to them, but which afterward we recognize to have been intentional. Many would also include lapses of awareness occurring during an emergency or other situation involving highly focused attention — for example, our not hearing the telephone while concentrating on extinguishing a fire on the stove, or not feeling pain while engrossed in a book (or while fighting for one's life). Some would also include another type of phenomenon that appears to be a component of every sensory perception, and perhaps also of perceptions of our ongoing thought processes. As far as sense perceptions are concerned, we regularly seem to be unaware of numerous details in our experiences, not only of items in our perceptual periphery, but also of more central details of our perceptual field (perhaps in order to reduce the overall amount of irrelevant sensory information or 'noise'). Nevertheless, we are often apparently capable (under hypnosis, for example) of recalling these items. Similarly, we might be unaware of many thoughts and feelings when they occur but able to recall them later under suitable circumstances. Hence, it may be that some degree of dissociation is a necessary condition for the mere focusing of conscious attention. Some also consider many instances of ordinary forgetting to be cases of dissociation, at least those cases in which the forgotten items are retrievable.

Furthermore, some consider *state-dependency* to be a sign of dissociation (see, e.g., Ross, 1989, pp. 88-89). For example, if I have certain thoughts, feelings, memories, or dispositions only after having entered a somewhat broadly characterized enduring type of state (e.g., a drunken or drugged state), then those subsidiary mental states would be dissociated from my normal consciousness. State-dependency, however, seems rather difficult to defend as a criterion of dissociation. Although the dependency on dramatically altered states may be dissociative (just as the dependency of some mental states on hypnosis seems dissociative), many of our mental states are state-dependent in a much less interesting way, and still seem to be part of our normal consciousness. For example, I might have certain thoughts, feelings, or dispositions only when I'm feeling depressed, giddy, sexual, or only when I'm feeling ironic (or even more specifically, Oscar Wildeish), or experiencing a wave of Kantian metaphysical grandiosity. But I think few would regard all these (if any) as instances of dissociation. Perhaps what is needed is an unprecedentedly clear definition of 'altered state', according to which such ordinary states as giddiness or irony would not count as altered. Then dissociation could be linked successfully to altered state-dependency. That ambitious project, however, goes beyond the scope of this chapter.

In any case, whatever the final inventory of normal dissociative phenomena turns out to be, it seems that the concept of dissociation has evolved somewhat since its first appearance in the work of Janet. Janet originally intended the concept to handle a distinctive and relatively limited class of phenomena in the domain of psychopathology. But many subsequently concluded that the processes at work in hysteria or double consciousness were also at work, to a lesser degree, in a broad range of non-pathological phenomena. It might seem, therefore, as if Janet's concept, rather than being significantly overhauled or revised, simply had its domain extended.

But in fact, this extension of the concept of dissociation marked a rather profound break with Janet. Since Janet took dissociation to be a phenomenon of psychopathology, he did not see it as a widespread human *capacity*, whose manifestations ranged from the normal to the pathological. Hence, he would not have accepted either the non-uniqueness or the diversification assumptions. Moreover, not only did Janet not view dissociation as a capacity, but, as Freud noted, he seems to have regarded it as a *weakness* in (or a *failure* of) one of our capacities — namely, our capacity to synthesize or integrate parts of consciousness and thereby maintain mental unity ('Five Lectures on Psychoanalysis', quoted in Crabtree, 1986, pp. 100-101).

There is also another major respect in which early thinking about dissociative phenomena has changed (although it is unclear to what extent this is a change away from Janet's view, rather than a view frequently misattributed to Janet or which developed along side that of Janet). Around the turn of the century, the prevailing view was that a dissociated idea (set of ideas, or dispositional system) became functionally *isolated*, both from conscious awareness and also from the mass of ideas and dispositions of which it had formerly been a part. At that point the dissociated elements could neither interfere with, nor be interfered with by, ongoing conscious thoughts or behavior. The early studies of automatisms encouraged this viewpoint, because it appeared as if the subject's conscious behavior (e.g., conversing with the experimenter) did not impede simultaneous communication with dissociated streams of consciousness as revealed (say) in automatic writing. And conversely, the subject's conscious behavior seemed unaffected by the ongoing automatic behavior. Eventually, many came to regard non-interference, not only as an empirical test for the existence of dissociative phenomena, but also as a necessary condition of dissociation.

Today, however, non-interference is no longer considered a necessary condition of dissociation. The non-interference criterion has been undermined by both clinical and experimental evidence. Beginning in the 1920s with the work of Messerschmidt (1927-8), a series of experiments in hypnotically divided attention demonstrated that even in automatic writing there was some interference or leakage between conscious behavior and subconscious tasks. Hence, either non-interference had to be dropped as a criterion of dissociation or else hypnosis could not properly be considered a form of dissociation. Most opted for the first alternative.

Furthermore, the non-interference criterion was undermined by clinical observations in cases of MPD — ironically, the very domain of phenomena in which the lack of interference had initially seemed most pronounced. Originally, investigators thought that alternate personalities were autonomous and functionally isolated from each other. But it did not take long for clinicians to realize that alters are often aware of the thoughts and behavior of others and that they can interfere with each other as well (e.g., by intruding their own thoughts or behavioral impulses into another alter's stream of consciousness or by inducing hallucinations). (For additional remarks on non-interference, see Hilgard, 1986, and Silberman, *et al.*, 1985.)

The dissociative barrier also turned out to be less extensive than Janet and his successors originally suspected. It is not clear whether Janet was seduced by his own spatial metaphor of dissociation as a kind of separation or breaking away into distinct masses or pieces of mental stuff (Hart, 1926), or whether a prior confusion led him to adopt that metaphor. But whatever the case, it is clear that the metaphor is misleading. Not only may dissociated systems interfere with each other (as if the dissociative barrier were, so to speak, permeable), but more important, dissociated mental systems appear to overlap or have common elements.[1] That would seem to explain why child alters often have at least partially adult vocabularies and grammar, and why adults hypnotically regressed to childhood retain certain adult linguistic skills (see, e.g., Orne, 1951, and O'Connell, Shor, and Orne, 1970). Indeed, it appears to explain why dissociated personalities often have common memories. Hence, even in cases where dissociation seems to be a kind of breaking away, it is clear that the break may only be partial.

Another important reason for conceding this point concerns the nature of traits or skills generally — at least the sort that become dissociated in cases of MPD and that often serve as an alter personality's centrally defining function. First of all, (as I will argue in the next chapter), these traits or skills represent only one way (out of many) of slicing up human functioning into illuminating units or regularities. Hence, one would expect — on quite abstract grounds — that our numerous categorizations of traits or skills would overlap to some extent. In fact, one would expect these descriptive categories to pick out complex *sets* of functions, many of which are *common* to other traits or skills. (See Chapter 7.4 for an extended discussion of this topic.)

This last point can also be defended on empirical grounds. For one thing, alters specializing in certain traits will usually share common language, motor skills, and memories with alters exhibiting different traits. And for another, traits or skills are expressed in numerous ways and in a variety of settings. In order to manifest the traits in different contexts, one must be able to draw on a considerable repertoire of ancillary or subsidiary abilities, many of which will be utilized in the expression of other traits or skills.

For example, helper personalities needn't have particular skills of which all other alter-types are deprived. Many alters will be able to advise, mediate, intervene, show compassion and understanding, or be able to express softness and warmth. Similarly, sexual, angry, childlike, or homicidal personalities will inevitably share many traits and abilities with alters of other kinds. In fact, other alters might still have the capacity to be (say) sexual or angry. And perhaps even a larger number of alters will share more mundane types of knowledge, skills, or capacities — for example, the ability to tie one's shoes, drive a car, screw in a light bulb, open a carton of milk, answer the telephone (along with the numerous everyday bits of knowledge these activities presuppose — e.g., what milk, thirst, voices, and telephones are), and of course linguistic ability and normal motor skills.

In general, the expression or execution of any one of a typical alter's functions involves a complex constellation of capacities. And although a specific personality, such as a helper personality, will probably have a distinctive *set* of traits, having particular traits in that set needn't involve a corresponding deprivation of traits for other alters. Generally speaking, then, what distinguishes one alter from another, and what gets dissociated in cases of MPD, is not a trait shared with no other alter or split-off completely from the rest of the multiple's activities. Rather, it is a distinctive *combination* of traits, any one of which might be shared with other alters.[2]

4.3 MORTON PRINCE AND CO-CONSCIOUSNESS

Janet was not the only early writer on dissociation whose views seem to have been distorted by focusing primarily or exclusively on the domain of abnormal psychology or psychopathology. Morton Prince may likewise have fallen into the trap. And curiously, despite Prince's staunch advocacy of dissociation as an explanatory concept (e.g., as opposed to, or in addition to, the concepts of Freudian dynamics), it is difficult to determine what, precisely, he took dissociation to be. One reason is that Prince never defined 'dissociation' specifically, even though he used the term often. Indeed, although he frequently used 'dissociation' and 'split-off' as synonyms and acknowledged similarities between his conception and that of Janet, Prince made no effort to analyze the concept and indicate clearly how his view differed from that of

Janet. In fact, he showed little interest in the analysis of dissociation. Instead, he repeatedly tried to clarify the concept of the
subconscious, and often merely mentioned dissociation in the process, almost as if it was clear what the term meant. As a result,
the reader has no choice but to construct Prince's concept of
dissociation from various indirect hints.

Unfortunately, however, Prince's remarks on the subject are
often confusing and apparently incompatible. Sometimes, he seems
to agree with Janet that dissociated ideas are merely split-off from
(and apparently independent of) the subject's normal conscious
awareness, although unlike Janet he recognized that dissociation
might therefore be a component in many normal experiences
(see, e.g., M. Prince, 1939, p. 354, 507 (or 1907, p. 79)). At other
times, however, Prince seems to go further, insisting on a very
close relation between dissociation and what he termed *co-consciousness*.[3] But there are two problems in understanding Prince's
position. First, it is unclear what Prince took co-consciousness to
be. I will make some detailed remarks on the subject shortly. For
now, however, we need only to observe that for Prince, the term
'conscious' in 'co-conscious' contrasts, not with '*un*conscious' or
'*sub*conscious', but with '*non*-conscious'. Presumably, we use the
former two terms to pick out occurrences of mental states of
which the subject is unaware, whereas 'non-conscious' would pick
out states of affairs *neither* above *nor* below the threshold of
awareness. The clearest indication of this is that the concept of
co-consciousness is supposed to help *explain* the kinds of under-
the-surface mental activity usually dubbed subconscious or unconscious. Hence, 'co-conscious' seems to pick out some form of
occurrent mental activity.

The second problem is that Prince never clarified what the
relation between dissociation and co-consciousness is supposed to
be. Sometimes he seems to *identify* dissociation and co-consciousness — for example, by stating explicitly that 'extra-conscious',
'doubling of consciousness', 'coconscious' and 'dissociation' are
all synonyms for 'subconscious' (1939, p. 354, 481). But at other
times Prince writes as if they are distinct. For example, on some
occasions, he suggests that co-consciousness accompanies only a
high degree of dissociation (1939, p. 69) or that it occurs only
when ideas are *far* outside the focus of attention (1939, p. 215).
And elsewhere, he writes as if dissociation and the co-activity of
different conscious systems are distinct but frequently correlated

(1939, p. 506, or 1907, p. 78). I prefer, however, not to get embroiled here in the intricacies of critical exegesis. Whether or not Prince actually wanted to identify dissociation with co-consciousness, or merely analyze the former in terms of the latter, it will be instructive to consider the advantages and disadvantages of that general approach.

Let us see, then, whether the weaker of these two positions has any merit (if it does not, then obviously the stronger position will not work either). Hence, let us try simply to explain dissociation (as Prince sometimes appeared to) in terms of the *co-activity* of another consciousness. From this Princean (Princely?) perspective, *x* is dissociated from *y* just in case *x* and *y* belong to distinct, simultaneously existing, co-embodied conscious systems. One conspicuous virtue of this approach is that it correctly downplays the importance of amnesia in understanding dissociation. Indeed, as Prince himself recognized, distinct alters in cases of MPD might be fully aware of each other's sensations, feelings, thoughts and actions. Nevertheless, as we observed in the previous chapter, one alter may neither experience the other alter's states as his own nor believe that those states are his own. To alter *A*, the states of alter *B* may be both non-autobiographical and non-indexical. Hence, Prince's approach permits the dissociative barrier to be either phenomenological or epistemological (or some hybrid), and it recognizes that amnesia is only one type of epistemological dissociative barrier. Another conspicuous feature of Prince's approach (although not obviously a virtue or a defect) is that unlike the two senses of 'dissociation' discussed earlier, Prince uses the term to stand for a *symmetrical* relation. The reason, of course, is that co-consciousness (and hence, dissociation) is analyzed in terms of the symmetrical relation of co-activity; if *x* is co-active with *y*, then clearly *y* is also co-active with *x*.

But the analysis of dissociation in terms of co-consciousness is highly problematical, both empirically and conceptually. Consider the conceptual difficulties first. To say that *x* and *y* are co-conscious is to say that they are (or belong to) different simultaneously-existing conscious systems. But how do we distinguish two different co-conscious systems from two different activities or sets of dispositions belonging to a single consciousness (e.g., attending to the activity one is engaged in while simultaneously experiencing grief over a recent death in the family)? One would think that co-conscious systems differ in a more radical way. But how should the separation between the two systems be explained?

For reasons already noted, we cannot appeal to functional independence or non-interference of the two systems. (Prince himself would probably have agreed.)[4] Nor, as we have seen (and as Prince acknowledged), can we appeal to the presence of an amnesic barrier. Amnesia appears to be an accidental, rather than essential feature of certain dissociative processes, and complete functional independence seems never to occur. Hence, the distinction has to be of another sort. Historically, it may be rooted in an intellectual trend discussed by Burnham (1986) — namely, an underlying anthropomorphism in turn-of-the-century mechanistic reductionism. Scientists of the period tended to believe in a kind of *dynamic atomicity*, according to which 'the functional units of the human machine each had an independent existence and purpose of their own' (p. 75). It would have been quite natural, then, to view co-consciousness — and, indeed, dissociation generally — in terms of relatively autonomous and purposeful underlying units.

But whatever its intellectual antecedents turn out to be, one would think that the concept of co-consciousness presupposes the existence of two distinct *agencies* or *subjects* of experience — perhaps even a pair of apperceptive centers. Granted, in the previous chapter we saw that among classic dramatic forms of dissociation, only MPD seems to require positing the existence of distinct apperceptive centers. But perhaps the other dissociative (and even non-dissociative) phenomena must be understood in terms of multiple agencies of other, presumably less robust, sorts. (In Chapter 6, we will consider to what extent non-dissociative phenomena require positing the existence of multiple agencies or selves within a single person.) Of course, whether mental functioning *generally* should be analyzed in terms of multiple agencies is one of the oldest and most tangled topics in the philosophy of mind. But it should not be necessary to take a stand on it simply in order to grasp the concept of dissociation. One would think that the concept of dissociation can have some utility no matter what position one takes with regard to basic questions concerning the nature of psychological explanation. Hence, it should be possible to provide a less ambitious account of dissociation, one which focuses more on phenomena than on theory. To be sure, we can never entirely escape conceptual problems even for such a modest enterprise, and quite probably we would have to deal with major philosophical issues in order to formulate a fully-developed *theory* of dissociation. But that shouldn't be necessary for present purposes. All we need to do now is to understand which domain of phenomena the concept of dissociation is supposed to cover, and how that concept differs from others that seem closely related to it.

But quite apart from abstract issues in the philosophy of mind, there seems to be little empirical support for analyzing dissociation in terms of co-consciousness. Granted, one can understand the temptation of explaining *multiple personality* in terms of two distinct repositories for different sets of states. But it is by no means clear that co-consciousness must be present in dissociative phenomena generally. For example, in order to explain cases of ordinary forgetting, lapses of awareness, overlearned behaviors, and perhaps also dreaming, we needn't suppose that there is a distinct secondary system of conscious activity in which the forgotten or subconscious (but retrievable) items have a function. In fact, not even classic fugue states demand the positing of co-conscious systems. (This is particularly ironic, given that Prince explicitly asserted the contrary (e.g., 1939, p. 500, or 1907, p. 72), and also given his belief in the particular value of the concept of co-consciousness in relation to psychopathology.) In fugue states, a person's normal traits, dispositions, and more or less unified stream of consciousness (including a sense of self) may disappear for a while, during which time they are replaced by a new set of traits, dispositions, and continuing inner life. When the old set finally returns, the new set disappears, usually forever. But in these cases there is no reason to insist either (a) that during the fugue the original set continued to operate as a simultaneously existing, more or less autonomous conscious system, or (b) that after the fugue the new set continues to exist as a co-conscious system. As far as (a) is concerned, the restored subject may forever have amnesia for the period when those traits disappeared, even following attempts at hypnotic retrieval. Hence, there is no reason to attribute to the original set a continuing conscious existence during the fugue — that is, something like an inner mental life that can later be recalled. And as far as (b) is concerned, the new set tends neither to reappear nor to give more subtle evidence of continuing to linger under the surface.

One might think that a co-conscious system could have a merely *dispositional* existence, so that during periods of its existence there might be no occurrent states that could later be recalled. Hence, during a fugue, the 'old self' might exist only dispositionally under the surface, rather than in terms of any occurrent experiences or thoughts. Now undoubtedly, dissociated states might exist only dispositionally; after all, some of those states were dispositions to begin with. But it seems as if the whole point of the concept of co-consciousness is to capture a form of existence more robust than mere dispositional continuing. At the very least, that seems to be what Prince had in mind. He says explicitly that he likes the term 'co-conscious' because it helps 'express the notion of co-*activity*' (1939, p. 495, or 1907, p. 67, italics added).

Of course, the term 'activity' might be stronger than necessary. But I suspect that it is not. I believe it points to a fundamental and (in this context) apparently fatal presupposition of the concept of co-consciousness. That concept seems particularly useful or appropriate in connection with certain phenomena of abnormal psychology and psychopathology. Indeed, as we have seen, the concept of co-consciousness is supposed to help explain so-called subconscious or unconscious phenomena. For example, in the case of automatisms, post-hypnotic suggestion, and MPD, one can easily see the attractiveness of appealing to the existence of a conscious system, distinct from the normal (or at least usual) waking consciousness. This co-conscious system is a kind of *active* repository of or locus for thoughts, feelings, experiences, and dispositions from which the normal (or main) consciousness is cut off. Therefore, calling it 'co-conscious' seems to suggest that it is a system comprised at least in part of *occurrent* mental states. Similarly, to say that a thought, feeling, etc. is co-conscious is to say either that it is (part of) an occurrent mental state, or (as in the case of traits or skills) that it is dispositionally related to a system of ongoing occurrent mental activity. Hence 'x is co-conscious with y' seems to entail that x and y are (components of) occurrent mental states, or at least dispositionally related to an ongoing system of occurrent mental activity.

But if co-consciousness requires the simultaneous existence of distinct systems of occurrent (and not merely dispositional) mental activity, then (as we have seen) it appears to require too much for certain types of dissociative phenomena — for example, ordinary forgetting, lapses of awareness, and fugue states. Moreover, many would agree that alternate personalities in MPD are dissociated from one another. But alters sometimes exist *only* dispositionally; sometimes they 'black out' or 'disappear' for extended periods, during which we may suppose they undergo or experience no occurrent mental states. One might think that two alters, neither of whom is engaged in any occurrent mental activity, may still be dissociated from one another. But if co-consciousness obtains only in the presence of distinct systems of occurrent mental activity, then it would be false to say that the dormant alters are co-conscious. Therefore, a Princean approach would fail also to countenance dissociative relations between systems *both* of which exist only dispositionally.

4.4 SUPPRESSION, REPRESSION, AND THE UNCONSCIOUS

A number of concepts are easily confused with, and apparently closely related to, the concept of dissociation. Probably the most important of these is the concept of repression. Although neither repression nor dissociation are precise concepts, they nevertheless seem to mark off different (if slightly overlapping) classes of psychological phenomena. Indeed, they seem to rest on different presuppositions.

Perhaps the best discussion of the differences between repression and dissociation is that of Hilgard (1986, pp. 80ff, 249ff). As Hilgard recognizes, we tend to employ different metaphors in describing the psychological barriers of repression and dissociation. For example, we think of repressive barriers as being horizontal; accordingly, we view repressed material as being *deeper* than what remains accessible to conscious awareness. By contrast, we think of dissocative barriers as being vertical; split-off parts of consciousness are not necessarily deeper than those accessible to conscious awareness.

As these spatial metaphors suggest, the central difference between repression and dissociation concerns their respective roles in a person's life. To begin with, repression is intimately related to dynamic psychological forces, such as active mental defenses, whose general function is to 'maintain the inhibition against recall' (Hilgard, 1986, p. 80). By contrast, dissociation may not affect memory, and if it does, that result may be only a by-product of the dissociative process, rather than its principal function. In fact, dissociation is only fortuitously related to the exigencies of psychological survival. For example, posthypnotic amnesia and ordinary forgetting can concern almost any kind of material, important and unimportant.

This difference between repression and dissociation rests on a more fundamental distinction. Generally speaking, the concept of repression is bound up with the psychoanalytic concept of a dynamic unconscious, which (among other things) acts as a kind of repository for repressed material. But the concept of a dynamic unconscious differs in crucial respects from the concept of a dissociated part of consciousness (Hilgard, 1986, p. 249). In particular, communication with the unconscious tends to be indirect, by means of its various by-products (e.g., dreams, slips of the tongue). Moreover, expressions of unconscious material tend to be distorted, either symbolically or by means of more primitive primary process thinking. Hence, unconscious mental activities can only be inferred from behavioral or phenomenological by-products, and not directly recovered. By contrast, communication with a dissociated part of consciousness can be direct, as in automatic writing, hypnosis, and interactions with alters in cases of MPD. Of course, some would argue that no third-person knowledge of an individual's states (especially mental states) is literally *direct* and that only first-person knowledge of those states can be direct. But this observation, however apt, needn't detain us. Clearly, the point here is simply that third- and first-person knowledge of dissociated — but not unconscious — states can be as direct as (respectively) third- and first-person knowledge of non-dissociated states. Moreover, dissociated mental activities needn't involve primary process thinking or symbolic transformation. Instead, they tend to be like normal mental activities, except for being separated by the sorts of phenomenological or epistemological barriers mentioned earlier.[5]

Hence, let us say that if x is repressed for S (in this sense of 'repressed'), then (a) S is not consciously aware of (or is amnesic for) x, and (b) third- and first-person knowledge of x is indirect as compared (respectively) to third- and first-person knowledge of both conscious and dissociated states (i.e., it must be *inferred* from its possibly distorted or primitive cognitive, phenomenological, or behavioral by-products).

But not all forms of repression seem to require the operation of a dynamic unconscious which can be accessed only indirectly. Consider, for example, amnesia for a memory we are motivated to forget, but which can be recovered directly through hypnosis.

Or consider behavior that reveals hidden feelings, but whose interpretation is clear to the person exhibiting it — for example, 'forgetting the keys to the office when you prefer to stay at home, or slipping into an unintended negative that tells the truth, when you were trying to falsify to be polite' (Hilgard, 1986, p. 251). Many regard these as types of repression, although they also seem to qualify as examples of dissociation. Nevertheless, what makes the concept of repression most interesting are the cases where one wants to posit the operation of deep (and only indirectly accessible) unconscious forces. And in those cases, the concepts of repression and dissociation differ in the ways just discussed. Perhaps some future psychological taxonomy will be neater. But for now, we need only observe, and then learn to live with, unclear and overlapping conceptual boundaries.

Regrettably, the concept of suppression is no clearer than that of repression. One difference between the two, according to Hilgard, is that 'amnesia is absent in suppression, present in repression' (1986, p. 251). Similarly, Braun suggests that suppression never results from unconscious activity. He writes, 'suppression...is a conscious putting-out-of-mind of something we don't want to think about' (1988, p. 5). But the concept of suppression seems to be used in a wide variety of ways, both in clinical and everyday discourse. No doubt many use the term 'suppression' in ways indistinguishable from those of 'dissociation' or 'repression'. But to keep matters as simple as possible, let us agree to use 'suppression' in a relatively narrow technical sense, in order to mark off the modest domain of phenomena hinted at by Hilgard and Braun. Let us say that when x is suppressed for S, (a) S consciously diverts attention from x (i.e., puts x 'out of mind'), and (b) S does not have amnesia for x.

Some, like Braun (1988), might think that *denial* is yet another distinct point on a continuum of awareness. But I question whether denial is distinct from suppression, repression, and dissociation. One would think that denial assumes many forms and that it could be analyzed in terms of these other concepts. In fact, one handy (if slightly oversimplified) way of doing this would be to think of repression as *unconscious denial*, dissociation as *subconscious denial*, and suppression as *conscious denial*.

Before leaving this topic, let us consider how or whether to apply these various concepts to certain cases. Since certain phenomena fall clearly into one category rather than another (e.g., hypnotic amnesia and anesthesia are clear examples of dissociation rather than repression), it will be most useful to look at cases that are rather more difficult to classify.

Consider, first, someone who neither cries nor experiences grief at a relative's funeral and who is surprised at not feeling any grief. Suppose, however, that two days later, the person finally begins to grieve and is then able to cry. Has that grief been dissociated, repressed, or suppressed? Obviously, this is not an example of suppression, because the person is surprised at not feeling grief, and suppression (we have agreed) would have been a conscious setting aside of those feelings. Hence, if the person had knowingly held his feelings in check until several days later, *that* would be an example of suppression. The case under consideration, however, seems to be an example of dissociation. But the dissociation of what, exactly? Here, we seem to have two options. On the one hand, we might want to regard the case as analogous to instances of hypnotic anesthesia in which the subject can later report sensations not experienced in the waking state. Hence, we could say that the feelings of grief existed at the time of the funeral but were cut off from conscious awareness. And in that case, we would say that some occurrent feelings of grief were dissociated. On the other hand, it might be more accurate to say that no feelings of grief were experienced at the time of the funeral (even subconsciously). And in that case, we would say that what has been dissociated is rather the subject's *ability* to grieve over the relative's death. Moreover, no matter which option we choose, the case might also count (for some) as an example of repression, but only of the sort that overlaps with the concept of dissociation. Since the grief is eventually experienced or recovered, and is not (say) simply inferred from other symbolic behavior or experiences, the case does not require positing the activity of a dynamic unconscious.

Consider, next, the case of someone who recalls abusive experiences but has no feelings attached to those memories (say, feelings of anger or fear). If the feelings can be directly (e.g., hypnotically) recovered or released and do not express themselves indirectly (e.g., symbolically) in other experiences or behavior, we should probably regard the case as one of dissociation. But suppose the subject exhibits certain kinds of obsessional or compulsive behavior, or suppose that he or she seems to have erected what Reich called *character armor* as an apparent defense against those feelings. For example, suppose the subject is a workaholic or continually and often inappropriately happy-go-lucky. Clinicians know that compulsivity of these sorts tends to diminish when the hidden feelings are released and acknowledged. In that case, we should perhaps say instead that the feelings have been repressed.

I should emphasize that the difference between repression and dissociation may have less to do with a person's mental condition and more to do with the conceptual framework that picks it out and in terms of which it is treated clinically. For instance, in the case just considered, the obsessional or compulsive behavior might be approached from a psychoanalytic perspective, using various indirect methods (e.g., free association) to uncover the reasons for the behavior. Alternatively, one might utilize hypnotic techniques to reveal hidden memories of events lying at the root of the problem. In principle, one would think that pathological conditions treatable from one perspective might equally well be treatable from the other. If so, it seems appropriate to say that there is but one psychological condition, which is simply identified and treated according to different criteria and methods. At any rate, we needn't worry here about whether cases diagnosed as instances of dissociation and repression are equally amenable to the same treatments; that is a matter for empirical investigation. For present purposes, it is sufficient to note the different criteria of individuation and methods of treatment by means of which we may distinguish the *concepts* of repression and dissociation.

4.5 HOW NOT TO DEFINE 'DISSOCIATION'

In the past few years, a large and growing number of academicians and clinicians have begun writing on the topic of dissociation, and (as one would expect) they often attempt to define the concept. Usually, their efforts are quite inadequate. Fortunately, however, their mistakes can be instructive. Therefore, I shall survey a representative sample of recent definitions, which clearly exemplify certain standard errors that need to be avoided. (The reader will recall that some problematic definitions have already been discussed, in section 4.2.)

Two different definitions have been offered by Zamansky and Bartis, each of which has distinctive difficulties. In their earlier definition (Zamansky and Bartis, 1984, p. 247), they list three criteria of dissociation:

(1) *S* is engaged in two or more cognitive processes concurrently.
(2) These processes occur simultaneously (rather than alternately).
(3) S perceives at least one (but not all) of these processes as autonomous, nonvolitional, or otherwise occurring below the level of conscious awareness.

A minor problem with this definition is that it is unclear how criteria (1) and (2) differ. One would think that concurrent processes are simultaneous. If not, then the first condition is superfluous, since the second and stronger condition is the one that counts. In any case, the requirement of simultaneity has the unfortunate effect of ruling out some paradigmatic examples of dissociation — for example, fugue states (in which the 'lost' personality or identity may be completely dormant), as well as any case where unexpressed dispositions, traits, or skills are dissociated. Moreover, a related problem with criterion (3) is that if dissociated states may be dispositional rather than occurrent, then it is false that *S* must perceive them as *occurring* at all, much less occurring autonomously, nonvolitionally, or subconsciously. In fact, a similar problem remains with criterion (3) even when the dissociated states are occurrent. For example, it is unclear how to describe cases of hypnotic anesthesia. But even if it is correct to say that the subject in some sense feels or registers the pain he does not experience consciously, it may be false to say that the subject perceives the pain *as having the properties of* being autonomous, nonvolitional, or subconscious. It is not clear that even a hidden observer could be properly described as perceiving the pain in this way. The subject may *retrospectively* conclude that the state occurred autonomously, etc., just as an outside observer would. But those judgments need not be components of the overall occurrent dissociative state.

Zamansky and Bartis's later definition suffers from rather different sorts of problems (Bartis and Zamansky, 1986). Moreover, it seems to be rooted in a very peculiar interpretation of the history of dissociation. The authors claim that historically, the term 'dissociation' has been intended to 'describe a conflictive relationship among different aspects of a single task or experience' (pp. 103-4). Armed with that falsehood, they propose the following definition.

117

The essential feature of dissociation is a conflict (or an inconsistency) between an individual's cognitive perspective on an event and other, *simultaneously held*, cognitive and/or behavioral aspects of that same event.

(Bartis and Zamansky, 1986, p. 104)

As an example, they note that 'a hypnotized subject may be aware that his arm is perfectly healthy and unrestrained, yet he may not be able to bend it' (p. 104).

Granted, the example fits their definition. But overall, the definition is both too inclusive and too restrictive. It is too inclusive because it is satisfied by a glut of non-dissociative phenomena — for example, cases of self-deception, cognitive dissonance or confusion, and outright ignorance or stupidity. An example of the latter would be a case in which a person knowingly and simultaneously holds contradictory beliefs but does not see the contradiction. An example of mere cognitive confusion would be a case in which a person believes both that her parents love and do not love her, recognizes the problem, but is unable to reconcile conflicting parental behaviors and the incompatible or clashing perspectives they foster.

Moreover, the definition is too restrictive, because it omits numerous classic dissociative phenomena. For one thing, the definition retains the unfortunate simultaneity condition from the previous definition; hence, it rules out fugue states as well as all cases where dispositions (rather than occurrent states) are dissociated. And for another, one would think that dissociative relations between occurrent states needn't all be conflicts or inconsistencies. Rather, they might be mere separations by the kinds of phenomenological or epistemological barriers discussed in the last chapter. For example, in cases of MPD, the states of alternate personality A can be dissociated from those of B even when A and B simultaneously have the *same* beliefs, perceptions, or feelings. There need be no conflict or inconsistency in *content* between dissociated states. The only disparity may be epistemological: A's belief would be embedded in a flow of indexical mental activity that B does not take to be his own. But this is no more clearly a conflict or inconsistency than similar disparities of indexicality between the shared beliefs of two different persons.

A rather different sort of definition has been proposed by Sanders, and it may be dismissed quickly. She claims that dissociation is characterized by modification of connections between affect, cognition, and perception of voluntary control over behavior, as well as modification in the subjective experience of affect, voluntary control, and perception.

(Sanders, 1986, p. 95)

Although this definition has the virtue of covering the dissociation of dispositions, it is far too inclusive. For example, it is satisfied by anxiety, depression and euphoria. In all these, we can find modifications of the sort mentioned by Sanders, including changes in the voluntary control of behavior (e.g., reduced control with depression and anxiety, and greater control — or a sense of empowerment or increased confidence — with euphoria). Sanders's definition may also *not* fit certain types of dissociation — in particular, those in which there is a mere separation of items of awareness. It is also difficult to see how it would cover the distinct inner lives of alternate personalities. The development of alters often seems to *create* new systems of connections, not modify previously existing connections. Unfortunately, the vagueness of Sanders's definition makes it difficult to determine how far it can be stretched.

In any case, whereas Zamansky and Bartis illustrate the dangers of defining 'dissociation' too specifically, Sanders's approach illustrates (among other things) the dangers of a certain kind of generality. One can't define 'dissociation' in terms of mere *modifications* of broad classes of psychological phenomena. That approach will always yield a definition that covers too much. Similarly, the DSM-III-R definition errs by defining 'dissociation' as a 'disturbance or alteration in the normally integrative functions of identity, memory, or consciousness' (see American Psychiatric Association, 1987, pp. 269-70). Presumably, the authors of this definition didn't want to include *every* disturbance or alteration of these integrative functions (whatever, exactly, that means). At the very least, they probably wanted to insist only on a kind of *prevention* or *absence* of integration. After all, one could find a disturbance or alteration of integrative functions in someone who suddenly remembers everything or who seems to remember or have another person's thoughts and feelings (as in ostensible ESP).

Lastly, we should take note of Spiegel's error of defining 'dissociation' as a *defense* (Spiegel, 1986a, p. 123). That seems clearly to be too restrictive, especially if we have been correct in allowing dissociation to cover numerous non-defensive features of ordinary life, as well as hypnotically induced states that may be dynamically and personally uninteresting. Even if most or many *spontaneous* dissociative states are defensive reactions, others surely are not — for example, many (or most) cases of forgetting, as well as automatic or overlearned behaviors. Besides, it is obvious that not all dissociations are spontaneous. Hence, Spiegel's definition clearly violates the diversification assumption.

4.6 CONCLUSION

Although no definition of 'dissociation' is likely to be fully satisfactory, and although a truly adequate definition will probably have to await the development of a robust theory of dissociation, we are in a position now to consider a tentative definition that avoids the problems noted above and that honors the intuitions about dissociation discussed in section 4.2. If nothing else, this definition should provide a useful focus for future discussions of the topic. Let us say, then, that x is dissociated from y just in case:

(1) (a) x is an occurrent or dispositional state of a human being S, or else a system of states (as in traits, skills, and alternate personalities), and (b) y is either a state or system of states of S, or else the person S.

(2) y may or may not be dissociated from x (i.e., dissociation is a nonsymmetrical relation).

(3) x and y are separated by a phenomenological or epistemological barrier (e.g., amnesia, anesthesia) erected by the subject S.

(4) S is not consciously aware of erecting the barrier between x and y.

(5) The barrier between x and y can be broken down, at least in principle.

(6) Third- and first-person knowledge of x may be as direct as (respectively) third- and first-person knowledge of the subject's non-dissociated states.

Condition (1) takes the ownership and diversification assumptions into account, and condition (5) acknowledges the accessibility assumption. Condition (4) requires that S erect the dissociative barrier either subconsciously or unconsciously; hence it attempts to rule out cases of mere suppression. Similarly, condition (6) attempts to rule out the appropriate set of cases of repression.

The point of insisting, in condition (3), that S actively *erects* a dissociative barrier is to rule out various cases where a subject's states seem to lie behind an epistemological barrier (i.e., they are non-indexical), but which we would probably not want to count as cases of dissociation. Most notably, this condition rules out numerous examples of conceptual naivete and various inevitable forms of self-ignorance. For example, S might desire or dislike something but lack the introspective sophistication or relevant information needed to recognize those states (this point takes on added significance in Chapter 6). For instance, although infants and small children have numerous mental states, they will tend to lack the conceptual categories necessary to grasp that they have those states. But of course, that kind of epistemological barrier is not something they erect. Similarly, adults may not recognize that they have certain mental states, either because they are insufficiently introspective or because they, too, lack the conceptual categories necessary to identify those states. For example, a person might not recognize that he enjoys and desires the experience of feeling sexually humiliated, because he does not even realize that this is a possible dimension of human sexuality. Or, a person may be unaware of his aversion to detective fiction, because he mistakenly believes that he dislikes only the two or three examples to which he has been exposed. It may take wider exposure to the genre before he realizes that his aversion is more general. But presumably this familiar type of self-ignorance is not a form of dissociation.

We are now in a position to understand the difference between the terms 'dissocia*ted*' and 'dissocia*tive*'. I suggest that x is dissocia*tive* for S just in case (a) x is a state or system of states of S, and (b) either x is dissociated from S or else it is produced by a process that is dissociated from S. Hence, some states of S may be dissociative but not dissociated (as we noted in section 4.2 in connection with automatic writing).

The distinction between these two terms also enables us to ward off a potential confusion about dissociation, perhaps encouraged by the ownership and accessibility assumptions. Although many recognize that amnesia is not a necessary condition of dissociation (though it may be sufficient), they might nevertheless insist that dissociation always obscures or removes a subject's states from conscious awareness. After all, the dissociative barrier might be anesthetic (and hence phenomenological) rather than amnesic (and epistemological). Moreover, since amnesia is a failure of *memory*, strictly speaking it is false to say that a subject has amnesia for spontaneously occurring states (e.g., volitions or actions) of which he is *presently* unaware. Hence, it might seem preferable to claim that an essential feature of dissociation is that it somehow *hides* states from conscious awareness or that it renders certain states subconscious or unconscious.[6]

But this would be a mistake. There are widely recognized forms· of dissociation in which the states in question are not hidden from conscious awareness. In particular, dissocia*tive* states clearly needn't be hidden. The automatist who observes his hand writing is obviously aware of his automatic behavior; but that behavior is nevertheless dissociative. Similarly, incongruous emotions or behavior produced dissociatively through post-hypnotic suggestion are likewise not hidden from the subject. But even more interestingly, there is at least one sort of case in which dissocia*ted* states needn't be hidden from awareness. As we have noted, alter personalities may know each other's thoughts, experiences, and actions but are nevertheless considered to be dissociated from each other. Even if each alter has complete knowledge of the other's thoughts and behavior, they remain separated by phenomenological and epistemological barriers of the sort discussed in Chapter 3. That is, states of one alter will tend to be neither autobiographical nor indexical for the other.

5

THE PRINCIPLE OF COMPOSITIONAL REVERSIBILITY

5.1 INTRODUCTION

My concern in the previous two chapters was to delineate various concepts central to our understanding of multiple personality. I want, now, to consider how theorizing about multiplicity has been contaminated by a widely held, but confused, assumption.

We saw in Chapter 1 how, in the eighteenth century, the Marquis de Puységur discovered (or at least drew widespread attention to) a sleeplike hypnotic trance state which he called 'magnetic sleep', and which appeared to reveal the existence of a persistent doubling of consciousness. The waking and magnetized persons, with their separate memories and other characteristics, were, he said, 'two different existences'. A few years later, Deleuze and Faria made similar observations (see, e.g., Crabtree, 1985b, 1993; Laurence and Perry, 1988). Since that time, dissociative phenomena — especially the dramatic phenomena of MPD — have inspired a great deal of theorizing over the structure of the mind and the nature of mental unity and disunity. Quite a lot of this theorizing, however, rests on highly questionable abstract presuppositions.

This chapter will examine a suspicious principle that has been widely accepted, at least tacitly, for well over a hundred years (probably since the time of Puységur). Although late nineteenth- and early twentieth-century authors adopted it fairly readily, it has seldom been articulated explicitly. Its pervasiveness, however, has done much to undermine discussions of dissociative phenomena. Indeed, this principle has led to a seriously distorted picture of the importance of dissociation (and especially MPD) for our understanding of the mind. We may call it the principle of *compositional reversibility*, or the *CR-principle*.

123

5.2 VARIETIES OF REVERSIBILITY

When the pioneers of hypnosis observed various forms of divided consciousness and multiple personality, they apparently saw themselves as having *uncovered* an aspect of mental functioning by means of magnetic techniques. They did not see themselves as having created the phenomena. From their perspective, the therapeutic techniques of animal magnetism disclosed and utilized a doubling of consciousness that existed already within the subject. Hence, they tacitly supposed that they were evoking phenomena that revealed to them something about the underlying structure or operation of the self or personality. In making that assumption, they were relying on a form of the CR-principle.

As far as I can tell, however, the early hypnotists never brought this assumption out into the open. The most prominent explicit proponents of the CR-principle were late nineteenth- and early twentieth-century advocates of the colonial view of the self — i.e., the view that a person is a kind of colony of lower-order selves or homunculi. For example, according to Myers (1903), 'observation of the ways in which the personality tends to disintegrate may suggest methods which may tend on the other hand to its more complete integration' (p. 3). And later, he says (rather less tentatively), 'Subjected continually to both internal and external stress and strain, its [i.e., the personality's] ways of yielding indicate the grain of its texture' (p. 39).

Similarly, a few years earlier, Ribot had stated, even more boldly, 'Seeing how the Self is broken up, we can understand how it comes to be' (1887, p. 20).

Fifty years later, William McDougall (1938) argued along the same lines. He claimed, first, that 'we cannot hope for clear and adequate understanding of the various ways in which the mind falls into disorder unless and until we have adequate insight into the conditions of its orderly and harmonious functioning and development' (p. 143). Then, after asserting that the *historical* structure or aspect of the mind 'is the product of, is built up by...associative links or bonds' (p. 144), he contends that dissociation is 'a weakening, or an undoing, or a failing of the work or product of the associative processes, the links of association' (p. 144).

What these authors seem to be asserting is a kind of historical or developmental claim — namely (and very roughly), that functional disorganization or splitting is a reversal of earlier processes leading to functional organization or unity. Hence, from the pheno-mena of dissociation, one ought to be able to infer the elements or organizing principles underlying prior functional unity. Stated in this general way, however, the CR-principle is ambiguous. In order to appreciate its weaknesses, we must consider it in two distinct forms.

The first, and stronger, version of the CR-principle holds that there is a correlation (or perhaps even an identity) between the *particular* clinical entities produced in dissociation and the com-ponents of the pre-dissociative self. Hence, from our discovery of the former, we can infer the existence of the latter. Let us call this the *Token* CR-principle; it is the view to which nineteenth-century writers came perilously close. The weaker version of the CR-principle asserts a correlation merely between the *kinds* of clinical entities produced dissociatively and the kinds of things composing the pre-dissociative self. Let us call this the *Type* CR-principle. (See Beahrs, 1982, and Watkins and Watkins, 1979-80, for perhaps the most explicit recent versions of this view.)

The Type CR-principle is weaker because type-correlations may exist even in the absence of token-correlations. For example, ac-cording to the Type CR-principle, the existence of a sexual (ag-gressive, angry) alternate personality would entail the pre-disso-ciative existence of a sexual (aggressive, angry) component of the personality. But it needn't be the case that the particular sexual (aggressive, angry) personality that we call Dorothy existed prior to dissociation, or that some specific Dorothy-personality ancestor or germ existed prior to dissociation. Furthermore, the Type CR-principle need only posit one sexual (aggressive, angry) pre-disso-ciative personality component for all post-dissociative members of that type. But the Token CR-principle requires a distinct pre-dissociative component for each distinct post-dissociative entity.

Both versions of the CR-principle are fatally flawed. Consider the Token CR-principle first. To begin with, it is not a *general* truth that things always divide or split along some pre-existing grain, or that objects divide only into their historically original components. For example, Humpty Dumpty may have been reduced to forty pieces of shell after his fall. But it would be a mistake to infer that he had previously been assembled and united out of forty parts, much less those forty parts. Similarly, I can break a table (or a board) in half with an axe. But it would be a mistake to conclude that the object resulted initially from the

125

uniting of those two halves. Furthermore, some cases of splitting are clearly *evolutionary*. For example, the familiar process of cell division *creates* entities that did not exist previously. Hence, if the Token CR-principle is true, it is not because it is an instance of a more general truth about the way things divide or break up. Presumably, it would be true in virtue of the special way the self breaks up.

But there is no reason to think that the self always breaks neatly, or along the grain, especially under extreme trauma or stress — for example, of the sort that apparently leads to MPD. For one thing, a multiple's total number of alters (full-blown personalities or fragments) can apparently range into the hundreds. Even if we grant the difficulty of taking a precise inventory of the number of distinct alters, must we suppose, on the Token CR-principle, that the pre-dissociative self consisted of *so many* distinct proto-personalities?

But more important, it is preposterous to suppose that the historically original components of personality are those (or correspond to those) that seem quite clearly to be *adaptational* — indeed, trauma- or situation-specific. Most alternate personalities appear to be formed in response to *contingent* stressful situations, and they appear to be similarly contingent *products* of a creative process of adaptation or defense. For example, I know a multiple who developed several animal personalities to deal with the incomprehensibility of parental abuse. The abuse occurred during early childhood, and at that time the only way she could grasp the acts into which she was coerced was by relating them to things she had seen dogs and horses do. (The significance and prevalence of animal alters is beginning to come under scrutiny. See, Hendrickson, *et al.*, 1989; Smith, 1989.) Bliss reports another sort of clearly adaptational alter, a personality who

> is blind, or virtually so, because her field of vision is fragmented into pieces, representing an intolerable event the patient witnessed at age six, when the patient's mother cut her live puppy into pieces as part of a voodoo ritual.
>
> (Bliss, 1986, p. 144)

Bliss (like many others) also notes that he has encountered alters who seem to have no physical sensations, apparently in order to cope with repeated sexual and physical assaults by a parent.

Moreover, once a multiple begins to dissociate habitually, as a

126

familiar and apparently effective technique for coping with virtually any kind of stress (traumatic or otherwise), one begins to see the emergence of highly specialized alters, some created to deal merely with inconveniences or relatively minor unpleasant situations. Some alters deal exclusively (or at least principally) with such circumscribed activities as eating, baking muffins, handling domestic finances, cleaning the toilet, participating in oral sex (but sex of no other kind), receiving enemas, and interacting with in-laws. Granted, they might engage in other identifiable types of activities in the process of executing these general functions. But it is nevertheless clear that certain functions rather than others make sense of the alter's role within the total personality system. These, we could say, are an alter's *centrally defining* functions, and there is no reason to suppose that they played any part in the original organization of the pre-dissociative self. There is simply no reason to suppose that an earlier united self consisted in part of components identical to (or correlated with) exactly these contingent post-dissociative entities. Hence, it is highly implausible to insist that the self always breaks along the grain or that it *has* a grain corresponding to situation-specific alternate personalities.

Furthermore, a multiple's inventory of alters often evolves over time in response either to therapeutic intervention or to day-to-day difficulties in life. The problem for the Token CR-principle is not simply that the inventory may continue to enlarge; hard-core advocates of that principle could always argue that additional alters reveal the finer structure of the pre-dissociative personality. Rather (as we observed in Chapter 2), the problem is that the personality-system might undergo *fundamental functional reorganization* into a different number of alters. Multiples might integrate (perhaps only partially) and then split again, but along novel functional lines. Hence, not only might the multiple create different alters (and a different number of alters) to deal with the same problems, but also the problems themselves might change and accordingly elicit a dramatically different set of alters. But then it becomes arbitrary to choose one temporal slice of an evolving system of alters and claim that it reveals the grain (or fundamental structure) of the pre-dissociative self. It is far more reasonable to maintain that a multiple's array of alters *at any time* represents merely one of many possible dissociative solutions to contingent problems in living.

Obviously, this point also works against the Type CR-principle. Since a multiple's system of alters at different times may divide along significantly different functional lines, it becomes arbitrary to select one set of alter-*types* as representing the deep functional divisions of the pre-dissociative self. Those functional divisions are clearly as contingent as the situations in response to which the alters were formed.

In other respects, however, the problems with the Type CR-principle differ somewhat from those afflicting the Token CR-principle. To begin with, it is very difficult to know what the principle means. In particular, to *which* types of post-dissociative entities is it supposed to apply? Presumably not *every* type — for example, personalities that hate Stephen Braude, eat only at McDonald's, or believe that Elvis still lives, or personalities that wear digital watches, enjoy rap music, or prefer Wordstar to WordPerfect. For one thing, that would imply that the historically original pre-dissociative personality components can have functions specific to things that did not exist at the time of birth or during early childhood (e.g., digital watches or computer programs). And for another, if post-dissociative kinds are identified too specifically — for example, the type that has *exactly* the characteristics and history of the personality called Dorothy — then the Type CR-principle is indistinguishable from the Token CR-principle.

Furthermore, even if we were to identify types less specifically, the Type CR-principle would still seem committed to an absurdly inflated inventory of original personality components. Suppose an alter emerged to handle witnessing the murder of one's parents. Does that mean that there already existed a personality component of the type suited specifically to dealing with the murder of one's parents? And if so, must we posit a distinct component waiting in the wings (so to speak) to deal specifically with the murder of siblings, and another for in-laws, or next-door neighbors, or friends in St. Louis, and another for total strangers? Moreover, if the parents' murder was committed with a gun, was the original personality component designed only to deal with the murder of parents with firearms? Would another component already exist just in case the the subject had to deal with murder by chain-saw, or by poison? Even if there needed only to be a personality component for dealing with murder, *of some kind or other*, of one's parent's (or of any loved one), would we then need to posit a component that could have been dissociated just in case the victims had been tortured instead, and another just in case they had been relentlessly harrassed?

5.3 AN APPEAL TO PSYCHOLOGICAL PRIMITIVES

Partisans of the Type CR-principle might reply that we need to identify post-dissociative entities very broadly. They might claim that the relevant types are those having to do only with the most *basic* general personality traits or functions — perhaps such as anger, fear, sexuality, helpfulness, compassion, etc. Presumably, these traits would transcend the familial, cultural, and social influences that help shape the more specific personality types found in MPD. For example, it may not matter that the personality claims to be a possessing spirit of the sort appropriate to a specific cultural milieu or more local belief-system of a family or religious cult, or that it displays the stereotypic traits of a Southern belle, 1960s hippie, or a street-wise tough from the Bronx. Similarly, it may not matter that an alter's centrally-defining function is to repair plumbing, write term papers, or deal with telephone solicitations. What would matter is whether the alter's more general and basic function is to be angry, helpful, sexual, etc. Hence, some might argue for a correlation between only the basic (or primitive) general personality traits or functions isolated dissociatively and component functions of the pre-dissociative self. This variant of the CR-principle, which we may call the *Minimal* Type CR-principle, would therefore seem committed to the existence of distinct pre-dissociative personality components, each of which specializes in a function corresponding to a basic post-dissociative function. And presumably, these corresponding pre-dissociative functions will be the primitive or fundamental functions around which the pre-dissociative self is organized. Undoubtedly, the Minimal Type CR-principle will strike some as commendably conservative. But it is still thoroughly unsatisfactory, for two reasons.

First and foremost, there is no justification for claiming that *any* set of general personality functions is absolutely primitive, either pre- or post-dissociatively. For example, our descriptive categories of anger, helpfulness, sexuality, etc., are hardly the only plausible ways of slicing up behavior into a set of putatively basic regularities or functions. Alternatively, one might prefer the inventory

129

of functions proposed in Transactional Analysis (into parent, child, etc.), while another might defend a Platonic division into reason, appetite, and emotion, and another might prefer a division along the lines of 5-element (or 8-element) diagnosis in Chinese medicine, or perhaps even Jungian archetypes. In fact, many different sets of categories can lay equal claim to dividing the self into basic functions. And they might all be able to countenance exactly the same particular behaviors. The different category-sets would simply take those behaviors to be instances of different sorts of regularities.

The moral, of course, is that these sets of personality functions, like descriptive categories of every sort, are no more than perspective- or context-appropriate divisions of nature into kinds. There is no reason to think that one of our categorizations is inherently preferable to another, or that it captures a built-in parsing of the self into discrete functions. On the contrary, it is only relative to a perspective or point of view, or against a background of continually-shifting needs and interests (both local and global), that certain categories rather than others will be appropriate. None are intrinsically appropriate or perspective-independent. Hence, it is only relative to a context, perspective, or background that we divide nature in one way rather than another and determine which general kinds of descriptive categories and which level of specificity are appropriate (Braude, 1986a, ch. 4).

It might help to think of sets of descriptive categories as conceptual *grids* through which we view the world around us. Since there is not one and only one way to parse reality into objects or events and relations between those things, we use different grids for different purposes. Hence, different conceptual grids will divide reality differently, accomodating certain types of things rather than others (namely, those that fit into the spaces in the grid), and also certain types of lawlike connections or natural regularities (namely, the sort that obtain between those kinds of things). And although some grids may bear lawlike relations to others, some may parse reality in mutually incommensurable ways. That is, a conceptual grid may countenance or reveal objects, properties, and relations that have few (if any), or perhaps only fortuitous, connections to alternative grids.

However (as I observed above), our choice of descriptive categories can be justified only with respect to a guiding background of interests or purposes — that is, some *perspective* relative to which those categories (rather than others) are appropriate. And in that case, the claim that some set of psychological predicates is inherently basic rests on the presupposition that some associated perspective on nature (some set of interests, etc.) is inherently fundamental, or more concerned with basic questions than other perspectives. But that presupposition is simply preposterous. In fact (as I have argued in detail elsewhere — viz., Braude, 1986a, ch. 4.4), the claim that some perspective or set of questions is inherently basic is no more than a thinly disguised and thoroughly indefensible chauvinism for merely one of many ways of looking at the world.

In some ways, then, the self is like a pie. We can slice a pie any number of ways — for example, along the radius, diameter, or by means of a vast array of conceivable grids or templates. And even if we select a general method of slicing the pie — say, along the radius, we still have to decide how large to make the slices. The self, too, can be divided functionally in a vast number of ways. And even if we prefer some general approach rather than others — say, into parent/child divisions, we still have numerous options concerning the finer structure we impose on the self. Do we need to distinguish mother from father, son from daughter, husband from wife, infant from adolescent? Do we need to appeal to grandparent/grandchild relations to understand the dynamics of the pre-dissociative self? Any method we choose, however, represents only one way of understanding, one sort of conceptual map we may trace over the surface of our subject. Moreover, like maps of any sort, our descriptive categories cannot be evaluated apart from a background of needs and interests or in isolation from an actual context of inquiry. And clearly, there is no reason to suppose that our conceptual maps, tailored to context-specific needs to understand, describe actual or natural partitions of the domain under investigation, any more than state or county borders on a map of the United States correspond to actual or natural features of the topography (see Heil, 1983, for an illuminating discussion of the map analogy).

Similarly, there is no reason to think that regional divisions on a map correspond to features of the terrain that are inherently basic (it is not even clear what that could mean). Granted, we might regard certain cartographic divisions as more important than others. But if certain divisions count as basic, that is only because we stipulate that they are basic. Both our parsings and our rankings of them are subject to revision and re-ordering. More generally, when we divide a region or domain of investigation in certain ways (rather than others) and consider some divisions to be more important or fundamental than others, that reflects not only a network of widely-shared assumptions and predispositions but also a range of specific and perhaps more ephemeral interests and concerns. In that respect, our choice and ranking (or hierarchical arrangement) of conceptual categories tells us at least as much about us as it does about the region or domain in question.

Apparently, then, the Minimal Type CR-principle suffers from two related, and very deep, conceptual flaws. First, it presupposes that in the classification of psychological functions some set of descriptive categories is absolutely basic. And second, it mistakes the merely pragmatically justifiable outlines of those categories for inherent divisions in nature. Hence, the Minimal Type CR-principle fails to transform the Type CR-principle into a viable theoretical claim.

5.4 ANOMALOUS MULTIPLICITY

Nevertheless, the foregoing arguments may still not be enough to subvert the CR-principle altogether. Many writers seem to subscribe to a kind of CR-principle, but refrain from endorsing any one version in particular. Perhaps that is because they don't realize they even have a choice. But whatever the reason, they betray their allegiance to the CR-principle by means of a seemingly modest claim. They argue that the self *cannot* be unitary, since if it were, MPD (and other dissociative phenomena) would be impossible. Binet, for example, wrote, 'What is capable of division must be made up of parts' (1896, pp. 348f). This principle, which we may call the *non-committal CR-principle*, also undergirds the work of Beahrs, Hilgard, the Watkins', and many others. Its adherents maintain only that pre-dissociative functional divisions of the self are necessary for the occurrence of post-dissociative functional divisions.

Some might protest that, because these writers take no stand on the nature of the correlation between pre- and post-dissociative entities, it is unclear whether they subscribe to a *reversibility* principle at all. Theoretically, at least, they have the option of affirming the existence of pre-dissociative divisions of the self while denying that post-dissociative divisions correlate with them in *any* meaningful or interesting way. (Borrowing another bit of terminology from recent work in the philosophy of mind, we could call this the *anomalous multiplicity principle*, since the correlations between pre- and post-dissociative divisions of the self would be anomalous — i.e., non-lawlike.) I suspect, however, that few (if any) researchers into MPD would be attracted to this rather skeptical position. If they believed that post-dissociative divisions afforded *no* clue as to the nature of pre-dissociative divisions — that is, if there were no lawlike connections between the two — then the entire enterprise of examining dissociative phenomena in detail would have had a markedly different and presumably less abstract cast. In the absence of such connections, one would not be able to generalize from post-dissociative to pre-dissociative phenomena, and infer features of the latter from those of the former.

Now granted, it may be that in order to ϕ post-dissociatively, one must already have had a pre-dissociative capacity for ϕing. But if *that* is all that partisans of the non-committal CR-principle are willing to claim, then the principle is theoretically vacuous. For one thing, it seems to be *trivially* true that for one to have ϕd, one must already have had a capacity for ϕing. And for another, dissociative phenomena would then be no more revealing than non-dissociative phenomena. After all, in order to manifest *any* trait, ability, etc., the agent must already have had the capacity for it. Furthermore, the non-committal CR-principle would in that case not support inferences about the development or formation of the pre-dissociative self — for example, about the nature of the elements or processes out of which the self was originally composed. But Binet and most other major figures in the history of the field have considered dissociative phenomena to be of enormous theoretical interest and not merely of relevance (say) to therapy. They believed that dissociation promised great and *distinctive* insights into the structure and function of the mind, insights presumably not forthcoming from the study of non-dissociative phenomena. Hence, it is extremely unlikely that in articulating the CR-principle, they were asserting no more than anomalous multiplicity.

To put the point somewhat less abstractly, consider why partisans of a Type CR-principle would ever consider the functional type of a dissociative entity or phenomenon to be of theoretical interest. We obviously do not need angry or sexually promiscuous alternate personalities (say) to demonstrate that people have a pre-dissociative capacity for anger or sexual promiscuity. So what is theoretically distinctive about the dissociation of anger (or any other trait or ability)? For example, what special sort of fact might advocates of a Type CR-principle hope to learn about the pre-dissociative self from the existence of an angry alter? The answer, presumably, is that an alter of that type would reveal something about how the pre-dissociative self *came to be* — that is, it would tell us something about the self's processes of organization and formation, or about the historically original components of the pre-dissociative self. If that were not the case, dissociated anger would apparently be no more theoretically illuminating than any other sort of anger or angry behavior.

More generally, it seems quite clear that researchers expect dissociative phenomena to illuminate the pre-dissociative divisions of the self that make *those* phenomena possible. They seem to be searching for a certain kind of non-trivial nomological connection between pre- and post-dissociative divisions. But that means they have to decide between the Token, Type, or Minimal Type CR-principles, all of which we have found to be fatally flawed. Thus, proponents of the non-committal CR-principle are impaled on the horns of a dilemma. On the one hand, they could decide that there are no — or only trivial — lawlike correlations between pre- and post-dissociative divisions of the self, in which case they would have to concede that MPD, hypnosis, and other dissociative conditions tell us virtually nothing about the nature or development of the pre-dissociative self. And on the other, they could assert the existence of non-trivial lawlike connections, which would require subscribing to one of the three views we have found to be false.

Interestingly, the non-committal CR-principle is widely used in physics, where it has contributed to the almost comical proliferation of 'fundamental' particles. Actually, physicists tend to endorse the Token CR-principle, and its weaknesses undermine the familiar argument that atomic collisions reveal deeper pre-existing structures and components of the atom. Of course, many physicists realize that they may be creating, rather than discovering, new particles. I am merely calling attention to the flawed principle underlying the standard argument in favor of the latter alternative. Even if physicists *are* discovering more fundamental units of matter, they will not establish it by appealing to the Token CR-principle, or even the non-committal CR-principle. In fact, we should perhaps call this defective general argument-form the *Humpty Dumpty Fallacy*.

5.5 THE SIGNIFICANCE OF DISSOCIATION

A few might still protest that *some* kind of CR-principle is required simply to explain the theoretical relevance of dissociative phenomena. After all, they might say, if that principle were false, how could dissociative phenomena ever teach us anything about the self? But one must understand that by abandoning the CR-principle, we needn't concede that it is impossible to learn about the self or the mind from the study of dissociation.

For example, it is clear that we could not dissociate at all, or in certain ways, unless we already had a capacity for it. Hence, dissociative phenomena promise to enhance our understanding of the limits and varieties of cognitive functioning. But of course one could not be *non-dissociatively* timid, long-winded, or anything else unless one already had the corresponding capacity. Hence, (as we've seen) dissociative phenomena are no more distinctively illuminating in that respect than non-dissociative phenomena. Naturally, one would hope to discover a range of unusual or enhanced capacities that occur rarely (if at all) outside of dissociative contexts — for example, hypnotic anesthesia, negative hallucinations, and the astonishing intelligence and literary talents of Patience Worth (Braude, 1980; Cory, 1919a; Litvag, 1972; W.F. Prince, 1927/1964). Indeed, one might *expect* dissociation to elicit infrequently used or displayed human capacities and yield insights into the conditions conducive to their manifestation. But the discovery of capacities unique to dissociation is of no greater *developmental* significance than the discovery that people are non-dissociatively capable of anger, sarcasm, or compassion. In discovering the existence of the capacity, we do not discover anything in particular about its role in the original formation or basic structure of the self. But it is only this latter sort of developmental claim that we reject when we abandon the CR-principle.

To avoid another possible misunderstanding, I should also emphasize that my criticisms of the CR-principle are not arguments against the view that the self has parts.[1] Nor are my criticisms arguments against the view that the pre-dissociative self is (in some sense) a colony of lower-order selves (that claim will be critically examined in Chapter 7). Granted, the etiological data

135

weighs heavily against the view that the pre-dissociative self consists of multiple *apperceptive centers*. From what we know of the life histories of multiples, it appears that new apperceptive centers *develop* in response to events in the subject's life, and that their development is an adaptive technique for handling trauma, one which perhaps only hypnotically-endowed individuals are capable of utilizing (see Bliss, 1986; Putnam, 1989; Ross, 1989). Of course, *how* additional apperceptive centers develop is still a mystery — perhaps the central mystery of MPD. But *when* they develop seems fairly clear. In any case, my arguments against the CR-principle are rather limited in scope. Their main purpose is to show that the principle fails to *establish* the colonial, or even the non-unitary, view of the self. The problem with the principle (in all of its versions) is that it infers the existence of pre-dissociative divisions of the self from the existence of post-dissociative divisions. But that strategy was doomed from the start. In order to argue successfully for the pre-dissociative complexity of the self, one must show that it is required to handle *non-dissociative* phenomena (we will consider such arguments in the next chapter). Otherwise, one can always maintain — quite plausibly — that alternate personalities and the like are simply products (rather than prerequisites) of dissociation.

5.6 POSTSCRIPT: COMMISSUROTOMY

Certain phenomena associated with brain bisection are nearly as striking as those found in cases of multiple personality, and they likewise suggest a profound form of mental disunity. Moreover, as in the case of dramatic dissociative phenomena, many researchers interpret the behavior of split-brain patients as demonstrating the existence, *prior to surgery*, of two distinct minds or selves, corresponding in this case to the two hemispheres of the brain. Of course, this position has been extremely influential, especially outside the academic community. Indeed, many seem to regard as dogma the idea that every person is a compound of two subsidiary selves, the left-brain self and the right-brain self. But not surprisingly, it seems as if the inference leading to that conclusion rests on a tacit application of the CR-principle, and if so, it would be no more legitimate than it was in connection with MPD. Hence, a few remarks about this relatively common use of the CR-principle seem in order.

136

As the reader may realize, the apparently disunified behavior of split-brain patients occurs only under highly artificial or otherwise exceptional conditions. In the majority of everyday situations their behavior seems as unified as that of most ordinary, non-dissociated persons. Nevertheless, on rare occasions in day-to-day life, a patient's left and right hands might seem to exhibit distinct and conflicting tendencies (although this generally occurs only in the few months following surgery). For example, the patient might embrace and push away his wife with different hands, or select different clothes to wear for the day.

However, these spontaneous and quite uncommon displays of disunity are perhaps less impressive than others. In particular, under conditions in which input to the two hemispheres is carefully segregated, the subject will tend to behave in some *predictably* curious ways. For example, suppose that we show a subject S two words — say, 'house boat', in such a way that the left visual field (going to the right hemisphere) contains only 'house' and the right visual field (going to the left hemisphere) contains only 'boat'. If we ask S what he saw, he will respond verbally by saying that he saw 'boat'. Moreover, if we ask S what kind of boat it is, he will not necessarily say 'house boat'. Apparently, he is as likely to name some other sort of boat — say, row boat or steam boat. But if we ask S to point with his left hand to a picture of what he saw from a display of several pictures (including pictures of a house, boat, and a house boat), he will probably point to the picture of a house. In general, when S's response is controlled by his left hemisphere, S will indicate that he was aware of 'boat' and not 'house'. Similarly, responses controlled by the right hemisphere will indicate that he was aware of 'house' and not 'boat'. One can perhaps understand, then, why some conclude that a split-brain patient has two minds, or that he is two persons (even if one disagrees with that position).

It is not my intention, however, to discuss the topic of commissurotomy in detail. Although it is unquestionably very interesting, in order to do it justice we would have to address numerous complex issues that would carry us quite far afield. I do not even wish now to consider whether or in what respect we might sensibly regard a human being as more than one person (we will look closely at that topic in Chapter 8). Similarly, I want to avoid for now the issue of whether the split-brain patient has two minds (or even just apperceptive centers).[2] Instead, I want merely to examine the claim that 'even in the normal, cerebrally intact human being there must be two persons, though before the era of commissurotomy experiments we had no way of knowing this' (Puccetti, 1973, p. 351).

And even then, I wish only to make a rather limited point — namely, that this inference seems to rest on the fallacious CR-principle. In the next chapter, we will survey problems facing a closely related sort of inference: Plato's argument from internal conflicts to the existence of a tripartite soul.

From our foregoing examination of the CR-principle, it should be clear by now that the apparent disunities exhibited by split-brain patients show *at most* that a person *can be made to have* two minds or that a person can be made to be two persons. Puccetti, however, in his influential paper (1973), seems quite oblivious to this. He says it is a mystery how brain bisection could *create* two minds when there was only one before. The reason, he claims, is that we would then have to choose *which* of the post-operative minds is new. Hence (he argues), there must have been two minds all along.

But this argument is clearly unconvincing. Assuming it makes sense to attribute two minds to one person, why *not* say that both post-operative minds are new? Analogously, in cell division (or in slicing a flatworm), one gets two new cells (or worms), *neither* of which existed as such before. There is simply no problem of having to decide which of the two worms (or cells) is new. Puccetti quite obviously commits the same error as those who argued from the complexity of the post-dissociative self to the complexity of the pre-dissociative self. Indeed, the trauma of surgery is the clear analogue of the trauma leading to the development of alternate personalities. In order to show that cerebrally intact individuals have two minds, one must argue that two minds are required to explain the apparent disunities of normal mental phenomena. Otherwise, it will always be more plausible to maintain that commissurotomy *causes* split-brain patients to have two minds.

Let us turn, then, to arguments purporting to show that various non-dissociative phenomena must be explained by reference to functionally distinct agencies ('selves' or minds) within a person.

6

MULTIPLE SUBJECTS OR MULTIPLE FUNCTIONS?

6.1 INTRODUCTION

In Chapter 5, we examined the standard arguments for parts of the self (or divided consciousness) based on the existence or characteristics of dissociative phenomena (and the almost equally dramatic results of brain bisection). We observed how those arguments commit the Humpty Dumpty Fallacy by relying on the fallacious principle of compositional reversibility. We noted that just because something is now in pieces, it does not follow that those pieces correspond to permanent or previously existing natural elements or divisions of that thing. That is why one cannot confidently argue from post-dissociative (or post-operative) divisions of the self to pre-dissociative (or pre-operative) divisions.

But some familiar arguments for a divided self make no special appeal either to the peculiarities of dissociation or to the principle of compositional reversibility. They focus on normal, non-dissociative phenomena, in which the person's mind does not seem (at least conspicuously) to be divided into parts — hence, in which there is no temptation to invoke the CR-principle. And they argue that even these common non-dissociative phenomena often require explanation in terms of functionally distinct subjects or parts of the self. Moreover, some take these arguments a step further. They claim that the need to posit parts of the self to explain both dissociative and non-dissociative phenomena shows that in some important sense we are all multiples, or at least that the difference between multiplicity and non-multiplicity is merely one of degree and not one of kind (see, especially, Beahrs, 1982; also, perhaps, Putnam, 1988, who seems to offer a less extreme version of the view).

139

These arguments do, indeed, avoid the Humpty Dumpty Fallacy. Nevertheless, they appear to suffer from different (and sometimes more subtle) flaws, which render them either totally unacceptable or at least too weak to be of much use. Moreover, we shall see (in the next chapter) that even the dramatically and deeply dissociative phenomena of MPD seem to require explanation with reference to a single unifying intelligence.

6.2 PLATO'S ARGUMENT

In *The Republic* (Book IV: 435-441 C), Plato presented what is probably the first, and what is most certainly the classic, argument for a kind of psychological multiplicity or disunity of consciousness. That is not to say that Plato himself argued (or at least clearly argued) against the commonsense view that there is only one mind to a person or one person to a body. (And there is no need to worry now over that particular issue of Platonic exegesis.) What matters here is Plato's dialectical strategy, which apparently is quite seductive. Writers have been adopting it in one form or another for about 2,500 years to argue for various degrees of psychic disunity. Nevertheless, Plato's argument is far from convincing, not only in its original version but also in those of its various descendants. The problem seems to lie in the central intuition on which the argument rests — namely, that unless we posit the existence of *multiple subjects* within a person, ascribing ordinary internal conflicts to that person will violate the law of non-contradiction.

In response, Plato's opponents usually argue that there are ways of describing internal conflicts that are both plausible and non-contradictory and that do not require positing distinct subjects within a person. Hence (they would urge), explanations in terms of multiple subjects are gratuitous as well as counter-intuitive. And that approach is not entirely without merit, as we will see. A more radical strategy would be to argue that the standard alternative methods of description are likewise gratuitous and that a deeper problem may lie in an illegitimate appeal to the law of non-contradiction. We will consider these two approaches in turn.

Let us begin by considering Plato's original version of the argument, which runs as follows. First, Plato states what at least appears to be the law of non-contradiction. The principle he invokes, tidied up a bit, is:

(NC): Nothing can be, at the same time, in relation to the same thing, and with respect to the same part of itself, both F and not-F.

Then, he argues that in cases where it looks as if a is simultaneously both F and not-F in relation to the same thing, there must be two parts of a, one of which is F and the other of which is not-F. One of Plato's examples is this. Suppose that a person simultaneously both wants and does not want to drink the liquid in the container before him (say, because he is thirsty but knows that the liquid is poison). If the subject who wanted to drink was the same as the subject who did not want to drink, (NC) would be violated. Hence, Plato concludes that there must be two parts to the person's soul — that is, two subjects within the person, one that wants to drink and another that does not. Therefore, the person is not literally in conflict with himself. Rather, different components of the person are in conflict with each other.

Not surprisingly, certain classic types of dissociation seem to cry out for a similar treatment. And, indeed, Plato's argument has played a central, if covert, role in discussions of dissociation. For example, it appears as if an hypnotically anesthetized individual may simultaneously feel and not feel the stimulus, and that the person with hypnotic amnesia may both know and not know that p. That is, at the same time, and in relation to the same thing, it seems as if the person is both F and not-F. But if we accept (NC), we may conclude instead that the subject who feels the stimulus (or knows that p) is distinct from the subject who simultaneously does not feel the stimulus (or does not know that p). Throughout the history of hypnosis, this has been the general strategy for arguing in favor of multiple subjects within a person (see, e.g., Binet, 1890, 1896; Hilgard, 1986), although the appeal to (NC) is usually tacit.

But is that strategy satisfactory? As I noted above, the standard objection is to argue, first, that the apparent internal conflicts (dissociative and non-dissociative) have been misdescribed, and second, that by redescribing those conflicts in a more perspicuous way one can eliminate the superficial appearance of a contradiction. In fact, several plausible strategies come to mind readily, some of which will be more suitable than others for specific cases. One approach would be to explain away the apparent contradictions, not in terms of distinct co-existing subjects, but in terms of disparities between a single subject's first- and second-order cognitive states. For example, in Plato's drinking case, we could say that the person wants to drink and in addition knows (or fears) that yielding to the desire would be fatal. Dissociative cases might be handled along similar lines. For example, rather than say that the subject both knows and does not know that p in cases of hypnotic amnesia, we could say that the subject knows that p, but does not know that he knows that p. Similarly, in cases of hypnotic anesthesia we could say that the subject feels the stimulus but does not know that he feels it.

A second method of redescription focuses on a subtle point about logical structure. One might argue that an ordinary language sentence such as 'S does not want x' is ambiguous between sentences of the form 'not-(S wants x)' and 'S wants not-x', and that the apparent contradiction between it and 'S wants x' disappears when we read it the second way. Similarly, one could read 'S does not believe that p' as 'S believes that not-p' rather than 'not-(S believes that p)'. For example, suppose (in the spirit of Plato) that S wants to have dessert (because he loves sweets) but that he doesn't want dessert (because he is dangerously overweight). The suggestion here is that although

(1) S wants to have dessert

is incompatible with

(2) not-(S wants to have dessert)

it is not incompatible with

(3) S wants not to have dessert

and that (3) is the more accurate sentence in this case. One can, indeed, want (believe) incompatible things, but it cannot be that the person both wants (believes) and does not want (believe) the same thing.

Yet another approach is similar to the first, except that it does not rely on a distinction between first- and second-order cognitive states. Quite apart from issues concerning logical form, one could simply redescribe the cases in question in other plausible ways. For example, we could say that S wants something sweet for dessert but does not want to exacerbate his weight problem, or that S wants to quench his thirst but does not want to poison himself.[1] Plato's opponents would contend that descriptions of these sorts are much more illuminating than (and hence, preferable to) descriptions in terms of multiple subjects. In fact, Plato's opponents would say that because their proposed redescriptions indicate precisely how the subject's goals or desires conflict, they explain more satisfactorily why the experience of that conflict *feels as if* it is the experience of a single subject.

I think there can be no doubt that these various approaches to redescribing ordinary internal conflicts may have considerable utility and that they may produce more perspicuous accounts of those conflicts than the descriptions in terms of multiple subjects favored by Plato. But in the wider context of discussing dissociative phenomena, I question whether those strategies are really appropriate. In fact, it may be that a reliance on them is question-begging. To see why, we must shift our attention back to some outstanding features of dissociation, even though dissociative phenomena are not the focus of this chapter.

Consider, for example, experiments in which the hypnotized subject displays apparent amnesia for some event *e* but through simultaneous automatic writing demonstrates a memory of *e*. Or consider cases in which an apparent hidden observer reports (or complains of) sensations (say, through automatic writing) of which the hypnotized subject seems unaware and for which he shows none of the customary *involuntary* responses associated with sensations of that type (e.g., pulling away from pain or the smell of ammonia, or the sneezes or watering eyes that the subject would ordinarily display when presented with the stimulus). Even those who recoil naturally from accepting that an individual can simultaneously be both *F* and not-*F* must admit that these are cases in which it is unusually tempting, *prima facie*, to say that there are distinct co-existing subjects of some non-trivial sort within the person. It looks as if distinct, and in some sense self-conscious, streams of experience exist simultaneously within the subject, one of which manifests through normal behavior and the other of which expresses itself through automatic writing. Moreover, this apparent doubling of consciousness seems even more pronounced when (as often happens) the personality manifesting automatically refers to the hypnotized subject in the third person. And of course, cases of MPD suggest even more strongly that profoundly distinct sorts of multiple subjects may co-exist in a person.

But since these cases so strongly suggest the presence of multiple subjects (of some kind or other), one cannot simply maintain that the aforementioned types of redescription are *antecedently* more plausible. After all, in light of the evidence for multiple personality, one cannot argue that such redescriptions are more plausible *as a rule*. Multiple personality demonstrates clearly the utility, in some cases at least, of explaining apparently contradictory psychological phenomena in terms of quite robust sorts of multiple subjects — namely, apperceptive centers. Hence, with regard to somewhat less imposing (but still dramatic) dissociative phenomena, and even with regard to humdrum internal conflicts, one would think that descriptions in terms of multiple subjects cannot be ruled out *a priori*.

I am not suggesting that one should always explain or describe cases of dissociative and non-dissociative internal conflicts with respect to multiple subjects. (Indeed, I am opposing that position in this chapter and the next.) The point is rather that we cannot simply *assume* that it is preferable to reject explanations in terms of multiple subjects in favor of the sorts of redescriptions mentioned above. After all, probably every phenomenon (and certainly, every psychological state) can be described *usefully* in quite different sorts of ways and from quite different points of view. But in that case, since some explanations in terms of multiple subjects have considerable utility, their rejection in the cases under consideration would seem to require something over and above the mere observation that illuminating redescriptions are available. At the very least, it requires some sort of defense. For example, one might argue that non-dissociative cases are relevantly different from at least the more dramatic dissociative cases and (accordingly) that the former neither require nor even benefit from an appeal to multiple subjects. Or, one might argue that Plato's argument is invalid or unsound. (My strategy will be to combine these approaches.) Hence, even if apparent internal conflicts can always be described without positing distinct subjects, that would show only that Plato's argument is not compelling. It would not show that the argument is actually defective. Hence, one might wonder whether it is possible to mount a stronger case against Plato's argument.

6.3 THE LAW OF NON-CONTRADICTION

It is in that spirit that I offer the following, admittedly debatable, suggestions. And I hasten to add that nothing else in the book stands or falls on the arguments of this section and the next. As we have seen, one need not accept Plato's argument for multiple subjects so long as alternative (and arguably, better) descriptions of the apparent conflicts are available. Hence, if my arguments below are correct, they would merely provide a different (albeit stronger) sort of reason for rejecting Plato's argument. Besides, as I note later, even if Plato's argument survives all attacks, it shows too little to support the view that everyone is a multiple to some extent.

I suggest, then, that we look more closely at the principle on which Plato's argument turns — namely, the law of non-contradiction. It is interesting how easily philosophers accept that law when considering the structure of the self. For example, Wilkes (1988) notes how the Platonic argument is used in connection with the disunities resulting from brain bisection, and although she disputes the claim that commissurotomy patients are multiple selves or that they are deeply disunified, she never challenges the appeal to the law of non-contradiction. Indeed, she claims that

> We break this law as soon as we permit ourselves to say that one and the same entity both knows and does not know that p, for nothing can, at time t, be said to ϕ and not to ϕ.
>
> (Wilkes, 1988, p. 142)[2]

Of course, to those without any philosophical axe to grind, cases of MPD might suggest that one can indeed be said to ϕ and not to ϕ at the same time. Since that could easily be taken to suggest that the law of non-contradiction has some hitherto unacknowledged limitation, and since one must always be open to the possibility that logical laws have limitations of one sort or another, let us examine the status of the law which dissociative and other phenomena appear to violate.

Notice, first, that Plato's version, (NC), is not, strictly speaking, a logical law. Certainly, it is not what logicians generally consider to be the law of non-contradiction. *That* law is usually taken to be either (a) the formal, syntactic law '$\sim(A \cdot \sim A)$' — usually rendered more informally as 'not-(A and not-A)', or else (b) a claim in logical semantics about truth-value assignments — namely, 'no sentence can be both true and false' (or alternatively, 'the conjunction of any sentence p and its denial not-p is false').

But the first of these is not violated by the cases under consideration, and the second is not even clearly a law.

Consider the syntactic law first. It concerns the *form*, rather than the content, of strings of symbols within a formal system. It takes any compound expression of the form 'not-(A and not-A)' to be a theorem, for *any* well-formed formula 'A'. But strictly speaking, the law does not pertain to sentences of any actual natural language. The syntactic law of non-contradiction does nothing more than sanction a particular arrangement of expressions within a certain set of formal systems. And although one can easily determine which symbolic expressions are theorems, those logical systems do not, in addition, offer a decision procedure for determining which sentences in a natural language are true or false. On the contrary, the relationship of formal to natural languages has to be both stipulated and investigated. And ultimately, the utility of a formal system of logic has to be evaluated empirically, by seeing whether or how well it applies to various domains of discourse — for example, by seeing whether the truth-values it would assign to actual sentences matches our independent judgments about what those truth-values should be.

In fact, formal logical systems do not even specify which expressions in a natural language count as legitimate instances of a simple (i.e., noncompound) formula 'A' — hence, which natural language expressions are instances (or violations) of its theorems. Although logicians generally agree that the simple formulae of the systems should represent declarative sentences, there is considerable debate over which particular *kinds* of declarative sentences are suitable. Interestingly, many would say that as far as the purely formal laws of logic are concerned, 'A' could stand even for sentences whose truth-value or meaning are indeterminate, such as 'unicorns are egregious', and 'Zeus is insecure'. But then it seems as if the uninterpreted formal law of non-contradiction is simply irrelevant to the cases under consideration. At best, those cases appear to challenge a semantic counterpart to the formal law, either

(NC$_1$): The conjunction of any sentence p and its denial not-p is false

or

(NC$_2$): No sentence can be both true and false

146

In a moment, I shall consider whether (or to what extent) either of these versions of the law of non-contradiction is satisfactory. First, however, we should note that even if the law of non-contradiction turns out to be a viable principle of logical semantics, it may still have a variety of significant limitations. In fact, the utility of formal logical laws varies widely, and the interpretation of those laws has proven to be a notoriously tricky business. As with all formal systems, no system of logic determines in which domains (if any) its expressions may be successfully applied. Students of elementary logic learn quickly that there are differences between the logical connectives 'and' and 'or' and many instances of the words 'and' and 'or' in ordinary language. Similarly, not all 'if...then...' sentences are adequately handled by the material conditional in standard systems of sentential logic, although that logical connective is undeniably useful in a great range of cases. Moreover, varieties of non-standard and 'modal' logics have been developed in attempts to represent types of discourse resistant to standard logical systems.

But even more relevantly, in most standard systems of logic, the formal law of non-contradiction, 'not-(A and not-A)', is demonstrably equivalent to the law of the excluded middle, 'A v $\sim A$' (i.e., 'A or not-A'). Like the formal law of non-contradiction, the law of the excluded middle concerns the form rather than the content of expressions. It takes any compound formula of the form 'A or not-A' to be a theorem (or logical truth), no matter what formula 'A' happens to be. Now the semantic sibling of that syntactic law is called the law of bivalence, which states that every sentence is either true or false. But the law of bivalence has faced numerous challenges throughout the history of logic (in fact, since the time of Aristotle). Many have argued that it fails for sentences in the future tense and sentences whose singular terms refer to non-existent objects. Moreover, some logicians consider these difficulties sufficiently profound to warrant the development of logical systems that retain the syntactic law of the excluded middle but reject the semantic law of bivalence (see, e.g., van Fraassen, 1966, 1968; Thomason, 1970). Now granted, these same logicians do not also reject the semantic version of the law of non-contradiction. Nevertheless, their reservations concerning bivalence should give us pause (especially in light of the caveats noted above regarding the limitations of formal systems generally). The debate over bivalence illustrates an important point — namely, that the relative impregnability of a formal logical law may not be inherited by its semantic counterpart (i.e., one of its interpretations). But at the very best, it is only the semantic counterpart — and in the case of our original (NC), an even more exotic interpretation — of a formal law that rests at the center of Plato's argument for the parts of the soul.

So let us now consider whether

(NC_1): The conjunction of any sentence p and its denial not-p is false

or

(NC_2): No sentence can be both true and false

can be relied on to help establish the existence of multiple subjects in cases of apparent psychological contradictions. First of all, (NC_1) is problematical; it has numerous counterexamples familiar to students of logic and the philosophy of language. For example, it seems to fail for sentences such as the aforementioned 'unicorns are egregious' and 'Zeus is insecure', which seem to lack truth-value. Many would say that when a sentence lacks truth-value, the conjunction of that sentence and its denial also lacks truth-value.

The somewhat more common (NC_2) has similar problems. Most notoriously, perhaps, it fails for the self-referential sentence 'this sentence is false', as well as for kindred expressions that do not seem even remotely suspicious inherently. For example, it fails for the innocent 'the sentence on the blackboard is false', when that sentence happens to be the only sentence on the blackboard. If these sentences have any truth-value at all, it seems as if they will be both true and false.

Furthermore, (NC_2) apparently fails for quite mundane present-tense sentences. For example, 'Socrates is sitting' may be true at one time and false at another. Of course, one standard response to such cases would be to claim that the sentence 'Socrates is sitting' contains an implicit reference to its time of production, so that it is not really the same sentence that is true at one time and false at another (i.e., those nonsimultaneous sentences would allegedly differ in meaning or express different propositions). For reasons too complex to be explored here, it seems to me that this particular maneuver creates more problems than it solves. Indeed, it seems to me that the standard Aristotelian notion of contradictories (stated

148

in terms of opposing truth-values) fails conspicuously for a tensed natural language, and that tensed contradictories can have the same truth-value (see Braude, 1986b, for a discussion of these issues). Although I recognize that this is most definitely a minority view, I submit that there are additional serious reasons here for challenging the straightforward application of (NC$_2$) to a real natural language — hence, for questioning its inviolability outside of the highly artificial or overly simplified linguistic situations to which logical laws apply easily.

Another standard way of avoiding problems with tensed sentences would be to amend (NC$_2$) as follows:

(NC$_3$): No sentence can be both true and false at the same time.

But even this principle seems to have exceptions, as Plato apparently realized. For example, the sentence 'Socrates is moving' can be both true and false at time t, as when Socrates sits still in a moving chariot. He is moving with respect to the ground, but not with respect to the chariot. Similarly, the sentence 'X is moving' might be considered simultaneously both true and false when different parts of X move and do not move with respect to a given object. Plato's examples are of a man standing still but moving his arms and of a spinning top whose axis is stationary. Hence, Plato resorts to a more complex version of the principle of non-contradiction, our original

(NC): Nothing can be, at the same time, in relation to the same thing, and with respect to the same part of itself, both F and not-F.

Contemporary philosophers would not be so quick to replace (NC$_3$) with (NC). They would probably have noted that 'x is moving' appears to violate (NC$_3$) because the predicate 'moving' (like many other predicates) is *relational*; one always moves *with respect to* something. That is why 'x is moving', treated non-relationally, can be both true and false at the same time. Hence, some might think that there is no problem with (NC$_3$) and that the aforementioned difficulties arise only when we ignore the underlying relational form of 'x is moving'. Such a sentence, they might claim, will always be elliptical for a more complex relational sentence.

But this position is far from convincing. One could reply that there is nothing inherently wrong with 'x is moving', treated non-relationally. Granted, when using the predicate 'moving', we may recognize that motion is always relative to an inertial frame, but we needn't recognize that at all in order to use the predicate successfully. Indeed, children (and others) often utter true sentences of the form 'x is moving' and communicate quite satisfactorily in the process, without grasping the relational character of the predicate 'moving'. And even when we do recognize the relativity of motion, we needn't have any particular inertial frame in mind when we say 'x is moving'. At most, we might assume only that x is moving relative to *something or other*.

More importantly, however, none of these assumptions must be understood as parts of the sentence's *content*. *Every* sentence we utter rests on numerous tacit background assumptions, which ordinarily needn't be considered, evaluated, or even understood by the speaker in order to determine what the sentence means or whether it is true. For example, when I say 'the table is brown', I make numerous assumptions about the nature of observation and the stability of physical objects and their properties over time.[3] If we engage in high-level philosophical speculations about the adequacy of these assumptions, we would inevitably and indirectly cast doubt on much of our ordinary talk about physical objects and their properties. But it is only at that level of discourse that the truth and meaning of 'the table is brown' hinges on the adequacy of our background assumptions. In most other contexts, we understand and assign truth-values to our sentences independently (and often, in total ignorance) of those assumptions.

Hence, the moral may be that (NC_3) is just not generally true, despite its utility in many contexts. But if (NC_3) can fail for some sentences containing relational predicates (such as 'moving'), we cannot simply assume that the principle must hold for all sentences containing psychological predicates. The problems posed by psychological predicates may be different than those posed by ordinary relational predicates. But once we acknowledge that the law of non-contradiction has some exceptions, we must be open to the possibility of others, particularly in those cases that seem most conspicuously to challenge the law.

Besides, we must be wary generally of treating a troublesome sentence such as 'Socrates is moving' as if it *must* be elliptical for a more complex sentence — for example, one which refers to times or mentions frames of reference. This is a customary maneuver in logic and the philosophy of language when trying to fit real-life sentences into a procrustean abstract framework, and it typically leads to various theoretical atrocities (see Braude, 1986b for the consequences of treating tensed sentences in this way). It is also antecedently incredible, because it requires that we attribute more informational (or propositional) content to those sentences than their utterers ever imagined.

But I must emphasize that these various examples do not show that the semantic law of non-contradiction is useless as a philosophical tool. And the moral is not simply that logical laws (like formal laws generally) may not hold in all domains (although that is certainly true and relevant here). Rather, the point is also that logical laws hold only for sentences we regard as *acceptable* (or *legitimate*) and *appropriate*, or as understood in certain ways rather than others. But these interpretations and classifications of linguistic entities are *practical* decisions, made as part of a much larger network of interrelated philosophical commitments.[4] Accordingly, those decisions do not stand or fall in isolation from others in various areas of philosophy and logic. In fact, they will continually be open for re-assessment in light of apparent difficulties arising at numerous points in our overall system of commitments (see Aune, 1970, for a relatively non-technical discussion of this point). But in that case, the apparent challenge to the law of non-contradiction posed by certain psychological phenomena must be viewed as indicating another possible exception to a law whose utility is already limited and whose acceptability in any case turns essentially on pragmatic considerations — indeed, considerations of precisely the sort that the cases in question seem to raise.

6.4 PSYCHOLOGICAL INDETERMINACY

In section 6.2, we considered several (admittedly plausible) ways of sidestepping apparent challenges to the law of non-contradiction posed by ordinary internal conflicts. Those maneuvers allowed us to preserve the law without positing distinct subjects within a person for each of the conflicting states. We noted that apparently contradictory states of affairs could be described in ways that are clearly non-contradictory, and which, therefore, eliminate the need to posit different subjects. For example, one could simply specify more thoroughly what the states were, or one could resort to the logical manuever of reading (say) 'S does not want x' as 'S wants not-x' rather than 'not-(S wants x)'.

In the previous section, however, we considered some reasons for questioning the straightforward and general application of logical laws to sentences in a natural language. Now, I want to examine another (related) set of reasons for thinking that sentences such as

(1) S wants to have dessert

and

(2) not-(S wants to have dessert)

can both be true at the same time.

First, I must emphasize again that the methods of redescription considered earlier are quite reasonable. What is at issue now is the *extent* to which they and the law of non-contradiction apply non-problematically to the domain of psychological states. And I suggest that quite apart from their admitted utility in connection with descriptions of psychological states, these analytical tools have equally important and revealing limitations in that domain.

To see why, it should help to note an interesting similarity between psychological states and natural languages. It is generally recognized that systems of natural deduction apply to ordinary discourse only by ignoring many of its subtleties and much (if not most) of its richness. Our languages are looser, and the meaning of our utterances more vague, than systems of natural deduction can tolerate. For those systems to work, we must treat sentences in our language as more clear-cut in meaning and structure than they are when produced in real-life situations. Indeed, the translation of sentences into symbols requires sometimes heroic but certainly creative acts of abstraction and interpretation, in which we focus on certain features of our utterances while ignoring others, and make decisions as to which readings of those utterances are appropriate or most illuminating. As every logic instructor knows, this crucial step in applying systems of natural deduction to everyday sentences is very difficult to teach, because the process is as much intuitive as it is rule-governed. Not surprisingly, the process of formalizing sentences and applying deductive techniques can be enormously helpful at those times when we need to clarify the meanings and implications of our utterances. But in many (and possibly most) situations, verbal communication succeeds quite nicely without such clarifications. Indeed, until problems emerge, we often do not even realize just how vague and ambiguous our remarks have been.

Granted, in many cases the analysis of our utterances and arguments is relatively straightforward. But that is seldom (if ever) because our utterances on those occasions are inherently clearer or more precise than on other occasions. Rather, it usually reflects the non-demanding nature of the prevailing context of inquiry. Although *in principle* the disambiguation[5] of ordinary discourse can proceed along an indefinite number of different lines, in practice our options tend to be highly circumscribed. Indeed, the disambiguation of our sentences is a challenge only in somewhat arcane contexts, or when the need for clarification is unusually pressing or the requirements particularly exacting. In most cases, however, we tolerate a great deal of ambiguity and vagueness, and we seldom need or demand further disambiguation. But that neither demonstrates nor requires that our utterances in those cases are inherently clear, or clearer than in contexts where disambiguation is more challenging or urgent. It merely reflects the pervasiveness of shared background assumptions underlying our linguistic practices generally and the specific topic of conversation in particular. That is why we might consider a sentence to be deeply obscure in certain contexts, whereas the same sentence would easily pass muster in situations where there is no need to question or examine our background assumptions. For example, the sentence, 'we create our own reality' might seem perfectly intelligible and acceptable at a conference celebrating the New Age movement, whereas in many traditional academic contexts it would be taken as mysterious at best and blatantly false at worst. Similarly, 'good neighbors come in all colors' may seem quite clear and true in the context of a town meeting on racial integration. But in many other contexts, (e.g., a logic or art class), one might properly note that the sentence is false, because no humans are (say) forest green, aquamarine, or vermilion.

I submit that an analogous situation obtains in connection with the domain of psychology, and that the vagueness and ambiguity of our linguistic productions parallels a similar indefiniteness in the thoughts and other psychological states behind those productions. The methods of redescription discussed in 6.2 are useful techniques for viewing and describing psychological states in ways that allow us to use our most powerful analytical tools. But there is no reason to think that the domain is as neat and tidy as the descriptions we find useful, or (recalling the discussion in Chapter 5.3) that the structure we justifiably attribute to thoughts, beliefs, and desires, etc., corresponds to natural features in the domain of mental states. It is more plausible to suppose that psychological states are typically as indeterminate in content or structure as ordinary sentences in a natural language.

To see why, consider the concept of *vagueness* as applied to ordinary language. A vague expression is one that does not have a precise application. For example, the term 'tall' (or 'tall person') is vague, because there are no precise or absolute criteria specifying at what height an object qualifies as tall. A vague term, then, is one for which there are no rules for the application of the term, or for which such rules as there are are insufficient to determine whether the expression applies in a given case.

Now generally speaking, our psychological predicates are vague. When we describe a person as depressed, remorseful, envious, irritated, intimidated, conciliatory, or hopeful, or when we attribute various beliefs or desires to a person, the expressions we use are no more straightforwardly applicable than the term 'tall'. As with other vague terms, the expressions we use to pick out mental states are vague in the sense that it is not always clearly true that a person is in that state or not in that state. In fact, in *most* cases it is unclear whether (or to what extent) mental states may be properly attributed to a person. But there is no reason to think that the vagueness of our psychological terms is either accidental or merely a feature (or defect) of our language or psychological concepts. It is more reasonable to suppose that psychological terms are vague because the mental states and state-kinds they pick out are comparably indeterminate and indistinct — that is, that there is nothing clear-cut or definite in the world for them to correspond to. In fact, if our psychological predicates pick out indefinite or inexact *kinds* of phenomena (as many philosophers concede), then there is no reason to think that the *objects* to which those predicate expressions apply are any more specific or definite (e.g., clearly specifiable states of the brain). To suppose otherwise is to make one of the deep errors sabotaging Davidsonian anomalous monism (Goldberg, 1977; Braude, 1979). At any rate, the vagueness of our psychological terms does not demonstrate our linguistic or conceptual incompetence — in particular, our inability to describe mental states in ways that permit their clear attribution. Rather, it

154

seems instead to reflect a deep fuzziness in the domain itself.

And in that case, one would expect to find parallels between the formal analysis of natural-language sentences and the analysis and descriptions of mental states. Just as we can employ logical or analytical techniques to impose a frequently useful degree of structure and specificity on our utterances, our conceptual analyses can impose structure and specificity on our desires and beliefs (say) and thereby help us to become clearer about what those desires and beliefs are. But just as the former activity clarifies something that was inherently indefinite and unclear before, the same would be true of our descriptions and analyses of psychological states. I am suggesting, then, that *prior* to the analytical work of describing and analyzing our subjective states, those states are relatively indistinct. They might *become* more specific and precise as the result of our cognitive elaborations, just as we can express ourselves more precisely when the situation demands. But even if (or when) we lack the power actually to transform our psychological states into more definite forms, our relatively precise descriptions of them may remain as heuristically and practically valuable as our careful analyses of verbal discourse. That is one reason we often indicate certain respects in which a person wants (believes) something, or specify more painstakingly what the objects of a person's desires (or the contents of a person's beliefs) are. But no matter how much precision we thereby achieve, at no point do we remove all vagueness from our terms. Success in such endeavors is always a matter of degree. Our relatively elaborate descriptions of mental states are simply attempts to reduce the natural indistinctness of those states to manageable proportions, so that we can profitably discuss them and attribute them successfully to ourselves and to others.

If these speculations are correct, then we should be no more perplexed about how

(1) *S* wants to have dessert

and

(2) not-(*S* wants to have dessert)

can both be true than about how

(3) Jones is tall

and

(4) Jones is not tall

can both be true. The sentences are not true or false *simpliciter*. They count as true only relative to certain criteria or assumptions as to what qualifies as wanting dessert or being tall. But we impose those criteria or rely on those assumptions only in situations where we need to make practical decisions about which sentence in each pair is true. In other contexts, however, we can simply and comfortably acknowledge that there is no clear fact of the matter.

Granted, it sounds somewhat counter-intuitive to say that both sentences in each pair may be true simultaneously. But that is because we are seldom willing to tolerate there being no such fact of the matter. The practical needs of real-life linguistic contexts tends to narrow our choices for us. For one thing, in most cases it *matters* whether we regard an individual as tall or not (or as wanting dessert or not); so we usually *need* to make a choice. And for another, in most conversational contexts our background assumptions and criteria for the application of vague terms are usually both shared and clear enough for the purposes at hand. However, that is simply a prerequisite for successful communication, and at best it is only a rough sort of concordance. Language use does not demand absolute clarity or the obliteration of all vagueness from our terms. It requires only enough clarity and agreement to permit practical decisions about which of our sentences should count as true. Hence, to insist that (1) and (2) *cannot* be true simultaneously is merely to express a form of logical rigidity, an unwillingness to admit that our analytical tools are just tools, which like tools of all sorts are more useful in some contexts (or for some tasks) than others, and which ultimately can only be as useful as the world allows.

6.5 THE UTILITY OF INTENTIONAL PARTS

At the very least, then, Plato's argument does not *demonstrate* the need for psychological explanation in terms of functionally distinct subjects in an individual, because one may always resort to the alternative methods of description discussed earlier. And if the arguments in the preceding two sections are correct, Plato's argument and those methods of redescription may all presuppose that the domain of the mental is inherently more determinate or

156

distinct than it actually is. But even if there were no persuasive reasons for challenging the utility of the law of non-contradiction, or any other central feature of Plato's argument, that argument would show relatively little — indeed, much less than many of its proponents seem to have thought.

Most notably, even if Plato's argument were to succeed in establishing the need for multiple subjects, it would not, by itself, determine what sort of subjects they are. At most, that argument would demonstrate the importance of positing what we might call *logically distinct subjects* for certain apparently incompatible predicates. That is, we might have to say that the subjects of those predicates are not *strictly* identical (in some suitably strong sense of 'strict' — e.g., satisfying Leibniz's Law). But that is scarcely more interesting than claiming (á la Heraclitus) that one cannot step into the same river twice, or (more relevantly) that I am not now strictly identical with the individual born to Mrs. Braude on April 17, 1945, because the adult Stephen Braude is F (say, bearded) and the infant Stephen Braude is not-F.

No doubt some will protest that one's distinct temporal parts *are* less impressive than what we might call one's distinct *intentional parts*. After all, we attribute incompatible predicates to a person's temporal parts only at different times, whereas we can attribute incompatible predicates to intentional parts at the same time. Hence, in the case of intentional parts, we are not dealing merely with the familiar (although conceptually complex) phenomenon of identity through change. It seems, however, that as long as we are dealing merely with failures of strict identity or the need to posit logically distinct subjects, it does not matter whether those subjects exist at the same or at different times. Generally speaking, failures of strict identity between a and b are compatible with a and b being identical in some other important respect.

In fact, in the present context, one's temporal parts seem crucially analogous to one's intentional parts. The concept of a person's temporal parts is a kind of convenient fiction; it is a philosophical construct which affords a handy and appropriate way (albeit only in certain and somewhat specialized philosophical situations) of speaking about an individual's life history. But the appropriateness of the locution does not show that a person's temporal parts are inherent divisions of the self. Sometimes we might find it appropriate to regard Braude-as-infant as a temporal part, whereas on other occasions we might consider the more specific Braude-at-age-6 months or Braude-at-October 6, 1945 to be temporal parts. But these divisions, however useful, needn't correspond to natural or built-in segments of my life history. Analogously (as we noted in Chapter 5.3), state or county borders on a map mark off parts of the country which we consider important to distinguish. But those geographical parsings needn't correspond to actual partitions on the surface of the land. The correspondences might obtain, and then again they might not; but in either case the parsings can have considerable utility.

Similarly, the appeal to intentional parts is sometimes a handy and appropriate maneuver in the attempt to explain human behavior, and intentional parts may or may not correspond to actual or natural divisions of the self. But if one's intentional parts are not simply convenient fictions (like a person's temporal parts, and some state and county borders), that must be established by a line of argument different from the one demonstrating nothing more than the utility of speaking of intentional parts. For example, one might argue, as I did in Chapter 3, that there are good reasons for regarding apperceptive centers as genuine divisions of the self. But of course, that line of argument focused on features specific to apperceptive centers, features not found in the sorts of intentional parts posited merely to explain ordinary internal conflicts.

Therefore, even if there were good reasons for saying that different parts of a person simultaneously want and do not want to drink, or know and do not know that p, they may not warrant the conclusion that those parts are more than useful fictions, much less that they they are complex or robust enough to demonstrate a deep disunity of consciousness — say, in the way distinct apperceptive centers appear to do in cases of MPD. (In Chapter 7, however, we will see that not even multiple apperceptive centers clearly demonstrate a fundamental disunity.) Moreover, even if we concluded that the intentional parts needed to explain internal conflicts are not merely convenient fictions, we cannot simply assume that those parts correspond to permanent divisions of the self or natural parts existing at some previous time. That argument would rest on the CR-principle, whose defects we examined in Chapter 5. Hence, even a successful version of Plato's argument might fail to establish the kind of multiplicity in non-dissociated persons that would support the position that in some interesting sense we are all multiples, or that the difference between multiplicity and non-multiplicity is merely one of degree and not one of kind.

At any rate, if Plato's argument is as weak as I have suggested, then there may be little reason for engaging in such speculations. That argument seems either presupposed by or explicitly invoked in most (if not all) attempts to argue for a deeply divided consciousness in normal persons. Hence, if the argument fails, there may be no grounds for positing *any* interesting sort of multiplicity in persons suffering from internal conflicts, or simply because they appear to be subjects of incompatible predicates.

6.6 A FREUDIAN VARIATION

In a recent paper, Eddy Zemach (1986) contends that Freud's arguments for the existence of an unconscious mind demonstrate instead the existence of multiple consciousnesses within one person. Although both Freud and Zemach seem to rely on a tacit and (for reasons considered earlier) possibly inappropriate appeal to the law of non-contradiction, they introduce some additional and more glaring errors, which now merit our attention.

As the reader may know, Freud argued that the inference to an unconscious mind is analogous to the everyday inference for the existence of minds in other persons. We attribute minds to others, because certain human behavior justifies the inference that it is caused by a mental state. But that inference works also in the case of our own behavior — most interestingly, in those instances where our behavior warrants the ascription of intentions of which we are consciously unaware. On the surface, then, it appears as if we can argue convincingly for the existence of other minds within ourselves.

Stated more systematically, Freud's argument (via Zemach) is as follows:

(1) Body B manifests behavior b_1, which is ordinarily sufficient to justify attributing mental state m to a subject x that we associate with B.

(2) B also manifests denial behavior b_2, which is ordinarily sufficient to attribute sincere *denial* of being in mental state m to a subject y that we associate with B.

(3) Necessarily, a mental state is a state of which its subject is conscious.[6]

(4) Therefore, since y sincerely denies being in m, y is not the subject of m.

(5) Therefore, $x \neq y$.

(6) Therefore, body B has more than one subject associated with it.

To see how this argument works, let us consider an example. Jones tells us, apparently quite sincerely, 'I'm not aware of any intention to ϕ' (or 'I don't want to ϕ'), but then Jones ϕs. Thus, we have two behaviors — a sincere avowal and an action — each of which normally warrants the ascription of a mental state. The former would ordinarily justify the inference that the individual making the avowal experienced no intention to ϕ. But the action would ordinarily justify the inference that its subject intended to ϕ. So it appears as if there must be at least two subjects within Jones, one who intended to ϕ and one who did not.

On the surface, it looks as if this argument begs the question by supposing that the same subject cannot simultaneously both intend and not intend to ϕ, which of course is the claim that Plato justified by his appeal to the law of non-contradiction. But Zemach avoids at least an overt appeal to that law and substitutes premise (3) in its place. Unfortunately, premise (3) is even more conspicuously flawed than the law of non-contradiction.

Zemach's third premise seems to be a curious relic from the days of Humean empiricism. In fact, Zemach explicitly endorses a 'Humean model of the mind [according to which] mental contents (ideas) are bits of self-conscious consciousness. Each idea is an awareness, and what it is immediately aware of is itself' (1986, p. 130). One might well protest that this position is incoherent (or at least that Hume said nothing of the kind). But even if Zemach's Humean model makes sense, it is problematic enough to sabotage his argument for multiple consciousnesses. Certainly, the model is obscure, and Zemach never clarifies what it means to be conscious of x, or aware of x, or if there is a difference between the two. For example, if ideas are bits of self-conscious consciousness or items having awareness, why does Zemach obviously take persons and other creatures to be subjects who are conscious or aware of mental states? The appeal to *subjects* of ideas seems gratuitous if ideas are themselves things that are aware. And if Zemach wants to say that both persons and ideas have awareness, in what sense is the consciousness of persons different from that of the ideas (or contents) of which they are presumably conscious? Similarly, if an idea is aware of itself immediately, in what sense of 'aware' are creatures 'aware of their surroundings' (p. 131)? And why does Zemach simultaneously endorse talk of subjects of mental states while rejecting the Kantian appeal to a transcendental ego, or a subject who is aware of his states?

Fortunately, we needn't dwell on these matters. Certain crucial features of Zemach's position are clear enough. Most important, Zemach equates the unconscious with the unknown (see, e.g., p. 131), and presumably, therefore, the conscious with the known. Apparently, then, 'S is conscious of state x' means something like 'S knows that state x obtains'. But then it is clear that Zemach's position is transparently false for reasons having nothing to do with the putative existence of multiple subjects within a person. One glaring problem is that not all of our mental states are occurrent; many are dispositional. And many of those dispositional states are revealed in our behavior *over time*. In fact, it is often *only* through the unfolding of that behavior that we learn of the existence of those states. There is simply no need to posit a subject who was aware of the states all along. (And certainly, there is no occurrent idea corresponding to the disposition, much less any sense in saying that the disposition has awareness or knowledge.)

For example, suppose it is true of Jones that he likes Smith, but not enough to risk his life for him. That mental state may be truly ascribable to Jones even before Jones discovers for himself that his feelings for Smith are limited in that way. Similarly, it is only over time that one discovers (say) a preference for companions with a penchant for whimsy, or an aversion to domineering lovers, or a dislike of musical theater. And although such dispositions may take time to manifest, persons may presumably have them all along, before realizing they have them. Indeed, we often understand that we have certain dispositions only after a considerable time, after our preferential patterns have become sufficiently clear. At first, we might wrongly think that our predilections are quite specific, rather than sweeping or systematic, and that they are merely individualized to certain particular objects. For example, we might think initially that we merely had an aversion to one or two particular domineering lovers, or one or two particular examples of musical theater, before discovering that our likes and dislikes were much more general.

Moreover, most of our memories are such that we are not conscious of them at every moment. For example, it is true to say of me that I remember the oral defense of my Ph.D. dissertation even when I am not thinking of it — that is, even when I am not conscious of any occurrent memory of that event. Similarly, while I'm absorbed in an intense conversation, I might reach instinctively for the housekey in my pocket to unlock my front door. I might not have had any occurrent memory of where my housekey was, but it was nevertheless true that I remembered where it was. Or perhaps even more relevantly, suppose I am notified that an emergency department meeting has been called, which forces me to cancel a lunch appointment I had made earlier. While I am on the phone arranging a new time to have lunch with my friend, it is true of me that I know I have an emergency department meeting to attend, and that I remember having received a phone call notifying me of that event. Indeed, my present behavior *presupposes* that knowledge and memory. But I need not have any occurrent cognitive state that we would identify as the knowledge or memory in question.

But Zemach's premise (3) is even more naive than these examples suggest. Another serious problem with it is that consciousness (or awareness) of one's intentions (desires, etc.) — that is, knowledge that the mental state obtains — often requires a certain amount of prior and relatively sophisticated knowledge or understanding of what intentions (desires, etc.) of the appropriate kind are. But merely *having* the intention (desire, etc.) does not. For example, small children, and even infants, have intentions and desires, even if they lack the conceptual categories needed to know what their intentions (desires, etc.) are — hence, to know that they have such mental states. Therefore, having a mental state does not require being conscious (aware) of it.

Moreover, even an adult's consciousness of his own mental states requires various conceptual preliminaries, including understanding what mental states of the appropriate kind are. For example, a person might be afraid of x, but not introspective, clever, or conceptually sophisticated enough to be aware of that fear. He might have to infer it from his own behavior after the fact, or have it pointed out to him. For example, I might have a fear of intimacy with a certain person, but realize it only after discovering how fearfully I behave given the opportunity for such intimacy, or only after someone explains to me how my behavior betrays my fear. Hence, before that revelation I might experience fear and not be aware of it. Similarly, Jones may not realize that his dislike of having bed sheets tucked tightly around him is a manifestation of a more general claustrophobia he knows he suffers from. Hence, because of his ignorance of that connection, he does *not* know that his preference for loose sheets is an instance of fear. Therefore, we see once again that a person may be afraid and not be conscious of it. One can easily multiply these examples. For instance, as I mentioned in Chapter 4, a sexually naive person may not recognize certain kinds of sexual desires in himself, because he does not realize that these fall within the range of human experience. Moreover, a person may be unaware of his aversion to (say) the sound of a fortepiano, and erroneously believe that he dislikes only the one or two such instruments he has heard.

We may conclude, then, that Zemach's argument is not a viable alternative to Plato's, and that it likewise fails to demonstrate the need for explaining either dissociative or non-dissociative phenomena in terms of functionally distinct subjects within a single individual. But perhaps a weaker and rather different sort of argument of multiple subjects has more promise. Perhaps we can justify positing multiple subjects simply by arguing that no compelling reason exists for maintaining that the self is deeply unified, at the very least in the case of multiple personality. So let us look once again at the dramatic phenomena of MPD, and consider what, if anything, can be said in favor of the unity of the self. After all, if we find reasons for saying that even multiples are deeply unified, then we needn't worry about the more mundane issues raised by ordinary internal conflicts.

7

THE UNITY BENEATH
MULTIPLICITY

7.1 INTRODUCTION

We saw in Chapter 3 that a multiple's apperceptive centers are distinct enough to be considered different *selves*, in what is not merely a trivial sense of that term. Since many alters are both autobiographically and indexically discontinuous from each other, to that extent they would seem to be different individuals, with corresponding distinct senses of themselves. One wonders, however, whether there is nevertheless some unity behind this diversity of apperceptive centers, some as yet unidentified and profound respect in which a multiple's apperceptive centers must be regarded, despite their relative autonomy, as functionally distinct parts of a more primitive unified whole. Certainly, some clinicians believe this is the case; in fact, one remarked to me that it seems as if a multiple's alters share a common unconscious.

Of course, we never observe a multiple's underlying self or common unconscious; rather, we observe only the subject's behavior. Still, it may be that in order to explain certain features of multiplicity the most reasonable interpretation of the evidence would be to posit some kind of underlying unity. That is what we must now consider. More specifically, we will examine reasons for rejecting what in Chapter 5 we called the *colonial* view of the self (although here I shall be using the term in a somewhat more restricted sense).[1] According to the colonialist, there is no ultimate psychological unity, only a deep and initial multiplicity of subjects, 'selves', or (for those smitten with recent work in cognitive science and artificial intelligence) 'modules' or subsystems within a person. Hence, we are born multiples in some sense — that is, we begin life as a collection of discrete states or processes (at the very least) or actual personalities (at most). These elements of the self undergo various evolutionary changes and developments — even types of integration, coordination, or cooperation — but they neither require nor display a deeper form of unification or synthesis.[2] From this perspective, one of a person's basic challenges in life is to find a way to organize these primitive and inherently distinct 'sides' of ourselves. And presumably, MPD illustrates graphically what happens when the ordinary strategies for organizing and coordinating those elements breaks down. Hence, what needs explaining, according to the colonialist, is not so much the apparently novel disunity found in MPD, but the semblance of unity maintained by most non-multiples most of the time.

7.2 TWO TYPES OF UNITY

Recently, Wilkes (1988) has offered a detailed and illuminating discussion of the unity of consciousness and its relevance to the concept of personhood. She correctly observes that gaps or breakdowns in the unity or continuity of consciousness (or experience) do not usually count against viewing an individual as one person. Indeed, when we consider periods of dreamless sleep, extensive memory gaps, and massive psychological conflicts, it is clear that 'our judgments of "sameness of person" allow for disunities and discontinuities on a large scale' (p. 105). That is why we do not routinely regard hypnotic subjects experiencing negative hallucinations or manifesting 'hidden observers' as more than one person. We quite naturally assume that it is one and the same person who experiences certain kinds of hypnotically-induced disunities and discontinuities. Thus, Wilkes properly observes that these dissociated states 'show how weakly the prejudice in favour of the unity and continuity of consciousness often needs to be taken' (p. 109). Hence, if MPD is to support the view that a multiple is (in some important sense) more than one person or self or that the multiple has more than one mind, it cannot simply be on the grounds of mental disunity and discontinuity.

Of course, colonialists would maintain that some disunities are deeper than others, and that the deepest ones (found in MPD) are explainable only in terms of functionally distinct agents, *whether or not* this gives us reason to call the multiple more than one person. (We will examine some varieties of personhood in the next chapter.) And that position seems correct, at least up to a point. As we saw in Chapter 3, only multiplicity seems to require positing the existence of two or more apperceptive centers in one person, never mind how that concession impacts on the concept of a person. The task before us now is to see whether there are grounds for positing the existence and activity of a unifying 'self' even deeper than the distinct apperceptive centers in MPD.

And, indeed, it appears that the aforementioned clinician's intuition is on the right track (whether or not we should regard the unifying self as a common 'unconscious'). Granted, our mental lives exhibit numerous, pervasive, and sometimes quite profound sorts of disunities and discontinuities. Nevertheless, certain features of experience seem to presuppose a type of psychological unity that can only be explained adequately in terms of a single underlying subject, even in cases of MPD. To see why, we must first look closely at a distinction that Wilkes correctly draws, but on which she does not lavish the attention it deserves. It is a distinction between two kinds of unity of consciousness, or what Wilkes describes as a distinction between the *unity* and *continuity* of consciousness.

To begin with, we must digress briefly to the modern history of philosophy and review Kant's response to Hume's skeptical reflections on the self.[3] Hume had noted that the self is never observed as an item in experience. No matter how carefully one introspects in the search for the self, one can never go behind or beyond one's experiences to encounter the thing *that has* those experiences. Rather, one only finds another experience. Hume concluded, therefore, that we are not justified in speaking of the self at all; that concept has no empirical content.

In reply, Kant pointed to a very interesting feature in all our experiences. He observed that we experience things in *sequence*, as coherent wholes spread out over time. For example, when we hear a melody, we do not merely hear the notes one by one, as if they had no connection to each other. We hear the notes as related to each other, forming a melody that exists only over time. The same is true of hearing (or reading) a sentence. We do not experience the sentence as disconnected strings of words or syllables; we experience those items as related into a meaningful whole. And Kant asked: How is this experience of a sequence of things possible? He proposed that in order for things to be experienced in sequence as connected wholes, there must be an underlying subject, a kind of synthesizing transcendental ego, for which it is a sequence. Without an undergirding ego or synthesizing self to *make* such phenomenological and conceptual connections between parts of experience, the experience of successive events as a unified whole would be impossible. Hume's mistake was to think that because the self is not an *object* of experience in the way that tables and chairs are, we have no reason to believe that there is such a thing.[4] Kant agreed that we do not observe or experience the self in that way. But he maintained that we are nevertheless justified in positing its existence, because the sorts of experiences we have could not occur in the absence of its synthesizing activity.

Notice, this dialectical move is distinct from Descartes' famous 'Cogito, ergo sum' ('I think, therefore I am'). Descartes was arguing for the existence of a thinking thing (or self) based on the mere existence of mental activity (never mind its character). Kant's point is more subtle. It focuses not on mental activity *per se*, but rather on certain of its features — in particular, its phenomenological spread and coherence. Ironically, Descartes' 'Cogito' is compatible with a Humean account of the mental, according to which the apparent cohesion and seamlessness of experience are ultimately inexplicable. Hence (although Descartes didn't recognize this), if the 'Cogito' were an acceptable inference, it could in principle establish a succession of momentary selves having no intimate connection to one another. Indeed, it is a notorious problem in Descartes' philosophy that his famous 'first principle' fails (among many other things) to establish that the self endures over time (see, e.g., Hintikka, 1962; Russell, 1912/1981). By contrast, Kant's argument for what he called (somewhat pedantically) the 'transcendental unity of apperception' shows that an enduring self is a *precondition* for having experiences of certain sorts.

But the sort of unity Kant considered was what we might more perspicuously call *diachronic* unity; this ties together successive parts of experience and is what Wilkes calls 'continuity'. Another sort of unity we might call *synchronic*; this connects simultaneous parts of experience and is what Wilkes calls 'unity'. Failures in these two sorts of unity might then be called (following Wilkes), 'diachronic gaps' and 'synchronic splits'.

Notice, though, that a Kantian argument can also show that a synthesizing self is presupposed in the synchronic unity of experience. If we grant that the activity of a transcendental ego is needed to explain the diachronic unity of such experiences as hearing a melody and understanding a sentence, consider what is required to explain our ability to experience as *simultaneous* two or more diachronically unified experiences — for example, hearing a melody *while* understanding a spoken (or written) sentence. Just as there must be a synthesizing self for a sequence of events to be experienced as a sequence, one would think that there must be a synthesizing self for simultaneously occurring (and diachronically continuous) events to be experienced together. Kant's point was that we need to posit a synthesizing self to account for a specific kind of phenomenological spread and coherence of experienced events — what we might regard as phenomenological *breadth*, or perhaps a *horizontal* cohesiveness in experience (running from earlier to later). But experience also has phenomenological *depth*, or a *vertical* dimension, resulting from the synthesis of two or more simultaneously occurring and diachronically continuous events. We often experience two distinct events, not simply as alternating or as disconnected. Rather, we experience them together and as standing in various sorts of simultaneous relations to each other. But since a synthesizing self is required to explain the horizontal connectedness of experience, presumably the same is true in the case of experiencing the vertical connectedness of experience. Just as there must be a self for a sequence of events to be experienced as a sequence, there must be a self for simultaneous events to be experienced as simultaneous.

For example, a person can hear a melody while reading, or drive a car while carrying on a conversation (and also while adjusting the rear view mirror). Granted, there may be cases in which the simultaneously occurring activities are experienced as rapidly alternating. In fact, one of the activities may even be dissociated from conscious awareness. We saw in Chapter 4 that overlearned or automatic behaviors (such as driving a car) often seem to qualify as dissociated. Nevertheless, most (if not all) readers have had the experience of synchronically unifying two (or more) distinct events or processes within oneself. And when that happens, we experience the two as occurring together, and as being related to each other vertically. Our experience is not simply (say) listening to music for a brief period and then reading, and then listening to music again. Rather, we listen to music *while* reading, and the simultaneity of the two diachronically continuous processes is part of what we experience. Indeed, numerous additional examples come to mind readily.

For instance, one might watch an instructor write a sentence on the blackboard (and understand the sentence) while copying it (or while carrying on a conversation with one's neighbor). Similarly, one might carry on a conversation with one's date and simultaneously experience sexual arousal (indeed, one might also be simultaneously aware that the former is providing the occasion for the latter). Again, one might simultaneously watch a movie and listen to the annoying conversation from the couple in the next row (and at the same time entertain angry thoughts over their lack of consideration). And again, one might simultaneously attend to the progress of and discomfort caused by a gastro-intestinal examination while discussing the procedure with one's physician and also while listening to the insipid music in the doctor's office and reflecting on its incongruity (or on the irony of the fact that the band is playing 'These Foolish Things').

We should also note that experienced events are never literally instantaneous but are instead always spread out over some (possibly quite brief) period of time. Hence, all such experiences (or at least parts of them) will be diachronically unified for the period during which they occur. In fact, even during breakdowns of more-or-less long-term diachronic continuity (such as bouts of amnesia), parts of one's experience nevertheless exhibit various sorts of diachronic and synchronic unity. For example, most sufferers of amnesia (including short-term amnesia) are still able to complete sentences, as well as simultaneously comprehend bits of language while doing something else (e.g., tying one's shoe laces). Similarly, persons experiencing synchronic splits (e.g., in 'hidden observer' studies) continue to experience forms of synchronic unity. For example, a person whose pain is relegated to a hidden observer may simultaneously carry on a conversation and serve coffee. Hence, even in the face of diachronic gaps and synchronic splits, we must still apparently posit the activity of self for which diachronically continuous events are unified synchronically.

But we have acknowledged the possibility — indeed, the pervasiveness — of diachronic gaps and synchronic splits in even a normal person's life, and certainly in dramatic dissociative phenomena. One may wonder, then, how far Kantian arguments can take us in the search for a kind of profound psychological unity. Hence, we need to consider whether certain features of experience require the synthesizing activity of a Kantian transcendental ego during the most massive failures of continuity and unity.

7.3 THE INDISPENSABILITY OF SYNTHETIC UNITY

As we noted earlier, although the splits between a multiple's alternate personalities may cut deep, alters nevertheless tend to overlap in many crucial respects. For example, in addition to sharing many memories, alters usually share a common language and often display the same linguistic idiosyncracies. A child alter, for instance, may talk in a conspicuously childlike way, yet share many adult words, expressions, and sometimes even physical mannerisms with 'older' alters. Perhaps the most plausible explanation for this would be that there is some single unifying intelligence or subject of experiences, dispositions, and other attributes, from which even autobiographically and indexically discontinuous alter personalities originate and from which they continue to draw when they develop their own idiosyncratic personalities. (Margolis and Margolis, 1979, argue along similar lines.)

But the overlapping of alters is apparently much more extensive than the foregoing examples would suggest, and it is extensive in ways that strengthen the case for explanations in terms of a single synthesizing ego. To see this, let us first recall some observations made in Chapter 4.2 concerning attribute-distribution among alternate personalities. We noted there that the functional specificity of alters does not require alters to have traits or abilities shared with no other alters (or split-off completely from the rest of the multiple's activities). The reason, we saw, is that when an alter expresses its characteristic function(s), it must usually draw on a range of additional or subsidiary capacities that need not be unique (or idiosyncratic) to that alter.

For example, suppose a multiple created an alternate personality whose function is to shop for groceries. Clearly, in carrying out that function the alter must rely on numerous other capacities — not simply relatively low-level perceptual and motor skills, but also a variety of other abilities and capacities, some of which require interacting with other persons. The grocery-shopping alter might need to be able to read a shopping list (or product labels), determine which product (or size of a product) is the best bargain (i.e., do arithmetic and make comparisons), ask the butcher to cut the meat in a particular way, and determine which fruit is ripe. The alter might also need to be able to interact with other shoppers (say, if someone asks for an opinion about a product, or if the shopper's cart is blocking the aisle). And of course, the alter will

170

presumably have to be able to interact with the cashier and pay for the groceries (possibly by writing a check). Similarly, sexual, angry, and helper personalities utilize various attributes and abilities in the execution of their functions. But of course, these attributes and abilities might be shared with other alters. For example, many alters might be able to understand language, read, push a cart, do simple arithmetic, write checks, and pay a cashier. Hence, we saw that what distinguishes one alter's function from that of another is a distinctive *set* or combination of traits and dispositions, any one of which might be shared with other alters.

In that case, however, the functional specificity of alters is — at the very least — compatible with the existence of a common reservoir of capacities on which all the alters rely. But if different alters can share the same capacity (e.g., the capacity to conduct financial transactions, or the capacity to listen attentively), why suppose that there are, within the person, as many different abilities to listen attentively (say) as there are alters who have the ability? The colonialist's position is that when two or more alters have the same ability (say, the ability to conduct financial transactions), the abilities of those alters are numerically distinct, similar to the way in which different human beings manifest numerically distinct instances of an ability. More generally, the colonialist contends that if n alters all have an ability of type A, then there are n discrete instances of A within the multiple, one for each alter, and there is no single ability of type A attributable to the person as a whole (and merely manifested differently in different alters). But such a proliferation of abilities of the same type seems (at best) difficult to explain and (at worst) arbitrary, pointless, and (as I will suggest in the next section) profoundly confused. Only one such ability was needed to explain the individual's behavior prior to becoming a multiple.

One might think that the colonialist position is actually more modest than I have made it out to be. Perhaps colonialists maintain only that n instances of ability A *may* be explained in terms of n different abilities, one for each alter, and that it is possible that there is only one ability of type A, attributable to the multiple as a whole. But that would be a fatal weakening of the colonialist position. It is a concession that one need not regard the various alters' manifestations of A as literally distinct abilities. But then it is not clear why one should *ever* do so.

Hence, it seems as if the colonialist must explain not only how

— and in fact, what it *means* to say that — numerically distinct abilities of the same type appear within a person, but also why one would ever have been tempted in the first place to resort to that mysterious hypothesis. After all, we have seen that there is no need to posit numerically distinct instances of an ability merely to explain how different alters exhibit the ability in idiosyncratic ways. That is easily explained in terms of different sets or combinations of abilities associated with each alter, but drawn from a common pool of capacities and dispositions attributable to a single unifying ego.

Similar observations apply even to what initially might seem to be a far less complex matter — namely, the dissociation of memories rather than more broadly-defined capacities or functions. To see the similarity, we need first to note that memories are not simply occurrent states. They are also dispositions, and the dissociation of a disposition requires not just establishing, but (more important) *maintaining* a different set of dispositions.

Consider, for example, what would be involved in dissociating the memory of a painful incident in one's past — say, an episode of sexual abuse by a parent. To begin with, dissociating that memory is a complex process having many intimate connections, not only to numerous other dispositions but also to psychological processes that occur with great regularity. It involves, among many other things, the continuing reinterpretation of past events as well as the sometimes contrived interpretation of present events (as conditions dictate), simply in the interest of obscuring the nature of the painful episode.

For example, it may involve erecting and maintaining a type of *a*sexual identity (or self-image) designed to distance oneself from one's sexuality generally, or a sexually promiscuous disposition formed to minimize one's horror of sexual encounters (of any kind). But for these coping strategies to work, it may be necessary to reconstruct one's past (and creatively interpret one's present) in order to bring various other memories and experiences into harmony with the life history one wishes to accept. And that process will likewise be ongoing, since everyday events may raise new issues or threaten to dredge up memories that would be incompatible with the story one has created. For example, it may be necessary to interpret the parent's continued sexual advances or innuendos as non-sexual, or construe those actions in some other way that preserves the desired illusion. Similarly, one may need to deflect inquiries from others who suspect that sexual abuse had occurred. And of course, it may be necessary to ignore, reinterpret, or otherwise cope actively and often with dreaded associations or memories linked to the dissociated memory, but connected with objects, persons, or locations one cannot avoid.

Clearly, this is a somewhat elaborate analogue of attempts by ordinary hypnotized subjects to preserve a suggestion in the face of events that tend to undermine it. For example, the subject who is hypnotized to *not* see the chair in front of him may struggle conspicuously to sustain the illusion. If he is told to walk toward someone standing behind the chair, the subject will not collide with the chair (as those attempting to simulate hypnosis have generally thought — see, e.g., Orne, 1971, 1972a). Rather, he walks (or stumbles) awkwardly around it. And then, when asked to explain that curious behavior, he displays confusion and perhaps consternation as he constructs a transparently artificial excuse, which he apparently accepts, despite its implausibility.

We see, then, that even humdrum dissociations — and clearly, the more dramatic and urgent ones found in MPD — are processes that exist over time and must be maintained. We have also seen that in order to remain dissociated (e.g., in the form of an alternate personality) one draws on attributes and abilities utilized for other activities as well, dissociative as well as non-dissociative. But then what would be the most plausible explanation of a person's ability to create alters (or adopt some other dissociative strategy) and then sustain that activity, all the while utilizing capacities which existed prior to dissociation and which may also be utilized in a dissociative state? Once again, it seems compelling to appeal to an underlying synthesizing subject who simply evolves into a multiple as a complex and creative response to various life situations. When the hypnotic subject resorts to what Orne called 'trance logic' and other ploys to sustain a suggested hallucination, we quite naturally explain the process with respect to a single subject. *That* one subject has certain specific needs and interests in virtue of which those particular dissociative strategies are appropriate. But since we can explain the dissociative strategies of MPD along the same lines, it is simply gratuitous to appeal to the colonial view of the self.

We can more fully appreciate the plausibility of this position by examining it from another angle. So far, we have focused primarily on the issues of overlapping abilities and the maintenance of dissociation. Now we should focus more closely on the topics of synthesis and adaptation. Notice first an important point about non-multiples, and non-dissociated individuals generally. For all such individuals there is a vital phenomenological datum that must be explained, and for which a Kantian explanation seems unavoidable — namely, the diachronic and synchronic unity of experience. But that unity is present even in the case of internal conflicts. For example, one may want both to go to the movies (rather than study for an exam) and to study for the exam (rather than go to the movies). Each desire is unified diachronically, and both conflicting desires are unified synchronically for the same subject. Indeed, without that synchronic unity, one could not experience the conflict of desires within oneself. For that experience to occur, there must be a synthesizing subject for whom the conflicting needs, desires, etc., conflict. If those needs, desires, etc., were only successive and did not overlap, the subject would not experience them as a present, occurrent internal conflict. At best, he would remember the previous need, desire, etc., as something he *had* felt. But of course, a previous and no longer existing desire to ϕ does not conflict with a present desire to not-ϕ. But then, if a kind of Kantian transcendental synthesizing self is needed in order to experience an internal conflict, the colonial view seems profoundly inadequate.

A number of related points lead to that conclusion. First of all, the ability to dissociate into alternate personalities *initially* is best explained in terms of a single pre-dissociative individual's experience of trauma, desire or need to cope with it, and ability to dissociate (i.e., *that* individual's experiences, needs, and high hypnotizability). One would think that we must continue to appeal to *that* individual's experiences and hypnotic ability to explain subsequent dissociative adaptational responses. That is, it seems plausible to explain later dissociations with respect to the same pre-dissociative synthesizing self that orchestrated (and needed to orchestrate) the initial dissociations.

More important, however, it is not clear that the development and maintenance of MPD make any sense without appealing to a single underlying synthesizing self. For one thing, in order to explain why subjects dissociate in certain ways rather than others (or form a certain set of alters rather than a different kind of set), it seems we must point to certain kinds of traumas or conflicts in the patient's (pre-dissociative) past, relative to which the dissociations are adaptationally appropriate. But since those traumas presumably all happened to the same subject, and since the conflicts and needs to which the traumas lead seem to make sense *only* with respect to a single agent, the subsequent dissociative coping strategies (and ongoing attempts to sustain them) likewise seem to make sense only with respect to a single agent.

For example, suppose that one alter's principal function involves suppressing a memory, while another's function involves recovering (or maintaining) awareness of it. Clearly, that conflict of interests does not force us to conclude that the alters are not more deeply unified, just as we are not forced to posit a deep disunity in the case of ordinary internal conflicts generally, including conflicts of moral principles (e.g., we may want simultaneously not only to be truthful but also to protect the feelings of others). Indeed, we saw in Chapter 6 that conflicts of needs, interests, or desire do not demand explanation in terms of different subjects within a person — and certainly not necessarily with respect to anything but logically distinct subjects. But more important, it now appears that we can best explain the creation of these (rather than different) alters relative to different aspects of a *single* subject's experiences, needs and interests — for example, short-term rather than long-term interests, or the desire to minimize pain and the often conflicting desire to know the truth.

Consider: if two alters (or their correlates) existed prior to dissociation (i.e., prior to developing the overt condition of MPD), multiplicity would make little or no sense adaptationally. In particular, it would be difficult to explain the causal role of the traumatic events that apparently triggered the dissociative response. If one pre-dissociative subject within the multiple needed to suppress a memory and another such subject needed to maintain awareness of it, there is not clearly a conflict that demands resolution of any kind. Similarly, if two (bodily) distinct persons had corresponding different needs, they would not necessarily have to find any way to resolve the differences.

Colonialists might respond that the traumatic events play a causal role, not in the *existence* of alters, but rather in their *appearance* or *emergence*. Hence, they might contend that the alters (or their correlates — perhaps even corresponding apperceptive centers) existed all along, and that despite continued attempts at cooperation various conflicts of interest get in the way, making it difficult to present a unified, coherent, or simply functional or

175

reliable 'self' to the world. Thus (they would argue), distinctive sorts of traumas initiate a struggle for dominance or control and simply elicit the overt manifestation of alters of the appropriate type.

It seems to me, however, that this maneuver has little plausibility and that it is actually difficult to reconcile with the conspicuous trauma-specificity and appropriateness of alters. For one thing, even if we grant that conflicts in cases of multiplicity may be interpreted as existing between distinct individuals, in many (if not all) cases of multiplicity there is reason to believe that the subject *experienced* trauma-induced conflicts prior to becoming a multiple. But that particular experience of conflicting needs, interests, etc. (relative to which alter-appearance would be a creative solution), seems to make sense only with respect to a single subject who synthesizes those conflicting needs, etc., synchronically. But in that case it seems plausible (if not obvious) that alters would be created — and, moreover, created by *that single subject* to deal with the trauma.

Second, from the colonialist's perspective a multiple's high hypnotizability becomes needlessly mysterious (if not entirely irrelevant). Indeed, it would seem to sever the quite obvious connection between multiplicity and other forms of dissociation, since on the colonial view it is unclear why the appearance of alters is dissociative at all. The alters (or their correlates) existed already on that view and had only to be called forth by triggering events.

Third (as we observed in Chapter 5), colonialists would be committed to an absurdly inflated inventory of pre-dissociative selves, waiting in the wings (so to speak) for the right kind of events to trigger their appearance. Colonialists cannot wriggle away from that problem by arguing that only *some* alters (or their correlates) existed pre-dissociatively and that others are created later. That would be a fatal concession that alters need not have pre-dissociative correlates. If some alters are merely products of dissociation, then one would think that they can *all* be. It becomes both arbitrary and gratuitous to single out certain alters (rather than others) as pre-dissociatively significant. And of course, colonialists cannot argue that trauma-appropriate alters (or selves) existed within the multiple all along just because they do now; that inference relies on the discredited CR-principle.

So far, our consideration of the adaptational nature of MPD has concentrated primarily on alter-appropriateness. But some additional observations on MPD as an apparently creative adaptive strategy now merit our attention. Notice first that alter-formation is only one of many possible ways of handling an intolerable situation, even for persons who are highly hypnotizable. An abuse victim needn't become a multiple. For example, she could simply yield and adopt a kind of attitude of acceptance (which itself can take various forms); she could respond violently and strike back; she could commit suicide and (in effect) decide not to cope more actively with the abuse; she could dissociate the trauma and develop amnesia for the episodes she could not accept; or she could dissociate more radically and become a multiple. Hence, alter-formation seems to be merely one of a number of adaptational options, and an apparently creative one at that.

In fact, a multiple can apparently develop any number of *different* alters as appropriate responses to a specific kind of abuse. For example, in order to cope with parental incest, the subject might develop an alter who is sexually indifferent and who yields passively to the parent's advances. Or, she might develop a sexually lustful alter who reacts more enthusiastically. Or, she might develop an aggressive and protective alter (possibly of the opposite sex) whose function is to hate the parent and respond violently to the parent's advances. Hence, in those cases where victims of childhood sexual abuse cope by developing alternate personalities, they need not create any particular *kind* of alter (say, a sexual alter). That, too, seems to be merely one of a number of different adaptational options.

Moreover, alter-formation is often *maladaptive* in some respects, in the way many of our life decisions are: When the decisions fail they may fail miserably, or they may help in some ways while creating new problems. For example, the alter one develops in response to parental sexual abuse may not succeed in minimizing the trauma; it might even exacerbate the situation. In that case the subject might develop an alter of a different sort. But even if the initial alter helps with the sexual abuse, it may create further difficulties in other areas of life — say, at school. In that case, the subject might have to develop yet another alter to deal with that situation. It appears, in fact, as if alter-formation is intelligently guided, at least in the early stages before it becomes more habitual.

Ross (1989, p. 123) argues that the question, 'Where do alter personalities come from, and who or what creates them?', 'prompts transcendental hypotheses. There seems to be a higher organizing principle or intelligence responsible for the rules and structure of the system'. (Interestingly, Ross compares this line of reasoning to the Argument from Design.) But whether or not we decide to regard adaptive responses as rule-governed and intelligent rather than more brutely instinctual (and that itself is a complex topic worthy of scrutiny), an important question remains: To what subject — or to how many subjects — do we attribute the ability to respond in one way rather than another, or the ability to respond successively in different ways (e.g., after earlier attempts fail)?

Notice that if a non-multiple were to respond to a stressful or traumatic situation in a similar manner, we would not hesitate to interpret the responses as attempts, *by that (single) person*, to cope with the pain of certain life situations. For example, suppose a child created an imaginary playmate to whom she could confide the horrible things she could not express to others. Or suppose she retreated whenever possible into an imaginary world where life was always pleasant and where parents invariably treated their children with kindness and love. And suppose the child eventually finds new ways of dealing with her pain, either as replacements for the old ways or simply as additions to those methods. For example, she could develop selective amnesia, turn to drugs or alcohol for escape, run away from home, or start taking out her rage on her siblings or friends. Clearly, we would explain the totality of the child's responses with respect to a single subject — in this case, the victim herself — who first experiences pain and conflict, and who then executes the strategies for dealing with them. Hence, we would say it is the same individual who, in the face of certain experiences, tries coping in a number of ways — for example, by retreating initially into an imaginary world, and at other times by means of amnesia or by escaping into a drugged stupor. And it is the same individual who, when one coping strategy fails to relieve the pain, resorts to a different tactic.

But presumably the same would be true of the victim who copes in a more dramatically dissociative manner by becoming a multiple, and who continues to split as part of an ongoing adaptational response to difficult circumstances. In fact (as I suggested earlier), the proliferation of alters in dramatically polyfragmented cases seems particularly mysterious from the colonialist point of view. Why should there be so many alters or alter-fragments?

178

Were they all present before the subject became a multiple? And if some of them are produced dissociatively (say, only the fragments, or only those alters who appear relatively late in the game), why not say all were? Naturally, if we posit a single synthesizing self undergirding the beginning and maintenance of MPD, the proliferation of alters is relatively easy to explain. Presumably the reason a multiple may develop a large inventory of alters is because dissociation has become the dominant coping mechanism of *that one subject*. The subject who dissociated initially by forming an alternate personality is the same as the subject who now habitually dissociates in the face of nearly every uncomfortable situation, creating numerous alters or fragments in the process.

The challenge for the colonialist, then, is complex, and seems to be overwhelming. A number of related matters must be explained together, all of which are easily accommodated only by positing a single synthesizing subject undergirding even the disunity of MPD. One must explain (a) the apparent adaptational nature of alter formation, and alter-appropriateness in general; (b) not only the initial appearance of alters but also the continued creative adaptations required to sustain or maintain them; (c) why those sustaining activities should be explained relative to multiple subjects, whereas the apparently analogous sustaining activities required for ordinary hypnotic dissociations are best explained relative to a single subject; (d) more generally, why if MPD is not genuinely dissociative (since on the colonial view alters or their correlates existed from the beginning), there are so many similarities between MPD and numerous less dramatic dissociative phenomena likewise most plausibly explained in terms of a single subject;[5] (e) the relevance of the fact that multiples seem significantly hypnotizable compared to non-multiples; (f) the pervasive overlapping of abilities between alters, which strongly suggests a shared reservoir of capacities attributable to a single unifying subject — namely, the multiple as a whole; (g) the apparent impossibility of *experiencing* an internal conflict without there being a single synchronically and diachronically synthesizing self for whom it is a conflict; and (h) the proliferation of alternate personalities and fragments in cases of polyfragmented MPD.

One last point, before moving on to a related topic. When Plato argued for the parts of the soul, he began by assuming some sort of unity of the self, and then he argued that internal conflicts demonstrate that the self is actually composed of parts underlying

179

that apparent unity. Now quite apart from the defects in that argument examined in Chapter 6, one of the arguments in this section, if sound, turns Plato on his head. I have begun by granting a kind of parthood or disunity — the existence of distinct apperceptive centers within multiples and the existence of at least logically distinct subjects within non-multiples — and have argued that the phenomenology of internal conflicts as well as other vertical features of experience demonstrate the need to posit a deeper unity of the self.

7.4 MAKING SENSE OF ABILITIES

We have been considering various obstacles facing the colonial view of the self. Now, we need to look more closely at perhaps the deepest underlying reason for those difficulties. It appears as if colonialists are caught in the grip of a seductive but misleading picture of abilities, personality traits, and other human capacities, and that by correcting the picture we can rob the colonial view even of its surface appeal.

We had a glimpse of the problem earlier, when we observed that an alternate personality's idiosyncratic abilities or capacities involve numerous other subsidiary capacities and traits which need not be unique (or idiosyncratic) to that alter. In the last section, however, we were concerned with the *explanatory* difficulties this posed for the colonialist. Now, we must consider how our earlier observation points to an even more fundamental problem with the colonial view.

The problem, in general terms, is that the colonial view quite subtly and perniciously treats an alternate personality's capacities, personality traits, etc., as things of a kind they could not possibly be — almost as if they were *objects* or *possessions* (like articles of jewelry). A necklace, for example, is the sort of thing which can have numerous (and numerous kinds of) instantiations. It can be replicated (with varying degrees of success) and its instances (or replicas) can come in many varieties. In this respect, at least, a necklace is indeed similar to a human capacity (trait, etc.), which likewise may exist in many people and in many forms. However, necklaces also have rather clear spatial boundaries and are easily isolable from each other. Hence, there is no problem in understanding how different necklaces (or different versions of the same necklace) can be possessed by different individuals. But the fatal temptation to which colonialists apparently succumb is to regard the capacities (traits, etc.) of different alters as if they were analogously distinguishable or separable.

The problem, clearly, is that an alternate personality's capacities, abilities, traits, skills, etc., are not comparably (much less literally) isolable features of a person. Rather, they are complex, overlapping, and indefinite webs of dispositions. Capacities, etc., overlap in the sense that the subsidiary capacities, etc., on which they rely may also be components of other capacities. And they are indefinite insofar as there is no way *in principle* to specify either in advance or in general what the features of a capacity (personality trait, etc.) are, even for a single person — for example, which other attributes one might need, or which sorts of activities one might have to engage in, in order to display that capacity (trait, etc.). That is because a capacity (trait, etc.) is both dispositional and typically as multifaceted as the virtually unlimited range of situations in which it can be expressed. Hence, unlike necklaces, there are no clear distinguishing features of a capacity (trait, etc.) or sharp boundaries separating one capacity (trait, etc.) from another. For that matter, there are no clear boundaries separating a capacity (trait, etc.) from nearly everything else a person may do.

Consider, for example, an ability found in many (but by no means all) employees in retail clothing stores — namely, the ability to take charge of the store while the manager goes to the bank. Clearly, this is not something having a complete or definite — much less antecedently specifiable — set of properties. Nor is it the sort of thing that can be isolated from the rest of the employee's traits and abilities. To begin with, it involves numerous motor and perceptual skills utilized in other capacities. But more interesting, in order to watch the store while the manager is away, the employee must draw on an enormous repertoire of additional and often comparably multifaceted capacities. One can't give a final (much less necessary and sufficient) list of these capacities, since one can't specify the virtually unlimited range of situations the employee *might* have to confront. Nevertheless, it is easy to anticipate certain of those situations, and thereby convey some of the richness of the capacity. The employee will presumably have to deal with customers, handle phone calls, talk to manufacturer's representatives, be pleasant to people she dislikes, work the register, turn away beggars, detect shoplifters, restrain unruly children while the parent tries on clothes, give instructions to (and possibly reprimand) another employee, dust and organize displays, not to mention being able to assist customers in the selection and care of clothing and (accordingly) make numerous aesthetic decisions about color, shapes, etc., as well as decisions about what customers will find pleasing. Moreover, there are numerous other capacities that the employee might have to draw on in the event of less predictable sorts of situations, such as an unexpected (or incorrect) delivery of merchandise, a broken register, a customer becoming ill, a group of rowdy teenagers, not to mention a robbery at gunpoint, fire in the stockroom, leaky roof, or a storewide electrical blackout.

And of course each of these various skills will involve many others. For example, to be able to deal with phone callers, salespersons, parents and their children, shoplifters, etc., a retail manager must utilize a broad and indefinite set of capacities common to the full range of human interactions. Similarly, the ability to advise customers on clothing is not clearly separable from the employee's ability to dress properly for work (or other occasions) or the ability to make aesthetic and other sorts of appropriate decisions in many areas of life (such as in decorating one's home or purchasing gifts).

Consider another example. The personality trait of being gregarious and friendly is not clearly separable from a person's other abilities and traits. It involves (among many other things) the ability to make conversation and the ability to talk to strangers (or mingle at parties). In some people, it may also involve the ability to host parties, go on blind dates, and actively participate in clubs or other organizations. But of course, all these abilities likewise involve a complex network of dispositions common to an enormous number of other traits and capacities. For example, the ability to make conversation is many-sided and is exhibited in varying degrees and styles. It involves not only the ability to use language but also (among many other things) the ability to pay attention to what others are saying, discuss unfamiliar subjects, and respond relevantly and appropriately. And once again, those abilities draw on a range of subsidiary capacities that extend throughout a broad spectrum of human activities. For example, in order to respond relevantly and appropriately in a conversation, one must be able to avoid cutting people off or in some other way dominating the conversation, determine when it is acceptable to change the subject or when it is important to suppress one's own opinion, show interest in what others are saying, draw people out by asking pertinent questions, etc. Moreover, the ability to respond relevantly and appropriately strongly overlaps with one of its subsidiary abilities — namely, the ability to show interest in what others are saying. Both require (among many other things) the ability to *understand* what others are saying (e.g., detect hidden messages or meanings behind people's words) and the ability to ascertain when a person is joking, teasing, insecure in one's opinions, revealing intimate secrets, fishing for compliments, being defensive, etc., so that one can determine whether to laugh, praise, express sympathy, seek additional information, feign horror in an appropriately jocular way, etc.

Die-hard colonialists might contend that the sorts of capacities (traits, etc.) I have been discussing (e.g., the ability to make conversation or manage a store) are not paradigmatic of human capacities generally. They might insist that paradigm human capacities are simple, basic sorts of dispositions that *are* clearly distinguishable from one another, and on which more complex capacities (such as those distinguishing one alter from another) are based or in terms of which they may be analyzed.

But at best, this maneuver is both irrelevant and self-defeating, and it also seems to be rather naive philosophically and methodologically. It is irrelevant because the colonialist hopes to explain the functional specificity of alternate personalities with respect to distinct isolable sets of capacities (traits, etc.) manifested by different alters. But the sorts of capacities and personality traits that in fact distinguish one alter from another are precisely the kind that overlap profoundly and cannot be isolated from each other.

For that reason (and somewhat ironically), it would be counterproductive for the colonialist to argue that high-level capacities and personality traits are analyzable in terms of lower-level capacities and skills. Quite apart from the profound deficiencies afflicting mechanistic analyses of the mental generally (see Braude, 1979, 1986a; Goldberg, 1982; Heil, 1981), that claim would work against the colonialist even if it were correct. Since the distinguishing features of alters overlap in the ways just considered, then if they could be analyzed in terms of more primitive traits and capacities, that would actually *support* the position that the distinct personalities of alters all issue from (or are explainable in terms of) a single reservoir of traits, etc., attributable to the multiple as a whole.

Moreover, quite apart from the details of anti-mechanistic arguments (which are too involved to consider here), it would be
surprising — if not totally unprecedented — if an alter's distinguishing traits, etc., could be analyzed in terms of putatively basic
traits, skills, and so on. That is because theories about human (or
organic) behavior modeled on allegedly simple cases have invariably failed to handle more interesting complex cases. And the
reason for that unimpressive track record is not difficult to fathom
(space does not permit detailed argument here; the reader will have
to settle for more of a methodological manifesto). The standard —
but completely wrongheaded — view in philosophy and the behavioral sciences is that human (organic) activities can be treated in a
manner analogous to that adopted in mathematics and the 'hard'
sciences. We assume that simple cases are (or are at least closest
to) a kind of theoretical ideal, and then we regard more complex
cases, not only as built up from, but also as increasingly degenerate instances of, the simple ideal cases.

This approach has led to some by now familiar theoretical
abominations. For example, in the philosophy of language it has
been customary to treat a sentence such as 'the cat is on the mat'
as paradigmatic — that is, as revealing some set of purportedly
fundamental features of language. The challenge is then to explain
how more characteristic sorts of human utterances exhibit (with
varying degrees of perspicuity) the principles or models developed
to analyze the more 'basic' sentences. But this approach has never
succeeded in yielding an adequate understanding of human linguistic behavior, or even a decent theory of meaning. Curiously, however, its proponents seldom grasp that the problem began right
from the start, in assuming that apparently simple sentences are
representative of language use generally. If we assume instead that
more complex or overtly ambiguous sorts of utterances are paradigmatic — for example,

(1) I wouldn't be caught dead in there.
(2) Jones wants to do something more with his life.

and (a terrific example from Goldberg, 1982),

(3) He didn't want to spend another year being Dr. No.

it is no mystery why the standard approach has failed. It has failed
because the 'simplicity' of a sentence like 'the cat is on the mat'
is largely artificial. That sentence, in fact, can be more profitably

viewed as a degenerate example of the more complex and ambiguous sorts of utterances that typify ordinary language use. From this perspective, the apparent simplicity of 'the cat is on the mat' is a kind of deficiency; it results from abstracting out or ignoring many pervasive and important features of language use (see Goldberg, 1982, for a good presentation of this opposing viewpoint). So it is no wonder that most human sentences fail to fit neatly into the procrustean linguistic theories developed, as it were, from the bottom up.

I submit that we would be making an analogous error if we assumed that there are simple, theoretically ideal, human capacities (traits, etc.) of which the multifaceted capacities and personality traits considered earlier are merely degenerate instances. It is more likely and more reasonable to suppose that the ability to make conversation (or to be gregarious, conciliatory, helpful, sensual, or sarcastic, or the ability to do well on multiple-choice tests, chair a philosophy department, project an air of confidence while interviewing for a job, or make commitments in relationships) are paradigmatic of human abilities, and that the apparent (or at least relative) simplicity of (say) the ability to raise one's arms or eyebrows, swallow, bend one's knees, or even the ability to brush one's teeth is a sign of how theoretically uninteresting and unilluminating those dispositions are.

Incidentally, it is interesting to note that subsidiary capacities do *not* tend to become increasingly simple, as one would expect if (as some colonialists and many workers in cognitive science like to maintain) capacities (traits, etc.) are built-up from a base of primitive (or atomic) functions hard-wired into specific discrete subsystems of the human machine. It is not that one cannot find certain capacities, etc., that are quite simple (e.g., the ability to blink, make a fist, or the more complex ability to hold a spoon). Rather, the point is that capacities, etc., do not fall into a natural (much less, a single) hierarchical system in which initially simple or basic items combine to form ever increasingly complex items. For example, the ability to express sympathy is no simpler than the ability to show interest in what others are saying. It merely involves a different extensive range of dispositions. Similarly, the ability to show interest in what others are saying is no more primitive than the ability to respond appropriately; the ability to respond appropriately is no less broad than the ability to make conversation; and the ability to make conversation is no simpler than the ability to be gregarious and friendly or the ability to manage a store. In each case, we are merely systematizing and categorizing a broad range of overlapping and interlocking human activities and dispositions, and drawing connections between distinctive sets of regularities and descriptive categories. We are not gradually approaching some single (much less inherently primitive) level of description.

Now if the foregoing remarks are on the right track, it is not even remotely plausible to suppose that the functional specificity of alternate personalities can be explained with reference to nothing deeper than '*lots of subsystems doing their own thing* without any central supervision' (Dennett, 1991, p. 358). We have seen that there *is* no clear thing that each alter does, much less something isolable from things other alters do. Similarly, we can see the inadequacy of Spiegel's contention (1990, p. 128) that alters are analogous to 'separate nets' or 'coherent subunits' in a parallel distributed processing model of the mind.

And this helps us to see why the somewhat fashionable comparison of a multiple (or human being) to a termite colony is ultimately rather shallow. The issue is not whether there are collections of individuals (such as termite colonies) whose overall coordination and apparent integration lead us to ascribe intentional properties to the colony as a whole (rather than to individuals or some overseeing intelligence). Undoubtedly, that is an acceptable practice in many contexts, although even in the case of termite colonies it remains unclear whether or to what extent it is merely a figure of speech to say that 'the colony as a whole builds elaborate mounds, gets to know its territory, organizes foraging expeditions, sends out raiding parties against other colonies, and so on' (Dennett, 1991, p. 358).[6] (It is clearly a figure of speech to attribute similar intentional properties to a country or government.) The problem for the colonialist is that there was never any reason *initially* for thinking that the comparison of a person to a termite colony was appropriate. We saw in Chapter 6 that mere conflicts within a person do not require positing distinct subsystems, one for each side in the conflict. And in this chapter, we have made two even more important observations. First, the personal conflicts and coping strategies at issue in the case of MPD seem to make sense only relative to a deeper synthetic psychological unity. And second, the functional specificity of alternate personalities actually discourages the appeal to distinct subsystems lacking a deeper unity, since the capacities, etc., that distinguish different alters are overlapping and interlocking parts of a *single individual's* full range of dispositions.

In fact, it appears as if the colonial view is unable to explain one of the most interesting features of MPD — namely, the (sometimes only) partial integration and re-disintegration of a multiple along *novel functional lines*. This seems understandable only from the perspective on capacities, etc., sketched above. If a multiple were merely a collection of discrete subsystems each doing their own (isolable) thing, it would be very difficult to understand how the multiple could become a different collection of discrete individuals each doing their own new thing. Since on the colonial view there is no shared pool of capacities, etc., from which alters draw, presumably one would have to posit processes within the person analogous to the birth and death (or worse, the sudden creation and disappearance) of members of a termite colony. This problem is clearest for colonialists who compare alters to subsystems (or modules) of the brain with their functions 'hard-wired', or to 'mutually inaccessible "directories" of stored information' in a computer (Dennett, 1991, p. 363). On the other hand, once we grasp that an alter's 'thing' is really no more than an arrangement of dispositions overlapping and intimately linked to other such arrangements within a single system of dispositions attributable to a unifying ego, it is not hard to imagine that the dispositions might get periodically rearranged or reorganized, and it is easy to grasp how those rearrangements might be intelligently guided and adaptationally appropriate. Similarly, it is not puzzling that this process of reorganization could be sudden.

7.5 MULTIPLICITY WITHIN UNITY

Let us assume, then, that the foregoing remarks are on the right track and that we are justified in positing a Kantian unity of the self underlying the dramatic splits of multiple personality. How, one might wonder, does that affect the position taken in Chapter 3, that alternate personalities are distinct apperceptive centers, autobiographically and indexically discontinuous from one another?

The answer, quite simply, is that the conclusions of this chapter are compatible with those of Chapter 3. That is, even if it is true that we must posit a transcendental ego in order to explain various central features of MPD, it may nevertheless be the case that alters are phenomenologically and epistemologically distinct in the ways described earlier. If the arguments in this chapter are sound, they would show, at most, that the dramatic disparities between alternate personalities rest ultimately on an even deeper psychological unity. But that would not force us to conclude that the disparities between alters are only apparent. If (as I have suggested) a kind of unifying Kantian ego underlies the phenomena of multiple personality, it would not be something that reveals itself as an item of experience. (In fact, that was part of Kant's point against Hume.) Rather, a Kantian or transcendental unity of consciousness would be revealed in the *form* of our experiences — say, in their diachronic and synchronic connectedness. Similarly, I suggest, it is revealed subtly in the overlapping and interlocking abilities of alters and in the adaptational nature of alter formation. Nevertheless, on a level of experience much closer to the surface of awareness, alters are distinct in the ways described in Chapter 3. Hence, we can hold both that alters are distinct psychic entities and also that a unifying self or ego is a precondition for their existence.

Similarly, if my speculations in section 7.4 about the nature of abilities are correct, it would seem as if a form of psychological unity is a precondition for the functional distinctness of alters. We have seen not only that an alter's characteristic functions inevitably overlap with those of other alters, but also that they cannot literally be isolated from a common pool of dispositions attributable to the multiple as a whole. In that case, however, we need not deny either the reality and functional distinctness of alters or the reality and functional complexity of the underlying subject to whom the entire repertoire of abilities belongs.

Somewhat ironically, we can now see one respect in which social psychologists skeptical about MPD are correct in insisting that multiples are not really divided persons, despite the serious flaws in their position surveyed in Chapter 2.6. We have noted (a) that a single individual's repertoire of abilities and dispositions undergirds the functional distinctness of alternate personalities, and (b) that a kind of transcendental ego is needed to explain important epistemological and phenomenological features of alters, as well as the adaptational nature of alter-formation. All these observations are compatible with the social psychological claim that alter creation is an idiom of distress having considerable (if only short-term) utility to the multiple.

But these observations do not force us to conclude that multiple personality is *nothing more than* an idiom of distress, or that it is a deception or an elaborate and refined form of role playing that allows the multiple to deflect responsibility for emotionally risky or deplorable behavior (Aldridge-Morris, 1989; Kenny, 1986; Spanos, 1986; Spanos, *et al.*, 1985, 1986). No matter how convenient or useful the creation of alternate personalities might be for the multiple, alters might still be distinct centers of consciousness in the sense explained earlier — namely, indexically and autobiographically discontinuous apperceptive centers. Similarly, the subjective reality and distinctness of alternate personalities are compatible with the fact that MPD is diagnosed much more often in the United States than anywhere else (see, e.g., Boon, S. and Draijer, N.,1993; Martínez-Taboas, 1989, 1991a; Putnam, 1993; Takahashi, 1990; van der Hart, 1993; van der Hart and Boon, 1990; Vanderlinden, *et al.*, 1991). And they are perhaps even more clearly compatible with the observation that MPD (and dissociative phenomena generally) seem to conform to the cultural and social milieu in which they occur. It is well known that cases of ostensible demonic or spirit possession have generally given way (in the West, at any rate) to cases of ostensible MPD. Moreover, cases of MPD in Brazil and India and reported cases among Hispanics exhibit what appear to be idiosyncratic but appropriate culturally-specific features (see, e.g., Adityanjee, *et al.*, 1989; Goodwin, *et al.*, 1990; Krippner, 1987; Steinberg, 1990; Varma, *et al.*, 1981). But these variations in the manifestation of apparently dissociative phenomena do not indicate that alters are nothing but roles adopted by the multiple. It is clearly possible that a genuine internal process or psychological disorder is simply being expressed in different ways. Hence, one can grant the appropriateness of dissociative disorders as idioms of distress while still insisting on the reality and depth of the subjective splits they seem to reveal.

The skeptical position of the social psychologist quite properly calls attention to certain social and adaptational dimensions of multiple personality, and it reminds us that some cases of ostensible MPD might be elaborate and more or less innocent forms of duplicity. (And no doubt, we will see more and more cases of malingering as detailed information about MPD becomes more widely disseminated and as the courts continue to uphold the legal precedent set in the Milligan case — see Keyes, 1982.) But that position does not do justice to the full spectrum of phenomena observed in

MPD, and it seems particularly useless for describing their pheno-menology and epistemology — that is, for describing those phenomena at the level of the subjects' experience. Moreover, skeptical explanations in terms of deception or mere role playing do not do justice to the numerous considerations (reviewed in Chapter 3) pointing to the indexical and autobiographical distinctness of alternate personalities. But that is hardly surprising, given the transparent inadequacy of social psychological attempts to explain away the totality of hypnotic phenomena as nothing more than a form of role enactment or social compliance (see Bowers, 1990; Gauld, 1988). Perhaps the most conspicuous shortcomings of that approach appear in connection with dramatic hypnotic phenomena, such as the sorts of anesthesias reported in Chapter 1 (see e.g., Braude, 1988a; Gauld, 1988).

In fact, one would think that positing the existence of apperceptive centers actually complements a kind of social psychological perspective on multiple personality. We have seen that there are good reasons for viewing multiple personality as a subjectively genuine and distinctive psychological condition, which apparently only some people are able to produce (or perhaps to which they are unusually susceptible). But clearly, one can also maintain that this ability or proclivity is socially advantageous in various ways. Hence, one need not jettison social psychological analyses of MPD simply because one concedes that alternate personalities are subjectively distinct psychic entities. One needs only to abandon the skeptical position that a satisfactory understanding of multiple personality can be presented *solely* in terms of such things as social compliance, role playing, deception, etc.

Moreover, even when a skeptical social psychological position is illuminating, it applies only to contexts in which it is appropriate to regard the *whole person* (i.e., a biological whole) as a subject of experiences. But of course, human experience and behavior can be profitably examined from many different perspectives and on many different levels of explanation, no one of which comes even close to affording a full characterization of human beings. Indeed, there are other contexts — some of them quite independent of the phenomena of multiple personality — in which we seem justified in regarding persons as something other than biological wholes. Let us turn our attention, then, to the concept of a person.

8

PERSONS AND PERSONALITIES

8.1 INTRODUCTION

One of the more intriguing aspects of multiple personality is the challenge it poses for our understanding of the concept of a person, as well as for the related concept of a personality. At the very least, cases of MPD suggest that one person may have several different, relatively autonomous, personalities. And when those personalities are quite robust, MPD tempts us to say that a multiple is — in some sense — several distinct persons.

Of course, the latter claim is more controversial than the former. Indeed, it conflicts with well-entrenched ways of speaking about persons. For example, we do not consider the husband of a multiple to be a polygamist; we do not grant a multiple more than one vote on election day, or require each alter to have its own social security number, health insurance, or driver's license; nor would a census taker count a multiple as more than one person. Hence, in many cases we apparently assume that there cannot be a one:many relation between human bodies and persons. Similarly, although alters are, in a sense, eradicated during integration, therapists do not feel they have committed murder in integrating their patients, even though they may mourn the loss of what had been interesting and enjoyable personalities (see, e.g., M. Prince's comments on the loss of Sally in 1905/1978).

On the other hand, we often treat different alternate personalities the way alters treat each other — namely, as distinct moral or prudential agents and as distinct moral objects. In these cases, we seem to employ different criteria of personhood. For example, we often consider one alter (but not another) as praiseworthy or blameworthy for certain actions. Similarly, we might feel obligated to give different alters distinct sorts of Christmas gifts, just as we would feel it to be both right and appropriate to select characteristically different sorts of gifts for friends or family members. Moreover, alters seem to mature with age, form attachments and express idiosyncratic sets of likes and dislikes, and in general have a sense of themselves apparently similar in crucial respects to a non-multiple's own sense of self. Presumably, that is why we are able to develop different sorts of relationships with different alters. In fact, we form attachments and experience distinctive feelings for certain alters just as we do for non-multiples, even when we know we are dealing with alternate personalities rather than distinct human organisms.

Of course, the temptation to regard alters as distinct agents or persons is strongest when the alters have reasonably full-blown personalities. In certain respects, then, the concept of a person would seem to be parasitic on the concept of a personality (or vice versa). In other respects, however, those concepts may not be so related. After all, as we noted above, there seem to be different concepts of a person, and those distinct concepts might be related in quite different ways to the concept of a personality.

Indeed, it would be foolish to think that 'person' has only one meaning, or even a meaning that is clearly preferred or privileged. Throughout the history of ideas, the term has taken on numerous meanings, and in fact the language of some cultures may possess no term even roughly equivalent to 'person'. Of course, in western philosophy the term 'person' has acquired various additional and sometimes quite specialized meanings, often associated with specific metaphysical doctrines, such as substance- (or Cartesian) dualism and certain theories of personal identity. But quite apart from the often arcane conceptions of persons developed in technical western philosophy, the concept of a person varies quite dramatically from one context or community of interests to another. What counts as a person from (say) certain theological points of view may differ considerably from what counts as a person in more thoroughly legal, sociopolitical, or biological contexts. For example, one might consider a fetus to be a person according to theological, but not sociopolitical, criteria of individuation. Moreover, each of these broad contexts accomodates its own set of — often profoundly distinct — conceptions of persons. For example, as Amélie Rorty correctly observes (1988, p. 7), Hobbes, Locke, Hume, Rousseau, and Kant each articulated different concepts of a person from within a shared set of sociopolitical interests.

Now it would clearly exceed the scope of this inquiry to present a comprehensive survey and evaluation of all the different concepts of a person, or even just those that have played an important role in the history of ideas. Fortunately, our present needs are more modest — namely, to understand how multiple personality challenges general widespread assumptions about the nature of persons. Hence, we need only consider those types of personhood to which the phenomena of multiple personality seem peculiarly relevant. Moreover, if these conceptions of persons blur the customary boundaries between, or issues characteristic of (say) legal and theological contexts, that would seem to be a matter of some interest rather than a cause for concern. It would demonstrate that the problems posed by multiplicity for the concept of a person transcend certain traditional distinctions and lines of demarcation.

8.2 PERSONS AS ORGANISMS

Let us begin by distinguishing several broad types of personhood or senses of 'person'. A number of these apply only to biological wholes — in particular, to living human organisms.[1] We may therefore call them *organismic* concepts of a person. The central unifying feature of these concepts is that they require a one:one correspondence between human bodies and persons.

The first organismic type of personhood we might call *normative*. To be a person in this sense, one must possess the functional integrity (or intactness), complexity, and development necessary to participate in social processes, assume responsibilities, and incur obligations — therefore, to be held culpable and either praiseworthy or blameworthy for one's actions. And presumably, these capacities require enough rational or cognitive sophistication to be able to evaluate one's actions and reason normatively. Persons in the normative sense, then, combine two features noted separately by Rorty (1988): They are both legal entities and autonomous agents. Hence, various types of thoroughly non-functional individuals ('basket-cases') would not count as persons in this sense — for example, adults who have fallen into a permanent coma. Although they may have the functional complexity required to participate in social processes, their organisms nevertheless lack the requisite functional integrity or intactness; they are simply too functionally impaired to take advantage of their organic complexity. Similarly, individuals whose organisms, although functioning, are malfunctioning dramatically — for instance, those who are severely brain-damaged at birth and who are unable to care for themselves — would likewise not count as persons in this sense.

It should be clear that one can be a person in the normative sense of the term while playing many roles in life (e.g., parent, politician, football coach, musician), and also while having different sides or aspects of oneself that are revealed or displayed selectively to others (e.g., tenderness, sensuality, combativeness, cruelty, etc). Hence, a person in this sense is not the same as (say) a Jamesian *social self* (1890/1981, pp. 281ff). In fact, it should be obvious that someone who is only one person in the normative sense can be many persons in other senses of the term.

The second organismic sense of 'person' we may call *forensic*. Although it retains the one:one correspondence between bodies and persons, it drops the requirement of functional integrity, complexity, and development. In this sense of the term, a person is a human organism deserving respect and consideration merely in virtue of existing, someone to be treated as an end rather than as a means. Although persons in this sense have rights, unlike persons in the organismic/normative sense, they need not have responsibilities or obligations. The reason, of course, is that responsibilities and obligations require enough functional intactness, complexity, and development to understand and control one's behavior and to participate in social obligation-incurring practices. Clearly, infants, idiots, basket-cases, and even fetuses might count as persons in the forensic, but not in the normative sense of the term. Moreover, since individuals severely impaired from birth may count as persons in the forensic sense, those who are persons forensically do not even need to have the *potential* to be persons normatively. Apparently, then, the class of persons in the forensic sense is approximately the same as the class of *human beings*. Indeed, the problem cases for those classifications seem to be the same. For example, doubts about whether fetuses are persons forensically are likewise doubts as to whether they are human beings.

The reader may have noticed that my use of the term 'forensic' here differs from that of Locke, who said that 'person'

is a forensic term appropriating actions and their merit; and so belongs only to intelligent agents capable of a law, and happiness and misery. This personality extends itself beyond present existence to what is past, only by consciousness; whereby it becomes concerned and accountable.

(*An Essay Concerning Human Understanding*, Book II,
Ch. XXVII)

That, of course, sounds very much like what I am calling the normative sense of 'person'. For Locke, persons are not only emotional creatures but also responsible (and potentially liable) agents. Indeed, they are individuals who are 'capable of a law'. But I would suggest that the term 'forensic' is more perspicuously applied to those who, in virtue of being moral *objects* (and not necessarily moral *agents*) deserve fundamental *protection* under the law. By contrast, someone counts as a person in the normative (or more or less Lockean) sense only if he can reason normatively and tailor his actions to his judgments, and (even more generally) only if he meets certain widely shared *norms* of functional integrity, complexity, and development in virtue of which we decide that the individual is a responsible agent, capable of incurring obligations and participating in social and legal practices. And these shared norms, I should add, are far from clear or uncontroversial. For example, it is not clear to what extent those regarded as mentally ill should be held accountable for their actions. In fact, as Rorty notes, even the related concepts of agency and social responsibility may vary with the idiosyncracies of culture and epoch.

A society's conception of agency is closely linked to the sorts of actions that are taken as central because they preserve or enhance that society's conception of its proper survival or development. In a society of hunters, cripples are thought incapable of action; but in a society of religious ascetics, cripples may be thought most capable of the sort of action that defines the true person.

(Rorty, 1988, p. 30)

At any rate, many would say that the organismic/normative sense of 'person' presupposes the organismic/forensic sense of the term. In fact, our usual assumption is that every human being is a person forensically, a bearer of rights, deserving to be treated as an end rather than as a means. Presumably, that is why the census taker counts those who are persons in the forensic sense (unless fetuses also belong in this class). Even more clearly, that is why persons in the forensic sense qualify for health insurance and have the right to protection under the law, whereas only persons in the normative sense marry, can hold driver's licenses, and are eligible to vote.

Some might think that we should identify a sense of 'person' intermediate between these two senses, by requiring that the individual be self-conscious or have a kind of minimal *sense of self*. For example, we could specify an organismic/*indexical* concept of a person, according to which those who are persons forensically take some of their states to be their own. Hence, to be a person in the indexical sense is to be a human organism possessing whatever degree of epistemic sophistication is required to believe that one's states are one's own (cf. the discussion of indexicality in Chapter 3). Apparently, then, the class of those who are persons in the indexical sense would include some who are persons in the forensic sense (e.g., at least some idiots and possibly older infants) while excluding others (basket-cases, fetuses, and newborns). Notice that one must become or develop into a person in the indexical or normative sense, whereas one automatically qualifies as a person in the forensic sense at birth (if not before).

Notice, by the way, that one might be a person in the indexical sense but fail to satisfy Frankfurt's (1971) minimal condition of having a certain class of second-order beliefs and desires (e.g., wanting to have certain desires or motives). Nevertheless, Frankfurt's standard of personhood is weaker than the requirement for being a person in the normative sense. One may have numerous second-order beliefs and desires but still be incapable of *evaluating* one's actions and participating in obligation-incurring activities. Hence, we should perhaps regard Frankfurt's account of personhood as being *strongly* indexical.

The failure to distinguish at least the normative from the forensic senses of 'person' has clouded certain otherwise illuminating discussions of personhood. For example, Ninian Smart (1972) argues that 'personhood is not simply something given, but something acquired, through the learning of language and through being inducted into a social mode of existence' (p. 22). This sounds vaguely like the normative sense of 'person'. Moreover, since linguistic ability and participation in social processes requires a fair amount of organic complexity and development, Smart notes, further, that 'some basic physiological and psychological equipment is necessary if the individual is to be capable of attaining personhood. For this reason, cats cannot properly speaking become persons' (p. 22). But possessing the basic physiological and psychological capacities is not the same as being a person. Personhood, according to Smart, must be *attained*. Accordingly, 'personhood is not something given biologically like being a biped. An individual has to *become* a person' (p. 22). Hence, Smart seems to be endorsing the normative sense and not acknowledging the forensic sense of 'person'. But at the same time he says

> at quite a primitive level recognizing an individual as a person involves being prepared to act toward him in certain ways [e.g., respectfully]...the person is seen as being the bearer, in principle, of certain rights...the concept of a person is not simply descriptive, but imperatival...the ascription of personhood...incorporates imperatives about not infringing certain rights etc.
>
> (Smart, 1972, pp. 23-4)

So apparently there is a 'primitive level' at which we regard persons as members of a Kantian kingdom of ends — that is, as persons in the forensic sense.

Smart also seems to endorse the view that personhood comes in degrees, since he insists that creatures without language and social initiation, like cats (and newborns, fetuses, or basket-cases?) are not *fully* persons. Now of course, one can easily understand the motivation for saying that persons in the normative (or indexical) sense are more fully persons than those who are persons only in the forensic sense. But I submit that the point may be more palatable if we state it less judgmentally, with respect to the distinct stages of personhood (forensic, indexical, normative) through which one can pass. That way, rather than saying that an individual is not fully a person, we can simply regard him as a person in a different sense. We can make virtually the same point somewhat more neutrally (as I attempted above), in terms of the degree of functional integrity and complexity required to be a person in the normative sense. Actually, since those who are persons only forensically are still bearers of rights and proper objects of respect and consideration, that classification has a positive moral tone missing from the claim that they are not (or are least) fully persons.

Interestingly, Smart observes that not all societies accept a forensic concept of personhood, since some societies do not regard persons as bearers of inherent rights, irrespective of their social group. (Rorty offers a similar observation in 1988, p. 37.) Indeed, in some societies, certain animals are treated more respectfully than humans belonging to specific social classes. Hence, it is not clear that the normative (or indexical) sense of 'person' presupposes the forensic sense in any deep way.[2] Granted, most contemporary western cultures may consider those who are persons normatively also to be persons forensically, or bearers of rights, etc. But other societies do not make that assumption. In fact, in such a society it would seem to be possible for a person to incur obligations (moral and legal) without having any inherent rights. For example, slaves could presumably be held culpable for crimes or failures to keep promises, even if their society grants them no inherent rights. We can see quite clearly, then, that the forensic concept of a person is normative in certain respects, because it expresses a certain moral view about the importance of human life. Indeed, since that view is not accepted in all cultures, the forensic concept of a person would seem to be a *universalistic* concept (i.e., *applying* to all humans), which is not itself universal.

We must be careful, then, about how we characterize the normative concept of a person. In a culture where that concept presupposes the forensic concept of a person, someone who is a person normatively is both a moral agent and a moral object, an individual having rights as well as responsibilities. But in a society where persons are not fundamentally bearers of rights or moral objects, not even moral agents need to be considered moral objects (as we observed above). Hence, to be a person normatively in such a society has to do with being functionally complex enough to incur obligations, etc., *whether or not* one belongs to a social class enjoying basic human rights. We would also have to characterize the indexical concept of a person somewhat differently. Instead of considering a person in the indexical sense to be (roughly) a self-conscious person in the forensic sense, we would have to say that a person in the indexical sense is simply a human organism enjoying self-consciousness, though not necessarily having either rights or responsibilities.

8.3 PERSONS AS MERE AGENTS OR SUBJECTS

So far, we have considered only organismic senses of 'person', presupposing a one:one correlation between bodies and persons. However, if we drop that requirement, we can identify types of personhood that parallel those already mentioned. We might call these *dispositional* senses of 'person', because they seem to capture the minimal requirements for being the kind of persisting individual we could regard as a moral or prudential agent or a moral object.

To begin with, we can isolate a dispositional/*normative* sense of 'person', according to which one is a person if one is a continuing subject of mental and physical states (and not merely a 'logical' subject, as discussed in Chapter 6), and also if one has enough functional complexity and versatility (mental and physical) to participate in social processes, have both rights and responsibilities, incur obligations, deserve praise or blame for one's actions, etc.[3] This concept of a person is probably quite close to the concept of a *rational agent*, at least in a suitably weak sense of 'rational' (we may not wish to demand that all rational agents qualify as sane). But no matter how we might approach the complex and troublesome issue of reconciling rationality with sanity (or degrees of sanity), a person in the dispositional/normative sense is (at the very least) an intelligent, self-conscious agent, enjoying whatever degree of internal coherence and unity is required for it to count as a single moral and prudential agent.

Of course, those who are persons in the organismic/normative sense are also persons in the dispositional/normative sense. But more interesting, in the latter sense of the term, some alternate personalities would count as persons. Granted, in the many contexts in which it seems quite natural to suppose that there is only one person per body, this use of the term 'person' may seem rather counterintuitive. We might feel that unless the term 'person' is (at least roughly) coextensive with 'human being', it does not apply to *real* persons (I shall return to this point in section 8.4). Nevertheless, the dispositional/normative sense of 'person' picks out a kind of personhood presupposed in other contexts. These include the many cultures and subcultures in which the possibility of spirit possession, mediumship, or discarnate survival is taken seriously, and of course (and perhaps somewhat closer to home), situations which tempt us to regard multiples as more than one agent with whom we can develop distinctive relationships.

Significantly, the relationships one forges with alters (ostensibly possessing spirits, etc.) may be no different than relationships established with those counting as persons in the organismic/normative sense, except (of course) in situations in which the bodily criterion matters. For example, we might feel it appropriate to reprimand, compliment, advise, joke with, or make love to an alter, just as we would a non-multiple. And of course, we might behave differently toward different alters. Moreover, different alters might respond to us in different ways, just as non-multiples do, and find our behavior annoying, amusing, stimulating, etc. Hence, the dispositional/normative sense of 'person' captures a type of personhood according to which what makes an individual a person is the set of psychological and behavioral attributes in virtue of which we are able to adopt certain attitudes toward that individual, interact with him as a more or less autonomous agent, and form a distinct relationship with him.

Curiously, it appears (at least on the surface) as if an alter might count as a person in the dispositional/normative sense, even though the multiple him/herself (or the system of alters taken together) does not. Although different alters might be able (in their idiosyncratic ways) to evaluate their actions and participate in obligation-incurring activities, it is unclear whether (or to what extent) the multiple *considered as a single individual* has any such ability. Granted, we saw in the last chapter that capacities of alters (even those that conflict or apparently contradict each other) seem ultimately to be capacities of the person whose alters they are. But that observation, however apt, is of little help in more practical contexts where we must assign responsibility for actions and determine an appropriate response. In such situations, we might regard one alter (rather than another) as blameworthy (say) for certain behavior, while at the same time refusing to consider the multiple as being able to evaluate his/her actions normatively. In fact, that seems to have been the thrust of the landmark legal decision in the case of Billy Milligan (Keyes, 1982).[4] Although one of Billy's alters was held responsible for certain crimes, Billy was not found to be criminally culpable and deserving of incarceration. Instead, he was found to be mentally ill and in need of psychiatric treatment, and he was accordingly institutionalized rather than imprisoned.

But we must be careful in interpreting this legal decision, or (more generally) cases in which we are tempted to assign responsibility for certain actions only to one or more alters but not to others (or to the multiple as a single individual). (I say 'one *or more* alters' because it is conceivable that we might hold a specific group of alters responsible for certain behavior, just as we would the members of a street gang or a group of mischievous siblings.) In the end, we might decide that these are, indeed, cases in which alters are persons in the dispositional/normative sense even though the multiple is not. But that decision is far from obvious. For example, in the Milligan case, one might think that it was Billy *the person* who was hospitalized and who required treatment for a psychiatric disorder. If so, we can apparently conclude only that Billy (the multiple) was simply not the same prudential or moral agent as the guilty alter. We would not be entitled to conclude that Billy failed to count as a person in the normative sense (either dispositional or organismic). On the other hand, one might argue that the reason Billy was institutionalized was that he (as a single individual) was unable to function as a responsible agent and that in virtue of his profound lack of functional integrity, he did not qualify as a person in the organismic/normative sense (although he might count as a person in the organismic/indexical or forensic sense).

Wilkes (1981) has suggested a similar, but perhaps more conspicuously controversial reason for claiming that alters might count as rational agents according to criteria that the multiple might not satisfy. Rational agents, she says,

> are Intentional systems whose behaviour can be explained and predicted by showing it to be intelligible and rational. Each of the trio [of Miss Beauchamp's personalities] separately met this condition, but the resulting aggregate did not. No amount of knowledge of *B*IV allowed one to predict what Sally or *B*I would do; *B*I's closest friends would have been horrified and alarmed to see her sitting naked on top of a wardrobe (one of Sally's crueller tricks). *B*I and *B*IV had little in common between 1899 and 1904, so that the understanding of one was irrelevant to an understanding of the other. Miss Beauchamp during this period was not one rational system but three, so it is difficult to call her *one* person.
>
> (Wilkes, 1981, p. 345)

201

Now it may be that an *aggregate* of alter personalities is a different entity than the multiple herself, to whom all the alters 'belong'. If so, it may be that the aggregate (or system) of alters does not count as a rational agent, even though the multiple herself does. But whether or not that was Wilkes's point, we should note that there are good reasons for thinking that the multiple herself is a rational agent, in terms of which even the surprising behavior of one alter *from the point of view of another alter* makes sense. Granted, an understanding of one alter may not help us to predict what other alters might do, but a thorough understanding of the multiple (as an individual) might help us to understand and explain everything that all the alters do. After all (as we have observed throughout this book), the distinctive behavior and character of different alternate personalities makes sense in terms of the multiple's need to adapt to unbearable physical or emotional pain, and the subsequent reliance on dissociative coping strategies that may eventually become habitual.

At any rate, it is clear that alternate personalities may be considered rational agents or persons in the dispositional/normative sense. Indeed, they would count as *distinct* persons in virtue of the different attitudes we take toward them as responsible and reciprocating agents and the correspondingly different relationships we establish with them — for example, if we held one (but not another) to be guilty of a crime or bound one to a promise that we feel another alter is not obligated to keep, or if we feel comfortable confiding in one alter but not another.

Notice that this is not the sort of distinction we make in more familiar situations where we like to say that an individual is a different person or that he is not himself. Consider, for example, situations in which a person (in either the organismic/ or dispositional/normative sense) is not held responsible for acts committed while (say) in a crazed or drugged state during which he did not know what he was doing (or did not recognize the difference between right and wrong). In such a case, when we say that the agent was a different person, etc., we might mean only that he was ill rather than criminally culpable, or that his capacity for responsible behavior was at least temporarily diminished (e.g., so that his act was one of manslaughter rather than first-degree murder).

Along the same lines, we are not required to say that a person (in the organismic/normative sense) becomes a different person (in the dispositional/normative sense) with every change of state (e.g., from grief or anger at one time to joy or tranquility at another). The reason is that persons in the latter sense (rational agents) may be complex enough to change and reveal different attributes or capacities over time. For example, an alternate personality might be angry at one moment but not at another, or interested in reading at one moment and then bored with reading but interested in food. Nevertheless, in the case of multiple personality, we often feel as if we miss something essential or crucially illuminating if we fail to link at least some changes in state with distinct agents. That is why we are sometimes willing to say, as in the case of Billy Milligan, that alter A incurred an obligation or is guilty of a crime, whereas B was under no such obligation or is innocent of the crime. Similarly, that is why we might find it appropriate to treat alter A as a female child alter who needs to play with her toys (and who never lies and hates asparagus), while we treat B as an adult male who has no interest in toys (and who lies frequently and loves asparagus).

These examples remind us of what is perhaps the most serious difficulty with the dispositional/normative sense of 'person'. In the organismic/normative sense, there is little problem in determining what counts as the *same* person, especially if we ignore classical thought-experiments about (say) brain-transplants, *doppelgängers*, and Lockean tales of body-swapping.[5] Generally speaking, we assume that identity is preserved through numerous sorts of diachronic gaps and synchronic splits, and we then simply rely on a relatively straightforward criterion of bodily continuity. But cases of multiple personality suggest that we need (at least sometimes) to adopt something like a dispositional/normative criterion of personhood. And in that case, it is not clear what counts as the same person or on what grounds an alternate personality counts as the same person after a protracted diachronic gap (e.g., an extended period of amnesia).

Of course, various suggestions come readily to mind, but they all seem to be problematical, at least in some situations. Obviously, we cannot rely on strict continuity or consistency of character or behavior, because alters (like most non-multiples) are sometimes complex enough to be erratic and unpredictable in their behavior and thoughts, and also capable of *evolving* as personalities. Hence, when we focus on apparent behavioral inconsistencies, dramatic mood swings, and changes in character over time, it is tempting to appeal to Lockean continuity of memory (or even simply *ostensible* memories), or perhaps a continuity of personality (in a sense of that term broad enough to encompass dramatic behavioral shifts and evolution), or perhaps continuity of indexical and autobiographical states. However, these various strategies are all likely to run into particular difficulty over cases of integration and subsequent re-disintegration (especially when that disintegration occurs along novel functional lines).

Neo-Lockeans might think that the following criterion of personhood for alters might sidestep these problems. Perhaps an alter is a person just in case (a) it has memories no other alter (or any individual, including non-multiples) has, and (b) some of those memories are systematically connected to (or associatively linked with) memories likewise not shared with any other individual. (Depending on what one means by 'systematic connections', this criterion might be a near relative of the account given in Chapter 3 of what it is to be a distinct apperceptive center. That is because experiencing and believing a state to be one's own gives that state certain distinctive and systematic connections to a broad set of additional phenomenological and epistemological states.) But this criterion runs into trouble over cases where different alters (with whom we have distinctive relationships) have the same ostensible memory.

Of course, it is by no means clear what it means to say that two alters have the same memory. Are they the same merely in the sense in which two different human beings can have the same memory — that is, a memory of the same event, or perhaps even subjectively or qualitatively similar memories of that event? Or must we suppose that alters' memories are the same in a stronger sense? For example, must they be qualitatively identical, or must they have the same or similar associative links to other ostensible memories? (When addressing these questions, the reader should recall the passages quoted from the Doris Fischer case in Chapter 3.2.)

Fortunately, we needn't settle all this here or even assume that there must be a single solution or criterion of sameness of persons in the dispositional/normative sense — much less a clear one. Indeed, in all cases where questions of identity arise, it is up to us to decide — rather than simply to discover — whether two things should count as the same, and those decisions inevitably rest on numerous and ever-changing pragmatic issues. Hence, our decisions may quite properly vary from one context of needs and interests to another. There is no reason to believe that a single criterion of identity will cover every case.[6] At any rate, it is clearly sufficient for present purposes to note the limitations of and difficulties with various relevant concepts of a person. Therefore, let us not dwell on the issues of identity and reidentification. Let us consider, instead, some additional dispositional senses of 'person', the counterparts to the other two organismic senses examined earlier.

Not surprisingly, we can distinguish a dispositional/*forensic* concept of a person, which (like its counterpart) drops the requirement of functional complexity and versatility. A person in this sense need not be a moral or legal agent, but it might nevertheless still be a moral object or member of a Kantian kingdom of ends, an individual with rights and deserving of respect and consideration. This sense of 'person' may apply to those alters (and even alter fragments) who apparently are not functionally complex enough to be held accountable for their actions, etc., but whom non-multiples and other alters regard as deserving of respect, consideration, affection, and so on. For example, an infant or catatonic alter might count as a person in the dispositional/forensic sense. And we might properly experience pity, concern, etc., for these alters just as we do for persons in the organismic/forensic sense.

We noted earlier that the organismic/normative sense of 'person' need not presuppose the organismic/forensic sense and that the possession of rights (for example) is not a fundamental attribute of persons in all societies. I suppose we must make an analogous observation about the dispositional concepts of a person and not insist that the dispositional/forensic sense of the term is fundamental. After all, if a society in which persons do not necessarily have rights has a concept of person that does not require a one:one correspondence between persons and bodies (e.g., if it regards alternate personalities or ostensibly possessing spirits as persons), then those who count as persons in the dispositional/normative sense may not necessarily be bearers of rights. For example, I suppose it is possible that only alters of multiples in certain social classes (or perhaps only alters taken seriously as members of the class they claim to belong to) would enjoy human rights.[7]

At any rate, we can also distinguish a dispositional/*indexical* concept of a person, intermediate between the normative and forensic concepts. In this sense of the term, an alter would count as a person if it lacked the complexity and versatility to incur obligations but was nevertheless sophisticated enough to take some of its states to be its own. For example, a paralyzed alter or an alter who is seriously impaired intellectually might count as a person in this sense.

8.4 THE CHALLENGE OF MPD

Can we draw any preliminary or tentative conclusions from all this? To begin with, it seems fair to say that multiple personality poses no threat to *the* concept of a person. There simply is no such concept. As we have seen, and as others have noted in rather different contexts (e.g., Rorty, 1988; Morton, 1990), there are a number of concepts of a person, no one of which is inherently more fundamental or preferable to another. It is up to us to decide — relative to a specific background of needs and interests — which concept of a person best applies to a given situation.

Hence, if multiple personality challenges our assumptions about personhood, the challenge seems directed at our (perhaps habitual, traditional, and unreflective) ways of regarding other human beings in certain specific kinds of situations. It does not undermine any particular concept of a person. Rather, MPD may influence our decision to apply certain of those conceptions rather than others in various circumstances. For example, it might encourage us, or make us more willing, to consider persons to be mere agents or subjects in contexts where previously we would have regarded them only as organisms. Thus, (as in the Milligan case) it might profoundly influence the legal stance we adopt toward multiples who have committed a crime, or (quite apart from legal contexts) it may broaden the range of situations in which we feel it appropriate to acknowledge different alters as distinct agents. Moreover, it might help legitimize and fortify an inclination that I suspect most friends of multiples feel already — namely, to establish distinct relationships with different alters and to treat the alters the way they treat non-multiples, as distinct moral or prudential agents, or at least as different moral objects. (And we should remember that this attitude is quite different (say) from the way we adjust our behavior to — and perhaps even patronize — a friend who experiences dramatic mood swings).

Apparently, then, we must simply live with the need to apply different criteria of personhood in different contexts. Our goal is not to find a concept of personhood adequate to every possible situation; rather, it is to select the most appropriate concept for the circumstances at hand. Hence, we may continue to hold (say) that the husband of a multiple is not a polygamist — at least in most circumstances — and that a multiple is entitled to only one vote on election day (or one social security number, driver's license, etc.). That is simply a tacit acknowledgment that in these contexts we consider it appropriate to apply an organismic concept of a person. But we might likewise tacitly acknowledge the appropriateness of using a dispositional concept of a person in other circumstances — for example, when we hold one alter (but not another) responsible for a certain act or when we buy different Christmas gifts for different alters.

In fact, those who know multiples well often find it quite natural to treat a multiple as they would an entire *family* (or some other collection of individuals). We might like (trust, respect) some family members but not others or have reservations about having the entire family over to dinner (rather than certain members of the family only). And of course, sometimes a particular family member acts as customary spokesperson for (or representative of) the group as a whole, just as a particular alter might assume the role of spokesperson for the other alters.

Probably some readers will feel that the contextualist account of personhood sketched above is indefensibly egalitarian. Even if they grant the multiplicity of concepts of a person, they might object that unless *some* concept of a person is privileged, any decision on whether alters are persons will be arbitrary, and a 'one person/one body' view of persons would be as plausible or acceptable as any other. But in fact, that is not a consequence of acknowledging the variety and context-dependence of criteria of personhood. Indeed, the concept of a person is analogous to the concept of *similarity* (or identity) in this respect. Objects are not intrinsically similar or dissimilar; we *take them to be similar* in virtue of context-relative criteria of relevance or importance. There is no absolutely privileged answer to a question of whether two things are similar or not — for example, two geometric figures or my table manners compared to the eating habits of my pet pig. Questions of similarity always arise in a living context in which certain interests and perspectives take precedence over others, and

207

in which certain aspects of things therefore matter more than others (see the discussions of similarity in Braude, 1979, 1983, 1986a). But decisions regarding personhood are also made against a real background of needs and concerns. So although in principle we can resolve questions of similarity in an indefinite number of ways, in practice our decisions are not arbitrary. Likewise, although none of the many concepts of a person is inherently privileged, it is not arbitrary (say) that we rely on a kind of (organismic) 'one person/one body' concept in issuing driver's licenses to multiples, or a (dispositional) 'many person/one body' concept in the purchasing of alters' gifts.

Hence, in one's day-to-day interactions with a multiple (say, a relative or friend), it may be appropriate and not at all arbitrary to adopt a dispositional concept of personhood and treat each alter as a distinct autonomous agent and moral object. A multiple's therapist, however, may need to shift frequently (and uncomfortably) between organismic and dispositional concepts of a person, adopting the former in connection with furthering the goal of integration and the latter in connection with establishing appropriate relationships with different alters.

Of course, one might object that we can *treat* alters as persons even if they are not really persons. For example, a therapist might recognize the need to forge distinct relationships with different alters and act toward them *as if* they are persons (in an organismic or any other sense), while (justifiably) refusing to believe that alters are persons at all. Hence, even if some concept of personhood (say, an organismic concept) were context-independently privileged, it might still be appropriate to behave toward multiples sometimes as many persons and sometimes as one person.

Now I grant that many people believe that alters are not persons even while acknowledging the importance of treating them as if they were. Consider, however, a rather different sort of attitude (or perhaps only a different way of characterizing the same attitude) toward multiples, one that may be somewhat more revealing. When interacting with multiples (especially on a frequent and familiar basis), it is very difficult to avoid facing a continuous conflict of instincts or intuitions about personhood. In most situations, it is not as easy or as practicable to separate and choose among competing criteria of personhood as it is to make one of our everyday decisions among competing criteria of similarity. For one thing, a great deal of ethical weight attaches to the former sort

208

of decision; it matters considerably how we view and treat one another. Moreover people interacting with multiples usually know *simultaneously* that it is appropriate to allow multiples only one driver's license, social security number, etc., and also that in many ways it feels right to interact with different alters the way we do with non-multiples — that is, as if they were individuals who needed *different* driver's licenses, social security numbers, etc. And usually, one cannot easily ignore either of these two sets of instincts. That is because one feels concern for the well-being and integration of the multiple while at the same time feeling the naturalness and importance of acknowledging the alters' distinctness and maintaining different relationships with different alters.

Granted, one might tend to feel all the while that an organismic concept of persons is more fundamental than a dispositional concept (i.e., that alters are not really persons). But we should not attach much metaphysical significance to that feeling. It probably indicates less about the inherent importance or priority of an organismic conception of persons and more about a perspective on our fellow human beings which we (but not necessarily others) find particularly natural, automatic, or familiar. Indeed, it seems to reflect nothing more than a contingent and culture-dependent intimacy with organismic criteria of personhood, rather than a feature of those criteria in virtue of which they are conceptually privileged. After all, if multiple personality were more common, or belief in spirit possession or discarnate survival more widespread, we might find ourselves more inclined to lean toward dispositional concepts as privileged. In that case we might feel that issuing a single driver's license to a multiple (or to anyone else) is merely a concession to the fact that many persons occupy (or animate) one body.

I mentioned above that we would not want to regard the husband of a multiple as a polygamist, and then added the caveat, 'at least in most circumstances'. That was because one can imagine a kind of case in which we would at least be tempted to decide otherwise. (Perhaps our readiness to decide otherwise will depend on our sympathy with the sort of decision reached in the Milligan case, or at least with the more general practice of treating different alters as distinct responsible and reciprocating individuals.) Consider a case in which at least some of a multiple's alters have both quite distinctive personalities and also distinctive physical appearance. That scenario is by no means farfetched; in fact, I know of a multiple one of whose alters is a rather plain-looking nurse, and another of whose alters is a successful high-fashion model with dramatically different facial and other physical features. Naturally, the two alters have different names, and they even work in different cities. Suppose then, that a person marries them both, unaware that his 'wives' are alternate personalities of the same human being, and, perhaps most important, actually *believing* himself to be committing bigamy (and, let us suppose, even feeling remorse for his actions). Although current formulations of statutes against polygamy may let the husband off the hook, in these unusual circumstances we might nevertheless feel that a case against him stands a chance of success. Or, at the very least, we might feel that the husband deserves condemnation, even if no legal action can be taken against him. In either case, presumably, we would be expressing the seriousness with which we treat the distinctness and relative autonomy of different alters, and (of course) also the husband's beliefs concerning his own actions.[8]

Incidentally, it is worth noting that although in some situations we are fairly comfortable treating different alters as distinct persons (in a dispositional sense of 'person'), we seem to adopt a different attitude toward hidden observers and pseudo-alters created experimentally through hypnosis. Not only do we regard them as mere artifacts (and certainly not as discrete moral or prudential agents), but also we do not even clearly regard them as moral *objects* distinct from the hypnotic subject. One reason, presumably, is that we take them to have no life history prior to the experimental situation and different from that of the hypnotized subject — that is, some sort of distinctive and already established web of relationships in the world. Moreover, in the case of hidden observers, we may recognize (if only tacitly and fuzzily) that they are not apperceptive centers distinct from the hypnotized subject (see Chapter 3). Hence, although we may treat these artifacts respectfully, our respect for them is not clearly distinct or separable from our respect for the individual under hypnosis.

A superficially similar situation obtains in connection with fragmentary alters whose functions and personalities are severely limited (e.g., an alter with a highly circumscribed personality whose principal activity is to clean toilets). But here, there may be more of a temptation to treat the alter-fragments as persons in the dispositional/indexical or forensic sense of 'person' — that is, at least as distinct moral objects. If so, it might reflect our tacit as-

210

sumption that alter fragments (unlike hidden observers, etc.) are not only distinct apperceptive centers, but also individuals who have a history and who serve a real function in the world. For that reason, if an experimentally created alter remained unintegrated and eventually developed the sort of robust history and network of relationships enjoyed by trauma-induced alters, we might well come to view that alter both as a genuine agent and an object of concern, respect, and affection. (We will return to the topic of alter-fragments shortly, when we examine the connection between personhood and personality.)

At any rate, we are now in a position to re-express a point made in earlier chapters. Even though alternate personalities are *at most* persons in the dispositional/normative sense, alters (or at least those associated with a single multiple) tend to consider one another as persons in the *organismic*/normative sense. Of course, that attitude is reinforced by the (sometimes dramatic) phenomenological and epistemic disparities between alters (most notably, their distinctive body-images) and also by their ability to experience one another in different spatial locations.

We should also remember that although multiple personality provides a variety of opportunities for shifting or questioning our assumptions about personhood, that sort of challenge is by no means unique to multiple personality (or to standard thought-experiments and puzzle cases). In western cultures, similar issues have traditionally arisen through taking seriously the possibility of spirit possession and mediumship. And not surprisingly, non-industrialized societies sometimes deal with analogous sorts of puzzles about personhood and agency.

In fact, the treatment of twins (triplets, etc.) in some African societies illustrates vividly (a) how the concept of a person is culturally variable and intimately connected to a much larger system of beliefs, and (b) how puzzles about types of personhood arise outside the context of multiple personality (see Gowler, 1972, pp. 42-3). These societies hold that human beings bear only one child at a time. But according to the prevailing and fairly rigid set of kinship rules that determine one's position in society, there is only one social slot for twins to occupy. As a result, twins are looked upon as mystically identical. Nevertheless, members of these societies clearly have difficulty reconciling that point of view with the obvious fact that twins are physically distinct, and they find their own ways of coping with that conflict. For example, the Bushman of the Kalahari will put one or both of the twins to death, and the Ashanti will accord one or both of them a special status.

Notice, moreover, that in virtue of believing that humans bear only one child at a time, the birth of twins (triplets, etc.) illustrates that these cultures do not clearly (or consistently) assume a one:one correspondence between persons and bodies. Of course, that in itself is unremarkable; after all, there are many contexts in our own western industrialized cultures in which the one:one correspondence between persons and bodies is rejected or at least questioned. What is curious, however, is the *way* twins (etc.) challenge the correspondence. The more familiar failure of correspondence represented by alternate personalities is many persons:one body. But in these African societies, twins seems to represent a case of one person:many bodies.

8.5 THE CONCEPT OF A PERSONALITY

We have noted that there appear to be at least tenuous sorts of connections between the concepts of personality and personhood. But what *is* a personality, and how robust or complex must a person's repertoire of attributes and capacities be for the person properly to be said to *have* a personality? One might have thought that the literature on MPD would shed light on these questions. But unfortunately, it seems only to add to the general confusion. Let us consider, then, what some of the issues are (at least in the present context), as a modest first step toward an eventual sharpening of the concept of a personality.

Most writers on MPD claim that alternate personalities exhibit varying degrees of well-roundedness in character or personality. But they disagree on *how* well-rounded they can be and on what we are to conclude from assessments of their degrees of complexity. Ludwig (1984, p. 161) says that the concept of a personality is 'exemplified almost in caricature in the manifestation of multiple personality', and Greaves (1980, p. 591) calls alters 'woefully incomplete as personality systems'. But others often note that alters tend to grow in maturity and complexity as they have more time in executive control of the body and are able to develop numerous distinctive relationships to the world around them. In fact, Braun, who concedes that some alters are mere fragments of a personality, nevertheless contends that others deserve to be classified as per-

212

sonalities. According to Braun, only members of this latter group exhibit an appropriate complexity of behavior, by which he means having 'an almost complete range of affect available to it' (1983a, p. 84).

But how complete is that supposed to be? For one thing, it should be clear that *no* person is capable of a literally *complete* range of affect or behavior. Once we grant, as we must, that even quite normal people differ (often dramatically) from one another in their capacities and abilities — including their repertoire of psychological attributes — we would expect even robust personalities to exhibit numerous limitations. Indeed, it is because of those limitations that people *do* differ from each other. Some people may be relatively, totally, or simply idiosyncratically incapable of (say) irony, trust, musical appreciation, or the ability to fantasize (or merely to fantasize visually). Similarly, they may be relatively, totally, or idiosyncratically humorless (i.e., humorless in quite specific ways — e.g., incapable of Shavian sarcasm, or unable to appreciate humor expressed by means of profanity, or sexually explicit humor, or humor appreciated primarily within certain ethnic minorities).

But quite apart from questions about personality-completeness, it is far from clear what even a *full* range of behavior or affect is for a normal person or for non-multiples generally. When demonstrating the personality limitations of alternate personalities, writers often note (say) how one alter might cry but be unable to laugh, whereas another alter might laugh but be unable to cry. But of course, similar observations apply to many non-multiples. More generally, non-multiples are often strikingly limited in their apparent repertoire of behavior and affect; that is why some alternate personalities seem at least as well-rounded as some non-multiples and often easily fool others into thinking that they are dealing with a normal (albeit possibly eccentric) non-multiple. In fact, non-multiples might not even be 'almost complete' in the sense intended by Braun. Many people have quite severely truncated or relatively one-dimensional personalities, and are nearly always (say) depressed, inhibited, passive, hostile, unemotional, or otherwise lacking in depth and breadth.

Hence, even if the most well-rounded alters have personality limitations that tend to become more apparent with time, those limitations do not detract from their personhood. In fact, we should keep in mind that in many cases of MPD, a single alter might control the body for long periods of time, with at least as much success as some non-multiples have managing their respective lives. Therefore, to the extent that being able to care for oneself, hold down a job, and participate in a range of interpersonal and social processes is a mark of personhood, these alters would count as persons. And of course, we would not hesitate to count a non-multiple with a quite one-dimensional personality as a person in the organismic/normative sense, so long as he too was able to participate in the appropriate range of personal, social and legal activities. At most, we might be justified in saying that the individual is simply not an *interesting* person.

Similarly, really extreme personality limitations would seem merely to influence how we assign an individual to a particular subset of persons (both in the organismic and dispositional sense). For example, an alter who seems to exist only to endure pain (or clean the house), but who has no capacity for reflection and evaluation of her actions, would not count as a person in the dispositional/normative sense, although she might count as a person in the dispositional/indexical sense. More generally, when we consider that various sorts of personality-less individuals (such as fetuses and coma victims) count as persons according to some organismic criteria of personhood, we must conclude that the absence of a personality (however complex a set of attributes that turns out to be) is a barrier, not to personhood in general, but only to some kinds of personhood.

8.6 CRITICAL REFLECTIONS ON THE CLINICAL LITERATURE

Most of the literature on MPD, not surprisingly, is written by mental health professionals, few (if any) of whom are directly concerned with the sorts of abstract topics discussed throughout this book. Nevertheless, they cannot avoid taking stands (sometimes unwittingly) on deep philosophical issues, simply in the course of discussing matters of more immediate clinical interest. Hence, although they are not to be faulted for what might count as conceptual errors in the context of a more relentlessly abstract discussion, we must now consider the respects in which prominent writers in the field have offered somewhat misleading or confusing descriptions of multiplicity and personhood.

For example, Putnam (1989) remarks that 'whatever an alter

personality is, it is *not* a separate person. It is a serious therapeutic error to relate to the alter personalities as if they were separate people' (p. 103). On the next page, however, he concedes that an alter will have its own '"self perceptions" that are important for its own sense of identity and overall role....The clinican must develop a degree of empathy for a personality's self-perceptions, if he or she is going to establish a working alliance with that personality' (p. 104).

Presumably, Putnam means only that it would be a serious mistake to treat alters as persons in an organismic sense, since he seems quite clearly to endorse treating them as distinct agents or objects, entities with whom one can forge distinctive relationships and working alliances. Hence, he seems content to treat (and 'relate to') alters as persons in a dispositional sense of that term. One can only wonder, then, whom Putnam meant to admonish. Only an alter would treat another alter as a person in an organismic sense.

Putnam also mentions two interesting characterizations of alters. First, he offers one of his own: 'I conceptualize the alters as highly discrete states of consciousness organized around a prevailing affect, sense of self (including body image), with a limited repertoire of behaviors and a set of state-dependent memories' (1989, p. 103). I realize that Putnam never intended this as a definition that would survive close philosophical scrutiny. Nevertheless, we must note that it has certain problematical features. First, we saw in Chapter 7 that it may not be very promising to characterize alters as 'highly discrete'. Granted, different alters seem to be distinct apperceptive centers; hence, the autobiographical and in-dexical states of one are largely non-autobiographical and non-indexical for the others. To that extent, they do seem quite discrete. Nevertheless, since a multiple's alters seem inevitably to draw on a large repertoire of *common* abilities and capacities, it may be more accurate to describe them as 'distinctive', in virtue of the differences between the contrasting sets of capacities exhibited by the various alters. Moreover, since we must grant that probably all persons (including non-multiples) have a 'limited repertoire of behaviors and a set of state-dependent memories', Putnam's definition hardly distinguishes alters from anyone else. In fact, since different human beings are more likely than alters to be 'highly discrete', Putnam's statement seems to be more of a definition of 'person' than of 'alternate personality' — one which

215

seems to fall somewhere between an organismic and dispositional sense of the term.

Similar problems afflict the second characterization of alters mentioned by Putnam, this one developed by Braun and Kluft. According to that definition an 'alternate personality' is

> an entity with a firm, persistent, and well-founded sense of self and a characteristic and consistent pattern of behavior and feelings in response to given stimuli. It must have a range of functions, a range of emotional responses, and a significant life history (of its own existence).

(Kluft, 1984c, p. 23)

Again, considering the wide variety of personality limitations of non-multiples, the attempt to characterize alters in terms of affective and behavioral attributes seems rather unpromising. Indeed, Kluft's definition (like Putnam's) fails to distinguish alters from persons generally. I would suggest that we return, instead, to the terminology introduced in Chapter 3 and simply note that alters are distinct apperceptive centers of a single human being, *whatever their personality limitations happen to be*. (Perhaps the authors had something like this in mind in using the obscure phrase 'well-founded sense of self'.)

A similar set of problems afflicts the description of alters offered by Ross (1989). He writes,

> alter personalities are not people....Alter personalities are highly stylized enactments of inner conflicts, drives, memories, and feelings....They are fragmented parts of one person: There is only one person. The patient's conviction that there is more than one person in her is a dissociative delusion and should not be compounded by a *folie à deux* on the part of the therapist.

(Ross, 1989, p. 109)

As was the case with Putnam's remarks considered above, Ross seems to be arguing (correctly, but gratuitously) that alters are not persons in an organismic sense of the term. And also like Putnam, Ross later advocates treating different alters empathically, and forming different sorts of alliances with them (e.g., treating the child alters differently from adult alters)(see, e.g., 1989, pp. 226-7, pp. 207ff). Hence, he also tacitly concedes that one interacts with alters as distinct moral and prudential agents, and perhaps also as

216

distinct moral objects (except as regards to their extinction in the process of integration). Moreover, there can be little doubt that the sort of interaction with alters advocated by Putnam and Ross is what most would consider appropriate at least for persons in the dispositional/normative or dispositional/indexical sense — that is, individuals with some sort of distinct (and perhaps robust) sense of self (Putnam is more explicit about this than Ross). It is different from what they might recommend in the case of people who are merely role playing (whom we might simply patronize, however sympathetically) or those whose behavioral eccentricities and changes we do not attribute to correspondingly distinct apperceptive centers (e.g., those who suffer from a non-dissociative psychopathology, such as schizophrenia).

Ross also makes a claim not found in Putnam.

> MPD is an elaborate pretending. The patient *pretends* that she is more than one person, in a very convincing manner. She actually believes it herself....
>
> The patient is acting *as if* she is more than one person, but she isn't. This is different from Hollywood acting because the patient is so absorbed in the different roles that she believes in their reality.
>
> (Ross, 1989, pp. 109-10)

Probably, the value of describing alters in terms of acting and pretending is that it focuses on the *creative* side of multiplicity; it is a way of expressing that alters are constructs of the multiple. And noting that (unlike professional actors) multiples thoroughly and deeply believe in their roles may account (in part, at least) for our willingness to treat different alters as distinct agents. But this way of characterizing multiples is actually difficult to reconcile with Ross's claim that alters are 'dissociated packets of behavior' (p. 109). Indeed, it fails to do justice to the distinct sense of self apparently enjoyed by an alternate personality (e.g., to the disparities of indexicality between alters). Similarly, it fails to explain the apparently *simultaneously* obtaining distinct senses of self in cases of co-conscious alters. After all, children believe in their role playing to a degree quite uncharacteristic of what Ross calls 'Hollywood' acting. But there is no reason to think that the thorough absorption of children in their role playing mirrors the involvement of multiples in the alters they create.

217

9

MULTIPLE PERSONALITY
AND MEDIUMSHIP

9.1 INTRODUCTION

It is intriguing that the resurgence of interest in multiple personality within the last twenty years has occurred alongside a resurgence of interest in mediumship — or 'channeling' as it is now often called. Both MPD and mediumship attracted widespread attention around the turn of the last century but then went into a kind of dormancy until the 1970s. It is not that either phenomenon totally disappeared; both seem merely to have gone underground. MPD apparently continued to occur, although it was seldom diagnosed as such. And the practice of mediumship was likewise ongoing, but usually only in the privacy of homes or in a small number of churches and relatively secluded Spiritualist enclaves (rather than for profit, publicity, or the scrutiny of psychical researchers).

The timing of this dual reappearance may not be coincidental. As scholars have recognized since the late nineteenth century, there may well be a deep link between multiple personality and mediumship. In fact, the investigation of this possibility was one of the principal activities of the founders of the Society for Psychical Research (SPR). For that matter, the SPR devoted much of its early energy to the study of hypnosis generally, and few today realize how much valuable pioneering research was printed in the pages of its *Proceedings* (conducted principally, but by no means exclusively, by Gurney). The founders of the SPR believed, along with many others, that dissociative phenomena promised insights into the nature of mind generally, including processes underlying normal mental phenomena. Moreover, certain SPR stalwarts suspected that the study of dissociation might also illuminate the nature of ostensibly *paranormal* mental phenomena. (Myers and Gurney were the most notable proponents of that position.) They recognized that even if psychic (or *psi*) functioning were not *explainable* in terms of dissociative processes, at the very least the forms of dissociation might be kinds of *bridge* phenomena, linking normal cognitive functions to paranormal cognitive functions.

It is easy to see why parapsychologists were drawn to these issues. For one thing, some of the early studies of hypnosis suggested that dissociative states might be psi conducive. Many of those studies contained fascinating reports of ostensibly paranormal occurrences, such as apparent apports, materializations, and especially varieties of 'lucidity' (i.e., clairvoyance and telepathy)(see, e.g., Dingwall, 1967). And for another, the early studies of hysteria and dual or multiple personality suggested possible connections with the phenomena of mediumship (and possession). As a result, some wondered whether mediumship might be nothing more than a type of dissociation, rather than a phenomenon indicative of survival of bodily death. Others, however (including Myers), took a more radical approach and proposed that dissociative phenomena of all sorts were best explained by adopting an analysis of the mind and human personality that embraced the reality of survival.

For various reasons, the parapsychological community (and scientific community generally) abandoned these lines of inquiry early in this century (see Braude, 1988b, for some possible explanations). Similarly, at about the same time, interest in mediumship went into a sharp decline (Braude, 1986a). But the renewed interest in both MPD and channeling seems to call for a reexamination of the old issues, especially in light of the vastly more detailed picture we now have of multiple personality.

Let us take a fresh look, then, at the comparison of mediumship to multiple personality. I suspect that our current understanding of MPD can help us to resolve some old disputes and dispel some old confusions. The familiar, and related, questions I want to address are these. What *are* we to make of the ostensibly discarnate personalities communicating through the medium? Are they merely ordinary alternate personalities claiming or appearing to be post-mortem entities? Are they really post-mortem individuals? Or — and this option was more popular around the turn of the century than it is today (perhaps with good reason) — are alternate personalities really discarnate entities parading as elements of a person's psyche?

More generally, the underlying issue before us is this. When we compare cases of mediumship to those of MPD, do we find evidence suggesting that the two types of phenomena are fundamentally distinct? Or does the evidence suggest that they are fundamentally alike, even if they fall along rather distant points on a single continuum of phenomena (dissociative or otherwise)?

Each of these options has had its partisans. And although commentators have advanced a number of quite different views, the literature divides into three major theoretical positions. Before examining these, however, it will help to clarify how I intend to use the terms 'dissociation' and 'dissociative phenomenon' in this chapter. Although I proposed a definition of 'dissociation' in Chapter 4, I do not want anything in this chapter to hinge on the acceptability of that proposal. Potentially controversial features of my earlier discussion are irrelevant to the issues under examination here. For present purposes, it will suffice to use the terms 'dissociation' and 'dissociative phenomenon' in a more theoretically neutral way, so that the conclusions reached in this chapter have an appropriate degree of generality. Hence, I shall now use those expressions merely to range over a class of phenomena explainable largely in terms of the states and properties of the individual said to be dissociated, rather than by reference to outside agencies, much less discarnate agencies. Dissociative phenomena, therefore, would be explainable in terms of such things as a person's perceptions, beliefs, needs, interests, desires, motivations, and cognitive capacities. Hence, I shall be using those terms in a way that takes only the most minimal stand on what dissociation is. As far as this chapter is concerned, it does not matter whether dissociation is primarily physiological, phenomenological, or even a form of social compliance or role enactment. (I will, however, ignore the possibility of malingering or fraud, because our concern here is clearly with those cases where there is no reason to suspect any form of duplicity.) My intention is simply to distinguish dissociation from processes or phenomena analyzable primarily or fundamentally with respect to an individual *other* than the individual who is said to be dissociated, whether that be another person (as in telepathy) or a discarnate entity (as would be the case in genuine mediumship or possession).

Naturally (and appropriately), this modest terminological con-

vention still leaves open the possibility that some *ostensibly* dissociative phenomena are not genuinely dissociative, and that they
result instead from external (e.g., telepathic or discarnate) influence of some kind. Similarly, it leaves open the possibility that
some cases of ostensible mediumship (or possession) are really
cases of genuine (and not merely ostensible) dissociation — hence,
that they are examples of dissociation manifesting in forms that
misleadingly suggest the activity of an outside agency. At any rate,
we are now in a position to state, fairly concisely, the three major
hypotheses concerning the relation of mediumship to multiple
personality.

Hypothesis 1: Mediumship and MPD are both forms of dissociation; neither requires explanation primarily in terms of an
outside agency, much less a survivalist explanation. Let us call this
the *dissociation hypothesis*. Notice, by the way, that I understand
the dissociation hypothesis to assert that *all* cases of ostensible
mediumship (and possession) are actually cases of dissociation.
The weaker hypothesis that *some* cases of ostensible mediumship
are not genuinely mediumistic (and are likely to be dissociative) is,
I shall assume, too obvious to be interesting.

Hypothesis 2: Although some cases of mediumship may be
nothing more than examples of dissociation, others are radically
different and manifest the agency of post-mortem individuals. This
is the hypothesis that the dissociation hypothesis usually challenges, and we may call it the *survival hypothesis*. (Clearly, it is
more specific than what is usually called the survival hypothesis —
namely, the general assertion that human beings survive bodily
death. By contrast, the present hypothesis is concerned merely with
the interpretation of mediumship.)

Hypothesis 3: Although some (or many?) cases of MPD may
be nothing more than examples of dissociation, others, like many
(or most?) cases of mediumship, require positing the existence
and influence of post-mortem individuals. In other words, some
alternate personalities are discarnate entities in disguise. Although
this hypothesis, like the last, asserts the survival of bodily death,
it attempts to account specifically only for certain phenomena of
psychopathology. And since, unlike cases of traditional mediumship, the phenomena happen to persons who do not overtly solicit
interaction with a discarnate agency, we may call it the *intrusion
hypothesis*.

Now how does one decide between these rival hypotheses? One

ambitious approach would be to determine first whether there is any evidence of any kind for survival, or — in case one doubts the very intelligibility of the concept of survival — whether there *could* be any such evidence. That approach, however, is not only a massive undertaking, but it would also take us too far afield. A more modest and workable alternative is to compare the symptoms of MPD to the behavior of entranced mediums, and then to look for outstanding similarities or differences. This has been a standard tactic for dealing with the aforementioned hypotheses (adopted even by those who, in addition, attempt to evaluate the evidence for survival in its totality), and we may call it the *comparative method*. Apparently, the assumption underlying this method is that if mediumship and multiple personality are distinct, one would expect to find telltale differences in their manifestations. On the other hand, if the phenomena are essentially the same, then one would expect to find only superficial differences in their manifestations.

Unfortunately, the comparative method is both risky and somewhat limited. It is risky because different (similar) underlying processes may have similar (different) manifestations or effects. For example, phenomenologically similar (distinct) headaches may be caused by distinct (similar) processes. Or more relevantly, distinct (similar) behavior may be due to similar (distinct) causes. Moreover, the method is limited because it is of little help in evaluating the very *possibility* of survival. The reason, obviously, is that one can defend or reject the possibility of survival quite independently of any similarities or differences between mediumship and MPD. Hence, not only might those similarities or differences be fortuitous, they might simply add nothing to already strong arguments for or against survival. Nevertheless, one cannot know *a priori* that the comparative method has no utility at all — that is, that the evidence has nothing to teach us, especially if one is undecided about the possibility of survival. Therefore, it is at least reasonable to see whether there are any *suggestive* differences or similarities between mediumship and MPD, even if they won't be conclusive. And I propose to make that the modest goal of this chapter. If (as I believe) the comparative method does not help us select one of the three hypotheses, that itself is a result worth knowing. And in any case, the very process of inquiry will force us to grapple with some interesting issues along the way.

It is important to remember, however, just how modest the

goal of this chapter is. To do full justice to the comparison of mediumship to multiple personality, one would have to assess fully the significance of mediumship as evidence for survival. And to do that one would sooner or later have to evaluate carefully, if not all the best evidence for survival (including cases of ostensible reincarnation, possession, and apparitions of the dead), at least those cases of mediumship whose features seem most difficult to explain *without* positing the survival of bodily death. Only then would one be in a position to assert confidently that no (all, or some) cases of ostensible mediumship are cases indicative of survival. Unfortunately, however, that project goes well beyond the scope of the present study (I intend, however, to undertake that investigation in a subsequent volume). At any rate, our immediate concern is merely to see what insights flow from the comparison of mediumship to MPD, and (as I noted above) we can assess the utility of the comparative method without having to decide whether survival is either actual or possible. To be sure, we will need to raise some central issues concerning the possibility of survival in the course of this chapter, but for the present, it should not be necessary to reach a decision one way or the other.

9.2 THE DISSOCIATION HYPOTHESIS

Let us consider, then, to what extent the comparison of mediumship to MPD supports the three hypotheses mentioned above. Our best course will be to focus on 'classic' cases, both of mediumship and MPD. I see no point in comparing recent cases of channeling to MPD, especially when there are numerous (generally older) cases that are, *prima facie*, considerably more suggestive of survival. Today's mediums typically present ostensible communications from entities claiming to be intergalactic beings, or else individuals from hopelessly remote periods of history, offering a great deal of advice on how to live, but very little in the way of potentially confirmable evidence of survival. But of course, the comparison of mediumship to MPD is most interesting when the evidence suggests strongly that mediums are what they purport to be. Moreover, the reason for concentrating on classic (generally older) cases of multiple personality is that those are the cases on which the best previous discussions have relied. And (as we shall see) the weaknessness of those discussions are often closely linked to their reliance on the older cases, as well as to a corresponding and rather outdated picture of MPD.

Consider, now, how one might argue, based on the comparison of mediumship to MPD, that mediumship is merely a form of dissociation rather than a phenomenon indicating survival.

(1) To begin with, the cognitive and behavioral traits of mediumistic personalities are sometimes suggestively similar to those of alternate personalities. This is particularly (but not exclusively) true of so-called 'control' personalities, who act as intermediaries (or masters of ceremony) between the medium and the rest of the spirit world. For example, controls might claim to deliver messages from other spirits, or they might simply announce the presence of a spirit who then communicates through the medium. Control personalities are frequently (but by no means always) highly artificial and do not appear to correspond to any formerly living person.

Consider, for example, the resemblances between (on the one hand) 'Sally' in the Miss Beauchamp case (M. Prince, 1905/1978) and 'Margaret' in the Doris Fischer case (W.F. Prince, 1915/16), and (on the other) the Feda-persona of the medium Mrs. Leonard (e.g., Salter, 1930; Troubridge, 1922). As C.D. Broad observed, Sally and Margaret were 'entertaining and likeable', but apparently also 'devoid of any deep feeling' (1962, p. 267). Moreover, they were prankish, and somewhat disdainful of and spiteful toward the host personality. They also showed little or no respect for the property of the host personality, but seemed strongly attached to items of their own. Feda, likewise, could be amusing or engaging in a childlike way and was somewhat contemptuous of Mrs. Leonard. She also showed little concern for Mrs. Leonard's possessions. For example, she would sometimes give away (or threaten to give away) jewelry or other items valued by the medium. On the other hand, Feda would display a strong attachment to objects given or promised to her — that is, given or promised to the medium when she (Feda) was in control. In addition, both Margaret and Feda distorted or perverted the language in childish ways. (See also Gauld, 1982, p. 112.)

Unfortunately, these similarities prove almost nothing. For one thing, alternate and mediumistic personalities display a wide range of behaviors. In fact, in some cases of MPD, *no* alters exhibit the childlike behavior of Sally or Margaret. Hence, it is clear that childlike behavior is not essential to cases of MPD. Furthermore, one would think that if communication with surviving spirits is possible, then the spirits needn't only be those of adults. Hence, the childlike behavior of some mediumistic communicators is not even clearly *suggestive* of dissociation. It is equally suggestive of the survival of a child (or childlike) spirit.

To avoid misunderstanding, I should mention that Broad would not have argued for the *prima facie* similarity of *all* ostensible communicators to alternate personalities. He wrote, 'It is only a regular control, like the Feda-persona, which bears much resemblance to any of the secondary personalities studied by psychiatrists' (1962, p. 268). Similarly, I take it that Broad would have been reluctant to defend the strong version of the dissociation hypothesis under discussion here. In addition, however, I suspect that, by emphasizing the comparison of a 'regular' control personality to alternate personalities, Broad was making a rather questionable (and perhaps until recently a somewhat familiar) assumption — namely, that alternate personalities are always relatively enduring and personality-like rather than ephemeral and fragmentary. But that assumption would be clearly false. No matter how unconvincing or inconclusive the similarities between alters and communicators may turn out to be, I think it is fair to say that some similarities (including similarities in childlike behavior) obtain between infrequent mediumistic communicators and alternate personality fragments. Broad may well have been relying too heavily on turn-of-the-century cases of MPD, which do not exhibit the transitory and functionally quite specific alters found in many cases today.

(2) Another initially interesting but ultimately unpromising cognitive or behavioral similarity between mediumship and MPD is the following: Sometimes a medium's personality is relatively bland compared to those of communicating personalities (especially the control personalities). This appears to be true of Mrs. Leonard, but it is much more conspicuous in other cases — for example, Pearl Curran (the case of Patience Worth — see W.F. Prince, 1927/1964; Litvag, 1972; Cory, 1919a) and Mrs. Chenoweth (Hyslop, 1917). Similarly, in cases of MPD, the presenting or host personality is often less interesting than its alternates, just as Doris Fischer and the 'real' Miss Beauchamp were less interesting than Margaret and Sally, respectively. One might argue, then, that an appeal to dissociation accounts nicely for these resemblances. What happens, according to the argument, is that a

dissociative process strips the subject of certain characteristics, or perhaps draws on latent or repressed attributes or traits, which then emerge in alternate personalities (or fragments) of one form or another. And of course, these emerging (or re-emerging) traits will sometimes be quite interesting or vital. Moreover, to support the argument, one could attempt to show how this kind of re-assignment of interesting personality traits has survival value for the formerly abused multiple, as well as a related utility for the medium, who can thereby avoid taking personal responsibility for the socially provocative or otherwise risky behavior of communicators.

Unfortunately, as was the case with childlike behaviors, the alleged parallel between mediumship and MPD holds — at best — for only a limited number of cases. In fact, exceptions are rather common. Not only are some presenting or host personalities quite interesting, mediums are often fascinating and very engaging characters (Mrs. Garrett and Mrs. Piper are clear examples). Even more seriously, in cases of MPD it is unclear which alter (if any) corresponds to the personality of the medium. We noted in Chapter 2.5 that the concept of a *primary* personality is problematical, and that although multiples often have a regular presenting personality or a host personality who takes charge of (or acts as spokeperson for) the others, neither that nor any other personality seems clearly to be *historically* primary, or primary in any other interesting — much less long term — sense. Hence, no alternate personality is clearly analogous to the medium's personality in the total system of alters.

(3) A different sort of similarity concerns epistemological relations between apparently dissociated parts of a subject's mind. For example, mediums are often unaware of what transpires when a communicator is in control, just as presenting or host personalities tend to be amnesic for periods when an alternate personality is in control. Moreover, some mediumistic communicators (such as Feda) claim to have access (if they wish) to all the medium's thoughts and feelings, just as some alternate personalities seem to know the thoughts and feelings of the presenting or host personality.

Now this observation might hold more generally for mediumship and MPD than the preceding two. But there are still numerous exceptions, especially in connection with amnesia and mediumship. Although amnesia is commonly found in a multiple's presenting or

226

host personality (as well as in some others), in general only *trance* mediums tend to be unaware of what transpires during ostensible communications. And even then, amnesia is common only in those trance mediums whose trance is *heavy*. By contrast, mediums who experience a lighter trance are often aware of what occurs during the trance. In fact, they may even carry on other activities while the communications are in progress. For example, mediums who receive communications through automatic writing or talking might simultaneously prepare food in the kitchen, write letters, or carry on a conversation.

But even when we focus only on those cases of mediumship where the similarity to MPD holds, there is no reason for taking the medium's amnesia (say) as a *prima facie* indicator of dissociation. For one thing, it is still unclear which (if any) alternate personality is analogous to the medium's personality. But more important, one would think that amnesia (like headaches and broken toes) can have different sorts of causes. Hence, for all we know, amnesic barriers between mediums and communicators might also be a natural result of a genuinely mediumistic process.

(4) A rather different similarity between MPD and mediumship concerns (on the one hand) the process of personality switching, and (on the other) the way mediums yield control to communicators. Mediums display a variety of ways in which they are 'taken over' by communicators. Some do it instantly, while others go through 'warm-up' periods of varying length, during which the medium's face sometimes acquires a vacant expression, and which may also be accompanied by groaning, eye-rolling, swaying, and other sorts of movements. But the same is true in cases of MPD. Until recently, the case literature (and motion picture industry) tended to support the mistaken impression that switching of personalities took the rapid and 'clean' form familiar from some classic cases. But (as we observed in Chapter 2) really clean, quick switching is the exception rather than the rule. Many cases of MPD exhibit slower switching, ranging from a few seconds to several minutes. And in all cases (but especially in the slower ones), the subject may temporarily acquire a vacant look, and there may also be accompanying physical movements (such as eye rolling or rhythmic swaying).

Now here, at last, we find a genuinely pervasive similarity between mediumship and MPD. But once again, it is compatible with a survivalist interpretation of mediumship. And one needn't be especially sympathetic to the possibility of survival to grant that point. It would simply be rather foolish to expect all mediums to relinquish control to a communicating spirit instantly or in the same way. Indeed, one would expect their 'reaction times', or styles of submission, to be as varied as the ways in which people normally respond to the everyday influence of others.

(5) Some cases of mediumship — particularly, trance mediumship — suggest that the medium is engaged in a kind of unconscious role playing, and that ostensible communicators are nothing more than trance-*impersonations*. These cases suggest that mediumistic communicators, like alternate personalities, result from the subject's own creative activity, however autonomous some of those creations might later become (as in cases of multiple personality). Of course, when the communicators are conspicuously artificial (e.g., as control personalities often are), this point seems both obvious and relatively uninteresting. It becomes interesting, however, in connection with more realistic communicators, especially those who offer information apparently unknown to the medium and sitters.

A famous and unusually obvious — though, unfortunately, also quite controversial — example is the case of Gordon Davis (Soal, 1925). In this case, the medium, Blanche Cooper, presented a trance impersonation of one Gordon Davis, whom she did not know. The sitter (Soal) had known Davis but claimed to believe his acquaintance had been killed in the First World War. The Gordon Davis manifesting in Mrs. Cooper's trance presented itself as a discarnate entity and offered information about Davis that was later found to be correct, but which was apparently unknown to those at the sitting. As it turned out, however, Davis was alive and well at the time, working at his real-estate business.

Now even if the Davis case turns out to be worthless, this line of argument might nevertheless be the most serious challenge so far to the survivalist interpretation of mediumship, especially for those undaunted by the possibility of refined unconscious psychic functioning. Not surprisingly, however, it is the most difficult to support by straightforward appeals to the evidence. Of course (as I've mentioned), when mediumistic communications are evidentially unimpressive, it is relatively easy to argue that the medium is engaged merely in a kind of role-playing. Examples of impressive mediumship, however, are more refractory. In fact, the Gordon Davis case (if genuine) would be quite exceptional, because it very clearly discourages a survivalist interpretation. But generally speaking, in cases where ostensible communicators give information not normally available to the medium, it is much more difficult to establish that the communicator is not a genuine discarnate spirit, and that the medium is simply exhibiting a form of psi-mediated dramatization.

Indeed, arguing for trance-impersonations in these cases is a complex and formidable project. To begin with, one would probably have to argue that the ostensible communicators are too flat as personalities to be genuine surviving spirits. And that, too, is no simple task, since it is unclear to what extent genuine communications from the deceased might be distorted, filtered, or 'watered down' by the process of communication. Of course, partisans of the survival hypothesis can rely all too easily on this point, in order to wriggle away from evidence apparently unfavorable to the hypothesis. But their opponents, likewise, can rely all too easily on the assumption that genuine mediumistic communicators will be robust personalities. The frustrating fact of the matter is that we have *no idea* what to expect of a genuine mediumistic communication. For all we know, it might be difficult or impossible for a communicator to control a medium's organism and still manifest his or her personality in all its robustness (e.g., without the medium's thoughts or personality getting in the way). For any number of reasons, it might be difficult to prevent trance-communications from seeming like personality caricatures. Still, one might argue that certain personality limitations are more revealing than others and that they strongly suggest dissociation rather than discarnate survival. That is part of Eisenbud's strategy in dealing with Mrs. Chenoweth's Cagliostro-persona (Eisenbud, 1983), and it is a strategy that requires a very deep grasp of human behavior and a keen eye for its nuances.

But quite apart from the issue of personality-robustness, major obstacles remain in the way of showing that communicators are merely trance-impersonations. For example, one must explain the *dynamic relevance* of the medium's behavior. One must explain why *this* particular individual appears to communicate, rather than someone else with different characteristics and offering different information. If the ostensible communicators are products of a dissociative process, then presumably there is a reason why the medium's trance-personality has the specific characteristics it has and offers the specific information it does (just as the specific features of alternate personalities make sense relative to the needs and interests of the multiple). But to establish this sort of claim in cases of mediumship, one would almost certainly have to make complex and inconclusive sets of conjectures about the lives, needs, and hidden agendas of the medium and sitters at a séance and the underlying psychodynamics between them. Once again, the classic model for such a study is Eisenbud's fascinating and compelling analysis of the Cagliostro-persona (1983). And finally, to make matters worse, even if one had the ability and available information to meet this part of the challenge successfully (and I know of no one besides Eisenbud who has pulled it off), one must still explain (in the best cases) the origin of communicated information presumably known only to the deceased person being impersonated. But that might require appealing, not simply to some psychic functioning or other, but to a *degree* of psychic functioning that even some parapsychologists find intolerable.

On the whole, then, these various comparisons of mediumship to MPD lend very little support to the dissociation hypothesis. Not only do they not *demonstrate* that mediumship is simply a dissociative phenomenon; they are not even especially suggestive. Perhaps only the argument from trance impersonations is at all promising. But it is very difficult to defend, and in any case it will appeal only to those who are open to the possibility of extremely refined psychic functioning. Of course, mediumship might still turn out to be nothing more than a form of dissociation (perhaps aided by virtuosic psychic functioning). The above considerations show only that this cannot be established (or even strongly supported) simply by comparing mediumship to MPD.

9.3 THE SURVIVAL HYPOTHESIS

Let us move on, then, to the survival hypothesis, and consider to what extent comparing mediumship to MPD supports the claim that at least some mediumistic communicators are post-mortem individuals. Just as many have felt that similarities between mediumship and MPD support the dissociation hypothesis, others have maintained that *differences* between the two types of phenomena support the hypothesis of survival. Most of the arguments I discuss below are relatively standard, but I will focus on their most persuasive formulations in works by C.D. Broad (1962) and Alan Gauld (1982).

(1) The first argument concerns the involuntary nature of MPD as compared to the relatively voluntary nature of mediumship. Some argue that alternate personalities tend to be independent of the host personality and that they often take control for extended periods against the will of the subject (or host personality), whereas mediumistic controls and communicators tend usually to appear only with the medium's knowledge or consent. As Gauld puts it, their 'comings and goings...unlike those of secondary personalities, are strictly circumscribed' (p. 113).

But this alleged difference may be challenged on several grounds. To begin with, in some cases of mediumship, communicators spontaneously take control of the medium. For example, sometimes Feda took over Mrs. Leonard without her knowledge or consent. Moreover, the literature contains numerous reports of so-called 'drop-in' communicators, whom sitters at a séance apparently do not know, and whom they certainly do not invite. And as far as MPD is concerned, the more functional multiples often have considerable control over which personalities appear and when they appear. The reason these multiples *are* functional, apparently, is that they have a high degree of internal cooperation between their various alternate personalities (e.g., some sort of ruling or organizing body or 'council').

Some might find it odd that I should raise the subject of drop-in communicators to *challenge* a point made in favor of a survivalist interpretation of mediumship. The reason is that drop-in cases sometimes provide outstanding *prima facie* evidence for survival. In the best of these cases, drop-in communicators offer information about themselves that is later verified, but of which those present at the sitting were presumably ignorant (see, e.g., Gauld, 1982; Haraldsson and Stevenson, 1975a, 1975b). But as Eisenbud's analysis of the Cagliostro drop-in demonstrates, the survivalist explanation seems most compelling only when one fails to probe beneath the psychological surface of a case, and only when one antecedently assumes that there are severe limits (or limits at all) to the scope and refinement of psychic functioning. In these respects, however, even the most promising cases suggestive of survival are rather disappointing. Despite their meticulous attention to details of other sorts, these cases are quite superficial psychodynamically (e.g., Haraldsson and Stevenson, 1975a, 1975b; Stevenson, 1984). Moreover, attempts to assign limits to psychic functioning have been highly controversial at best and extremely naive at worst (for criticisms of those attempts, see Braude, 1986a, 1987, 1989; Eisenbud, 1982, 1983).

Furthermore, as Gauld has observed,

> I do not know of a single instance in which a drop in communicator has tried to put the same message through two different mediums. Yet surely we might expect that some of them would try. In fact, cases in which any kind of communicator has convincingly manifested through more than one medium *without the presence of the same sitter* are fairly uncommon.
>
> (Gauld, 1982, pp. 110-11, italics added)

What that suggests, obviously, is that drop-in communicators are more dependent on the needs and interests of the sitters than they appear to be. But then, they are not clearly *prima facie* indications of post-mortem survival. Rather, they seem at least equally well explained in terms of hidden ante-mortem needs and motivations, as well as subconsciously stored and paranormally obtained information.

Nevertheless, it may well be that the comings and goings of mediumistic communicators are, *on the whole*, more restricted than those of alternate personalities. But it is not clear whether that difference would be significant. As Broad realized (1962, p. 267), it might only be a difference in degree rather than a difference in kind. In fact, it is obvious that one can explain the difference (if it exists) without positing radically distinct sorts of underlying processes, much less the existence of post-mortem individuals. After all, dissociation can play different sorts of roles in a person's life. For the multiple, the creation of alternate personalities apparently begins as a reaction to intolerable suffering, and eventually dissociation tends to become a somewhat habitual means of coping with a broad range of stressful situations. For the medium, however, dissociation might not be linked (at least so conspicuously) to the exigencies of psychological survival. Perhaps it is not rooted in earlier disturbing traumas of the sort that lead to full-fledged cases of multiplicity. It might instead illustrate how a person can use dissociative capacities to reinforce a belief or world view (e.g., the belief in survival). And clearly, if dissociation is merely playing a different sort of role in mediumship from that in MPD, the comparatively controllable nature of mediumistic communications is easy to understand. After all, mediums tend to place themselves voluntarily in situations where they can exercise their mediumistic capacities, either by holding séances or by making themselves psychologically open to mediumistic communications at any time. By contrast, the multiple does not (at least consciously) seek the stressful situations that trigger the switching of personalities.

(2) Gauld also suggests that multiple personality is a form of psychopathology, whereas mediumship is not. So perhaps that is a reason for thinking that mediumistic communicators are not merely dissociative constructs (like alters). But we must be careful here. For one thing, mediumship *might* be pathological, but its pathology might simply be more subtle or less severe than that found in MPD. Once again, Eisenbud's (1983) conjectures about the sexual repressions of medium and sitters are a model of the deeper analyses we must make before drawing hasty conclusions about mediumship and psychopathology.

Besides, pathology is inevitably a matter of degree. Even if mediumship *is* a dissociative disorder, the fact that MPD appears more pathological may (again) reflect no more than a difference in etiology or a difference in the role dissociation plays in the subject's life. For example, the problems leading to classic cases of MPD might simply be more dramatic than those conducive to the development of mediumship. Whereas MPD arises from severe trauma or abuse, the generally less disruptive phenomena of mediumship may reflect a milder causal history. But then the phenomena of MPD and mediumship might not be fundamentally different. Not only might they both be dissociative phenomena linked to an underlying psychological instability or weakness, but they might also both be ultimately maladaptive (though to different degrees).

Moreover, we should remember that not all cases of MPD are as dramatic or life-disrupting as the classic or best-known cases. In fact, not only are some multiples far more functional than others, some mediums are clearly *less* functional than others and have varying degrees of difficulty coping with their mediumship and with everyday life. Hence, when we consider the extent to which MPD and mediumship are pathological or maladaptive, there are reasons for thinking that the various cases can all be spread out along a single continuum.

(3) Now Gauld never explicitly said that MPD is pathological and that mediumship is not; he only suggests it. His explicit point

is somewhat different. He claims 'There does not seem to have been anything disturbed about the normal personalities of Mrs. Piper, Mrs. Leonard, and other leading trance mediums' (1982, p. 112). Presumably, Gauld means that the host or dominant personalities in cases of MPD *are* disturbed, by contrast.

But one must be careful here as well. It is not clear what Gauld means by 'disturbed'. One would think he means something like 'not well-adjusted' — that is, that disturbed persons behave erratically, or that they respond inappropriately or self-destructively to life's daily turmoil, or that in some other way they show little ability to handle everyday situations. But if that is what Gauld means, then MPD and mediumship may not differ in the way he suggests. For one thing, some alternate personalities (including dominant personalities) show few (if any) signs of being disturbed in this sense. In fact, they often appear quite stable and functional, and at least as normal and well-adjusted as many non-multiples and non-mediums. Granted, those alters might be relatively one-dimensional or flat as personalities compared to some (or most) non-multiples. But their personality limitations are often quite subtle and need not interfere with the multiple's ability to navigate through the day. And in any case, many quite functional non-multiples are comparably limited as personalities.

Moreover, criteria of normality are very tricky; and usually, one's important personality disturbances are not evident on the surface, or even under the sort of scrutiny accorded most great mediums. In fact, one should remember that mediums, unlike multiples, are not typically investigated by mental health professionals on the lookout for personality disturbances and poised (if not eager) to make a diagnosis. But in any case, there is no reason to suppose that mediums generally are well-adjusted, even if Mrs. Piper and Mrs. Leonard seemed to be. Quite probably, mediums are no better-adjusted on the whole than members of other occupational or avocational groups, most (if not all) of which contain their fair share of troubled individuals. '(Consider, for example, weekend golfers, amateur photographers, bird-watchers, construction workers, airline personnel, account executives, ministers, politicians, and most certainly academics.) But even if all mediums *were* well-adjusted, the difference between well-adjusted mediums and poorly-adjusted alternate personalities may still be no more than a by-product of their distinctive sorts of histories (severely traumatic, presumably, only in the case of MPD). It may not point to any fundamental difference in underlying processes — for example, in the origin of mediumistic communicators as compared to alternate personalities.

Perhaps Gauld should have made a somewhat different, but related point — namely, that the dominant personalities seem more incomplete, or less well-rounded, than those of mediums. And *that* claim may be defensible, since a multiple's various alternate personalities (even the most robust ones) often seem somewhat flat by comparison to many non-multiples (well-adjusted or otherwise). Nevertheless, I know of no sufficiently detailed comparative study of mediums and multiples to support the view that mediums are generally more robust as personalities than even the most fully developed alters.

In any case, the view is problematical. For one thing, as I noted earlier it is often very hard to tell which (if any) of a multiple's alternate personalities is historically primary — hence, which should be compared to the medium's personality. But even if the personalities of mediums were, on the whole, more well-rounded than *any* alternate personalities in cases of MPD, that, too, needn't be understood as indicating that alternate personalities and mediumistic communicators differ radically in kind or origin. It might show only that mediums and multiples exemplify somewhat different dissociative processes.

For example, perhaps it is true (as we considered in Chapter 2) that the formation of alternate personalities always *subtracts* something from the multiple's total remaining cognitive, perceptual, emotional, or behavioral repertoire, so that both dominant and subordinate alters will inevitably be somewhat flat as personalities. But even if that is the case, it may still be of little use to proponents of the survival hypothesis. It might be that mediums and multiples alike dissociate into temporary or long-term alternate personalities or fragments, but that mediumistic dissociation, in virtue of being less profound or serving somewhat different functions than the dissociation in MPD, does not greatly deplete the personality of the medium.

Moreover, it is unclear how one could defend *any* sweeping generalization about the complexity or robustness of mediumistic communicators as compared to alternate personalities. It is difficult enough to evaluate the relative complexity of two ordinary personalities, but it is substantially more imposing to make such comparisons across *populations* of personalities. Besides, we must remember that the personality of a *non*-multiple may be restricted (even severely) in a variety of ways and for a variety of reasons. Hence, even if we were to find suggestive *limitations* in the personalities of mediums and their communicators, we should not leap to the conclusion that mediumship is merely dissociative. As we noted in connection with the dissociation hypothesis, those limitations might result from something other than dissociative depletion — for example, natural constraints of the process of communicating with discarnate entities.

Perhaps some will feel that an important point is being overlooked. It concerns the fact that the most elaborate alternate personalities tend to be those that have had considerable time in executive control of the body — that is, time in which to develop and mature. Now if it could be shown that mediumistic communicators are robust *to begin with*, with little or no time to develop into well-rounded personalities, that might indeed suggest a significant difference between alternate personalities and ostensible communicators. Perhaps the complexity of mediumistic communicators could be explained most parsimoniously by positing the action of an already complete post-mortem intelligence. Unfortunately, though, mediumistic communicators have not been notoriously robust, or conspicuously (if at all) more robust than well-rounded alternate personalities.

But even if one *could* demonstrate that communicators are distinctively more complex than alternate (including dominant or host) personalities, it would still be difficult to build a case for survival on that fact. One would first of all have to justify the underlying assumption that dissociated personalities *cannot* emerge full-blown or well-rounded, without first having time to develop while in control of the body. And that project is made no easier in the face of reports from some multiples that certain of their alters developed covertly, before first assuming executive control.[1]

(4) A rather different kind of comparison of mediums and multiples seems particularly questionable in the light of recent evidence. Broad (1962, p. 268) mentions the once familiar point that in cases of MPD, personalities do not present themselves as discarnate entities. But of course that is clearly false; some alternate personalities do claim to be post-mortem individuals. (I will have more to say about this below.) Granted, most of the examples of such personalities are described in reports written considerably after Broad's *Lectures*, but earlier examples can be found in the

236

literature, even in the major cases Broad considers. For example, in the Doris Fischer case, 'Sleeping Margaret' claims to be a surviving spirit (W.F. Prince, 1915/16, p. 1264).

Nevertheless, most alternate personalities make no such claim. But that still does not clearly support the survival hypothesis. For that matter, even if *no* alters claimed to be surviving spirits, that would not show that mediumistic communicators are what they purport to be. It might show only that the underlying psychodynamics of mediumship are unusually conducive to the production of alternate personalities or fragments that pass themselves off as discarnate individuals. That is, there might be perfectly understandable depth-psychological reasons why some alternate personalities (particularly, those of mediums) claim to be discarnate. (I will return to this point also.)

(5) Another point apparently undermined by recent evidence is the following. Gauld claims 'that the number of distinct personalities which may control a trance medium during the course of her career greatly exceeds anything for which the annals of multiple personality provide a parallel' (1982, p. 112). But this, too, seems plainly false, given the now relatively common reports of huge inventories of alters and fragments in polyfragmented cases of MPD.

Of course, I have noted that it is unclear what to make of recent evidence, due to the difficulty of accurately *individuating* alters — in particular, determining when one is dealing with two different alters as opposed to one alter assuming different names. Ironically, this is equally a problem for determining the actual number of communicators expressing themselves through mediums (whether they be dissociated parts of the medium's psyche or genuine post-mortem individuals). If we count personalities and communicators simply on the basis of the number of *names* claimed or the number of separate identities claimed by or through the subject, then mediums and multiples have comparably extensive inventories. But because alternate personalities and ostensible communicators often exhibit only the most subtle behavioral differences (and differ primarily in what they *claim* about themselves), and because the appearance of counterfeit new personalities or communicators can sometimes be explained in terms of demand characteristics of the therapeutic or mediumistic situation, one can't be certain how large the actual inventories really are. Therefore, this sort of 'head counting' is unlikely to yield any useful information about the relationship between mediumship and MPD.

(6) Gauld also says that he knows of no 'complete parallel for the simultaneous and apparently quite full manifestation of two personalities (one through the hand and one through the voice), which occurred quite commonly during one period of Mrs. Piper's mediumship' (1982, p. 112). But first of all, Mrs. Piper's case is not unique in that respect, although it is uncommon. Another impressive case is that of Mrs. Curran, who could converse or write letters with one hand, while the other hand produced the Patience Worth scripts on the ouija board (see Litvag, 1972; W.F. Prince, 1927/1964; Braude, 1980; Cory, 1919a).

Moreover, it is unclear why this phenomenon would count in favor of the survival hypothesis. The literature on MPD contains numerous reports of submerged personalities expressing themselves through automatic writing while another alter is in executive control of the body. But even if some mediums exhibit simultaneous and robust personalities to a degree unmatched by any case of MPD, that phenomenon would still be consistent with the dissociation hypothesis. As we have already seen, it might (for all we know) be a rare form of dissociation, perhaps explained in terms of etiological differences between mediumship and MPD, or perhaps in terms of differences in demand characteristics. After all, dissociative phenomena come in many varieties, whose differences might reflect nothing more than a corresponding variety of dissociative functions or contexts for dissociation.

(7) Some might think that etiological differences between mediumship and MPD support the survival hypothesis. For example, in most cases of MPD, the phenomena begin in childhood, and alternate personalities often have extended histories out in the world. Mediumship, however, can begin in adulthood, and more important, the communicators tend to pop in and out of the medium's life, just like the 'visitors' or possessors they claim to be.

But as with the other differences I have discussed, this does not show very much. Although it might (at best) support the view that mediumship is not a form of MPD, mediumship could still be a form of dissociation. Once again, we must remember that dissociative phenomena come in varieties and degrees. For example, mediumship could be similar in some respects to hysterical fugue, which typically occurs later in life than MPD. Moreover, fugue states seem less profound and more ephemeral than alternate personalities, presumably because the subject's personality after a certain age is too solidified and developed to be more deeply and more permanently fragmented. Another possibility is that ostensible communicators are analogous to certain artifacts of hypnosis (such as the 'hidden observer'). That is, they might be products of a kind of self-hypnosis, and their features might be influenced by demand characteristics of the séance.

(8) Perhaps a related point about etiology will fare somewhat better. It concerns the different degrees to which alternate personalities and mediumistic communicators make sense in terms of the subject's life history. Generally speaking, we can understand why alternate personalities develop and why they have their distinct sets of attributes. We can understand their functions relative to traumas or other incidents in the multiple's history, and we can see how they fit both into a larger personality *system* and also into the multiple's ongoing efforts to cope with everyday problems. By contrast, mediumistic communicators seem to play no comparable role in the medium's life; they seem to be dynamically fortuitous. But then, perhaps they are not simply created by the subject and are instead genuine discarnate communicating entities.

It should be clear by now that this suggestion can be attacked for reasons considered earlier. While it might be true that mediumistic communicators do not play the *same* role in the medium's life as alters play in the multiple's life, it would be rash to conclude that they play no role at all. As Eisenbud's analysis of the Cagliostro-persona reminds us, mediumistic communicators might simply serve a different kind of function. Granted, communicators might not be created in response to traumas, either directly or as a by-product of what eventually becomes an habitual dissociative coping technique. But dissociative processes might serve a wide variety of needs and interests, and their role in the life of a medium might be far more subtle than in cases where subjects experience major traumas, and in which alternate personalities are clearly trauma-specific.

(9) Of course, partisans of the survival hypothesis would argue that mediums sometimes display abilities or knowledge for which there is no parallel in the case of ordinary multiplicity, and which seems explicable only in terms of the persistence of consciousness after bodily death. This is probably the only sort of difference which — if it could be defended — would clearly favor the survival

hypothesis over the dissociation hypothesis. Unfortunately, however, it is the difference we can least afford to examine in detail, since to do so we would have to grapple with most of the central issues concerning the evidence for survival, quite apart from the comparison of mediumship to MPD.

At any rate, before this alleged difference can be invoked in favor of the survival hypothesis, one would have to evaluate very carefully the nature of the unusual knowledge and abilities sometimes displayed by mediums. As far as the knowledge is concerned, one would have to show why the so-called *super-psi hypothesis* would not explain things more neatly in terms of highly refined psychic functioning — that is, in terms of mere extensions of abilities for which (according to some) we already have considerable evidence. The unusual abilities sometimes displayed by mediums — for example, apparent responsive xenoglossy (the ability to conduct conversations in a language one has never learned) — pose somewhat different problems (see Stevenson, 1984). Here, the challenge is to show (a) that the ability is more extensive than what might be acquired normally, but unconsciously, from information picked up unwittingly in day-to-day life, and (b) that the unusual abilities transcend in refinement and complexity the enhanced capacities sometimes exhibited in apparent cases of dissociation not suggestive of survival, or at least in borderline cases (such as that of Patience Worth). And to meet that challenge, one must examine very carefully the cases most strongly suggestive of survival, and also assess numerous skeptical arguments intended to show that those cases can be more parsimoniously explained without positing survival. (For a debate on these issues, see Braude, 1989, 1992a, 1992b, and Stevenson, 1992.)

Clearly, at this point we arrive at the heart of the problems of survival. And it is at this point that the issues go well beyond the mere comparison of mediumship to MPD. Since we cannot afford what would amount to a book-length digression assessing the best mediumistic evidence for survival, we will have to settle for a modest and rather tentative conclusion. Based on the foregoing considerations, I think it is safe to say that the comparison of mediumship to MPD does not offer any particular support to the survival hypothesis, at least over and above whatever relatively independent support comes from examining the unusual knowledge and abilities occasionally displayed by mediums.

9.4 THE INTRUSION HYPOTHESIS

That brings us, finally, to the intrusion hypothesis, the claim that some alternate personalities are really discarnate entities passing themselves off as mere fragments of the person's psyche. This hypothesis differs in important respects from the other two. First, it has relatively few advocates. And second, it is seldom supported by means of the comparative method. It is also the easiest of the three to evaluate. In fact, it can be fairly easily evaluated *whether or not* one accepts the hypothesis of survival. Indeed, even those sympathetic to survival tend to reject the intrusion hypothesis. The reasons are relatively straightforward.

(1) As McDougall (1905) observed, in cases where *integration* of personalities seems to have occurred, it is not especially plausible to interpret alternate personalities as post-mortem individuals. Integration, he argued, is presumably a form of *making whole* again or *re*integration. Hence, it suggests a process of simply putting back together elements that previously had formed a whole. But *ex hypothesi*, post-mortem individuals were not parts of the subject to begin with.

No doubt, some will find McDougall's argument unconvincing. For one thing, it may rest on his tacit acceptance of the CR-principle (see Chapter 5), since it seems to require that alternate personalities (or their correlates) were originally parts of the person's psyche, rather than something *created* post-traumatically. But quite apart from problems concerning the CR-principle, there are good reasons for thinking that 'integration' and 'reintegration' are not synonymous expressions, especially in the present context. There are many reasons for thinking that 'integration' may denote a process that is not merely a reuniting of parts that once formed a whole. Perhaps after integration, a *new* person can result from a synthesis of old parts and new ones either created dissociatively or imported from the spirit realm. Or, if that seems too bizarre, perhaps in the integrated subject, the original self acquires skills and traits from formerly invading spirits who then depart.

Or, if that still seems too bizarre, one could always argue that the integration may simply be illusory. For one thing (as we noted in Chapter 2), attempted integrations are often quite unstable. One possible reason that we did not consider in that earlier chapter, but which partisans of the intrusion hypothesis are free to propose, is that a multiple's post-mortem and ante-mortem personalities may be unable to merge. Perhaps, like oil and water, those entities simply don't mix (or mix only temporarily). And of course, a multiple's integration may be illusory for some of the other, more pedestrian, reasons considered in Chapter 2 (e.g., it may only be feigned, or the clinician and patient may not realize that alters remain unintegrated). But in that case, McDougall's point is (at best) quite limited in scope, because the number of genuine or full integrations may be quite small.

(2) Other arguments, however, apply to a greater range of cases. For one thing, as I noted above, it is generally clear how alternate personalities fit into the multiple's life history and how they together form a kind of personality *system*. That is, it is generally clear why multiples develop the kinds of personalities they display and what role those personalities play in the life of the patient. But in that case, the intrusion hypothesis seems unnecessary and unparsimonious.

In fact, that seems to be true even in cases where alternate personalities claim to be communicating spirits. For example, Cutler and Reed (1975) discuss a case of MPD in which the patient had one personality claiming to be from the eighteenth century and another from the twenty-first century. The patient's other personalities were transparently — and quite typically — adaptive; their roles concerned types of behavior and situations she had difficulty handling, especially those involving her sexuality. But the temporally-displaced personalities likewise seemed clearly adaptive. They, too, appeared to have an important function in the patient's overall emotional and psychological makeup.

Of course, not all personalities in a multiple's personality-system have clearly identifiable functions and reasons for existing. But that hardly warrants treating those alternate personalities as discarnate spirits in disguise. A more reasonable conjecture is that not enough is known about the multiple to be able to identify the personality's role and causal history.

Moreover, we should remember that many multiples have various alters who appear 'stuck' in time — often child personalities representing specific traumatic periods or episodes in the multiple's past. It would clearly be foolish to assume that those alters are spirits of individuals who lived at those times. Their claiming to belong to another period is straightforwardly explainable in terms of the multiple's history and the problems in living which that history has created. We ordinarily (and quite properly) treat the temporal displacements of alters as part of an overall creative adaptive strategy that the multiple adopts in order to cope with painful events occurring at earlier times. But *prima facie*, the same is true of many central features of alters, such as their sex, chronological age, body image, sexuality, and (presumably) whether or not they claim to be a discarnate spirit.

Moreover, the type of individual an alter claims to be may also be a function of the culture in which the multiple lives. Significantly, multiples in Brazil frequently manifest alters claiming to be spirits. But these conform closely to rather idiosyncratic spiritist belief-systems widely held only in Brazil (see Krippner, 1987). Reported cases of MPD in India and among Hispanics likewise exhibit what appear to be culture-specific characteristics (see, e.g., Adityanjee, *et al.*, 1989; Steinberg, 1990; Varma, *et al.*,1981). And Ross claims that 'personalities of different races are similarly culture-bound. I suspect we have far fewer black alters in white bodies in Canada than in the United States (1989, p. 120). He also asserts,

> I suspect that the frequency of demon alters varies with geographical area in North America, with more demons in the 'Bible belts'. MPD patients as individuals are probably more likely to have demon alters if they belong to a fundamentalist church, irrespective of geographical location.
>
> (Ross, 1989, p. 119)

Similarly, alters described in very early accounts of MPD often have quaint characteristics appropriate to the period and prevailing beliefs (e.g., the 'angels' reported in Despine's case of Estelle — see Fine, 1988).

(3) Ralph Allison (1985) reported that many of his patients manifested personalities claiming to be spirits of deceased people (some of whom had been multiples in earlier incarnations). Others claimed to be spirits never previously embodied. Usually, these personalities claim that their function is to help cure the patient. Allison called alternate personalities who help the patient *Inner Self Helpers* (ISHs), and this subset of the ISHs he called *Higher Helpers* (HHs).

Obviously, Allison's data may be interpreted along either survivalist or non-survivalist lines. A survivalist would contend that at least some HHs really are discarnate individuals. Opinions may then divide over why certain post-mortem individuals (rather than others) intervene in the subject's life, and which situations are conducive to that intervention. For example, one fairly obvious approach would be to argue, first, that invading spirits have needs and interests converging somehow with those of the subject, and second, that a multiple's psychological weaknesses and already existing fragmented state give them 'room' to enter. A non-survivalist, however, would simply regard the HHs as a particular class of personalities or personality fragments, taking a form psychologically useful or appropriate to the subject.

Although it is not entirely clear to what extent Allison himself endorses the intrusion hypothesis, he does take it seriously, and many others (particularly laypersons) seem to have adopted the hypothesis enthusiastically. Nevertheless, Allison's encounters with HHs offer very little support to the intrusion hypothesis.

(i) One might think that the problem concerns the issue of personality-robustness. If HHs are temporarily embodied or re-embodied spirits, why should they be relatively one-dimensional personalities, like most alters? Why should they seem so much like helpful, circumscribed parts of a fragmented psyche, rather than more full-bodied personalities using an extensive repertoire of affect and behavior to aid the patient? The fact is, HHs simply *seem* only to be personality fragments who claim to be spirits. Except for claiming to be non-corporeal, they are not conspicuously different from other helpful alters (say, with regard to their limitations or functions in the subject's overall psychology).

But as we have seen, one cannot simply assume that discarnate individuals would suffer no limitations during possession or in the process of communication. To be fair to partisans of the survival and intrusion hypotheses, we must admit that we have no idea what sorts of personality distortions might occur under the circumstances. Moreover, there is no reason to insist that a possessing or communicating spirit is either compelled or motivated to appear in its most robust form. Perhaps it reveals or gives only as much of itself as the situation demands. After all, human beings seldom reveal their total personality over the course of a few interactions, especially if those interactions are relatively brief.

(ii) A more serious problem with Allison's position concerns the reliability of his descriptions. According to Allison, one reason for believing that HHs are not merely alternate personalities is that they remain after the patient is integrated. But for the reasons considered in Chapter 2.4, Allison could easily be mistaken about whether his patients were fully integrated. Hence, like others in the field, he may well have misjudged the success of his integration attempts, whether or not the error was motivated by a prior belief in survival.

(iii) Moreover, quite apart from the issue of successful integration, Allison's accounts suggest iatrogenic contamination. We know that pseudo-personalities and personality fragments may be created in hypnotic and therapeutic settings, and it appears as if Allison was inclined to accept the possibility (if not the reality) of survival prior to uncovering HHs. So we might wonder just how antecedently sympathetic Allison was to the survival or intrusion hypotheses and how he might have subtly communicated that to suggestible patients. Moreover, we should recall an important fact from the history of hypnosis — namely, that practitioners of different schools of hypnosis tended to see correspondingly different sorts of hypnotic symptoms. Those researchers, in other words, observed the distinctive sorts of dissociative phenomena they expected. Clearly, this could also have occurred with Allison's subjects.

(iv) But perhaps the most important objection to the intrusion hypothesis generally (i.e., not simply in connection with HHs) concerns the psychological utility of HHs and other apparent alters claiming to be discarnate entities. Considering how much HHs resemble ordinary alternate personalities in their clinical presentation, we should ask: Why might it be important for a multiple to regard certain alternate personalities as temporarily embodied spirits? Three reasons in particular stand out.

First, as Ross observes, the alter might simply 'represent a clear-cut identification' with some individual close or important to the subject. For example, if the personality is identified as a dead relative, and if the patient's

> identification is with an abuser, the alter will be an abuser. If it is with a nurturing grandmother, it will be a protector. One patient had an alter that was a seagull named Jonathan. Not surprisingly, this alter soared in freedom above the patient's troubles, much like Jonathan Livingston Seagull.
>
> (Ross, 1989, p. 120)

Second, when the ostensible spirit serves the function of a helper personality, the patient might feel as if his guidance and cure are directed by something transcendent, something inevitably more powerful or wise than the patient feels himself (or his therapist) to be. Besides, as Allison concedes, HHs do not offer *evidence* of survival; they merely claim to be spirits. Therefore, since helper personalities appear in many (if not most) cases of MPD, it seems reasonable to suppose that HHs are merely a subset of the set of helper personalities. They would be those ISHs who, for reasons of deep psychological importance to the patient, claim to be entities who possess the wisdom gained from higher plains or from the experience of a former life.

Third, in cases where the ostensible spirit is not a helper, the patient might benefit in a rather different way. Unlike part of one's own fractured self, an invading entity would conveniently deflect responsibility for behavior (or simply thoughts or emotions) away from the patient and onto the spirit realm. The patient would not have to feel personally responsible for behavior (thoughts or emotions) that would normally be provocative or psychologically risky. Interestingly, some skeptics about the genuineness of MPD (e.g., Kenny, 1986) think that *every* alternate personality results from a kind of role playing and offers similar advantages to the multiple. Although that more extreme view seems to be indefensible (see Braude, 1988a), it is clear that by assigning risky thoughts, feelings, or behavior to a discarnate entity, the subject can deflect responsibility to a greater degree than would be possible by assigning them to another part of oneself (such as an alter).

9.5 CONCLUSION

These last considerations lead us back to mediumship. Obviously mediumistic communicators might play a role similar to that of a multiple's apparently intruding discarnate alters. In fact, there are two major reasons why a medium might prefer (at least unconsciously) to see communicators as genuinely discarnate, rather than as elements or creations of her own psyche. First, quite apart from the social utility or appealing notoriety some might find in being a medium, there is considerable psychological value in believing that the messages emanate from something other than a mere mortal. The medium might neither trust nor respect words of wisdom, comfort, guidance, or even bits of mundane information, if she felt they came from her own mind. And of course, the medium's sitters might share and reinforce that point of view. Second, a belief in one's mediumship psychologically takes the medium off the hook, with regard to successes as well as failures. Since a medium believes that she is merely an intermediary for communications and information provided by post-mortem individuals, she never has to feel responsible when a séance goes awry (i.e., when no phenomena, or only disappointing phenomena, occur). And perhaps more important, when successes occur (i.e., when good information is communicated), the medium never has to fear the extent of her powers, particularly when the séance is over. She does not need to attribute successes to her own ESP, which for a first-rate medium would raise the terrifying spectre of omniscience — or at the very least a degree of psychic functioning that most people find deeply frightening (Braude, 1987, 1989). And when we consider the profound psychological needs that the communicator's information or behavior might satisfy — needs that we might be reluctant to acknowledge — how convenient, then, if the information or behavior is provided by a third party, a communicator for whom we can feel (say) contempt. Once again, the medium herself can feel blameless for anything the sitters find objectionable. (And again, I recommend Eisenbud's essay on Cagliostro.)

Of course, these considerations do not rule out the possibility that some mediums really do provide evidence for survival. But as we deepen our grasp of the etiology and dynamics of multiplicity, we inevitably see how the underlying dynamics of mediumship might also be more complex than they have seemed. (That is hardly surprising; after all, cases of mediumship are seldom given the sort of depth-psychological scrutiny accorded cases of multiplicity.) As a result, it becomes easier to make conjectures about the ways in which dissociative phenomena might manifest in forms appropriate to a mediumistic séance. Indeed, that seems to be a major irony in the parapsychological study of MPD. Ever since the founding of the Society for Psychical Research, many have expected the study of dissociation to help *strengthen* the case for survival (for example, that seems to have been Myers's view (1903)). But in fact, it only furnishes deeper reasons for treating mediumship as one of many possible forms of dissociation.

10

UPDATE AND AFTERTHOUGHTS

10.1 INTRODUCTION

In the few years since this book first appeared, several developments in the study and treatment of MPD have altered the empirical and conceptual landscape. Although none of them require
modifications to the positions taken in earlier chapters, it seems
appropriate to bring the discussion up to date.

Changes — even rapid changes — in our thinking about MPD
should come as no surprise. For one thing, as clinicians have seen
additional patients and logged more hours with patients already in
treatment, they have inevitably and gradually refined their perceptions of multiple personality and developed a deeper appreciation of the diversity and subtlety of its manifestations. Clinicians
also have continued to explore various approaches to the treatment
of MPD, and their results likewise have had an impact on their
thinking.

These developments are not simply matters of interest to mental
health professionals and historians of psychology, psychiatry, and
medicine. Changing conceptions of psychopathology are also evo-
lutions in our thinking about persons generally, and as such they
deserve careful scrutiny.

10.2 DISSOCIATIVE IDENTITY DISORDER

Perhaps the most striking conceptual innovation is that the category
of MPD has been eliminated in the new DSM-IV (American Psychiatric Association, 1994) and superseded by the category of *Dissociative Identity Disorder* (DID).[1] As one would expect of a work
tailored to the needs of mental health professionals, the reasons for

this change seem (at least on the surface) to be clinical and pragmatic rather than philosophical. Indeed, apart from the systematic
replacement of certain terms, the diagnostic criteria for DID differ
little from those of its predecessors.

According to the DSM-IV, those diagnostic criteria are as
follows.

A. The presence of two or more distinct identities or personality states (each with its own relatively enduring pattern
   of perceiving, relating to, and thinking about the environment and self).
B. At least two of these identities or personality states
   recurrently take control of the person's behavior.
C. Inability to recall important personal information that is
   too extensive to be explained by ordinary forgetfulness.
D. The disturbance is not due to the direct physiological
   effects of a substance or a general medical condition.

Apart from the terminological novelty of emphasizing identities
over personalities, the major change in the diagnostic criteria
seems to be condition C, which reflects the growing consensus
among clinicians that amnesia plays a central role in dissociative
disorders. Moreover, considering that the category of DID is
designed to overcome alleged problems with the concept of
personality presupposed by MPD, it might seem odd that the new
diagnostic criteria and the accompanying discussion continue to
make frequent use of the term 'personality'. What *is* new, however, is that the DSM-IV downplays the importance of the term by
referring to personality *states* rather than personalities *simpliciter*.
The reason for this will be considered below.

Predictably, the clinical community is divided over the merits of
and the need for this new diagnostic category. In fact, it may be
significant that the World Health Organization's counterpart to the
DSM, the ICD-10, is retaining the term 'MPD'. Although the
terminological change in the DSM appears in part to have been
politically motivated,[2] the major official justification for the change
is that the concept of multiple personality fosters counter-therapeutic clinical interventions. In particular, clinicians worry that they
might inadvertently encourage either the proliferation or the
perpetuation of alters. Janet had long ago contended that the
naming of personality states tended to legitimate them and con-

tribute to their maintenance and further elaboration. Moreover, clinicians have known for some time that alter-like states can be created hypnotically (see Chapter 2, p. 61). Since most clinicians consider the goal of treatment to be the integration and disappearance of functionally distinct and apparently autonomous alters, they naturally want to avoid treatment strategies that would tend to thwart those objectives. Hence, many hope that the new terminology will deter both clinicians and patients from acting as if alters are distinct individuals or relatively autonomous and enduring things, and that they will instead view them merely as states, confusions, or types of behavior into which patients may shift, and from which they need to be weaned or discouraged.

These clinical concerns have been reinforced by an observation made by an increasing number of mental health professionals treating MPD. They have found that an effective — and possibly the most effective — way of preventing their patients from acting out or engaging in other forms of counter-therapeutic behavior is to treat them as if they are fundamentally unified individuals capable of understanding and controlling their actions. Hence, some clinicians simply demand — say, under threat of cutting off treatment — that their patients behave responsibly.

The success of what we may call this *hard-line* approach is not easy to interpret. Some clinicians believe that it illustrates that patients are unitary rather than genuinely multiple and that they simply believe mistakenly (although perhaps for good reasons) that some of their situationally-appropriate roles are distinct individuals. And of course, from this clinical perspective, it would be counter-productive to treat alters as distinct moral or prudential agents, because that would simply reinforce patients' delusions. (For a discussion of MPD and moral responsibility, see Braude, in press.)

Of course, not all clinicians regard patients' compliant behavior under these conditions as evidence of their deep unification. Some believe that the hard-line approach merely encourages dishonest acquiescence. For example, since patients are strongly motivated to please their therapists, they might simply act *as if* they are unified and responsible. Perhaps a group of alters will conspire to create this illusion, and perhaps certain alters will simply go undercover (so to speak), never emerging (at least conspicuously) in therapy sessions and emerging only covertly at other times.

Others adopt a middle-of-the-road position and maintain that the success of the hard-line approach is simply ambiguous, and that it affords no clue as to the ultimate nature of multiplicity. Interestingly, some of these agnostics support the new terminology on the grounds that it might help discourage attitudes and treatment strategies that either reinforce the divisions between personality states or encourage the creation of new ones.

But most advocates of the new terminology do not worry about the proper interpretation of the hard-line approach to treatment. They concede that the change from MPD to DID was never intended to address philosophical questions about the nature and autonomy of alters (or identities)[3] and that the virtues of this innovation (if genuine) would be largely pragmatic. As we have noted, some clinicians hope it will promote behavior toward alters that leads to more effective treatment strategies. And some believe that 'MPD' has become a pejorative term for many patients, hospitals, and insurance companies (a state of affairs possibly reinforced by sensationalist television talk shows dealing with the subject). As a result, they believe that the switch to DID may relieve the patient of the stigma presently attached to the diagnosis of MPD. Perhaps that is one reason why clinicians are beginning to report that their patients like the new diagnostic category.

Still, legitimate concerns remain about the category of DID and its associated terminological shifts. According to some clinicians, many patients are convinced at the start of treatment that their alters are clear and rigid divisions within the self. And when that occurs, they often insist on the reality of those divisions even when the clinician denies it and approaches them with a presumption of underlying unity. For example, even when the therapist tells the patient that alters are merely ego states and not real individuals, the patient may protest and enumerate apparently significant differences (including body type, sex, age, etc.). In these cases, there may be nothing to gain by the mere expedient of talking about and relating to alters as if they are less distinct or independent than the patient experiences them to be.

In fact, that strategy might even be counter-productive. Most MPD patients are not only intelligent but also quite clever and perceptive. They also tend to be masters of adaptation. One would expect many of them to perceive this strategy as a way of trying to trick them conceptually into less rigid personality divisions. Hence, this approach could lead to dishonesty and feigned unity in therapy sessions (of the sort some clinicians fear in connection

251

with the hard-line approach mentioned earlier), especially if patients are antecedently convinced about the distinctness or autonomy of alters. After all, it is hardly uncommon for MPD patients to withhold information from their therapists, usually out of fear and sometimes to satisfy what they take to be the therapist's expectations.

But quite apart from this issue, there is another reason for questioning whether the aims of treatment are more likely to be met by talk of alternate identities than by talk of alternate personalities. The problem, in a nutshell, is that the DSM-IV account of DID does not eschew the sort of language that it was presumably intended to eliminate. Although one no longer finds references to alternate personalities, one now finds frequent references, not simply to personality *states* but to alternate *identities*. And most important, those latter references are couched in the same allegedly unhelpful language previously used to describe alternate personalities. For example, the DSM-IV notes that 'there is a primary identity that carries the individual's given name and is passive, dependent, guilty, and depressed' (American Psychiatric Association, 1994, p. 484).[4] And it says that alternate identities

> may deny knowledge of one another, be critical of one another, or appear to be in open conflict. Occasionally, one or more powerful identities allocate time to the others. Aggressive or hostile identities may at times interrupt activities or place the others in uncomfortable situations.
>
> (American Psychiatric Association, 1994, p. 484)

We have considered reasons for thinking that multiples can be encouraged in the course of therapy to develop new personalities and that old personalities can harden when they are treated as distinct individuals (or even when they are simply named or referred to). The problem, however, is not that alters are simply called (or regarded as) personalities. The danger (if there is one) is in the way we conceptualize and describe alters' behavior and mental states, not simply in the decision to classify them as personalities rather than identities. It is ironic, then, that the passages quoted above ascribe to alter identities the same sorts of behavior and intentional states that previously had been attributed to alter personalities. The DSM-IV notes that alternate identities do such things as criticize one another, allocate time to others, and engage in aggressive or hostile acts. And it is the apparent aptness of those ascriptions that encourages the treatment of alters as distinct moral and prudential agents. So it is doubtful that the mere terminological switch from 'personalities' to 'identities' represents a major change in underlying metaphysical presuppositions or that it is likely to lead to substantially improved success rates in treatment. Hence, one would expect the problem (if there is one) to persist no matter which of those classifications one chooses.

Moreover, by continuing to ascribe to alter identities the sorts of intentional states previously ascribed to alter personalities, the DSM-IV seems tacitly to concede that alter identities are distinct *apperceptive centers,* as discussed in Chapter 3. That is, they still seem to be phenomenologically and epistemologically robust loci of self-awareness, indexically discontinuous from one another. That continues to be the most interesting feature of a multiple's inner life, and it continues to be what distinguishes MPD (or DID) from other complex and deeply involved role enactments. (And curiously, it is a feature of multiple personality about which clinicians still have relatively little to say.)

I would urge caution, therefore, about rejecting wholesale the well-entrenched terminology developed to describe MPD. Some clinicians continue to use the old terminology, if for no other reason than to communicate successfully with the many non-clinicians who have no reason to abandon the older terminology and also to preserve the link with more than a century of careful investigation of the disorder. Time will tell whether the new diagnostic category succeeds. In fact, Kluft may well be correct in observing that 'identity is as problematic a concept as personality — it just has been spared the invidious scrutiny afforded to "personality" in MPD'.[5]

10.3 THE 'FALSE MEMORY' DEBATE

The controversy over the concept of DID seems relatively tame and straightforward when compared to the debate regarding the possible creation of false memories of childhood abuse. This complex and highly-charged dispute centers around an attack on a broad assortment of mental health professionals, including those who treat MPD/DID and who take seriously the apparent link between MPD and early childhood trauma and abuse.

In what has become an occasionally strident and heated exchange, a growing number of critics have argued that therapists are making serious errors. First, they unwittingly (or intentionally) suggest false memories of abuse to malleable patients, especially when they utilize hypnotic and other memory retrieval techniques to uncover those allegedly hidden memories. The main reason for this, according to the critics, is that therapists often are predisposed to believe that their patients' problems stem from childhood abuse; hence, they keep probing until they get the responses they desire. Second, therapists too readily accept their patients' memory reports, because they underestimate both the variety of ways in which people can fabricate apparently vivid memories and the sorts of distortions to which even genuine memories are vulnerable. As a result, critics argue, patients (often at the urging, or at least with the approval, of their therapists) wrongly accuse parents, caretakers, or others of various forms of abuse. And naturally, such confrontations lead to wrongful convictions, expensive and wrenching lawsuits, and the destruction of family ties or other previously close relationships, all of which ruin the lives of innocent persons. Proponents of this skeptical position have even formed a well-financed and media-sophisticated organization, the False Memory Syndrome Foundation (FMSF), whose purpose seems to be to expose and prosecute the therapists it holds responsible for this state of affairs.

The ensuing debate is interesting not only for its substance and its potential impact on clinicians and the treatment of trauma, but also for its tone. One can't help but note the almost evangelical fervor on both sides of the debate and the apparent ineptitude and dishonesty of much of the criticism directed against clinicians. As I will illustrate shortly, critics often resort to transparently fallacious arguments and shoddy dialectical tactics that they presumably would not employ in other contexts, or whose defects they would probably be quick to spot if they had been the targets of that criticism instead.

Even the name of the FMSF might evoke suspicion, because there simply was no false memory syndrome recognized by any scientific body prior to the FMSF's formation. Granted, in medicine, naming a syndrome is easy; virtually anyone can do it, and unlike the classification of *disease*, it requires no broad professional consensus. In fact, the FMSF's designation of false memory syndrome has no more authority or antecedent credibility than my capricious invention of *premature seat belt release syndrome* to describe a familiar activity of impatient arriving

254

airline passengers, or *delusions of invisibility syndrome* to characterize drivers of automobiles who think people in other cars can't see them picking their nose. So although the mere naming of false memory syndrome is neither illegitimate nor unprecedented, it seems primarily to be a ploy to confer scientific respectability on an organization whose aims are largely political. After all, the purpose of the organization would have been communicated just as effectively if the word 'syndrome' had been dropped from its name.

Members of the clinical community have responded swiftly and (on the whole) intelligently and soberly to the challenge from FMSF spokespersons. In fact, many acknowledge that memory is a complex phenomenon. They note that because it is partially a creative act of cognitive construction and because multiples and other highly hypnotizable subjects are capable of responding to very subtle cues, ostensible memories reported in therapy should not be assumed to be the whole truth and nothing but the truth.

Of course, many (and perhaps most) clinicians knew this already, and they understandably bristled at their critics' gratuitous and apparently condescending admonitions about the complexity and fallibility of memory and the suggestibility of highly hypnotizable patients. After all, the concern about subject suggestibility has been a hot topic since the early days of Mesmerism (see, e.g., Laurence and Perry, 1988), and the contemporary literature on MPD has routinely cited studies bearing on the suggestibility and malleability of patients in therapy or under hypnosis.

Nevertheless, FMSF spokespersons undoubtedly are justified in claiming that some (presumably incompetent or naive) therapists are ignorant about the complexities of memory and the pitfalls of suggestibility, and also that some suggest memories of abuse to their patients. That is one reason why, even if the problem is not widespread, the debate over false memories is by no means trivial. Of course, the debate also matters to competent and sophisticated clinicians whose activities are being called into question and who are understandably torn about how to handle patients' ostensible memories of abuse. Although therapists are not in the detective business and although they are obligated to protect their patients' confidentiality, many find it difficult to ignore memory reports that could lead to the apprehension of abusers and thereby prevent the additional vicitimization of other innocent persons. Moreover, the false memory debate raises interesting legal issues, because lawsuits based on ostensibly recovered memories might be filed many years after the reported events took place.

But what needs to be addressed here is a matter of conceptual (rather than professional) housecleaning — namely, the quality of the reasoning deployed in the skeptical literature on false memories. Indeed, it is striking how that argumentation deteriorates once critics move beyond the aforementioned truisms about memory and suggestibility. At that point, skeptics' claims tend to range from the merely contentious to the absurd. The literature on this topic is already too vast to be dealt with comprehensively in several pages. But a few remarks seem to be in order.

10.4 THE RECORDER VIEW OF MEMORY

One of the most common skeptical tactics is to attribute to clinicians a view of memory — call it the *recorder view* — that they do not hold and that (contrary to the skeptics) their efforts to uncover hidden memories does not presuppose. For example, McHugh (1993) says that therapists who attempt to recover hidden memories are 'committed to the belief that memories are always true' (p. 18). Lindsay and Read (1994) describe this as the belief that memory is 'infallible' (p. 284). They claim that 'many proponents of memory recovery therapies…think of memory as a sort of video library of their personal histories, and of remembering as akin to replaying a video of the past' (p. 284). They maintain that therapists accept the 'implication of this metaphor…that memory is perfect and complete, requiring only the proper cues to allow people to retrieve accurate records of past experiences' (p. 284). Along the same lines. Ofshe and Watters (1993) say, 'Recovered memory therapy's fundamental conception of how memory functions assumes that the human mind records and stores everything perceived' (p. 5).

In a moment, I will consider in more detail what the recorder view of memory is supposed to be. But first we need to observe that it is simply false that so-called memory recovery therapy is committed to any such view. The mere attempt to uncover or search for hidden traumatic memories rests on two relatively modest assumptions: (a) that it is possible for memories to be rendered inaccessible by some form of traumatic amnesia, and (b) that it is possible to reverse traumatic amnesia with the aid of appropriate cues or memory recovery techniques.

But neither of those assumptions presupposes the completeness or infallibility of memory. In fact, assumption (a) is compatible with the view that we permanently forget some experienced events. It presupposes only that events or information may be remembered while being unavailable to conscious recall. In other words, it requires the further non-controversial assumption that remembering can be dispositional, and that one may not always be able to manifest that disposition in occurrent memory episodes. Similarly, assumption (b) does not presuppose that memory recovery elicits infallible or totally accurate memory reports. It requires only that the reversal of traumatic amnesia can uncover previously inaccessible details about one's past. But more important, assumption (b) is compatible with the view that some forgotten events may be irretrievable. That is, the clinical viability of memory recovery techniques does not require *every* memory to be recoverable; it is enough that some of them can be retrieved. Apparently, then, proponents of this familiar criticism are simply (and transparently) setting up a straw man.

Another way to approach the issue is to consider what clinicians might mean when (or if) they say that 'proper cues [or triggers]...allow people to retrieve accurate records of past experiences' (Lindsay and Read, 1994, p. 284). For present purposes, that claim can be interpreted in two ways. The first, and stronger, version is the one FMSF spokespersons seem to ascribe to clinicians who attempt to elicit hidden memories of abuse.

(M1): Every experienced past event can be recalled with the aid of an appropriate cue.

This claim, which is not presupposed by memory recovery techniqes, is easily falsified. It would be false so long as there is *some* experienced past event that can't be recalled under any circumstances. Since most clinicians probably believe that many events (including events from one's earliest days, but even many from later in life) are permanently forgotten, it is improbable that the use of memory retrieval techniques rests on a tacit acceptance of (M1). It is more likely that the majority of clinicians subscribe to the relatively modest claim:

(M2): Many experienced past events can be recalled with the aid of an appropriate cue.

But (M2) is neither radical nor particularly naive, and it would not be undermined by gratuitous skeptical reminders that some experienced events may never be recalled or that attempts to trigger the recovery of hidden memories sometimes result in false memory reports.

Another confused piece of reasoning figures prominently in an oft-cited paper by Elizabeth Loftus (1993). Loftus begins by quoting authors who claim that 'traumatic events leave some sort of indelible fixation in the mind' (p. 530) — that is, a lasting residue, impression, or trace (choose your metaphor) that, as one author puts it, does not erase. She counters this position with the claim that 'memory is malleable even for life's most traumatic experiences' (p. 530). As her subsequent remarks illustrate, what she means by this is that even veridical memory reports can change in their details from one occasion to another and that those details often are incorrect. In fact, she argues that traumatic memories can be 'radically changed' (p. 530).

The first thing to notice about Loftus's position is that it is irrelevant to at least a sensible interpretation of the view she is challenging. The claim that traumatic events leave indelible impressions on the mind does not have to be understood as meaning that traumatic events get recalled perfectly in all details or that memories of traumatic events never vary. But it is only that absurdly strong claim that Loftus can undermine by observing that genuine traumatic memories might be wrong in certain details.

Loftus makes this obvious error repeatedly. For example, in one of a series of replies to Loftus's 1993 paper, Olio articulates the view to which most clinicians dealing with trauma and dissociation probably subscribe.

> All memories contain inaccuracies and distortions in the details that are recalled. For adult survivors of childhood sexual abuse, however, it is not the small details (e.g., the exact age, the number of incidents) that are essential. Rather, it is the validation of the reality of the abuse itself that is crucial. The question is not whether there are inaccuracies in memory but whether memory retains essential truths.
>
> (Olio, 1994, p. 442)

But when Loftus responds to the commentaries in which Olio's article is included, she argues against a position none of the commentators defended, and she does not address the more reasonable position articulated by Olio. Olio concedes that not even veridical memories need to be accurate in all respects; however, Loftus writes,

> not every memory about the past is accurate, whether it is about child abuse or something else. And some false memories about the past come about because of powerful or even subtle suggestion.
>
> (Loftus, 1994, p. 443)

Lindsay and Read (1994) seem to commit a similar error. They suggest that the view that 'proper triggers [will elicit] accurate records of the past' (p. 284) conflicts with the view that 'remembering involves inference-like reconstructive processes' (pp 284-285). But those claims are incompatible only according to a simplistic recorder view according to which memory experiences are unadulterated playbacks of (all details of?) past events. But for reasons I will consider shortly, it is unclear whether *anybody* really subscribes to that view. The claim that memory is reconstructive means only that memory experiences are always subject to some degree of cognitive overlay, distortion or 'noise'. And that is a position that most clinicians seem quite clearly to accept.

Incidentally, this sort of exchange highlights why one must be careful in calling memories *true*, *false*, *accurate*, etc. As Olio's remarks make clear, what is usually at issue is whether certain crucial *components* of a memory report are accurate. Hence, when skeptics note (correctly, but gratuitously) that memories may not be entirely true because people misremember many details of past events, the terms 'true', 'accurate', etc., do not pick out properties straightforwardly ascribable to memories as a whole. At other times, however, it seems as if authors ignore or overlook the truth-value complexity of memory reports — for example, Loftus's remarks above, and in McHugh's warning that 'we must differentiate the true from the pseudo-memories' (McHugh, 1993, p. 18).

Returning, however, to Loftus's argument, it is also striking that her example of a radical change in a traumatic memory is not what it purports to be. In fact, she seems unwittingly to play into her opponents' hands. Loftus cites baseball pitcher Jack Hamilton's memory of hitting batter Tony Conigliaro in the face with a fastball. Although Hamilton claimed to remember the event perfectly, he remembered it as happening during a day game, when in fact the game was played at night. Of course, it is contentious (to say the least) that this was a 'critical' detail (Loftus, 1993, p. 531). But the important point is that Hamilton did not forget having hit Conigliaro in the face. So one would think that this is precisely the sort of case that would be embraced by the authors Loftus was opposing. After all, the allegedly critical detail concerning the time of the game was not traumatic; hence, Hamilton's failure to remember it is compatible with the claim that traumatic events leave an indelible impression on the mind. However, the traumatic part of the event, hitting the batter, seems to have been etched in Hamilton's memory (see Olio, 1994, for a similar observation).

Loftus's position here is particularly odd, because she has argued vigorously for the view that people remember certain types or details of events better than others (see Loftus, 1979). That is why, in an earlier work, she approvingly quoted D.S. Gardner's observation that

The extraordinary, colorful, novel, unusual, and interesting scenes attract our attention and hold our interest, both attention and interest being important aids to memory. The opposite of this principle is inversely true — routine, common-place and insignificant circumstances are rarely remembered as specific incidents.

(Loftus, 1979, p. 27)

Ironically, Loftus's point here tends to support the view she now opposes. It would seem to buttress the position that traumatic events (like hitting a batter in the face) are more indelible than non-traumatic features of the incidents (such as the time of day).

We have seen that memory recovery techniques do not presuppose a simplistic recorder view of memory, and we have also considered reasons for thinking that at least some reasonable clinicians do not subscribe to that view. But now we need to ask directly: does *anyone* really believe that memory is perfect and complete or infallible? After all, it is hard to imagine that any minimally reflective person would claim sincerely never to have forgotten or misremembered. Even Lindsay and Read admit, 'most readers can likely recall everyday experiences in which past events were misremembered' (p. 286). So who holds the recorder view? Presumably, the clinicians in question also are shrewd enough to recognize that they, too, have misremembered on occasion. But in that case, it is important to specify more carefully what those subscribing to memory recovery techniques actually believe.

Let us begin by granting that the class of mental health professionals is as diverse as other occupational groups and that it certainly has its share of fools and incompetents. But it is obviously illegitimate to attack all clinicians who use hypnosis, or who treat dissociative disorders, or who try to reverse traumatic amnesia, on the basis of confused or careless statements made by some practitioners. That is as indefensible as impugning the entire class of sociologists on the basis of Richard Ofshe's apparent inability to formulate a sound argument. One needs to determine not simply what proponents of memory recovery techniques seem to believe on the basis of popular self-help literature, offhand remarks, or inevitably oversimplified responses to superficial or misleading questionnaires, but what their more considered responses and careful professional writings suggest they actually believe.[6]

And it is not being overly charitable to think that most believe something like the following. It is possible for people to remember many events with considerable accuracy and in considerable detail, but their ability to gain conscious access to the remembered details of those events is situation-dependent or state-dependent. More-over, it is possible to retrieve some (and perhaps many) presently inaccessible memories or details by producing appropriate cues or recreating the appropriate states. Another way of putting this point (one that is less conspicuously wedded to the analogy of memory as a recording process) would be to replace the potentially misleading phrase 'memory *recovery* techniques' with 'memory *enhancement* techniques', and then to claim that such techniques can sometimes improve the accuracy or completeness of recollections of past experiences. Put this way, the more modest view apparently presupposed or held by reasonable clinicians is analogous to the view that the taste of food can be enhanced by the judicious application of spices — that is, flavor enhancement techniques. In fact, in both cases the techniques have their pitfalls. Memory enhancement techniques can produce various artifacts, and flavor enhancement techniques can likewise produce anomalies or undesired results.

10.5 THE APPEAL TO REPRESSION

Another way in which FMSF spokespersons frequently set up a

straw man concerns their illegitimate conflation of repression with dissociation or traumatic amnesia. For example, Loftus (1993) and Ofshe and Watters (1993) attack clinicians who attempt to recover hidden memories on the grounds that they assume the existence of a phenomenon for which there is no solid empirical evidence — namely, Freudian repression. But as some have observed (e.g., Gleaves, 1994), those clinicians are not committed to the existence of repression, and the skeptics' arguments against that concept are clearly irrelevant. Curiously, Ofshe and Watters seem tacitly to concede this, because they acknowledge the existence of traumatic amnesia, which is all the search for hidden memories of abuse ever required.[7]

It is difficult to view this skeptical assault on repression as anything other than dishonest. But disheartening as that conjecture may be, it is more credible than the leading alternative — namely, that Loftus, Ofshe, and others are too naive or ignorant about the professional literature on dissociation and memory to realize that processes besides repression could lead to the selectivity of perception and recall. Interestingly (and perhaps revealingly), in response to the several commentaries in which Gleaves's article was included, Loftus (1994) does not even acknowledge Gleaves's criticism of her improper focus on repression. Indeed, she continues to argue that 'the evidence for the delayed recovery of valid repressed memories is "rather thin"' (p. 444).

The irrelevance (and apparent dishonesty) of the FMSF's attack on repression is highlighted by another of Loftus's tactics. Loftus cites Holmes's survey of the evidence for repression (1990) to support her negative assessment of that evidence. Others cite Holmes's paper in the same manner (e.g., Ofshe, in press; Yapko, 1994). For example, Ofshe (in press) refers readers to Holmes's paper when he says 'none of the luminaries of the recovered memory movement take the time to instruct readers as to the flimsy to non-existent foundations on which the traditional repression concept rests'. But as Gleaves observes, Holmes states clearly (pp. 97-98) that other processes besides repression might generate selective memories and perceptions. It is presumably no accident that more sophisticated skeptical authors do not commit this error (e.g., Lindsay and Read, 1994).

Interestingly, Gleaves could have cited additional ways in which Holmes's paper fails to support the positions of Loftus, Ofshe, Yapko and others. In fact, one can only wonder whether those authors actually read Holmes's paper. Most notably, not only does Holmes explicitly ignore processes other than repression that might lead to selective recall, he focuses only on 'after expulsion' repression rather than 'primary repression'. In the former, 'an individual consciously recognizes something as threatening (anxiety provoking) and then represses the thought to avoid the anxiety' (p. 86). But the type of amnesia at issue in many (if not most) cases of ostensible childhood sexual abuse seems, rather, to be closer to the latter, 'in which threatening material is relegated to the unconscious before it is consciously recognized as stressful' (p. 86). Hence, even if Holmes's conclusions about the lack of evidence for repression are correct, they would be irrelevant to the aims of the FMSF.

Holmes does claim that there is a lack of 'controlled evidence' for primary repression (p. 96), and he dismisses anecdotal clinical evidence for the phenomenon. Of course, one could argue plausibly that *only* anecdotal clinical evidence could demonstrate the phenomenon that is really at issue, and (moreover) that the demand for controlled experimentation is simply the methodologically naive sort of physics envy[8] that one finds all too frequently in the behavioral sciences. But in any case, Holmes's survey of the evidence for both sorts of amnesia is hardly comprehensive. Most important, he ignores interesting experiments for something at least very close to primary repression cited elsewhere in the same volume by Kihlstrom and Hoyt (1990) — for example, Luria, 1932; Huston, *et al.*, 1934 — as well as research not mentioned in that paper (e.g., Eisenbud, 1937, 1939). So Holmes's assurances about the lack of experimental evidence carry little weight.

Actually, the confusions surrounding the skeptics' attack on repression are legion. For example, Ofshe (in press) also attacks clinicians for positing what he says is a novel form of repression, and which he claims is 'more powerful...than has ever been recognized in human history'. Ofshe calls this 'the newly discovered (total) repression phenomenon' or 'robust repression'. According to Ofshe, the reason this form of repression is so distinctive and extreme is that patients 'enter therapy confident that they *have never been sexually abused* or...suspicious but *completely lack*[ing] *any actual knowledge* of sexual abuse'. But since the evidence for that assertion can only consist of testimony from the patients, all this means is that patients entering therapy sincerely *claim* that they remember no abuse. But then it is unclear why Ofshe calls this form of repression 'new'. For one thing, what Ofshe describes has been reported throughout the history of dissociation. Moreover, sincerely (and sometimes adamantly) claiming not to have repressed or forgotten anything is a familiar feature, not only of traditional repression (and dissociation), but also of everyday cases of forgetting.

10.6 ADDITIONAL SKEPTICAL ERRORS

Some of the most astonishly weak arguments in the false memory debate have been offered by Paul McHugh, one of the FMSF's most visible and influential spokespersons. For instance, he claims that ostensibly recovered memories of abuse have met with 'direct contradictions' (McHugh, 1993, p. 18), an example of which he says is 'the patient's failure to mention any mistreatment in diaries kept at the time of the alleged abuse' (p. 18). Of course, that is ridiculous. Unless the diaries specifically state that no abuse occurred, there is no direct contradiction to the patient's memory claim. In fact, for the mere absence of reports of abuse in diaries to be significant in the way McHugh suggests, one would have to assume (preposterously) that diaries report the whole truth and nothing but the truth.

McHugh also maintains that recovered memories of abuse are refuted by 'the way the claims shift' (p. 18) regarding the identity of the abuser. But of course there are many reasons why genuine memories of abuse can be embedded within a fluxuating nexus of confusions and errors over details of the abusive situations. Hence, although such shifts in testimony merit caution about charging a specific person with abuse, they do not show that no abuse occurred.

McHugh also claims that accused parents are often in 'stable, enduring, and satisfactory intimate relationships' (p. 18), and that this counts against the charges of abuse. But what is McHugh's standard of evidence? Does he base his assessment of the accused family members solely on statements made by the parents or others reasonably motivated to deny the abuse, or perhaps on his own personal observations of their behavior? If so, then McHugh is obviously subscribing to an indefensible double standard. Unless there is independent testimony of intimate details of the family's life (a highly improbable occurrence), McHugh is assigning more *prima facie* antecedent credibility to the parents' (or the alleged victimizers') testimony and behavior than to that of the alleged victim.

Ofshe and Watters commit an equally glaring blunder. They write, 'only pre-therapy accounts of a person's history can be treated as a normal memory with only the ordinary component of error' (1993, p. 14). But clearly, that position is plausible only on the untenable assumption that there are no abnormally potent constraints on testimony prior to therapy, or that therapy is inherently a more psychologically coercive environment than the family environment or any other situation one may encounter outside of therapy.

By contrast, and to their credit, Lindsay and Read admit that 'reconstructive memory processes...could also contribute to the creation of illusory beliefs and memories of a non-abusive childhood', so that 'people who were abused [would] think that they were not' (Lindsay and Read, 1994, p. 294). Regrettably, however, they bury this concession in a footnote.

Lindsay and Read also offer a questionable evaluation of the evidence regarding human suggestibility. One of the most pivotal underlying issues in the false memory debate is whether false memories of traumatic events (rather than their peripheral details) can be created by suggestion. FMSF spokespersons like to argue that this is possible, and they often support their position by appealing to allegedly relevant experiments. That has led to a debate over whether traumatic situations are psychodynamically distinct or discontinuous from experimental environments, and whether (or to what extent) experimental 'evidence of suggesti-bility can be generalized to therapy situations' (Read and Lindsay, 1994, p. 410) in which false memories are allegedly produced. These issues are too complex to be settled here, and it is likely that the evidence is neither as bad as defensive clinicians argue nor as good as the skeptics contend. Still, it is worth noting that even sophisticated skeptics such as Lindsay and Read seem insensitive to the peculiar intensity and devastating nature of traumatic experiences.

For example, they claim that 'recent studies have demonstrated that suggestions can give rise to false reports about dramatic (and even traumatic) life experiences (Read and Lindsay, 1994, p. 410). But they defend this point by citing a study in which children misremembered who gave them an injection. Although a 40-year-old male doctor had administered the injections, many of the children thought it had been a 22-year-old female research assistant.

It seems that Lindsay and Read err in several respects with this example. First, there is no reason to think that the case is psycho-dynamically similar to cases of genuine trauma. Injections are a relatively common, and admittedly unpleasant, occurrence in a child's life. But although most children probably dislike the experience, it is rarely (if ever) traumatic, and it is arguably not even particularly dramatic. In fact, doctors usually take steps to minimize their young patients' fear. Second, one could argue plausibly that children (especially young ones) are more vulnerable to memory distortions than adults. And if that is the case, then one could easily challenge the relevance of this sort of experiment to the possible memory distortions created in adults undergoing psychotherapy. (See Loftus, 1993, for additional examples of this questionable reliance on studies with children.) Third, Lindsay and Read commit the error noted above in connection with Loftus — namely, confusing peripheral and undisturbing details of the event with the central unpleasant event. The children may have misremembered the age, sex, and occupation of the person administering the injection, but they did not forget the injection. Hence, it seems plainly false that the childrens' memory errors are 'rather dramatic and potentially important' (Read and Lindsay, 1994, p. 410).

Lindsay and Read's second example seems more promising, at least on the surface. They cite research in which, as the result of suggestion, subjects reported having been lost in a shopping mall as a young child (Loftus, 1993; Loftus and Coan, in press). Although Loftus has apparently conceded that 'being lost in a shopping mall is completely different from being sexually abused' (quoted in Olio, 1994, p. 442), the study does seem to show that suggestion can lead at least some sorts of subjects to report remembering unusually unpleasant experiences. But that is still far from demonstrating that suggestion can implant false memories of traumatic experiences.

Moreover, Loftus's study is vulnerable to a number of serious criticisms. First, the subject pool was too small to permit any useful generalization ($N = 5$). Second, since those subjects were all friends or family of Loftus' research assistants, they cannot be considered a random or uncontaminated sample. Third, this study examines 'only the possibility of implanting a single generic memory with which most people can identify' (Olio, 1994, p. 442). Presumably, relatively few people have been sexually abused. But most people have had the experience of being lost at some time. Hence, one would think it is easier to create a pseudo-memory of the latter than of the former. Evidence of the experimental creation of false memories would be more relevant if those memories were significantly different from the subjects' personal experiences — for example, inducing typical U.S. citizens to believe they went to high school in India.[9] Fourth, Loftus's subjects received their suggestions from 'a trusted family member who played a variation of "Remember the time that...?"' (Loftus, 1993, p. 532). But then one would think that Loftus's experimental setting differs in an important respect from the environment of a therapy session. Although therapists, like family members, may be viewed as trustworthy sources, they are not in the authoritative and influential position of having been present for the subject's ostensibly remembered childhood experience.

FMSF spokespersons have also been criticized for focusing too narrowly on only certain types or manifestations of memory, or for failing to recognize important differences between distinct types of memory. For example, Olio claims that Loftus 'does not recognize traumatic memory as a different phenomenon from everyday narrative memory' (personal communication, August 27, 1994). Others note that memories needn't always manifest as occurrent conscious states. Byrd criticizes Loftus (1993) for not 'attending [more thoroughly] to the physiological aspects of memory formation (1994, p. 439). He notes that although 'much of the narrative content of traumatic memories may be particularly subject to repression, confabulation, or contextual biasing...the somatic and affective features of the memory...[may] remain as the root of the patient's symptomatology' (p. 439). Similarly, Ewin notes that memories might be expressed, not only physiologically, but by means of ideomotor responses — that is, a kind of imprinting (Ewin, 1994, p. 175). In particular, he has in mind David Cheek's experiments, in which the sequential head and shoulder movements of the birth process were unknowingly replicated by adults during hypnotic age regressions to birth (see Rossi and Cheek, 1988). For additional provocative research on the physiological residue or retention of traumatic experiences, see De Bellis, Chrousos, Dorn, Burke, *et al.*, 1994; De Bellis, Lefter, Trickett, and Putnam, 1994; Rösler, 1994; and van der Kolk, 1991.

Overall, I think it is safe to say that the skeptical contributions to the false memory debate comprise an uneven and often undistinguished body of literature. That is particularly regrettable, considering the practical and theoretical importance of many of the issues. Of course, the preceding discussion has been far from comprehensive. I can only hope that my comments will resolve some pervasive confusions and contribute to a relatively speedy resolution of at least some of the central disputes.

NOTES .

1 A BRIEF HISTORY OF HYPNOSIS

1 See also Martínez-Taboas, 1991a. Kenny (1986) offers a detailed examination of the social and cultural influences on the manifestations of MPD. But although he raises many valuable points and draws attention to many important external forces affecting the expression of the disorder, he adopts the indefensibly strong position that MPD is *nothing* but an idiom of distress. For a detailed criticism of his view, see Braude, 1988a. And see Chapters 2.6 and 7.5 for discussions of some social and cultural dimensions of multiple personality.

2 For more detailed accounts of the early history and theories of hypnosis, see Bliss, 1986; Laurence and Perry, 1988; Crabtree, 1985, 1988, 1993; Gauld, 1992; and Ellenberger, 1970.

3 Puységur noted that sleepwalkers tend not to respond to attempts at communication. By contrast, magnetized somnambulists have entered into an intimate rapport with the magnetizer, and that enables them to respond in a profound way to the magnetizer's communications. Indeed, Puységur maintained that his subjects could often respond to his unstated thoughts and wishes. He therefore called sleepwalkers 'independent somnambulists' and magnetized subjects 'subordinated somnambulists' (see Crabtree, 1993, and Gauld, 1992, for more complete accounts of Puységur's views).

4 Mesmer, aware that Puységur often conducted successful treatment without eliciting disruptive or violent crises in his subjects, insisted that magnetic sleep was merely a type of crisis, which he called 'critical sleep' or 'sommeil critique'. Puységur, on the other hand, claimed that crises were not essential to the healing process.

5 The view that the secondary consciousness was 'entirely cut off' from one's normal consciousness was widely held around this time. However, it was eventually undermined by subsequent experimentation, which revealed various forms of interference between dissociated parts of consciousness (see, e.g., Hilgard, 1986, Messerschmidt, 1927-8). Curiously, though, there were ample indications by the 1880s that such interference occurred (see, e.g., Gurney, 1887a, p. 317, 319ff).

6   Hilgard is more circumspect than many of his predecessors in
    drawing inferences about the nature of the hidden observer. He
    mentions repeatedly that hidden observer phenomena can be elicited
    only with highly hypnotizable subjects (and not even with all of
    those), and he emphasizes that the '"hidden observer" metaphor was
    intended only to imply a temporary division' (1986, p. 299) rather
    than a persisting or permanent part of consciousness.

2 MULTIPLE PERSONALITY DISORDER: A SURVEY OF THE EVIDENCE

1   I prefer this term to the currently accepted term 'directional aware-
    ness'.
2   I know of one multiple whose best friend sustained precisely this
    view of her for a long time. When the multiple finally found the
    courage to tell her friend she suffered from MPD, the friend rejected
    her.
3   Those wishing to subscribe to *Many Voices* should write to P.O. Box
    2639, Cincinnati, Ohio 45201-2639.
4   This is due in part to Prince's attempts to conceal his patient's identi-
    ty. But a more important reason may be 'his insensitivity to, or
    inhibitions about, certain dynamic influences, sexual and symbolic,
    that he regarded as Freudian extravagances' (Rosenzweig, 1987, p.
    27).
5   It should not be surprising that alternate personalities both interfere
    with and overlap each other. It has been known for some time that
    dissociated states tend not be functionally independent. See Chapter
    4 for a discussion of this issue.
6   A somewhat different sort of sociological/psychological account is
    offered by Kenny (1986), who claims that MPD is an 'idiom of dis-
    tress' appropriate to a certain set of social and cultural conditions.
    Kenny's arguments, however, are complex and often confused, and
    it is not clear to what extent he regards MPD as nothing more than
    role playing. See Braude (1988a) for an extended critical discussion
    of Kenny's position.
7   Incidentally, considering the controversial nature of the evidence,
    Watkins and Watkins's recent reliance on the Bianchi case in their
    sympathetic (i.e., non-skeptical) account of MPD (1986) seems quite
    bizarre − in fact, a rather thinly disguised case of special pleading.
    For more details on that case, see Watkins, 1984; Allison, 1984; and
    Orne, Dinges, and Orne, 1984.
8   I am grateful to Frank Putnam for pointing this out to me in conver-
    sation.

3 THE NATURE OF MULTIPLICITY

1   For example, if the nun does not experience her body's hunger as *her
    own* hunger, why does she eat at all? For that matter, why would she

believe or recognize that there is a causal connection between feeding a certain body and making the sensation of hunger disappear? And how would she explain the fact that the sensation's disappearing is not causally related to the feeding of any other body? In fact, how would she make sense, generally, of her ability to perceive (allegedly impersonal) sensations uniquely associated with one body?

2   This issue seems to be analogous to that of explaining what hallucinations are in a phenomenalist epistemology. Beginning philosophy students often ask, 'How would a phenomenalist tell if he's hallucinating?', as if this was a potential problem for the theory. But the correct answer is that this is as practically difficult for a phenomenalist as it would be for a materialist or dualist. And it is not a problem for the phenomenalist (which is not to say that phenomenalism is a viable theory). The phenomenalist would say that hallucinations are explained in terms of certain kinds of actual or possible discrepancies between the experiences of different minds, no matter how difficult it might be to determine for oneself whether those discrepancies obtain in any given real-life case.

3   I am indebted to Ray Martin for this example.

4   Cutler and Read (1975) use the term 'co-consciousness' where I use the term 'co-sensory'. But since Prince often seems to use 'co-consciousness' for situations where alters may be both co-sensory and intra-conscious, and since other authors seem to use the term more or less as Prince did, I prefer to follow Prince's lead. On the other hand, Prince sometimes seems to regard 'co-conscious' and 'co-active' as synonyms (see Chapter 4). And in that case, I think we are justified in diverging from Prince's use of 'co-conscious' in order to make what appears to be a valuable distinction.

5   We needn't worry about what, precisely, Wilkes means by 'mind'. What matters here is the approach she takes to identifying the distinctive disunities of MPD. I suspect, however, that her use of 'mind' is close to my use of 'apperceptive center'.

4 THE CONCEPT OF DISSOCIATION

1   van der Hart has reminded me (in correspondence) that there *are* times when Janet seems to recognize this. Unfortunately, his writings are not as clear or as consistent as one would like.

2   This point is compatible with observations made in Chapter 2 concerning attribute depletion and distribution. The functional specificity of one alter, and the disappearance of that function elsewhere in the system of alters, has to do with distinctive *arrangements* or *sets* of capacities, any of which may be found — in different combinations — with other alters. Hence, attribute depletion and distribution are compatible with the sharing or overlapping of functions and traits among alters.

3   The reader will notice that the use here of 'co-conscious' is not exactly the same as the more precise use mentioned in the previous

chapter. The use of 'co-conscious' in Chapter 3 was intended only to be in the general spirit of Prince's somewhat more indefinite use of the term.
4   In connection with automatic writing, he observes, 'Certainly in many cases there is a halting in the flow of thought of the principal intelligence, indicating that the activity of the secondary intelligence tends to inhibit the untrammelled flow of the former'. (1939, p. 488)
5   Interestingly, William McDougall (1938) came close to recognizing this difference between repression and dissociation. He regarded repression as a breakdown in *dynamic* relations between parts of consciousness, rather than a breakdown of logical or associative links. But McDougall writes as if repression is a relation between two *conscious* things, almost as if repression presupposes Prince's concept of co-consciousness. And, in fact, McDougall does consider parts of consciousness to be *monads* (1938, p. 145). By contrast, Hilgard is more metaphysically conservative, or at least non-committal.
6   Clinicians writing about dissociation and MPD tend to overlook this point and say it is an amnesic (or 'amnestic', one of the uglier words in the professional lexicon) barrier that blocks even ongoing states from conscious awareness. However, this error seems relatively innocuous and so far (at least) has not led to any theoretical calamities.

5 THE PRINCIPLE OF COMPOSITIONAL REVERSIBILITY

1   I have, however, observed that no set of descriptive categories or psychological predicates is inherently fundamental; hence, no parsing of the self into functional units is inherently basic.
2   I must note, however, that I find no evidence suggesting that split-brain patients have two apperceptive centers, corresponding to the two surgically separated hemispheres.

6 MULTIPLE SUBJECTS OR MULTIPLE FUNCTIONS?

1   At least some dissociative cases could perhaps be handled along similar lines. For example, in cases of hypnotic amnesia we might say that S remembers that p but is presently unable to gain access to that memory. However, if that maneuver is satisfactory, one wonders if there is any distinction between cases of hypnotic or dissociative amnesia and ordinary forgetting (of things that can later be recalled). That issue is considered briefly in Chapter 4.
2   This simplification of (NC) is not really acceptable, as Plato realized. He noted how a person could be both moving and not moving at t, with respect to different objects (e.g., sitting still in a moving vehicle). That is why he said that nothing can, at t, *and in relation to the same thing*, be both F and not-F. Hence, when we say that S is both moving and not-moving with respect to the same thing, there must be two parts of S, one of which is moving and the other of which is not (e.g., as when I move only my finger; at t, part of me

moves while another part does not move, with respect to the same object).

3 For example, I tacitly assume (say) that observation of an object's color is a relatively passive process in which the object affects me (rather than the reverse, as some ancient Greek philosophers believed), and which does not alter the object's color. Similarly, I tacitly assume that the object is of a kind which does not spontaneously undergo transmogrifying alterations in atomic and molecular structure (at least in relatively short periods of time.)

4 Indeed, one can even doubt whether logic applies to sentences at all. According to some, it applies instead to statements or propositions. At any rate, consider the following example of how the acceptability (or meaning) of a logical law is part of a larger network of commitments. Whether we accept the law of identity, '$(x)(x=x)$' — roughly, 'anything is identical to itself', depends on numerous other considerations. If we allow, for instance, that 'Zeus = Zeus' is true, then in many systems of deductive logic containing the rule of Existential Generalization, we can infer that Zeus exists. To many, that result is intolerable. But one can handle it in several ways. One can stipulate that 'Zeus' is not a genuine name, and that genuine names pick out only real existent individuals. One can reject the rule of Existential Generalization and endorse a so-called (existence) *free* logic. Or one can adopt a substitutional interpretation of the existential quantifier. The reader needn't understand all these options. The point, however, is that the law of identity — like logical laws generally — is not simply true *no matter what*. Its truth turns on a number of other decisions as to which logical laws or principles are acceptable, and the whole package of decisions can only be evaluated on pragmatic grounds.

5 I use the term 'disambiguation' here to refer to the general process of clarifying the meaning of our utterances, which involves rendering them *both* less ambiguous and less vague.

6 I trust this is a fair restatement of Zemach's somewhat more careless (or at least ambiguous) version of this premise. Zemach's original is, 'On general grounds, we maintain that a mental state is a state of which its subject must be conscious' (1986, p. 124).

7 THE UNITY BENEATH MULTIPLICITY

1 As I used the term in Chapter 5, one could presumably assert that the self is composed of lower-order selves and also maintain that a psychological unity underlies the lower-order selves.

2 Consider, for example, the following statement from Putnam: 'We are not born into this world with a single, unified personality. Rather...we come organized as a basic set of behavioral states with the capacity to generate new states and develop and modify complex sequences of behavioral states' (1992a, p. 101).

3 I. Kant, *Critique of Pure Reason*, B 129-140. D. Hume, *A Treatise of Human Nature*, Book I, Part IV, Sec. VI. In order to explain Kant's point while doing justice to the rest of his philosophy, one

would have to present it in his own, highly idiosyncratic, terms. However, that would clearly exceed the scope of this book and the needs of the present discussion. Hence, I shall not worry about the details and subtleties of Kant scholarship here (or Hume scholarship, for that matter). Rather, I shall content myself with explaining what may fairly be described as a 'Kantian' account of the synthetic unity of experience.

4   Of course, Hume's point is somewhat more complicated. For example, he also rejects any *a priori* argument for the existence of the self, on the grounds that such arguments are empirically insignificant; they merely reveal relations of ideas. But if the self exists, that would be a matter of fact.

5   Together, (c) and (d) amount to the problem of explaining why multiplicity should not be construed as lying at the far end of a continuum of dissociative phenomena, all explainable ultimately with respect to a single subject. For the reasons we examined in Chapters 3 and 4, that position has considerable antecedent plausibility.

6   For example, it is not clear that the colony *organizes* foraging expeditions. It is clear only that foraging expeditions leave the colony.

8 PERSONS AND PERSONALITIES

1   There is some debate in the literature over whether intelligent non-humans (say, aliens) could count as persons. For example, Wiggins writes,

> An alien intelligence is not a person. A person is a creature with whom we can get onto terms, or a creature that is of the same animal nature and psychophysical make-up as creatures with whom we can get onto terms.
>
> (Wiggins, 1987, p. 72)

For the moment, however, we may sidestep this issue. Our immediate concern is whether there is a one-one or one-many correspondence between bodies and persons (alien or terrestrial) and whether (at least in the case of MPD) persons should be viewed normatively or forensically. For additional discussion of whether persons may be non-human, see Morton, 1990, and Smith, 1990. Morton also offers further reasons for thinking that there is no single privileged concept of a person.

2   In that case, Smart may not be justified in claiming (as he appears to do) that being a person in the (normative) sense he describes requires being a person at the more primitive level (i.e., a member of a Kantian kingdom of ends).

3   Probably, a person in the dispositional/normative sense is one who meets Dennett's well-known six conditions of personhood (1976), at least if we relax his first condition, that of rationality. I suspect that at least many whom we would consider insane, or whose behavior is largely inscrutable and unpredictable, would still count as persons in the dispositional/normative (and for that matter, in the organismic/

normative) sense of the term.

4   We need not worry here over whether Billy is genuinely a multiple rather than a skillful malingerer. Our present concern is how to understand Billy's case on the assumption that he *is* a multiple.

5   I tend to concur with Wilkes (1988) that traditional thought-experiments concerning personal identity do more harm than good, and that we gain more by concentrating on the real puzzles handed us in life. Wilkes puts the point succinctly in the Preface to her book. Regarding thought-experiments, she writes,

> these alluring fictions have led discussion off on the wrong tracks; moreover, since they rely heavily on imagination and intuition, they lead to no solid or agreed conclusions, since intuitions vary and imaginations fail. What is more, I do not think that we need them, since there are so many actual puzzle-cases which defy the *imagination*, but which we none the less have to accept as facts.
>
> (Wilkes, 1988, p. vii)

In a similar — but rather more restrained — vein, Rorty complains that 'thought experiments of this kind are always underdescribed' (1988, p. 28). Likewise, Johnston notes that the 'inconstancy in our intuitive reactions...suggests that our ordinary capacity to make correct judgments about personal identity is not well engaged by such bizarre cases. (1987, p. 81)

6   Aune has been quite properly making this point for years. See, e.g., 1985, Chapter 5. And of course, these observations apply equally to the concept of *similarity*. See the discussion of similarity in Braude, 1979, 1983, 1986a.

7   Similarly, if such a society takes spirit possession seriously, certain individuals might count as persons in some dispositional (rather than organismic) sense. But whether they are regarded as bearers of rights may depend on whether their *claims* concerning their social origin are taken seriously.

8   Interestingly, a prominent clinician and authority on MPD told me of a similar attitude adopted by the boyfriend of one of his patients. Since the multiple had numerous female alters representing different styles of sexuality and femininity (e.g., a Southern belle, New York hooker), he felt that (among other things) he had a harem at his disposal.

9 MULTIPLE PERSONALITY AND MEDIUMSHIP

1   Interestingly, Gauld observes that Doris Fischer developed into a versatile medium after her original hysterical symptoms and their associated alternate personalities had disappeared. But Gauld considers this a point *in favor of* interpreting mediumistic communicators as alternate personalities, and I agree. The Doris case might indicate only that the manifestations of alternate personalities took on a

different form as Doris's psychological well-being improved. For all we know, once Doris became a medium, her dissociative capacities were serving a different set of needs and simply manifested in a healthier (or at least less profoundly or cripplingly maladaptive) form.

10 UPDATE AND AFTERTHOUGHTS

1   Psychogenic Fugue has also been renamed; it is now called *Dissociative Fugue*.
2   See the comments on the name change in the *ISSD News*, Vol 12 (4), August, 1994.
3   Not surprisingly, clinicians are no longer certain what to call alters. Although they are not alter *personalities* according to the DSM-IV, they are still considered to be alter identities. So perhaps the term 'alter' is still acceptable, despite its having been coined as an abbreviation for 'alternate personality'. Some clinicians seem inclined to talk instead just of 'ego states'. It is perhaps even less clear what to call multiples. Had the name of their disorder been 'multiple identity disorder', the term 'multiple' might still have been appropriate. Personally, I like Richard Loewenstein's suggestion to use the term 'whatchamacallits'.
4   The appeal to a *primary* identity seems particularly curious and reactionary, in view of the generally sensible reasons clinicians had been drifting away from talk of primary personalities (see Chapter 2).
5   *ISSD News* Vol. 12 (August, 1994), p. 10.
6   For example, Yapko (1994) found that 31% of those responding to his survey agreed with the statement, 'When someone has a memory of a trauma while in hypnosis, it objectively must actually have occurred'. Quite apart from legitimate concerns over whether Yapko's population of respondents differs substantially from the population of mental health professionals generally (see Gravitz, 1994), one can only wonder what sort of response Yapko would have obtained had he substituted 'ostensible memory' for 'memory'. For many people, the term 'memory' *means* 'true (accurate, veridical) memory'. If the subjective experience in question or verbal report failed to correspond in the right way to some past event, one could reasonably consider it a false memory. And if one couldn't be sure about whether the correspondence obtained, it would be an ostensible memory.
7   Actually, it is difficult to know what, exactly, Ofshe and Watters concede, because they present thoroughly muddled and inaccurate descriptions of both repression and traumatic amnesia. Moreover, it is not only skeptics who confuse those two phenomena. See, e.g., Lamm, 1991, p. 23. But I do question whether the majority of clinicians suffer from this particular confusion.
8   I thank Sherry Turkle for this appropriately disdainful phrase.
9   This example is Olio's (personal communication, Oct. 1, 1994). Olio also notes that this may be why Loftus's young subjects were told that

they were lost in a shopping mall, whereas older subjects were told that they were lost in a department store (subjects ranged in age from 8 to 42). The reason, apparently, is that older subjects would be less likely to have had *any* mall experiences as a child, and the discrepancy between the attempted suggestion and their history would reduce the likelihood of creating a false memory. See Loftus and Coan (in press).

BIBLIOGRAPHY

Abrams, S. (1983). 'The Multiple Personality: A Legal Defense'. *American Journal of Clinical Hypnosis* 25: 225-231.

Adityanjee (1990). 'Letter to the Editor'. *American Journal of Psychiatry* 147: 1260-1261.

Adityanjee, Raju, G.S.P. and Khandelwal, S.K. (1989). 'Current Status of Multiple Personality Disorder in India'. *American Journal of Psychiatry* 146: 1607-1610.

Albini, T.K. and Pease, T.E. (1989). 'Normal and Pathological Dissociations of Early Childhood'. *Dissociation* 2: 144-150.

Aldridge-Morris, R. (1989). *Multiple Personality: An Exercise in Deception*. Hillsdale, N.J.: Erlbaum.

Allison, R.B. (1974). 'A New Treatment Approach for Multiple Personalities'. *American Journal of Clinical Hypnosis* 17: 15-32.

Allison, R.B. (1981-82). 'Multiple Personality and Criminal Behavior'. *American Journal of Forensic Psychiatry* 2: 32-38.

Allison, R.B. (1982-83). 'The Multiple Personality Defendant in Court'. *American Journal of Forensic Psychiatry* 3: 181-192.

Allison, R.B. (1984). 'Difficulties Diagnosing the Multiple Personality Syndrome in a Death Penalty Case'. *International Journal of Clinical and Experimental Hypnosis* 32: 102-117.

Allison, R.B. (1985). 'Spiritual Helpers I Have Met'. Paper presented at meeting of Association for the Anthropological Study of Consciousness, Menlo Park, CA, Apr. 11-14.

Allison, R.B. and Schwarz, T. (1980). *Minds in Many Pieces*. New York: Rawson, Wade.

Alvarado, C.S. (1989). 'Dissociation and State-Specific Psychophysiology During the Nineteenth Century'. *Dissociation* 2: 160-168.

Alvarado, C.S. (1991). 'Iatrogenesis and Dissociation: A Historical Note'. *Dissociation* 4: 36-38.

American Psychiatric Association (1987). *Diagnostic and Statistical Manual of Mental Disorders (3rd Edition, Revised)*. Washington, D.C.: APA.

American Psychiatric Association (1994). *Diagnostic and Statistical Manual of Mental Disorders (4th Edition)*. Washington, D.C.: APA.

278

BIBLIOGRAPHY

Anderson, C.-E. (1991). 'Uninformed Consent'. *ABA Journal* January: 28.

Anderson, R.I. (1980). 'The Watseka Wonder: A Critical Re-Evaluation'. *Theta* 8(4): 6-10.

Anderson, R.I. (1981). 'The Therapist As Exorcist: James H. Hyslop and the Possession Theory of Psychotherapy'. *Journal of Religion and Psychical Research* 4: 96-112.

Armstrong, J. (1991). 'The Psychological Organization of Multiple Personality Disordered Patients As Revealed in Psychological Testing'. *Psychiatric Clinics of North America* 14: 533-546.

Atlas, G. (1988). 'Multiple Personality Disorder Misdiagnosed As Mental Retardation'. *Dissociation* 1: 77-83.

Aune, B. (1970). *Rationalism, Empiricism, and Pragmatism: An Introduction*. New York: Random House.

Aune, B. (1985). *Metaphysics: The Elements*. Minneapolis: University of Minnesota Press.

Baldwin, L. (1984). *Oneselves: Multiple Personalities, 1811-1981*. Jefferson, N.C. & London: McFarland.

Barkworth, T. (1889). 'Duplex Versus Multiplex Personality'. *Journal of the Society for Psychical Research* 4: 58-60.

Barlow, D.H., Abel, G.G. and Blanchard, E.B. (1977). 'Gender Identity Change in a Transsexual: An Exorcism'. *Archives of Sexual Behavior* 6: 387-395.

Bartis, S.P. and Zamansky, H.S. (1986). 'Dissociation in Posthypnotic Amnesia'. *American Journal of Clinical Hypnosis* 29: 103-108.

Basmajian, J. (1963). 'Control and Training of Individual Motor Units'. *Science* 141: 440-441.

Basmajian, J. (1972). 'Electromyography Comes of Age'. *Science* 176: 603-609.

Beahrs, J.O. (1982). *Unity and Multiplicity: Multilevel Consciousness of Self in Hypnosis, Psychiatric Disorder and Mental Health*. New York: Brunner/Mazel.

Beahrs, J.O. (1983). 'Co-Consciousness: A Common Denominator in Hypnosis, Multiple Personality, and Normalcy'. *American Journal of Clinical Hypnosis* 26: 100-113.

Benner, D.G. and Evans, C.S. (1984). 'Unity and Multiplicity in Hypnosis, Commissurotomy and Multiple Personality'. *Journal of Mind and Behavior* 5: 423-431.

Benson, D.F., Miller, B.L. and Signer, S.F. (1986). 'Dual Personality Associated With Epilepsy'. *Archives of Neurology* 43: 471-474.

Berger, D., Ono, Y., Nakajima, K., Suematsu, H. (1994). [Letter to Editor]: 'Dissociative Symptoms in Japan'. *American Journal of Psychiatry* 151: 148-149.

Bernstein, E.M. and Putnam, F.W. (1986). 'Development, Reliability, and Validity of a Dissociation Scale'. *Journal of Nervous and Mental Disease* 174: 727-735.

Bernstein Carlson, E. and Putnam, F.W. (1989). 'Integrating Research

279

On Dissociation and Hypnotizability: Are There Two Pathways to Hypnotizability?'. *Dissociation* 2: 32-38.

Binet, A. (1890). *On Double Consciousness*. Chicago: Open Court.

Binet, A. (1896). *Alterations of Personality*. New York: D. Appleton & Co.

Binns, P. (1994). 'Affect, Agency, and Engagement: Conceptions of the Person in Philosophy, Neuropsychiatry, and Psychotherapy'. *Philosophy, Psychiatry, & Psychology* 1: 13-23.

Bliss, E.L. (1980). 'Multiple Personalities. A Report of 14 Cases With Implications for Schizophrenia and Hysteria'. *Archives of General Psychiatry* 37: 1388-1397.

Bliss, E.L. (1983). 'Multiple Personalities, Related Disorders and Hypnosis'. *American Journal of Clinical Hypnosis* 26: 114-123.

Bliss, E.L. (1984a). 'Spontaneous Self-Hypnosis in Multiple Personality Disorder'. *Psychiatric Clinics of North America* 7: 135-148.

Bliss, E.L. (1984b). 'A Symptom Profile of Patients With Multiple Personalities, Including MMPI Results'. *Journal of Nervous and Mental Disease* 172: 197-202.

Bliss, E.L. (1984c). 'Hysteria and Hypnosis'. *Journal of Nervous and Mental Disease* 172: 203-206.

Bliss, E.L. (1986). *Multiple Personality, Allied Disorders, and Hypnosis*. New York & Oxford: Oxford University Press.

Bliss, E.L. (1988). 'Commentary: Professional Skepticism About Multiple Personality'. *Journal of Nervous and Mental Disease* 176: 533-534. Comment on Dell, 1988a.

Bliss, E.L. and Jeppsen, E.A. (1985). 'Prevalence of Multiple Personality Among Inpatients and Outpatients'. *American Journal of Psychiatry* 142: 250-251.

Bliss, J. and Bliss, E.L. (1985). *Andrea's World*. New York: Onyx.

Boon, S. and Draijer, N. (1991). 'Diagnosing Dissociative Disorders in the Netherlands: A Pilot Study With the Structured Clinical Interview for DSM-III Dissociative Disorders'. *American Journal of Psychiatry* 148: 458-462.

Boon, S. and Draijer, N. (1993). *Multiple Personality Disorder in the Netherlands*. Amsterdam: Swets & Zeitlinger.

Boor, M. (1982). 'The Multiple Personality Epidemic: Additional Cases and Inferences Regarding Diagnosis, Etiology, Dynamics, and Treatment'. *Journal of Nervous and Mental Disease* 170: 302-304.

Boor, M. and Coons, P.M. (1983). 'A Comprehensive Bibliography of Literature Pertaining to Multiple Personality'. *Psychological Reports* 53: 295-310.

Bowers, K.S. (1979). 'Hypnosis in Healing'. *Australian Journal of Clinical and Experimental Hypnosis* 7: 261-278.

Bowers, K.S. (1990). 'Unconscious Influences and Hypnosis'. In J.L. Singer (ed.), *Repression and Dissociation*. Chicago & London: University of Chicago Press: 143-179.

Bowers, K.S. (1991). 'Dissociation in Hypnosis and Multiple Personality

Disorder'. *International Journal of Clinical and Experimental Hypnosis* 39: 155-176.

Bowers, K.S. and Meichenbaum, D. (eds) (1984). *The Unconscious Reconsidered*. New York: Wiley-Interscience.

Bowman, E.S., Blix, S. and Coons, P.M. (1985). 'Multiple Personality in Adolescence: Relationship to Incestual Experiences'. *Journal of the American Academy of Child Psychiatry* 24: 109-114.

Bowman, E.S. and Coons, P.M. (1990). 'The Use of Hypnosis in a Deaf Patient With Multiple Personality Disorder: A Case Report'. *American Journal of Clinical Hypnosis* 33: 99-104.

Bowman, E.S., Coons, P.M., Jones, R.S. and Oldstrom, M. (1987). 'Religious Psychodynamics in Multiple Personalities: Suggestions for Treatment'. *American Journal of Psychotherapy* 41: 542-553.

Bramwell, J.M. (1896a). 'James Braid; His Work and Writings'. *Proceedings of the Society for Psychical Research* 12: 127-166.

Bramwell, J.M. (1896b). 'Personally Observed Hypnotic Phenomena'. *Proceedings of the Society for Psychical Research* 12: 176-203.

Bramwell, J.M. (1896c). 'What Is Hypnotism?'. *Proceedings of the Society for Psychical Research* 12: 204-258.

Brandsma, J.M. and Ludwig, A.M. (1974). 'A Case of Multiple Personality: Diagnosis and Therapy'. *International Journal of Clinical and Experimental Hypnosis* 22: 216-233.

Brassfield, P.A. (1983). 'Unfolding Patterns of the Multiple Personality Through Hypnosis'. *American Journal of Clinical Hypnosis* 26: 146-152.

Braude, S.E. (1979). *ESP and Psychokinesis: A Philosophical Examination*. Philadelphia: Temple University Press.

Braude, S.E. (ed.) (1980). 'Selected Poems of Patience Worth'. In *New Directions in Prose and Poetry 40*. New York: New Directions Press: 155-166 .

Braude, S.E. (1983). 'Radical Provincialism in the Life Sciences: A Review of Rupert Sheldrake's *A New Science of Life*'. *Journal of the American Society for Psychical Research* 77: 63-78.

Braude, S.E. (1986a). *The Limits of Influence: Psychokinesis and the Philosophy of Science*. New York & London: Routledge & Kegan Paul.

Braude, S.E. (1986b). 'You Can Say That Again'. *Philosophic Exchange* 17: 59-78.

Braude, S.E. (1987). 'Psi and our Picture of the World'. *Inquiry* 30: 277-294.

Braude, S.E. (1988a). 'Some Recent Books On Multiple Personality and Dissociation'. *Journal of the American Society for Psychical Research* 82: 339-352.

Braude, S.E. (1988b). 'Mediumship and Multiple Personality'. *Journal of the Society for Psychical Research* 55: 177-195.

Braude, S.E. (1989). 'Evaluating the Super-Psi Hypothesis'. In G.K. Zollschan, J.F. Schumaker, and G.F. Walsh (eds), *Exploring the Para-*

normal: Perspectives on Belief and Experience. Dorset: Prism: 25-38.

Braude, S.E. (1992a). 'Survival or Super-Psi?'. *Journal of Scientific Exploration* 6:127-144.

Braude, S.E. (1992b). 'Reply to Stevenson'. *Journal of Scientific Exploration* 6: 151-156.

Braude, S.E. (in press). 'Multiple Personality and Moral Responsibility'. In M. Gainer (ed.), *Self Reflections: Philosophical Issues in Dissociation*. Lanham, MD: University Press of America.

Braun, B.G. (1983a). 'Neurophysiologic Changes in Multiple Personality Due to Integration: A Preliminary Report'. *American Journal of Clinical Hypnosis* 26: 84-92.

Braun, B.G. (1983b). 'Psychophysiologic Phenomena in Multiple Personality and Hypnosis'. *American Journal of Clinical Hypnosis* 26: 124-137.

Braun, B.G. (1984a). 'Towards a Theory of Multiple Personality and Other Dissociative Phenomena'. *Psychiatric Clinics of North America* 7: 171-193.

Braun, B.G. (1984b). 'Hypnosis Creates Multiple Personality: Myth or Reality?'. *International Journal of Clinical and Experimental Hypnosis* 32: 191-197.

Braun, B.G. (1984c). 'Uses of Hypnosis With Multiple Personality'. *Psychiatric Annals* 14: 34-40.

Braun, B.G. (1985). 'The Transgenerational Incidence of Dissociation and Multiple Personality Disorder: A Preliminary Report'. In R.P. Kluft (ed.), *Childhood Antecedents of Multiple Personality*. Washington, D.C.: American Psychiatric Press: 128-150.

Braun, B.G. (1986). *The Treatment of Multiple Personality Disorder*. Washington, D.C.: American Psychiatric Press.

Braun, B.G. (1988). 'The BASK (Behavior, Affect, Sensation, Knowledge) Model of Dissociation'. *Dissociation* 1: 4-23.

Braun, B.G. (1989). 'Iatrophilia and Iatrophobia in the Diagnosis and Treatment of MPD'. *Dissociation* 2: 66-69.

Braun, B.G. and Sachs, R.G. (1985). 'The Development of Multiple Personality Disorder: Predisposing, Precipitating, and Perpetuating Factors'. In R.P. Kluft (ed.), *Childhood Antecedents of Multiple Personality*. Washington, D.C.: American Psychiatric Press: 38-65.

Brende, J.O. (1984). 'The Psychophysiologic Manifestations of Dissociation. Electrodermal Responses in a Multiple Personality Patient'. *Psychiatric Clinics of North America* 7: 41-50.

Brende, J.O. and Rinsley, D.B. (1981). 'A Case of Multiple Personality With Psychological Automatisms'. *Journal of the American Academy of Psychoanalysis* 9: 129-151.

Brick, S.S. and Chu, J.A. (1991). 'The Simulation of Multiple Personalities: A Case Report'. *Psychotherapy* 28: 267-272.

Broad, C.D. (1962). *Lectures On Psychical Research*. London: Routledge & Kegan Paul.

Bruce-Jones, W. and Coid, J. (1992). 'Identity Diffusion Presenting As

Multiple Personality Disorder in a Female Psychopath'. *British Journal of Psychiatry* 160: 541-544.

Buck, O.D. (1983). 'Multiple Personality As a Borderline State'. *Journal of Nervous and Mental Disease* 171: 62-65.

Buranelli, V. (1975). *The Wizard from Vienna: Franz Anton Mesmer.* New York: Coward, McCann & Geoghegan, Inc.

Burnham, J.C. (1986). 'The Fragmenting of the Soul: Intellectual Prerequisites for Ideas of Dissociation in the United States'. In J.M. Quen (ed.), *Split Minds/Split Brains*. New York & London: New York University Press: 63-83.

Bursen, H.A. (1978). *Dismantling the Memory Machine.* Dordrecht, Boston, London: D. Reidel.

Butterfield, M.I. (1993). 'Do Patients' Recovered Memories of Sexual Abuse Constitute a "False Memory Syndrome"?' *Psychiatric News* 28 (23):18.

Byrd, K.R. (1994). 'The Narrative Reconstructions of Incest Survivors'. *American Psychologist* 49: 439-440.

Cardeña, E. (1992). 'Trance and Possession As Dissociative Disorders'. *Transcultural Psychiatric Research Review* 29: 287-300.

Carlson, E.T. (1981). 'The History of Multiple Personality in the United States, I. The Beginnings'. *American Journal of Psychiatry* 138: 666-668.

Carlson, E.T. (1984). 'The History of Multiple Personality in the United States: Mary Reynolds and Her Subsequent Reputation'. *Bulletin of the History of Medicine* 58: 72-82.

Carlson, E.T. (1986). 'The History of Dissociation Until 1880'. In J.M. Quen (ed.), *Split Minds/Split Brains*. New York & London: New York University Press: 7-30.

Carlson, E.T. (1989). 'Multiple Personality and Hypnosis: The First One Hundred Years'. *Journal of the History of the Behavioral Sciences* 25: 315-322.

Carlson, E.T. and Simpson, M.M. (1971). 'Tarantism or Hysteria? An American Case of 1801'. *Journal of the History of Medicine* 26: 293-302.

Caws, P. (1994). 'Commentary On "Affect, Agency, and Engagement"'. *Philosophy, Psychiatry, & Psychology* 1: 25-26. Commentary on Binns, 1994.

Chodoff, P. (1987). 'Correspondence: More On Multiple Personality Disorder'. *American Journal of Psychiatry* 144: 124.

Chu, J.A. (1991). 'On the Misdiagnosis of Multiple Personality Disorder'. *Dissociation* 4: 200-204.

Chu, J.A. (1993). 'Critical Issues Committee Report: Criminal Responsibility and MPD'. *ISSMP&D News* 11: 4-5.

Clary, W.F., Burstin, K.J. and Carpenter, J.S. (1984). 'Multiple Personality and Borderline Personality Disorder'. *Psychiatric Clinics of North America* 7: 89-99.

Cleary, M.F. (1983). 'Dissociative States — Disproportionate Use As a

Defense in Criminal Proceedings'. *American Journal of Forensic Psychiatry* 4: 157-165.

Condon, W.S., Ogston, W.D. and Pacoe, L.V. (1969). 'Three Faces of Eve Revisited: A Study of Transient Microstrabismus'. *Journal of Abnormal Psychology* 74: 618-620.

Confer, W.N. and Ables, B.S. (1983). *Multiple Personality: Etiology, Diagnosis and Treatment*. New York: Human Sciences Press.

Congdon, M.H., Hain, J. and Stevenson, I. (1961). 'A Case of Multiple Personality Illustrating the Transition from Role-Playing'. *Journal of Nervous and Mental Disease* 132: 497-504.

Coons, P.M. (1980). 'Multiple Personality: Diagnostic Considerations'. *Journal of Clinical Psychiatry* 41: 330-336.

Coons, P.M. (1984). 'The Differential Diagnosis of Multiple Personality. A Comprehensive Review'. *Psychiatric Clinics of North America* 7: 51-67.

Coons, P.M. (1985). 'Children of Parents With Multiple Personality Disorder'. In R.P. Kluft (ed.), *Childhood Antecedents of Multiple Personality*. Washington: American Psychiatric Press: 152-165.

Coons, P.M. (1986). 'Treatment Progress in 20 Patients With Multiple Personality Disorder'. *Journal of Nervous and Mental Disease* 174: 715-721.

Coons, P.M. (1988). 'Psychophysiologic Aspects of Multiple Personality Disorder: A Review'. *Dissociation* 1: 47-53.

Coons, P.M. (1989). 'Iatrogenic Factors in the Misdiagnosis of MPD'. *Dissociation* 2: 70-76.

Coons, P.M. (1991). 'Iatrogenesis and Malingering of Multiple Personality Disorder in the Forensic Evaluation of Homicide Defendants'. *Psychiatric Clinics of North America* 14: 757-768.

Coons, P.M. (1993). 'Critical Issues Committee Report: Criminal Responsibility and MPD'. *ISSMP&D News* 11: 3.

Coons, P.M., Bowman, E.S., Kluft, R.P. and Milstein, V. (1991). 'The Cross-Cultural Occurrence of MPD: Additional Cases from a Recent Survey'. *Dissociation* 4: 124-128.

Coons, P.M., Bowman, E.S. and Milstein, V. (1988). 'Multiple Personality Disorder: A Clinical Investigation of 50 Cases'. *Journal of Nervous and Mental Disease* 176: 519-527.

Coons, P.M. and Bradley, K. (1985). 'Group Psychotherapy With Multiple Personality Patients'. *Journal of Nervous and Mental Disease* 173: 515-521.

Coons, P.M. and Milstein, V. (1986). 'Psychosexual Disturbances in Multiple Personality: Characteristics, Etiology, and Treatment'. *Journal of Clinical Psychiatry* 47: 106-110.

Coons, P.M., Milstein, V. and Marley, C. (1982). 'EEG Studies of Two Multiple Personalities and a Control'. *Archives of General Psychiatry* 39: 823-825.

Cory, C.E. (1919a). 'Patience Worth'. *Psychological Review* 26: 397-407.

Cory, C.E. (1919b). 'A Divided Self'. *Journal of Abnormal Psychology* 14: 281-291.

Coryell, W. (1983). 'Multiple Personality and Primary Affective Disorder'. *Journal of Nervous and Mental Disease* 171: 388-390.

Crabtree, A. (1985a). *Multiple Man: Explorations in Possession and Multiple Personality*. London & New York: Holt, Reinhart & Winston.

Crabtree, A. (1985b). 'Mesmerism, Divided Consciousness, and Multiple Personality'. In N.M. Schott (ed.), *Franz Anton Mesmer Und Die Geschichte Des Mesmerismus*. Stuttgart: Franz Steiner: 133-143.

Crabtree, A. (1986). 'Explanations of Dissociation in the First Half of the Twentieth Century'. In J.M. Quen (ed.), *Split Minds/Split Brains*. New York & London: New York University Press: 85-107.

Crabtree, A. (1988). *Animal Magnetism, Early Hypnotism, and Psychical Research, 1766-1925: An Annotated Bibliography*. White Plains: Kraus International.

Crabtree, A. (1993). *From Mesmer to Freud: Magnetic Sleep and the Roots of Psychological Healing*. New Haven: Yale University Press.

Cutler, B. and Reed, J. (1975). 'Multiple Personality – A Single Case Study With a 15-Year Follow-Up'. *Psychological Medicine* 5: 18-26.

Damgaard, J., Van Benschoten, S. and Fagan, J. (1985). 'An Updated Bibliography of Literature Pertaining to Multiple Personality'. *Psychological Reports* 57: 131-137.

Dawson, M.E. (1980). 'Physiological Detection of Deception: Measurement of Responses to Questions and Answers During Countermeasure Maneuvers'. *Psychophysiology* 17: 8-17.

De Bellis, M.D., Chrousos, G.P., Dorn, L.D., Burke, L., *et al.* (1994). 'Hypothalamic-Pituitary-Adrenal Axis Dysregulation in Sexually Abused Girls'. *Journal of Clinical Endocrinology and Metabolism* 78: 249-255.

De Bellis, M.D., Lefter, L., Trickett, P.K., and Putnam, F.W. (1994). 'Urinary Catecholamine Excretion in Sexually Abused Girls'. *Journal of the American Academy of Child and Adolescent Psychiatry* 33: 320-327.

Decker, H.S. (1986). 'The Lure of Nonmaterialism in Materialist Europe: Investigations of Dissociative Phenomena, 1880-1915'. In J.M. Quen (ed.), *Split Minds/Split Brains*. New York & London: New York University Press: 31-62.

Dell, P.F. (1988a). 'Professional Skepticism About Multiple Personality'. *Journal of Nervous and Mental Disease* 176: 528-531.

Dell, P.F. (1988b). 'Not Reasonable Skepticism, but Extreme Skepticism'. *Journal of Nervous and Mental Disease* 176: 537-538. Response to Bliss, 1988; Hilgard, 1988; Spiegel, 1988.

Dennett, D.C. (1976). 'Conditions of Personhood'. In A.O. Rorty (ed.), *The Identities of Persons*. Berkeley & Los Angeles: University of California Press: 175-196. Reprinted in D.C. Dennett (1978), *Brainstorms*. Cambridge, Mass.: Bradford Books: 267-285.

Dennett, D.C. (1991). 'The Origin of Selves'. In D. Kolak and R.

Martin (eds), *Self and Identity: Contemporary Philosophical Issues*. New York & Toronto: Macmillan: 355-364.

Dessoir, M. (1889). 'Dr. Albert Moll's "Hypnotism"'. *Proceedings of the Society for Psychical Research* 5: 566-574.

Dingwall, E.J. (ed.) (1967). *Abnormal Hypnotic Phenomena: A Survey of Nineteenth-Century Cases, 4 Vols*. New York: Barnes & Noble.

Donovan, D.M. (1989). 'The Paraconscious'. *Journal of the American Academy of Psychoanalysis* 17: 223-251.

Downs, J., Dahmer, S.K. and Battle, A.O. (1990). 'Letter to the Editor: Multiple Personality Disorder in India'. *American Journal of Psychiatry* 147: 1260.

Eisenbud, J. (1937). 'The Psychology of Headache: A Case Studied Experimentally'. *Psychiatric Quarterly* 11: 592-619.

Eisenbud, J. (1939). 'A Method for Investigating the Effect of Repression on the Somatic Expression of Emotion in Vegetative Functions: A Preliminary Report'. *Psychosomatic Medicine* 1: 376-387.

Eisenbud, J. (1970). *Psi and Psychoanalysis*. New York: Grune & Stratton.

Eisenbud, J. (1982). *Paranormal Foreknowledge: Problems and Perplexities*. New York: Human Sciences Press.

Eisenbud, J. (1983). *Parapsychology and the Unconscious*. Berkeley, California: North Atlantic Books.

Ellenberger, H.F. (1970). *The Discovery of the Unconscious*. New York: Basic Books.

Elliotson, J. (1843/1982). 'Numerous Cases of Surgical Operations Without Pain in the Mesmeric State: With Remarks Upon the Opposition of Many Members of the Royal Medical and Chirurgical Society and Others to the Reception of the Inestimable Blessings of Mesmerism. London: H. Baillière'. Reprinted in F. Kaplan (ed.), *John Elliotson on Mesmerism*. New York: Da Capo.

Elliott, D. (1982). 'State Intervention and Childhood Multiple Personality Disorder'. *Journal of Psychiatry and the Law* 10: 441-456.

Ervin, F.R., Palmour, R.M., Pearson Murphy, B.E., Prince, R. and Simons, R.C. (1988). 'The Psychobiology of Trance: II: Physiological and Endocrine Correlates'. *Transcultural Psychiatric Research Review* 25: 267-284. See Simons, et al, 1988, for Part I.

Esdaile, J. (1846). *Mesmerism in India, and Its Practical Applications in Surgery and Medicine*. London: Longman, Brown, Green & Longmans.

Esdaile, J. (1852). *Natural and Mesmeric Clairvoyance, With the Practical Application of Mesmerism in Surgery and Medicine*. London: Hyppolyte Baillière.

Evans, F.J. and Orne, M.T. (1971). 'The Disappearing Hypnotist: The Use of Simulating Subjects to Evaluate How Subjects Perceive Experimental Procedures'. *International Journal of Clinical and Experimental Hypnosis* 19: 277-296.

Ewin, D.M. (1994). 'Many Memories Retrieved With Hypnosis Are Accurate'. *American Journal of Clinical Hypnosis* 36: 174-176.

Fagan, J. and McMahon, P.P. (1984). 'Incipient Multiple Personality in Children: Four Cases'. *Journal of Nervous and Mental Disease* 172: 26-36.

Fahy, T.A. (1988). 'The Diagnosis of Multiple Personality Disorder: A Critical Review'. *British Journal of Psychiatry* 153: 597-606.

Fahy, T.A. (1989). [Letter to the Editor]. *British Journal of Psychiatry* 154: 878.

Fahy, T.A. (1990). [Letter to the Editor]. *British Journal of Psychiatry* 156: 906.

Fahy, T.A., Abas, M. and Brown, J.C. (1989). 'Multiple Personality: A Symptom of Psychiatric Disorder'. *British Journal of Psychiatry* 154: 99-101.

Fine, C.G. (1988). 'The Work of Antoine Despine: The First Scientific Report On the Diagnosis and Treatment of a Child With Multiple Personality Disorder'. *American Journal of Clinical Hypnosis* 31: 33-39.

Fine, C.G. (1989). 'Treatment Errors and Iatrogenesis Across Therapeutic Modalities in MPD and Allied Dissociative Disorders'. *Dissociation* 2: 77-82.

Fleming, J.A.E. (1989). [Letter to the Editor]. *British Journal of Psychiatry* 154: 877.

Frankel, F.H. (1990). 'Hypnotizability and Dissociation'. *American Journal of Psychiatry* 147: 823-829.

Frankfurt, H. (1971). 'Freedom of the Will and the Concept of a Person'. *Journal of Philosophy* 68: 5-20.

French, A.P. and Shechmeister, B.R. (1983). 'The Multiple Personality Syndrome and Criminal Defense'. *Bulletin of the American Academy of Psychiatry and the Law* 11: 17-25.

French, O. (1987). 'Correspondence: More On Multiple Personality Disorder'. *American Journal of Psychiatry* 144: 123-124.

Freud, S. (1925/1961). 'Moral Responsibility for the Content of Dreams.' In J. Strachey (ed. & trans.), *The Standard Edition of the Complete Psychological Works of Sigmund Freud, Vol. 19*. London: Hogarth: 131-134.

Frischholz, E.J. (1985). 'The Relationship Among Dissociation, Hypnosis, and Child Abuse in the Development of Multiple Personality Disorder'. In R.P. Kluft (ed.), *Childhood Antecedents of Multiple Personality*. Washington, D.C.: American Psychiatric Press: 100-126.

Frischholz, E.J. and Braun, B.G. (1990). 'Commentary On Takahashi (1990)'. *Dissociation* 3: 60-61.

Gainer, M.J. (1990). 'A Descriptive Analysis of Communication Between Alternate Personalities in Multiple Personality Disorder'. Paper presented at the Seventh International Conference on Multiple Personality and Dissociative States, Chicago, Nov. 9.

Ganaway, G.K. (1989). 'Exploring the Credibility Issue in Multiple Personality Disorder and Related Dissociative Phenomena'. Paper presented at Fourth Regional Conference on Multiple Personality and Dissociative States, Akron, Ohio, April, 1989.

Gauld, A. (1982). *Mediumship and Survival*. London: Heinemann.

Gauld, A. (1988). 'Reflections On Mesmeric Analgesia'. *British Journal of Experimental and Clinical Hypnosis* 5: 17-24.

Gauld, A. (1992). *A History of Hypnotism*. Cambridge: Cambridge University Press.

Gillett, G. (1986a). 'Brain Bisection and Personal Identity'. *Mind* 95: 224-229.

Gillett, G. (1986b). 'Multiple Personality and the Concept of a Person'. *New Ideas in Psychology* 4: 173-184.

Gillett, G. (1987). 'Reasoning About Persons'. In A. Peacocke and G. Gillett (eds), *Persons and Personality*. Oxford: Blackwell: 75-88.

Gleaves, D.H. (1994). 'On "The Reality of Repressed Memories"'. *American Psychologist* 49: 440-441.

Goldberg, B. (1977). 'A Problem With Anomalous Monism'. *Philosophical Studies* 32: 175-180.

Goldberg, B. (1982). 'Mechanism and Meaning'. In C. Ginet and S. Shoemaker (eds), *Knowledge and Mind*. Oxford & New York: Ox-ford University Press: 191-210.

Goodman, F.D. (1988). *Possession and Exorcism in the Modern World*. Bloomington & Indianapolis: Indiana University Press.

Goodwin, J. (1985). 'Credibility Problems in Multiple Personality Disorder Patients and Abused Children'. In R.P. Kluft (ed.), *Childhood Antecedents of Multiple Personality*. Washington, D.C.: American Psychiatric Press: 2-19.

Goodwin, J. (1988). 'Munchausen's Syndrome As a Dissociative Disorder'. *Dissociation* 1: 54-60.

Goodwin, J., Hill, S. and Attias, R. (1990). 'Historical and Folk Techniques of Exorcism: Application to the Treatment of Dissociative Disorders'. *Dissociation* 3: 94-101.

Gowler, D. (1972). 'On the Concept of the Person: A Biosocial View'. In R. Ruddock (ed.), *Six Approaches to the Person*. London & Boston: Routledge & Kegan Paul: 37-69.

Gravitz, M.A. (1994). 'Are the Right People Being Trained to Use Hypnosis?'. *American Journal of Clinical Hypnosis* 36: 179-182.

Greaves, G.B. (1980). 'Multiple Personality: 165 Years After Mary Reynolds'. *Journal of Nervous and Mental Disease* 168: 577-596.

Greaves, G.B. (1988). 'Common Errors in the Treatment of Multiple Personality Disorder'. *Dissociation* 1: 61-66.

Greaves, G.B. (1989). 'Observations On the Claim of Iatrogenesis in the Promulgation of MPD: A Discussion'. *Dissociation* 2: 99-104.

Green, E. and Green, A. (1977). *Beyond Biofeedback*. New York: Delta.

Greenberg, W.M. and Attia, S. (1993). 'Multiple Personality Disorder and Informed Consent'. *American Journal of Psychiatry* 150: 7.

Greenwood, E. (1903). 'Some Experiments in Hypnotism'. *Proceedings of the Society for Psychical Research* 17: 279-289.

Gruenewald, D. (1971). 'Hypnotic Techniques Without Hypnosis in the Treatment of Dual Personality'. *Journal of Nervous and Mental Disease* 153: 41-46.

Gruenewald, D. (1977). 'Multiple Personality and Splitting Phenomena: A Reconceptualization'. *Journal of Nervous and Mental Disease* 164: 385-393.

Gruenewald, D. (1984). 'On the Nature of Multiple Personality: Comparisons With Hypnosis'. *International Journal of Clinical and Experimental Hypnosis* 32: 170-190.

Gruenewald, D. (1986). 'Dissociation: Appearance and Meaning'. *American Journal of Clinical Hypnosis* 29: 116-122.

Gurney, E. (1884a). 'The Stages of Hypnotism'. *Proceedings of the Society for Psychical Research* 2: 61-72.

Gurney, E. (1884b). 'An Account of Some Experiments in Mesmerism'. *Proceedings of the Society for Psychical Research* 2: 201-206.

Gurney, E. (1884c). 'The Problems of Hypnotism'. *Proceedings of the Society for Psychical Research* 2: 265-292.

Gurney, E. (1887a). 'Peculiarities of Certain Post-Hypnotic States'. *Proceedings of the Society for Psychical Research* 4: 268-323.

Gurney, E. (1887b). 'Stages of Hypnotic Memory'. *Proceedings of the Society for Psychical Research* 4: 515-531.

Gurney, E. (1888a). 'Recent Experiments in Hypnotism'. *Proceedings of the Society for Psychical Research* 5: 3-17.

Gurney, E. (1888b). 'Hypnotism and Telepathy'. *Proceedings of the Society for Psychical Research* 5: 215-259.

Gurney, E. and Myers, F.W.H. (1885). 'Some Higher Aspects of Mesmerism'. *Proceedings of the Society for Psychical Research* 3: 401-423.

Hacking, I. (1986). 'The Invention of Split Personalities (An Illustration of Michel Foucault's Doctrine of the Constitution of the Subject)'. In A. Donagan, A.N. Perovich, and M.V. Wedin (eds), *Human Nature and Natural Knowledge: Essays Presented to Marjorie Grene On the Occasion of Her Seventy-Fifth Birthday*. (Boston Studies in the Philosophy of Science, vol. 89.) Dordrecht: D. Reidel: 63-85.

Hacking, I. (1991). 'Double Consciousness in Britain 1815-1875'. *Dissociation* 4: 134-146.

Hall, P.E. (1989). 'Multiple Personality Disorder and Homicide: Professional and Legal Issues'. *Dissociation* 2: 110-115.

Halleck, S.L. (1991). 'Dissociative Phenomena and the Question of Responsibility'. *International Journal of Clinical and Experimental Hypnosis* 38: 298-314.

Hamilton, D.M. and Ondrovik, J. (1993). 'Automatism Versus Insanity: Defenses to Crimial Responsibility'. *ISSMP&D News* 11: 7.

Haraldsson, E. and Stevenson, I. (1975a). 'A Communicator of the "Drop in" Type in Iceland: The Case of Runolfur Runolfsson'. *Journal of the American Society for Psychical Research* 69: 33-59.

Haraldsson, E. and Stevenson, I. (1975b). 'A Communicator of the "Drop in" Type in Iceland: The Case of Gudni Magnusson'. *Journal of the American Society for Psychical Research* 69: 245-261.

Harré, R. (1987). 'Persons and Selves'. In A. Peacocke and G. Gillett (eds), *Persons and Personality*. Oxford: Blackwell: 99-115.

Harriman, P.L. (1942a). 'The Experimental Production of Some Phenomena Related to the Multiple Personality'. *Journal of Abnormal and Social Psychology* 37: 244-255.

Harriman, P.L. (1942b). 'The Experimental Induction of a Multiple Personality'. *Psychiatry* 5: 179-186.

Harriman, P.L. (1943). 'A New Approach to Multiple Personality'. *American Journal of Orthopsychiatry* 13: 638-643.

Hart, B. (1926). 'The Concept of Dissociation'. *British Journal of Medical Psychology* 6: 241-263.

Hastings, A. (1991). *With the Tongues of Men and Angels: A Study of Channeling*. Fort Worth: Holt, Rinehart & Winston.

Haule, J.R. (1986). 'Pierre Janet and Dissociation: The First Transference Theory and Its Origins in Hypnosis'. *American Journal of Clinical Hypnosis* 29: 86-94.

Heil, J. (1978). 'Traces of Things Past'. *Philosophy of Science* 45: 60-67.

Heil, J. (1981). 'Does Cognitive Psychology Rest On a Mistake?'. *Mind* 90: 321-342.

Heil, J. (1983). *Perception and Cognition*. Berkeley & Los Angeles: University of California Press.

Hendrickson, K.M., McCarty, T. and Goodwin, J.M. (1989). 'Edgar Allen Poe and the Animal Alters'. Paper presented at Sixth International Conference on Multiple Personality/Dissociative States. Chicago, October, 1989.

Herzog A. (1984). 'On Multiple Personality: Comments On Diagnosis, Etiology, and Treatment'. *International Journal of Clinical and Experimental Hypnosis* 32: 210-221.

Hess, D.J. (1990). 'Ghosts and Domestic Politics in Brazil: Some Parallels Between Spirit Possession and Spirit Infestation'. *Ethos* 18: 407-438.

Hicks, R.E. (1985). 'Discussion: A Clinician's Perspective'. In R.P. Kluft (ed.), *Childhood Antecedents of Multiple Personality*. Washington, D.C.: American Psychiatric Press: 240-258.

Hilgard, E.R. (1984). 'The Hidden Observer and Multiple Personality'. *International Journal of Clinical and Experimental Hypnosis* 32: 248-253.

Hilgard, E.R. (1986). *Divided Consciousness: Multiple Controls in Human Thought and Action (Expanded Edition)*. New York: Wiley-Interscience.

Hilgard, E.R. (1988). 'Professional Skepticism About Multiple Personality'. *Journal of Nervous and Mental Disease* 176: 532. Reply to Dell, 1988a.

Hilgard, J. (1970). *Personality and Hypnosis*. Chicago: University of

Chicago Press.

Hirsch, E. (1991). 'Divided Minds'. *Philosophical Review* 100: 3-30.

Hodgson, R. (1891). 'A Case of Double Consciousness'. *Proceedings of the Society for Psychical Research* 7: 221-257.

Hodgson, R. (1898). 'A Further Record of Observations of Certain Phenomena of Trance'. *Proceedings of the Society for Psychical Research* 13: 284-582.

Holmes, D.S. (1990). 'The Evidence of Repression: An Examination of Sixty Years of Research'. In J. Singer (ed.), *Repression and Dissociation: Implications for Personality, Theory, Psychopathology and Health*. Chicago: University of Chicago Press: 85-102.

Hopenwasser, K. (1994). 'When It All Comes Back'. New York Times Op-Ed, June 8.

Horevitz, R.P. and Braun, B.G. (1984). 'Are Multiple Personalities Borderline? An Analysis of 33 Cases'. *Psychiatric Clinics of North America* 7: 69-87.

Hornstein, N.L. and Putnam, F.W. (1992). 'Clinical Phenomenology of Child and Adolescent Dissociative Disorders'. *Journal of the American Academy of Child and Adolescent Psychiatry* 31: 1077-1085.

Huston, P.E., Shakow, D. and Erickson, M.H. (1934). 'A Study of Hypnotically Induced Complexes By Means of the Luria Technique'. *Journal of General Psychology* 11: 65-97.

Howle, W.P. (1895). 'The Oldest, but Latest Fad — Hypnotism'. *Journal of the American Medical Association* 25: 1056.

Hughes, D.J. (1992). 'Differences Between Trance Channeling and Multiple Personality Disorder On Structured Interview'. *Journal of Transpersonal Psychology* 24: 181-192.

Hughes, J.R., Kuhlman, D.T., Fichtner, C.G. and Gruenfeld, M.J. (1990). 'Brain Mapping in a Case of Multiple Personality'. *Clinical Electroencephalography* 21: 200-209.

Hyslop, J.H. (1917). 'The Doris Fischer Case of Multiple Personality: Part III'. *Proceedings of the American Society for Psychical Research* 11: 5-866.

Institute of Noetic Sciences (1985). 'Multiple Personality — Mirrors of a New Model of Mind?'. *Investigations* 1(3/4): .

James, W. (1887). 'The Consciousness of Lost Limbs'. *Proceedings of the American Society for Psychical Research* 1: 249-258.

James, W. (1889/1986). 'Notes On Automatic Writing'. *Proceedings of the American Society for Psychical Research* 1: 548-564. Reprinted in *The Works of William James: Essays in Psychical Research*. Cambridge: Harvard University Press: 37-55.

James, W. (1890/1981). *The Principles of Psychology*. 2 vols. Cambridge, Mass. & London: Harvard University Press.

Janet, P. (1886). 'Les Actes Inconscients Et Le Dédoublement De La Personnalité Pendant Le Somnambulisme Provoqué'. *Revue Philosophique* 22: 577-592.

Janet, P. (1887). 'L'Anesthésie Systématisée Et La Dissociation Des

291

Phénomènes Psychologiques'. *Revue Philosophique* 23: 449-472.

Janet, P. (1888). 'Les Actes Inconscients Et La Mémoire Pendant Le Somnambulisme'. *Revue Philosophique* 25: 238-279.

Janet, P. (1889). *L'Automatisme Psychologique: Essai De Psychologie Expérimentale Sur Les Formes Inférieures De L'Activité Humaine*. Paris: Felix Alcan.

Janet, P. (1907). 'A Symposium On the Subconscious'. *Journal of Abnormal Psychology* 2: 58-67.

Janet, P. (1907/1920). *The Major Symptoms of Hysteria*. New York: Macmillan.

Johnson, G.L. (1900). 'Psychic Projection of Suggested Visualised Impressions'. *Annals of Psychic Science* 9: 71-73.

Johnston, M. (1987). 'Human Beings'. *Journal of Philosophy* 84: 59-83.

Kampman, R. (1976). 'Hypnotically Induced Multiple Personality: An Experimental Study'. *International Journal of Clinical and Experimental Hypnosis* 24: 215-227.

Kenny, M.G. (1981). 'Multiple Personality and Spirit Possession'. *Psychiatry* 44: 337-358.

Kenny, M.G. (1986). *The Passion of Ansel Bourne: Multiple Personality in American Culture*. Washington, D.C.: Smithsonian Institution.

Keyes, D. (1982). *The Minds of Billy Milligan*. New York: Bantam Books, Inc.

Kleinman, A. (1991). 'The Psychiatry of Culture and the Culture of Psychiatry'. *Harvard Mental Health Letter* 8(No. 1): 4-6.

Kihlstrom, J.F. and Hoyt, I.P. (1990). 'Repression, Dissociation, and Hypnosis'. In J. Singer (ed.), *Repression and Dissociation: Implications for Personality, Theory, Psychopathology and Health*. Chicago: University of Chicago Press: 181-208.

Kline, M.V. (1984). 'Multiple Personality: Facts and Artifacts in Relation to Hypnotherapy'. *International Journal of Clinical and Experimental Hypnosis* 32: 198-209.

Kluft, R.P. (1982). 'Varieties of Hypnotic Interventions in the Treatment of Multiple Personality'. *American Journal of Clinical Hypnosis* 24: 230-240.

Kluft, R.P. (1984a). 'Treatment of Multiple Personality Disorder. A Study of 33 Cases'. *Psychiatric Clinics of North America* 7: 9-29.

Kluft, R.P. (1984b). 'Multiple Personality in Childhood'. *Psychiatric Clinics of North America* 7: 121-134.

Kluft, R.P. (1984c). 'An Introduction to Multiple Personality Disorder'. *Psychiatric Annals* 14: 19-24.

Kluft, R.P. (ed.) (1985a). *Childhood Antecedents of Multiple Personality*. Washington: American Psychiatric Press.

Kluft, R.P. (1985b). 'Childhood Multiple Personality Disorder: Predictors, Clinical Findings, and Treatment Results'. In R.P. Kluft (ed.), *Childhood Antecedents of Multiple Personality*. Washington, D.C.: American Psychiatric Press: 168-196.

Kluft, R.P. (1985c). 'The Natural History of Multiple Personality Disorder'. In R.P. Kluft (ed.), *Childhood Antecedents of Multiple Personality*. Washington, D.C.: American Psychiatric Press: 198-238.

Kluft, R.P. (1985d). 'Making the Diagnosis of Multiple Personality Disorder (MPD)'. *Directions in Psychiatry* 5(23): 1-10.

Kluft, R.P. (1985e). 'The Treatment of Multiple Personality Disorder (MPD): Current Concepts'. *Directions in Psychiatry* 5(24): 1-10.

Kluft, R.P. (1985f). 'Hypnotherapy of Childhood Multiple Personality Disorder'. *American Journal of Clinical Hypnosis* 27: 201-210.

Kluft, R.P. (1985g). 'Using Hypnotic Inquiry Protocols to Monitor Treatment Progress and Stability in Multiple Personality Disorder'. *American Journal of Clinical Hypnosis* 28: 63-75.

Kluft, R.P. (1986a). 'Preliminary Observations On Age Regression in Multiple Personality Patients Before and After Integration'. *American Journal of Clinical Hypnosis* 28: 147-156.

Kluft, R.P. (1986b). 'Correspondence: The Prevalence of Multiple Personality'. *American Journal of Psychiatry* 143: 802-803.

Kluft, R.P. (1986c). 'High Functioning Multiple Personality Patients'. *Journal of Nervous and Mental Disease* 174: 722-726.

Kluft, R.P. (1986d). 'Personality Unification in MPD: A Follow-Up Study'. In B.G. Braun (ed.), *Treatment of Multiple Personality Disorder*. Washington, D.C.: American Psychiatric Press: 29-60.

Kluft, R.P. (1986e). 'Treating Children Who Have Multiple Personality Disorder'. In B.G. Braun (ed.), *Treatment of Multiple Personality Disorder*. Washington, D.C.: American Psychiatric Press: 79-105.

Kluft, R.P. (1987a). 'Correspondence: More On Multiple Personality Disorder'. *American Journal of Psychiatry* 144: 124-125.

Kluft, R.P. (1987b). 'First-Rank Symptoms As a Diagnostic Clue to Multiple Personality Disorder'. *American Journal of Psychiatry* 144: 293-298.

Kluft, R.P. (1987c). 'An Update On Multiple Personality Disorder'. *Hospital and Community Psychiatry* 38: 363-373.

Kluft, R.P. (1987d). 'Unsuspected Multiple Personality Disorder: An Uncommon Source of Protracted Resistance, Interruption, and Failure in Psychoanalysis'. *Hillside Journal of Clinical Psychiatry* 9: 100-115.

Kluft, R.P. (1987e). 'The Parental Fitness of Mothers With Multiple Personality Disorder: A Preliminary Study'. *Child Abuse and Neglect* 11: 273-280.

Kluft, R.P. (1987f). 'The Simulation and Dissimulation of Multiple Personality'. *American Journal of Clinical Hypnosis* 30: 104-118.

Kluft, R.P. (1988a). 'The Postunification Treatment of Multiple Personality Disorder: First Findings'. *American Journal of Psychotherapy* 42: 212-228.

Kluft, R.P. (1988b). 'The Phenomenology and Treatment of Extremely Complex Multiple Personality Disorder'. *Dissociation* 1: 47-58.

Kluft, R.P. (1988c). 'On Treating the Older Patient With Multiple Personality Disorder: "Race Against Time" or "Make Haste Slowly?"'. *American Journal of Clinical Hypnosis* 30: 257-266.

Kluft, R.P. (1989a). 'Editorial: Thoughts On the Issue of Iatrogenesis'. *Dissociation* 2: 59-60.

Kluft, R.P. (1989b). 'Iatrogenic Creation of New Alter Personalities'. *Dissociation* 2: 83-91.

Kluft, R.P. (1991). 'Clinical Presentations of Multiple Personality Disorder'. *Psychiatric Clinics of North America* 14: 605-630.

Kluft, R.P., Steinberg, M. and Spitzer, R.L. (1988). 'DSM-III-R Revisions in the Dissociative Disorders: An Exploration of Their Derivation and Rationale'. *Dissociation* 1: 39-46.

Kolb, L.C. (1986). 'Comments On Post-Traumatic Stress Disorder and Dissociation'. In J.M. Quen (ed.), *Split Minds/Split Brains*. New York & London: New York University Press: 171-178.

Krippner, S. (1987). 'Cross-Cultural Approaches to Multiple Personality Disorder: Therapeutic Practices in Brazilian Spiritism'. *Ethos* 15: 273-295.

Krippner, S. and George, L. (1986). 'Psi Phenomena As Related to Altered States of Consciousness'. In B.B. Wolman and M. Ullman (eds), *Handbook of States of Consciousness*. New York: Van Nostrand Reinhold: 332-364.

Kroger, W.S. (1979). *Clinical and Experimental Hypnosis in Medicine, Dentistry and Psychology*. 2nd ed. Philadelphia: J.B. Lippincott.

Lamm, J.B. (1991). 'Easing Access to the Courts for Incest Victims: Toward an Equitable Application of the Delayed Discovery Rule'. *The Yale Law Journal* 100: 2189-2208.

Larmore, K., Ludwig, A.M. and Cain, R.L. (1977). 'Multiple Personality — An Objective Case Study'. *British Journal of Psychiatry* 131: 35-40.

Laurence, J.-R. and Perry, C. (1981). 'The "Hidden Observer" Phenomenon in Hypnosis: Some Additional Findings'. *Journal of Abnormal Psychology* 90: 334-344.

Laurence, J.-R. and Perry, C. (1988). *Hypnosis, Will, and Memory: A Psycho-Legal History*. New York & London: The Guilford Press.

Leavitt, F. and Braun, B. (1991). 'Historical Reliability: A Key to Differentiating Populations Among Patients Presenting Signs of Multiple Personality Disorder'. *Psychological Reports* 69: 499-510.

Leavitt, M.C. (1947). 'A Case of Hypnotically Produced Secondary and Tertiary Personalities'. *Psychoanalytic Review* 34: 274-295.

Lewis, D.O. and Bard, J.S. (1991). 'Multiple Personality Disorder and Forensic Issues'. *Psychiatric Clinics of North America* 14: 741-756.

Li, D. and Spiegel, D. (1992). 'A Neural Network Model of Dissociative Disorders'. *Psychiatric Annals* 22: 144-147.

Lichtenberg, J.D. (1975). 'The Development of a Sense of Self'. *Journal of the American Psychoanalytic Association* 23: 453-484.

Lindsay, D.S. and Read, J.D. (1994). 'Psychotherapy and Memories of Childhood Sexual Abuse: A Cognitive Perspective'. *Applied Cognitive Psychology* 8:281-338.

Litvag, I. (1972). *Singer in the Shadows*. New York: Macmillan.

Loewenstein, R.J., Hamilton, J., Alagna, S., Reid, N. and deVries, M. (1987). 'Experiential Sampling in the Study of Multiple Personality Disorder'. *American Journal of Psychiatry* 144: 19-24.

Loewenstein, R.J. and Putnam, F.W. (1988). 'A Comparison Study of Dissociative Symptoms in Patients With Complex Partial Seizures, Multiple Personality Disorder, and Posttraumatic Stress Disorder'. *Dissociation* 1: 17-23.

Loftus, E.F. (1979). *Eyewitness Testimony*. Cambridge, Mass.: Harvard University Press.

Loftus, E.F. (1993). 'The Reality of Repressed Memories'. *American Psychologist* 48: 518-537.

Loftus, E.F. (1994). 'The Repressed Memory Controversy'. *American Psychologist* 49: 443-445.

Loftus, E.F. and Coan, D. (in press). 'The Construction of Childhood Memories'. In D. Peters (ed.) *The Child Witness in Context: Cognitive, Social and Legal Perspectives*. New York: Kluwer.

Loftus, E.F., Garry, M., Brown, S.W. and Rader, M. (1994). 'Near-Natal Memories, Past-Life Memories, and Other Memory Myths'. *American Journal of Clinical Hypnosis* 36: 176-179.

Lucas, O.N. and Tocantins, L.M. (1964). 'Problems in Hemostasis in Hemophilic Patients Undergoing Dental Extractions'. *Annals of the New York Academy of Science* 115: 470-480.

Ludwig, A.M. (1983). 'The Psychological Functions of Dissociation'. *American Journal of Clinical Hypnosis* 26: 93-99.

Ludwig, A.M. (1984). 'Intoxication and Sobriety: Implications for the Understanding of Multiple Personality'. *Psychiatric Clinics of North America* 7: 161-169.

Ludwig, A.M., Brandsma, J.M., Wilbur, C.B., Benfeldt, F. and Jameson, D.H. (1972). 'The Objective Study of a Multiple Personality. Or, Are Four Heads Better Than One?'. *Archives of General Psychiatry* 26: 298-310.

Lundeholm, H. (1928). 'An Experimental Study of Functional Anesthesia Induced By Suggestion in Hypnosis'. *Journal of Abnormal and Social Psychology* 23: 337-355.

Luria, A.R. (1932). *The Nature of Human Conflict*. New York: Liveright.

Lynn, S.J., Myers, B. and Sivec, H. (1994). 'Psychotherapists' Beliefs, Repressed Memories of Abuse, and Hypnosis: What Have We Really Learned?'. *American Journal of Clinical Hypnosis* 36: 182-184.

Lynn, S.J. and Nash, M.R. (1994). 'Truth in Memory: Ramifications for Psychotherapy and Hypnotherapy'. *American Journal of Clinical Hypnosis* 36: 194-208.

Margolis, J. and Margolis, C.G. (1979). 'The Theory of Hypnosis and the Concept of Persons'. *Behavior* 7: 97-111.

Marks, C.E. (1980). *Commissurotomy, Consciousness and Unity of Mind*. Montgomery, VT: Bradford Books.

Marmer, S.S. (1980). 'Psychoanalysis of Multiple Personality'. *Inter-*

national Journal of Psychoanalysis 61: 439-459.

Marmer, S.S. (1991). 'Multiple Personality Disorder: A Psychoanalytic Perspective'. *Psychiatric Clinics of North America* 14: 677-694.

Martínez-Taboas, A. (1989). 'Preliminary Observations On MPD in Puerto Rico'. *Dissociation* 2: 128-131.

Martínez-Taboas, A. (1990). 'Commentary On Takahashi (1990)'. *Dissociation* 3: 62-63.

Martínez-Taboas, A. (1991a). 'Multiple Personality Disorder As Seen From a Social Constructionist Viewpoint'. *Dissociation* 4: 129-133.

Martínez-Taboas, A. (1991b). 'Multiple Personality in Puerto Rico: Analysis of Fifteen Cases'. *Dissociation* 4: 189-192.

Martínez-Taboas, A. and Anderson, R.I. (1982). 'Final Comments On the Watseka Wonder'. *Theta* 10(1): 23-24.

Martínez-Taboas, A., Anderson, R.I. and Chari, C.T.K. (1981). 'The End of the Watseka Wonder'. *Theta* 9(4): 20-24.

Marx, O.M. (1970). 'Morton Prince and the Dissociation of a Personality'. *Journal of the History of the Behavioral Sciences* 6: 120-130.

Mason, A.A. (1952). 'A Case of Congenital Ichthosiform Erythroderma of Broca Treated By Hypnosis'. *British Medical Journal* Aug. 23: 422-423.

Mason, A.A. (1955). 'Ichthyosis and Hypnosis'. *British Medical Journal* July 2: 57-58.

Mason, R.O. (1893). 'Duplex Personality'. *Journal of Nervous and Mental Disease* 18: 593-598.

Mason, R.O. (1894). 'Case of Hysteria, Catalepsy and Unstable Consciousness, Accompanied By Supernormal Perception'. *Journal of the Society for Psychical Research* 6: 361-365.

Mason, R.O. (1895a). 'Duplex Personality — Its Relation to Hypnotism and to Lucidity'. *Journal of the American Medical Association* 25: 928-933.

Mason, R.O. (1895b). 'Hypnotism and Double Personality'. *Journal of the American Medical Association* 25: 1103.

Mason, R.O. (1896). 'Alternating Personalities; Their Origin and Medico-Legal Aspect'. *Journal of the American Medical Association* 27: 1082-1085.

Mathew, R.J., Jack, R.A. and West, W.S. (1985). 'Regional Cerebral Blood Flow in a Patient With Multiple Personality'. *American Journal of Psychiatry* 142: 504-505.

McDougall, W. (1905). 'Review of B. Sidis and S.P. Goodhart, *Multiple Personality*'. *Proceedings of the Society for Psychical Research* 19: 345-353.

McDougall, W. (1906). 'The Case of Sally Beauchamp'. *Proceedings of the Society for Psychical Research* 19: 410-431.

McDougall, W. (1911). *Body and Mind: A History and Defense of Animism*. Boston: Beacon Press.

McDougall, W. (1938). 'The Relation Between Dissociation and Repression'. *British Journal of Medical Psychology* 17: 141-157.

McHugh, P.R. (1993). 'Do Patients' Recovered Memories of Sexual Abuse Constitute a "False Memory Syndrome"?' *Psychiatric News* 28 (23):18.

Mersky, H. (1992). 'The Manufacture of Personalities: The Production of Multiple Personality Disorder'. *British Journal of Psychiatry* 160: 327-340.

Messerschmidt, R.A. (1927-8). 'Quantitative Investigation of the Alleged Independent Operation of Conscious and Subconscious Processes'. *Journal of Abnormal and Social Psychology* 22: 325-340.

Miller, R.D. (1984). 'The Possible Use of Auto-Hypnosis As a Resistance During Hypnotherapy'. *International Journal of Clinical and Experimental Hypnosis* 32: 236-247.

Miller, S.D. (1989). 'Optical Differences in Multiple Personality Disorder'. *Journal of Nervous and Mental Disease* 177: 480-486.

Miller, S.D., Blackburn, T., Scholes, G., White, G.L. and Mamalis, N. (1991). 'Optical Differences in Multiple Personality Disorder: A Second Look'. *Journal of Nervous and Mental Disease* 179: 132-135.

Mitchell, T.W. (1912a). 'Some Types of Multiple Personality'. *Proceedings of the Society for Psychical Research* 26: 257-285.

Mitchell, T.W. (1912b). 'A Study in Hysteria and Multiple Personality, With Report of a Case'. *Proceedings of the Society for Psychical Research* 26: 286-311.

Mitchell, T.W. (1920). 'The Doris Fischer Case of Multiple Personality'. *Proceedings of the Society for Psychical Research* 31: 30-74.

Mitchell, T.W. (1922). 'Presidential Address'. *Proceedings of the Society for Psychical Research* 33: 1-22.

Moerman, D.E. (1981). 'Edible Symbols: The Effectiveness of Placebos'. In T.A. Seboek and R. Rosenthal (eds), *The Clever Hans Phenomenon. Annals of the New York Academy of Sciences. 34.* New York: New York Academy of Sciences: 256-268.

Morton, A. (1990). 'Why There Is No Concept of a Person'. In C. Gill (ed.), *The Person and the Human Mind: Issues in Ancient and Modern Philosophy*. Oxford: Oxford University Press: 39-59.

Münsterberg, H. (1907). 'A Symposium On the Subconscious'. *Journal of Abnormal Psychology* 2: 25-33.

Mulhern, S. (1991). 'Embodied Alternative Identities: Bearing Witness to a World That Might Have Been'. *Psychiatric Clinics of North America* 14: 769-786.

Myers, F.W.H. (1885). 'Human Personality in the Light of Hypnotic Suggestion'. *Proceedings of the Society for Psychical Research* 4: 1-24.

Myers, F.W.H. (1887). 'Multiplex Personality'. *Proceedings of the Society for Psychical Research* 4: 496-514.

Myers, F.W.H. (1888a). 'The Work of Edmund Gurney in Experimental Psychology'. *Proceedings of the Society for Psychical Research* 5: 359-373.

Myers, F.W.H. (1888b). 'French Experiments On Strata of Personality'. *Proceedings of the Society for Psychical Research* 5: 374-397.

Myers, F.W.H. (1889). 'Correspondence: Reply to Barkworth (1889)'. *Journal of the Society for Psychical Research* 4: 60-63.

Myers, F.W.H. (1898). 'The Psychology of Hypnotism (Address Delivered At Meeting of British Medical Association)'. *Proceedings of the Society for Psychical Research* 14: 100-109.

Myers, F.W.H. (1903). *Human Personality and Its Survival of Bodily Death*. 2 vols. London: Longmans, Green, & Co.

Nace, E.P. and Orne, M.T. (1970). 'Fate of an Uncompleted Posthypnotic Suggestion'. *Journal of Abnormal Psychology* 75: 278-285.

Nace, E.P., Orne, M.T. and Hammer, A.G. (1974). 'Posthypnotic Amnesia As an Active Psychic Process'. *Archives of General Psychiatry* 31: 257-260.

Nagel, T. (1971). 'Brain Bisection and the Unity of Consciousness'. *Synthese* 22: 396-413.

Nash, M.R., Lynn, S.J. and Givens, D.L. (1984). 'Adult Hypnotic Susceptibility, Childhood Punishment, and Child Abuse: A Brief Communication'. *International Journal of Clinical and Experimental Hypnosis* 32: 6-11.

Nash, M.R., Lynn, S.J. and Stanley, S.M. (1984). 'The Direct Hypnotic Suggestion of Altered Mind/Body Perception'. *American Journal of Clinical Hypnosis* 27: 95-102.

Nogrady, H., McConckey, K.M., Laurence, J.-R. and Perry, C. (1983). 'Dissociation, Duality, and Demand Characteristics in Hypnosis'. *Journal of Abnormal Psychology* 92: 223-235.

Noll, R. (1989). 'Multiple Personality, Dissociation, and C.G. Jung's Complex Theory'. *Journal of Analytical Psychology* 34: 353-370.

O'Brien, P. (1985). 'The Diagnosis of Multiple Personality Syndromes: Overt, Covert, and Latent'. *Comprehensive Therapy* 11: 59-66.

O'Connell, D.N., Shor, R.E. and Orne, M.T. (1970). 'Hypnotic Age Regression: An Empirical and Methodological Analysis'. *Journal of Abnormal Psychology* 76 (Monograph Supplement No. 3): 1-32.

Oesterreich, T.K. (1921/1966). *Possession: Demoniacal and Other* (trans. D. Ibberson). New Hyde Park, N.Y.: University Books.

Ofshe, R. (in press). 'Making Grossly Damaging but Avoidable Errors: The Pitfalls of the Olio/Cornell Thesis'. *Journal of Childhood Sexual Abuse* 3 (3).

Ofshe, R. and Watters, E. (1993). 'Making Monsters'. *Society* 30 (3): 4-16.

Olio, K.A. (1994). 'Truth in Memory'. *American Psychologist* 49: 442-443.

Ondrovik, J. and Hamilton, D.M. (1990). 'Multiple Personality: Competency and the Insanity Defense'. *American Journal of Forensic Psychology* 11: 41-65.

Orne, M.T. (1951). 'The Mechanisms of Hypnotic Age Regression: An Experimental Study'. *Journal of Abnormal and Social Psychology* 46: 213-225.

Orne, M.T. (1959). 'The Nature of Hypnosis: Artifact and Essence'.

Journal of Abnormal and Social Psychology 58: 277-299.

Orne, M.T. (1962). 'Implications for Psychotherapy Derived from Current Research On the Nature of Hypnosis'. *American Journal of Psychiatry* 118: 1097-1103.

Orne, M.T. (1966). 'On the Mechanisms of Posthypnotic Amnesia'. *International Journal of Clinical and Experimental Hypnosis* 14: 121-134.

Orne, M.T. (1969). 'Demand Characteristics and the Concept of Quasi-Controls'. In R. Rosenthal and R. Rosnow (eds), *Artifact in Behavioral Research*. New York: Academic Press: 143-179.

Orne, M.T. (1971). 'The Simulation of Hypnosis: Why, How, and What It Means'. *International Journal of Clinical and Experimental Hypnosis* 19: 277-296.

Orne, M.T. (1972a). 'On the Simulating Subject As a Quasi-Control Group in Hypnosis Research: What, Why, and How'. In E. Fromm and R.E. Shor (eds), *Hypnosis: Developments in Research and New Perspectives*. Chicago: Aldine-Atherton: 399-443.

Orne, M.T. (1972b). 'Can a Hypnotized Subject Be Compelled to Carry Out Otherwise Unacceptable Behavior?'. *International Journal of Clinical and Experimental Hypnosis* 20: 101-117.

Orne, M.T. (1977). 'The Construct of Hypnosis: Implications of the Definition for Research and Practice'. *Annals of the New York Academy of Science* 296: 14-33.

Orne, M.T. (1979). 'The Use and Misuse of Hypnosis in Court'. *International Journal of Clinical and Experimental Hypnosis* 27: 311-341.

Orne, M.T., Dinges, D.F. and Orne, E.C. (1984). 'On the Differential Diagnosis of Multiple Personality in the Forensic Context'. *International Journal of Clinical and Experimental Hypnosis* 32: 118-169.

Orne, M.T. and Evans, F.J. (1966). 'Inadvertent Termination of Hypnosis With Hypnotized and Simulating Subjects'. *International Journal of Clinical and Experimental Hypnosis* 14: 61-78.

Orne, M.T., Sheehan, P.W. and Evans, F.J. (1968). 'Occurrence of Posthypnotic Behavior Outside the Experimental Setting'. *Journal of Personality and Social Psychology* 9: 189-196.

Owen, A.R.G. (1971). *Hysteria, Hypnosis and Healing: The Work of Jean-Martin Charcot*. New York: Garrett Publications.

Parfit, D. (1984). *Reasons and Persons*. Oxford: Oxford University Press.

Parfit, D. (1987). 'A Response' [to Gillett, 1987]. In A. Peacocke and G. Gillett (eds), *Persons and Personality*. Oxford: Blackwell: 88-98.

Pattison, E.M., Kahan, J. and Hurd, G.S. (1986). 'Trance and Possession States'. In B.B. Wolman and M. Ullman (eds), *Handbook of States of Consciousness*. New York: Van Nostrand Reinhold: 286-310.

Perry, C. (1984). 'Dissociative Phenomena of Hypnosis'. *Australian Journal of Clinical and Experimental Hypnosis* 12: 71-84.

Perry, C. and Laurence, J.-R. (1984). 'Mental Processing Outside of Awareness: The Contributions of Freud and Janet'. In K.S. Bowers and D. Meichenbaum (eds), *The Unconscious Reconsidered*. New York: Wiley-Interscience: 9-48.

299

Perry, C. and Walsh, B. (1978). 'Inconsistencies of Response As a Defining Characteristic of Hypnosis'. *Journal of Abnormal Psychology* 87: 574-577.

Pettinati, H.M. (1988). *Hypnosis and Memory*. New York & London: The Guilford Press.

Pierce, A.H. (1895). 'Subliminal Self or Unconscious Cerebration?'. *Proceedings of the Society for Psychical Research* 11: 317-325.

Podmore, F. (1895). 'Subliminal Self or Unconscious Cerebration?'. *Proceedings of the Society for Psychical Research* 11: 325-332.

Podmore, F. (1909/1963). *From Mesmer to Christian Science: A Short History of Mental Healing*. New Hyde Park, N.Y.: University Books.

Powers, S.M. (1991). 'Fantasy Proneness, Amnesia, and the UFO Abduction Phenomenon'. *Dissociation* 4: 46-54.

Presser, A.L. (1991). 'Publicity and Justice'. *ABA Journal* April: 20.

Prince, M. (1898-99). 'A Contribution to the Study of Hysteria and Hypnosis'. *Proceedings of the Society for Psychical Research* 14: 79-97.

Prince, M. (1901). 'The Development and Genealogy of the Misses Beauchamp: A Preliminary Report of a Case of Multiple Personality'. *Proceedings of the Society for Psychical Research* 15: 466-483.

Prince, M. (1905/1978). *Dissociation of a Personality*. Oxford: Oxford University Press.

Prince, M. (1907). 'A Symposium On the Subconscious'. *Journal of Abnormal Psychology* 2: 22-5, 67-80.

Prince, M. (1909). 'Experiments to Determine Co-Conscious (Subconscious) Ideation'. *Journal of Abnormal Psychology* 3: 33-42.

Prince, M. (1914). *The Unconscious*. New York: Macmillan.

Prince, M. (1939). *Clinical and Experimental Studies in Personality, With Introduction and Notes By A.A. Roback*. Cambridge, Mass.: Sci-Art.

Prince, M. (1975). *Psychotherapy and Multiple Personality: Selected Essays*. Edited With an Introductory Essay By N.G. Hale, Jr. Cambridge, Mass.: Harvard University Press.

Prince, W.F. (1915/16). 'The Doris Case of Multiple Personality Parts I & II'. *Proceedings of the American Society for Psychical Research* 9 & 10: 23-700; 701-1419.

Prince, W.F. (1916). 'The Doris Case of Quintuple Personality'. *Journal of Abnormal Psychology* 11: 73-122.

Prince, W.F. (1923a). 'The Mother of Doris'. *Proceedings of the American Society for Psychical Research* 17: 1-216.

Prince, W.F. (1923b). 'Heinrich Meyer Case: The Rise and Education of a Permanent Secondary Personality'. *Proceedings of the American Society for Psychical Research* 17: 217-272.

Prince, W.F. (1926). *The Psychic in the House*. Boston: Boston Society for Psychic Research.

Prince, W.F. (1927/1964). *The Case of Patience Worth*. New Hyde Park, N.Y.: University Books.

Puccetti, R. (1973). 'Brain Bisection and Personal Identity'. *British Journal for the Philosophy of Science* 24: 339-355.

300

Puccetti, R. (1981). 'The Case for Mental Duality: Evidence from Split Brain Data and Other Considerations'. *Behavioral and Brain Sciences* 4: 93-99.

Putnam, F.W. (1984a). 'The Psychophysiologic Investigation of Multiple Personality Disorder. A Review'. *Psychiatric Clinics of North America* 7: 31-39.

Putnam, F.W. (1984b). 'The Study of Multiple Personality Disorder: General Strategies and Practical Considerations'. *Psychiatric Annals* 14: 58-61.

Putnam, F.W. (1985a). 'Multiple Personality Disorders and Related Dissociative Reactions'. *International Medicine* 5: 13-15.

Putnam, F.W. (1985b). 'Multiple Personality Disorder'. *Medical Aspects of Human Sexuality* 19: 59-74.

Putnam, F.W. (1985c). 'Dissociation As a Response to Extreme Trauma'. In R.P. Kluft (ed.), *Childhood Antecedents of Multiple Personality*. Washington: American Psychiatric Press: 65-97.

Putnam, F.W. (1986a). 'The Treatment of Multiple Personality: State of the Art'. In B.G. Braun (ed.), *The Treatment of Multiple Personality Disorder*. Washington: American Psychiatric Press: 175-198.

Putnam, F.W. (1986b). 'The Scientific Investigation of Multiple Personality Disorder'. In J.M. Quen (ed.), *Split Minds/Split Brains*. New York & London: New York University Press: 109-125.

Putnam, F.W. (1988). 'The Switch Process in Multiple Personality Disorder'. *Dissociation* 1: 24-32.

Putnam, F.W. (1989). *Diagnosis and Treatment of Multiple Personality Disorder*. New York: Guilford.

Putnam, F.W. (1991). 'Recent Research On Multiple Personality Disorder'. *Psychiatric Clinics of North America* 14: 489-502.

Putnam, F.W. (1992a). 'Discussion: Are Alter Personalities Fragments or Figments?'. *Psychoanalytic Inquiry* 12: 95-111.

Putnam, F.W. (1992b). 'Altered States: Peeling Away the Layers of a Multiple Personality'. *The Sciences* November/December: 30-36.

Putnam, F.W. (1993). 'Diagnosis and Clinical Phenomenology of Multiple Personality Disorder: A North American Perspective'. *Dissociation* 6: 80-86.

Putnam, F.W., Guroff, B.S., Silberman, E.K., Barban, L. and Post, R.M. (1986). 'The Clinical Phenomenology of Multiple Personality Disorder: Review of 100 Recent Cases'. *Journal of Clinical Psychiatry* 47: 285-293.

Putnam, F.W. and Loewenstein, R.J. (1993). 'Treatment of Multiple Personality Disorder: A Survey of Current Practices'. *American Journal of Psychiatry* 150: 1048-1052.

Putnam, F.W., Loewenstein, R.J., Silberman, E.K. and Post, R.M. (1984). 'Multiple Personality Disorder in a Hospital Setting'. *Journal of Clinical Psychiatry* 45: 172-175.

Putnam, F.W., Zahn, T.P. and Post, R.M. (1990). 'Differential Autonomic Nervous System Activity in Multiple Personality Disorder'.

Psychiatry Research 31: 251-260.

Quen, J.M. (ed.) (1986). *Split Minds/Split Brains: Historical and Current Perspectives*. New York & London: New York University Press.

Radden, J. (1989). 'Chemical Sanity and Personal Identity'. *Public Affairs Quarterly* 3: 64-79.

Read, J.D. and Lindsay, D.S. (1994). 'Moving Toward a Middle Ground on the "False Memory Debate": Reply to Commentaries on Lindsay and Read [1994]'. *Applied Cognitive Psychology* 8: 407-435.

Ribot, T. (1887). *Diseases of Personality*. New York: Fitzgerald.

Ribot, T. (1907). 'A Symposium On the Subconscious'. *Journal of Abnormal Psychology* 2: 33-37.

Richards, D.G. (1991). 'A Study of the Correlations Between Subjective Psychic Experiences and Dissociative Experiences'. *Dissociation* 4: 83-91.

Richeport, M.M. (1992). 'The Interface Between Multiple Personality, Spirit Mediumship, and Hypnosis'. *American Journal of Clinical Hypnosis* 34: 168-177.

Riley, R.L. and Mead, J. (1988). 'The Development of Symptoms of Multiple Personality Disorder in a Child of Three'. *Dissociation* 1: 41-46.

Ronquillo, J. and E.B. (1991). 'The Influence of "Espiritismo" On a Case of Multiple Personality Disorder'. *Dissociation* 4: 39-45.

Rorty, A.O. (1988). *Mind in Action: Essays in the Philosophy of Mind*. Boston: Beacon Press.

Rosenbaum, M. (1980). 'The Role of the Term Schizophrenia in the Decline of Diagnoses of Multiple Personality'. *Archives of General Psychiatry* 37: 1383-1385.

Rosenfeld, I. (1993). *The Strange, Familiar, and Forgotten: An Anatomy of Consciousness*. New York: Vintage.

Rosenzweig, S. (1987). 'Sally Beauchamp's Career: A Psychoarcheological Key to Morton Prince's Classic Case of Multiple Personality'. *Genetic, Social, and General Psychology Monographs* 113: 5-60.

Rosenzweig, S. (1988). 'The Identity and Idiodynamics of the Multiple Personality "Sally Beauchamp": A Confirmatory Supplement'. *American Psychologist* 43: 45-48.

Rösler, A. (1994). 'Editorial: Long-Term Effects of Childhood Sexual Abuse on the Hypothalamic-Pituitary-Adrenal Axis'. *Journal of Clinical Endocrinology and Metabolism* 78: 247-248.

Ross, C.A. (1984). 'Diagnosis of Multiple Personality During Hypnosis: A Case Report'. *International Journal of Clinical and Experimental Hypnosis* 32: 222-235.

Ross, C.A. (1985). 'DSM-III Problems in Diagnosing Partial Forms of MPD: Discussion Paper'. *Journal of the Royal Society of Medicine* 78: 933-936.

Ross, C.A. (1989). *Multiple Personality Disorder: Diagnosis, Clinical Features, and Treatment*. New York: Wiley.

Ross, C.A. (1990). 'Commentary On Takahashi (1990)'. *Dissociation* 3: 64-65.

Ross, C.A. (1991a). 'The Dissociated Executive Self and the Cultural Dissociation Barrier'. *Dissociation* 4: 55-61.

Ross, C.A. (1991b). 'Epidemiology of Multiple Personality Disorder and Dissociation'. *Psychiatric Clinics of North America* 14: 503-518.

Ross, C.A. and Gahan, P. (1988). 'Cognitive Analysis of Multiple Personality Disorder'. *American Journal of Psychotherapy* 42: 229-239.

Ross, C.A., Heber, S., Norton, G.R. and Anderson, G. (1989a). 'Somatic Symptoms in Multiple Personality Disorder'. *Psychosomatics* 30: 154-160.

Ross, C.A., Heber, S., Norton, G.R. and Anderson, G. (1989b). 'Differences Between Multiple Personality Disorder and Other Diagnostic Groups On Interview'. *Journal of Nervous and Mental Disease* 177: 487-491.

Ross, C.A., Miller, S.D., Bjornson, L., *et al.* (1991). 'Abuse Histories in 102 Cases of Multiple Personality Disorder'. *Canadian Journal of Psychiatry* 36: 97-101.

Ross, C.A., Norton, G.R. and Fraser, G.A. (1989). 'Evidence Against the Iatrogenesis of Multiple Personality Disorder'. *Dissociation* 2: 61-65.

Ross, C.A., Norton, G.R. and Wozney, K. (1989). 'Multiple Personality Disorder: An Analysis of 236 Cases'. *Canadian Journal of Psychiatry* 34: 413-418.

Ross, D.F., Read, J.D. and Toglia, M.P. (eds) (1994). *Adult Eyewitness Testimony: Current Trends and Developments*. Cambridge: Cambridge University Press.

Rossi, E.R. and Cheek, D.B. (1988). *Mind-Body Therapy: Methods of Ideodynamic Healing in Hypnosis*. New York: W.W. Norton.

Russell, B. (1912/1981). *The Problems of Philosophy*. Oxford: Oxford University Press.

Salter, M.W.H. (1930). 'Some Incidents Occurring At Sittings With Mrs. Leonard Which May Throw Light On Their Modus Operandi'. *Proceedings of the Society for Psychical Research* 39: 306-332.

Saltman, V. and Solomon, R.S. (1982). 'Incest and the Multiple Personality'. *Psychological Reports* 50: 1127-1141.

Sanders, S. (1986). 'The Perceptual Alteration Scale: A Scale Measuring Dissociation'. *American Journal of Clinical Hypnosis* 29: 95-102.

Savitz, D.B. (1990). 'The Legal Defense of Persons With the Diagnosis of Multiple Personality Disorder'. *Dissociation* 3: 195-203.

Saxe, G.N. *et al.* (1994). 'Somatization in Patients with Dissociative Disorders'. *American Journal of Psychiatry* 151: 1329-1334.

Schacter, D.L., Kihlstrom, J.F., Kihlstrom, L.C. and Berren, M.B. (1989). 'Autobiographical Memory in a Case of Multiple Personality Disorder'. *Journal of Abnormal Psychology* 98: 508-514.

Schafer, D.W. (1986). 'Recognizing Multiple Personality Patients'. *American Journal of Psychotherapy* 40: 500-510.

Schiller, F.C.S. (1915). Review of *The Unconscious*, By M. Prince. *Proceedings of the Society for Psychical Research* 27: 492-506.

Schiller, F.C.S. (1917). Review of *Proceedings of the American Society for Psychical Research*, 'The Doris Fischer Case of Multiple Personality'. *Proceedings of the Society for Psychical Research* 29: 386-403.

Schopp, R.F. (1991). *Automatism, Insanity, and the Psychology of Criminal Responsibility*. Cambridge: Cambridge University Press.

Schreiber, F.R. (1974). *Sybil*. New York: Warner Books, Inc.

Schultz, R., Braun, B.G. and Kluft, R.P. (1989). 'Multiple Personality Disorder: Phenomenology of Selected Variables in Comparison to Major Depression'. *Dissociation* 2: 45-51.

Selye, H. (1956). *The Stress of Life*. New York: McGraw-Hill.

Sheehan, P.W. and Orne, M.T. (1968). 'Some Comments On the Nature of Posthypnotic Behavior'. *Journal of Nervous and Mental Disease* 146: 209-220.

Shelley, W.B. (1981). 'Dermatitis Artefacta Induced in a Patient By One of Her Multiple Personalities'. *British Journal of Dermatology* 105: 587-589.

Sidis, B. (1898). *The Psychology of Suggestion*. New York: Appleton-Century.

Sidis, B. (ed.) (1902/1908). *Psychopathological Researches: Studies in Mental Dissociation*. Boston: Richard G. Badger.

Sidis, B. and Goodhart, S.P. (1905). *Multiple Personality: An Experimental Investigation into the Nature of Human Individuality*. New York: D. Appleton & Co.

Sidtis, J.J. (1986). 'Can Neurological Disconnection Account for Psychiatric Dissociation?'. In J.M. Quen (ed.), *Split Minds/Split Brains*. New York & London: New York University Press: 127-147.

Silberman, E.K., Putnam, F.W., Weingartner, H., Braun, B.G. and Post, R.M. (1985). 'Dissociative States in Multiple Personality Disorder: A Quantitative Study'. *Psychiatry Research* 15: 253-260.

Simon, J. and Goldberg, C. (1984). 'The Role of the Double in the Creative Process and Psychoanalysis'. *Journal of the American Academy of Psychoanalysis* 12: 341-361.

Simons, R.C., Ervin, F.R. and Prince, R.H. (1988). 'The Psychobiology of Trance: I: Training for Thaipusam'. *Transcultural Psychiatric Research Review* 25: 249-266. See Ervin, et al, 1988, for Part II.

Simpson, M.M. and Carlson, E.T. (1968). 'The Strange Sleep of Rachel Baker'. *The Academy Bookman* 21: 2-13.

Sizemore, C.C. and Pittillo, E.S. (1977). *I'm Eve*. Garden City, N.Y.: Doubleday & Co., Inc.

Slovenko, R. (1991). 'How Criminal Law Has Responded in Multiple Personality Cases'. *The Psychiatric Times* 3: 22-26.

Slovenko, R. (1993). 'The Multiple Personality and the Criminal Law'. *Medicine and Law* 12: 329-240.

Smart, B. (1974). 'Persons and Selves'. *Philosophical Studies* 26: 331-336.

Smart, N. (1972). 'Creation, Persons and the Meaning of Life'. In R. Ruddock (ed.), *Six Approaches to the Person*. London & Boston:

Routledge & Kegan Paul: 13-36.

Smith, P. (1990). 'Human Persons'. In C. Gill (ed.), *The Person and the Human Mind: Issues in Ancient and Modern Philosophy*. Oxford: Oxford University Press: 61-81.

Smith, S.G. (1989). 'Multiple Personality Disorder With Human and Non-Human Subpersonality Components'. *Dissociation* 2: 52-57.

Soal, S.G. (1925). 'A Report On Some Communications Through Mrs. Blanche Cooper'. *Proceedings of the Society for Psychical Research* 35: 471-594.

Society for Psychical Research (1898). 'Addresses On Hypnotism Delivered At the British Medical Association. By J.M. Bramwell, F.W.H. Myers, and Others'. *Proceedings of the Society for Psychical Research* 14: 98-110.

Solomon, R.S. and Solomon, V. (1982). 'Differential Diagnosis of the Multiple Personality'. *Psychological Reports* 51: 1187-1194.

Spanos, N.P. (1983). 'The Hidden Observer As an Experimental Creation'. *Journal of Personality and Social Psychology* 44: 170-176.

Spanos, N.P. (1986). 'Hypnosis, Nonvolitional Responding, and Multiple Personality: A Social Psychological Perspective'. *Progress in Experimental Personality Research* 14: 1-62.

Spanos, N.P. and Chaves, J.F. (1989). 'Hypnotic Analgesia and Surgery: In Defence of the Social-Psychological Position'. *British Journal of Experimental and Clinical Hypnosis* 6: 131-139.

Spanos, N.P. and Hewitt, E.C. (1980). 'The Hidden Observer in Hypnotic Analgesia: Discovery or Experimental Creation?'. *Journal of Personality and Social Psychology* 39: 1201-1214.

Spanos, N.P., Weekes, J.R. and Bertrand, L.D. (1985). 'Multiple Personality: A Social Psychological Perspective'. *Journal of Abnormal Psychology* 94: 362-376.

Spanos, N.P., Weekes, J.R., Menary, E. and Bertrand, L.D. (1986). 'Hypnotic Interview and Age Regression Procedures in the Elicitation of Multiple Personality Symptoms: A Simulation Study'. *Psychiatry* 49: 298-311.

Spiegel, D. (1984). 'Multiple Personality As Post-Traumatic Stress Disorder'. *Psychiatric Clinics of North America* 7: 101-110.

Spiegel, D. (1986a). 'Dissociating Damage'. *American Journal of Clinical Hypnosis* 29: 123-131.

Spiegel, D. (1986b). 'Dissociation, Double Binds, and Posttraumatic Stress in Multiple Personality Disorder'. In B.G. Braun (ed.), *Treatment of Multiple Personality Disorder*. Washington, D.C.: American Psychiatric Press: 61-77.

Spiegel, D. (1988). 'Commentary: The Treatment Accorded Those Who Treat Patients With Multiple Personality Disorder'. *Journal of Nervous and Mental Disease* 176: 535-536. Reply to Dell, 1988a.

Spiegel, D. (1990). 'Hypnosis, Dissociation, and Trauma: Hidden and Overt Observers'. In J.L. Singer (ed.), *Repression and Dissociation*. Chicago & London: University of Chicago Press: 121-142.

Spiegel, H. (1963). 'The Dissociation-Association Continuum'. *Journal of Nervous and Mental Disease* 136: 374-378.

Stade G. (1986). 'Horror and Dissociation, With Examples from Edgar Allan Poe'. In J.M. Quen (ed.), *Split Minds/Split Brains*. New York & London: New York University Press: 149-170.

Steinberg, M. (1990). 'Transcultural Issues in Psychiatry: The Ataque and Multiple Personality Disorder'. *Dissociation* 3: 31-33.

Stephens, G.L. and Graham, G. (1994). 'Self-Consciousness, Mental Agency, and the Clinical Psychopathology of Thought-Insertion'. *Philosophy, Psychiatry, & Psychology* 1: 1-10.

Stern, C.R. (1984). 'The Etiology of Multiple Personalities'. *Psychiatric Clinics of North America* 7: 149-159.

Stern, D.N. (1985). *The Interpersonal World of the Infant*. New York: Basic Books.

Stevenson, I. (1970). 'A Communicator Unknown to Medium and Sitters: The Case of Robert Passanah'. *Journal of the American Society for Psychical Research* 64: 53-65.

Stevenson, I. (1984). *Unlearned Language: New Studies in Xenoglossy*. Charlottesville: University Press of Virginia.

Stevenson, I. (1992). 'Survival or Super-Psi: A Reply'. *Journal of Scientific Exploration* 6: 145-150.

Stevenson, I. (1994). 'A Case of the Psychotherapist's Fallacy: Hypnotic Regression to "Previous Lives"'. *American Journal of Clinical Hypnosis* 36: 188-193.

Stevenson, I. and Pasricha, S. (1979). 'A Case of Secondary Personality With Xenoglossy'. *American Journal of Psychiatry* 136: 1591-1592.

Suryani, L.K. and Jensen, G.D. (1993). *Trance and Possession in Bali*. Oxford: Oxford University Press.

Sutcliffe, J.P. and Jones, J. (1962). 'Personal Identity, Multiple Personality, and Hypnosis'. *International Journal of Clinical and Experimental Hypnosis* 10: 231-269.

Takahashi, Y. (1990). 'Is Multiple Personality Disorder Really Rare in Japan?'. *Dissociation* 3: 57-59. Commentaries and response: 60-69.

Taylor, E. (1984). *William James On Exceptional Mental States*. Amherst: University of Massachusetts Press.

Taylor, W.S. and Martin, M.F. (1944). 'Multiple Personality'. *Journal of Abnormal and Social Psychology* 39: 281-300.

Terr, L. (1988). 'What Happens to Early Memories of Trauma? A Study of 20 Children Under Age Five at the Time of Documented Traumatic Events'. *Journal of the American Academy of Child and Adolescent Psychiatry* 27: 96-104.

Thigpen, C.H. and Cleckley, H.M. (1957). *The Three Faces of Eve*. New York: McGraw Hill.

Thigpen, C.H. and Cleckley, H.M. (1984). 'On the Incidence of Multiple Personality Disorder: A Brief Communication'. *International Journal of Clinical and Experimental Hypnosis* 32: 63-66.

Thomason, R.H. (1970). 'Indeterminist Time and Truth-Value Gaps'.

Theoria 36: 264-281.

Thomson, M.M., Forbes, T.W. and Bolles, M.M. (1937). 'Brain Potential Rhythms in a Case Showing Self-Induced Apparent Trance States'. *American Journal of Psychiatry* 93: 1313-1314.

Torem, M. (1989). 'Iatrogenic Factors in the Perpetuation of Splitting and Multiplicity'. *Dissociation* 2: 92-98.

Troubridge, U. (1922). 'The Modus Operandi in So-Called Mediumistic Trance'. *Proceedings of the Society for Psychical Research* 32: 344-378.

van der Hart, O. (1990). 'Commentary On Takahashi (1990)'. *Dissociation* 3: 66-67.

van der Hart, O. (1993). 'Multiple Personality Disorder in Europe: Impressions'. *Dissociation* 6: 102-118.

van der Hart, O. and Boon, S. (1989). 'Correspondence: Multiple Personality Disorder'. *British Journal of Psychiatry* 154: 419.

van der Hart, O. and Boon, S. (1990). 'Contemporary Interest in Multiple Personality Disorder and Child Abuse in the Netherlands'. *Dissociation* 3: 34-37.

van der Hart, O. and Friedman, B. (1989). 'A Reader's Guide to Pierre Janet On Dissociation: A Neglected Intellectual Heritage'. *Dissociation* 2: 3-16.

van der Kolk, B.A. (1991). 'The Biological Response to Psychic Trauma: Mechanisms and Treatment of Intrusion and Numbing'. *Anxiety Research* 4: 86-88.

van der Kolk, B.A. and van der Hart, O. (1989). 'Pierre Janet and the Breakdown of Adaptation in Psychological Trauma'. *American Journal of Psychiatry* 146: 1530-1540.

Vanderlinden, J., Van Dyck, R., Vandereycken, W. and Vertommen, H. (1991). 'Dissociative Experiences in the General Population in the Netherlands and Belgium: A Study With the Dissociative Questionnaire (DIS-Q)'. *Dissociation* 4: 180-184.

van Fraassen, B. (1966). 'Singular Terms, Truth-Value Gaps, and Free Logic'. *Journal of Philosophy* 63: 481-495.

van Fraassen, B. (1968). 'Presupposition, Implication, and Self-Reference'. *Journal of Philosophy* 65: 136-152.

Varma, V.K., Bouri, M. and Wig, N.N. (1981). 'Multiple Personality in India: Comparison With Hysterical Possession State'. *American Journal of Psychotherapy* 35: 113-120.

Vijselaar, J. and van der Hart, O. (1992). 'The First Report of Hypnotic Treatment of Traumatic Grief: A Brief Communication'. *International Journal of Clinical and Experimental Hypnosis* 40: 1-6.

Wagner, E. and Heise, M. (1974). 'A Comparison of Rorschach Records of Three Multiple Personalities'. *Journal of Personality Assessment* 38: 308-331.

Watkins, J.G. (1984). 'The Bianchi (L.A. Hillside Strangler) Case: Sociopath or Multiple Personality?'. *International Journal of Clinical and Experimental Hypnosis* 32: 67-101.

Watkins, J.G. and Watkins, H.H. (1979-80). 'Ego States and Hidden Observers'. *Journal of Altered States of Consciousness* 5: 3-18.

Watkins, J.G. and Watkins, H.H. (1984). 'Hazards to the Therapist in the Treatment of Multiple Personalities'. *Psychiatric Clinics of North America* 7: 111-119.

Watkins, J.G. and Watkins, H.H. (1986). 'Hypnosis, Multiple Personality, and Ego States As Altered States of Consciousness'. In Wolman, B.B. and Ullman, M. (eds), *Handbook of States of Consciousness*. New York: Van Nostrand Reinhold: 133-158.

Watkins, J.G. and Watkins, H.H. (1988). 'The Management of Malevolent Ego States'. *Dissociation* 1: 67-72.

Weiss, M., Sutton, P.J. and Utecht, A.J. (1985). 'Multiple Personality in a 10-Year-Old Girl'. *Journal of the American Academy of Child Psychiatry* 24: 495-501.

Wiggins, D. (1980). *Sameness and Substance*. Cambridge: Harvard University Press.

Wiggins, D. (1987). 'The Person As Object of Science, As Subject of Experience, and As Locus of Value'. In Peacocke, A. and Gillett, G. (eds), *Persons and Personality*. Oxford: Blackwell: 56-74.

Wiggins, O.P. (1994). 'Commentary On "Self-Consciousness, Mental Agency, and the Clinical Psychopathology of Thought-Insertion"'. *Philosophy, Psychiatry, & Psychology* 1: 11-12. Commentary on Stephens and Graham, 1994.

Wilbur, C.B. (1984). 'Multiple Personality and Child Abuse. An Overview'. *Psychiatric Clinics of North America* 7: 3-7.

Wilbur, C.B. (1985). 'The Effect of Child Abuse On the Psyche'. In Kluft, R.P. (ed.), *Childhood Antecedents of Multiple Personality*. Washington, D.C.: American Psychiatric Press: 22-35.

Wilbur, C.B. (1988). 'Multiple Personality Disorder and Transference'. *Dissociation* 1: 73-76.

Wilkes, K.V. (1981). 'Multiple Personality and Personal Identity'. *British Journal for the Philosophy of Science* 32: 331-348.

Wilkes, K.V. (1988). *Real People: Personal Identity Without Thought Experiments*. Oxford: Oxford University Press.

Williams, B. (1973). 'Personal Identity and Individuation'. In *Problems of the Self*. Cambridge: Cambridge University Press: 1-18.

Wilson, A. (1904). 'A Case of Multiple Personality'. *Proceedings of the Society for Psychical Research* 18: 352-415.

Wingfield, H. (1888). 'The Connection of Hypnotism With the Subjective Phenomena of Spiritualism'. *Proceedings of the Society for Psychical Research* 5: 279-287. Published anonymously.

Wolff, P.H. (1987). *The Development of Behavioral States and the Expression of Emotions in Early Infancy*. Chicago: University of Chicago Press.

Worrall, W.A. (1987). 'Multiple Personality Disorder in Alaska'. Paper presented at 4th International Conference on Multiple Personality/Dissociative States, Chicago, Nov. 6, 1987.

308

Yank, J.R. (1991). 'Handwriting Variations in Individuals With Multiple Personality Disorder'. *Dissociation* 4: 2-12.

Yapko, M.D. (1994a). 'Suggestibility and Repressed Memories of Abuse: A Survey of Psychotherapists' Beliefs'. *American Journal of Clinical Hypnosis* 36: 163-171.

Yapko, M.D. (1994b). 'Response to Comments'. *American Journal of Clinical Hypnosis* 36: 185-187.

Young, W.C. (1987). 'Emergence of a Multiple Personality in a Posttraumatic Stress Disorder of Adulthood'. *American Journal of Clinical Hypnosis* 29: 249-259.

Young, W.C. (1988). 'Dissociation and Psychodynamics: All That Switches Is Not Split'. *Dissociation* 1: 33-38.

Zamansky, H.S. and Bartis, S.P. (1984). 'Hypnosis As Dissociation: Methodological Considerations and Preliminary Findings'. *American Journal of Clinical Hypnosis* 26: 246-251.

Zamansky, H.S. and Bartis, S.P. (1985). 'The Dissociation of an Experience: The Hidden Observer Observed'. *Journal of Abnormal Psychology* 94: 243-248.

Zemach, E. (1970). 'The Unity and Indivisibility of the Self'. *International Philosophical Quarterly* 10: 542-555.

Zemach, E. (1986). 'Unconscious Mind or Conscious Minds?'. In French, P.A., Uehling, T.E., Jr., and Wettstein, H.K. (eds), *Midwest Studies in Philosophy X*. Minneapolis: University of Minnestota Press: 121-149.

INDEX

abilities, nature of 95-6, 105-6, 180-8
abuse 39-40, 48, 62, 115, 126, 172-3, 177, 226, 233, 245, 253-5, 257-9, 262-7; *see also* trauma
Achilles 26-7
Adityanjee, R. 189, 243
Aldridge-Morris, R. 61, 63-4, 109
Allison, R.B. 243-6, 270
alternate personalities: animal personalities 84, 126; blending of 79-80 (*see also* co-presence); complexity of 58-60, 62, 64-5, 84-5, 212-16, 229-30, 234-6, 244; cultural specificity of 37-8, 189, 243; functional specificity of 41, 48, 55, 56-61, 63, 84, 126-9, 170-3, 175-6, 183, 187, 207, 210, 225, 251-2; grounding behavior 43, 63; individuation of 55-6, 81, 84-5, 126; number of 41, 47, 58-9, 127, 178-9, 237-8, 249-52; overlapping of 105-6, 170-3, 180-7, 200, 215, 270-1; social-psychological interpretation of 8, 61-5, 188-90, 220, 269-70, 276; switching of 41-7, 227; temporally displaced 242-3, 245-6; *vs* fragments 41, 47, 179, 210-11, 225; *see also*

personality; primary personality
amnesia 28, 85, 93, 96-7, 108-110, 112, 114-5, 120-2, 141-3, 169, 177-8, 203, 226-7, 249, 256-7, 262, 272, 276; in alternate personalities 40-1, 43, 46, 82, 99-100, 108, 111-12, 249
analgesia, hypnotic 21, 23, 143
anesthesia: hypnotic 19-24, 27-31, 85, 96-7, 115, 117, 120, 122, 135, 141-3, 190; in alternate personalities 45-6, 48; systematized 29-34 (*see also* negative hallucination); total *vs* complete 23-4
anomalous monism 154
apperceptive center 77-86, 88-92, 109, 136-7, 144, 158, 164, 166, 175, 180, 187, 190, 204, 210-11, 215-16, 253-5, 271-2
Arnold, J.N. 36
artificial intelligence 164
attribute-depletion 54, 57-60, 235-6, 271
attribute-distribution 54, 57-9, 170, 271
Aune, B. 151, 275
automatic writing 25-8, 34-6, 76, 89, 97-100, 104, 113, 121-2, 143, 227, 272

Bartis, S.P. 116-19

310